Husserl and Analytic Philosophy

Husserl and Analytic Philosophy

Edited by
Guillermo E. Rosado Haddock

DE GRUYTER

ISBN 978-3-11-061178-6
e-ISBN (PDF) 978-3-11-049737-3
e-ISBN (EPUB) 978-3-11-049418-1

Library of Congress Cataloging-in-Publication Data
A CIP catalog record for this book has been applied for at the Library of Congress.

Bibliographic information published by the Deutsche Nationalbibliothek
The Deutsche Nationalbibliothek lists this publication in the Deutsche Nationalbibliografie; detailed bibliographic data are available on the Internet at http://dnb.dnb.de.

© 2018 Walter de Gruyter GmbH, Berlin/Boston
This volume is text- and page-identical with the hardback published in 2016.
Printing and binding: CPI books GmbH, Leck

♾ Printed on acid-free paper
Printed in Germany

www.degruyter.com

Preface

Since the origins of analytic philosophy in the hands of Bertrand Russell, Ludwig Wittgenstein, G. E. Moore and later the Vienna Circle group around Moritz Schlick, Rudolf Carnap and Otto Neurath, the immense philosophical legacy of Edmund Husserl has been either completely ignored or distorted, whereas Gottlob Frege's also extremely important legacy has been distorted by the filter of empiricism and nominalism, and a caricature of the rationalist and mathematical as well as logical Platonist has been proclaimed in Neo-Kantian clothes the grandfather of analytic philosophy. Since the 1970s that received view both of the origins of analytic philosophy and of Husserl's philosophy has been questioned, but more than forty years later, the myths still have the upperhand.

It is the purpose of this book to help eradicate that myth completely, and to contribute to give Husserl his due place among the greatest philosophers. But the book will also show that the relation of Husserl with some of the foremost so-called analytic philosophers is very different to what the received view has tried to instil in the minds of its followers. Husserl's influence on a wide variety of authors working in the analytic tradition cannot be longer put under the carpet. Bertrand Russell, for example, was very enthusiastic of Husserl's *magnum opus Logische Untersuchungen*, which he read while in prison during the First World War. And Husserl's influence on some members of the Polish School of logicians, especially on Ajdukiewicz' syntactic connection and on Lesniewski's mereology are well-known. Finally and very especially, the mystery of the mostly unknown relation between Husserl and the young Carnap will be definitely established, and there is no way back thereafter to the doubly innocent rendering of Carnap as the scientific-philosopher *par excellence*, be it as a born empiricist or as a Neo-Kantian in his younger years.

For the development of this book two colleagues were of utmost importance, even without contributing to the book itself: Dr. Rafael Hüntelmann and Prof. Roberto Poli. Rafael Hüntelmann founded and ran the philosophical Ontos Verlag that now belongs to De Gruyter Publishing Company. Roberto Poli – who has been so helpful to me so many times in my scholarly career – is the editor of the Ontos (now De Gruyter) book series *Categories*, in which I published my collection of papers *Against the Current* in 2012. Both wholeheartedly supported my project on Husserl and Analytic Philosophy and also put me in contact with Dr. Gertrud Grünkorn at De Gruyter, who has been very supportive of the project as well.

Furthermore, this book would not have been possible without the help of many people. First of all, I owe a special debt to each of the contributors to this volume, not only for accepting the invitation to contribute to the volume, but also because of their great interest in the project. In particular, I would like to thank three of them, which I have never met personally. Firstly, Uwe Meixner for some suggestions, and very especially Carlo Ierna and Verena Mayer, who have been so helpful at different points of the development of this project. In fact, Prof. Mayer has been so helpful on so many points that I do not know whether I would have been able to finish the project without her very valuable help.

I would also like to thank Prof. Dr. Ulrich Melle, Director of the Husserl Archives in Leuwen, for the permission to publish here as Appendix I an edited version, by Dr. Carlo Ierna and Prof. Dr. Dieter Lohmar, of the first part (pages 1a-28b) of Husserl's A I 35 manuscript on the paradoxes; as well as the Steinheim-Institut für deutsch-jüdische Geschichte at the University of Duisburg-Essen and its director, Dr. Margret Heitmann, for the permission to publish as Appendix II an unpublished letter of Rudolf Carnap to Jonas Cohn; and Dr. Thomas Vongehr, of the Husserl Archives in Leuwen for his valuable commentary on Cohn's relation with Husserl, published here as Appendix III.

Last but not least, I want to thank my wife, Dr. Tinna N. Stoyanova for her encouragement and patience.

Table of Contents

Preface —— V

Guillermo E. Rosado Haddock
Introduction —— 1

Part I: **Husserl and Analytic Philosophy: A General Assessment**

Guillermo E. Rosado Haddock
Husserl as Analytic Philosopher —— 15

Jairo José da Silva
The Analytic/Synthetic Dichotomy
    Husserl and the Analytic Tradition —— 35

Uwe Meixner
Husserl's Classical Conception of Intentionality – and Its Enemies —— 55

Part II: **Husserl and some Analytic Philosophers**

Claire Ortiz Hill
Husserl and Frege on Functions —— 89

Carlo Ierna
The Reception of Russell's Paradox in Early Phenomenology and the School of Brentano: The Case of Husserl's Manuscript A I 35α —— 119

David Woodruff Smith
Husserl and Tarski: the Semantic Conception of Intentionality and Truth —— 143

Verena Mayer
Der *Logische Aufbau* als Plagiat
    Oder: Eine Einführung in Husserls System der Konstitution —— 175

Guillermo E. Rosado Haddock
The Old Husserl and the Young Carnap —— 261

Part III: **Appendices**

Carlo Ierna and Dieter Lohmar
Husserl's Manuscript A I 35 —— 289

A Letter of Rudolf Carnap to Jonas Cohn from 26 September 1925 —— 321

Thomas Vongehr
Jonas Cohn und Edmund Husserl. Eine Skizze ihrer Beziehung —— 323

Name Index —— 331

Subject Index —— 335

Guillermo E. Rosado Haddock
Introduction

Philosophy in the XXth century was usually, but also arbitrarily, divided into analytic philosophy and so-called continental philosophy, a presumed distinction usually made by so-called analytic philosophers. Under 'analytic philosophy' it was understood philosophy mostly done in Anglo-American countries, namely, England, the United States of America and Canada, and was supposed to be empiricist, presumably scientific, and pretended to make free usage of the tools of contemporary logic and mathematics. On the other hand, continental philosophy was supposed to lack any source of rigour, being not even informed of scientific developments, and was inclined towards metaphysics and irrationality. Both characterizations were completely misleading and the dichotomy clearly did not have any serious grounding. On the so-called analytic side, you had, on the one hand, logical positivism – which is mainly an Austrian product inherited by the Anglo-American world- and, on the other hand, the so-called philosophy of ordinary language, a trend without the least scientific rigour, which has been sharply criticized by philosophers like Katz and Fodor from the standpoint of contemporary (scientific) linguistics. And, of course, what the logical empiricists believed science to be was completely false. Their successive criteria of scientific significance were all shown to be inadequate. In fact, the most developed empirical sciences, like physics, are mostly a theoretical enterprise, and though clearly no presumed empirical science can operate disconnected from experience, the relation to experience is much looser and more complicated than what the logical empiricists and other less liberal empiricists have thought. By the way, more radical empiricists, for example, Quine, not only have opted to assume an uncritical standpoint with regard to science – in his case: to what he conveniently understands by science –, but have even based many philosophical argumentations on the presumed scientific character of questionable primitive behaviouristic assertions.

On the other hand, the rubric 'continental philosophy' was conceived by so-called analytic philosophers as a sort of waste basket, in which you could put at the same time philosophers like Kant or Husserl, even Popper, as well as Neo-Kantians, German idealists, hermeneutics, existentialists of all sorts and, of course, Marxism, so-called 'post-modernism' and other varieties of irrationalism. But the biggest problem of all was that so-called analytic philosophers mostly did not read so-called continental philosophers, nor the latter read the former. The result was complete miscommunication and misunderstanding.

Analytic philosophers, however, had a big problem. Some of them, especially those dealing with the philosophy of mathematics and semantics, wanted to consider Frege as their intellectual grandfather, though it is perfectly clear that Frege had nothing to do with empiricism nor with their beloved stance in the philosophy of mathematics, namely, nominalism. They were delighted with Frege's logicism, since it is a sort of reductionism, the magical word that makes them salivate like Pavlov's dogs. And they were also very impressed by the Frege-Husserl distinction between (in Fregean terminology) sense and referent, which, of course, they solely attributed to their presumed putative grandfather Frege. Thus, they re-discovered Kant, the great German philosopher of the XVIII century, who had developed a philosophy that tried to combine aspects both of rationalism and of empiricism. And although Frege was certainly nearer to rationalism than even to Kant's philosophy, commentators of Frege from the analytic circles began to conceive Frege as a sort of Kantian. And though Frege was most of all a philosopher of mathematics and of logic, who entered hesitatingly the fields of semantics and philosophy of language in order to round up his philosophy, but said very little about epistemology -because he feared to be led into psychologism-, they began to render Frege as a sort of epistemologist, moreover, as a Kantian epistemologist. Certainly there are coincidences with respect to Kant's and Frege's conceptions of geometry, though Frege's arguments are different from Kant's, and Frege's definition of analyticity seems to be inspired in Kant's Principle of Analytic Judgements –not, however, on Kant's official definition of analyticity-, but with respect to other issues the differences are overwhelming. Frege conceived non-geometrical mathematical statements as analytic –whereas Kant considered them as synthetic *a priori*; Frege was a mathematical and logical Platonist, and a logicist, having nothing to do with constructivism in mathematics, whereas Kant was a mathematical constructivist, neither a Platonist in any sense nor a logicist, and was, of course, an epistemologist.

Some of the more sophisticated analytic philosophers more recently "discovered" that Quine's and other's renderings of the young Carnap's *Der logische Aufbau der Welt* as a work in the tradition of Mach's positivism or of Russell's empiricism were too primitive and poorly based. Thus, they also "discovered" that after all the young Carnap was no positivist or empiricist at all, but a Kantian or Neo-Kantian of some sort. Thus originated the new fable of the young Kantian Carnap of *Der Raum* and *Der logische Aufbau der Welt,* and its originators have been very active in defending that new dogma, not by arguments that they do not have, nor by examining the textual evidence, which they cannot find, but by trying to silence dissident renderings of their hero.

Edmund Husserl, on the other hand, is usually acknowledged to be the founder of phenomenology, probably the second most important school of philosophy in the twentieth century. Certainly, the publication of the first volume of *Ideen zu einer reinen Phänomenologie und phänomenologischer Philosophie I* in 1913 served many young philosophers and later generations of philosophers to group themselves under the banner of transcendental phenomenology, sometimes presumably doing phenomenology in ways that Husserl would probably not acknowledge as his own. And that phenomenological school consciously distanced itself from the sciences, while believing that they had in their hands a new method that would bring them to the philosophical paradise, and without taking knowledge of how far away from Husserl they were. Thus, though Husserl is the founder of transcendental phenomenology, one should not fail to appreciate the distance that separates Husserl from his transcendental phenomenological epigones. A short biographical overview of Husserl would make things somewhat clearer.

As Frege, Husserl was originally a mathematician. He studied mathematics in Leipzig, Berlin (with Weierstrass and Kronecker) and in Vienna, where he obtained his doctorate at the very beginning of 1883 with Weierstrass' former student Leo Königsberger. He also studied physics, astronomy and philosophy as minor studies – in German: Nebenfächer. After finishing his doctoral studies he was called by Weierstrass to return to Berlin in order to be his assistant. That was certainly a special recognition for Husserl, not only because any professor chooses as assistants only his most promising students or former students, but, moreover, because Weierstrass was one of the two or three greatest mathematicians of his time. However, when a few months later Weierstrass became ill, Husserl abandoned Berlin and his teacher to pursue a career as philosopher, in fact, originally, as philosopher of mathematics. Thus, he worked on his professorship's thesis *Über den Begriff der Zahl* and presented it in 1887 in Halle, where a former student of Weierstrass, Georg Cantor, and Carl Stumpf, a former student of Franz Brentano, who had also been Husserl's philosophy professor in Vienna, gave their approval. Husserl's much maligned but rarely studied *Philosophie der Arithmetik* (1891) is an extension of his professorship's thesis. In Halle Husserl was especially near to Cantor, for whom Husserl was a sort of academic younger brother. Immediately after the publication of his *opus magnum*, *Logische Untersuchungen*, Husserl moved to Göttingen, where the former mathematician and then philosopher was by far better accepted by the mathematicians than by the philosophers. In particular, Felix Klein and David Hilbert invited Husserl immediately to address the mathematical colloqium, and Husserl did it in a famous double lecture in 1901. From then on, Husserl developed a friendship with Klein and especially with his contemporary David Hilbert considered by many as the greatest mathematician of the first half of the XXth century –, and such friendships continued to the end of their lives. David Hilbert encouraged his students to take courses with Husserl and to study philosophy as one of their minor studies. Two of those students were Max Born, who took a seminar with Husserl on the philosophy of mathematics around 1902, and Hermann Weyl, who followed a little later. Interestingly enough, both of them were to develop a friendship with Husserl that lasted until the latter's death. Hilbert's trust in Husserl was so great that in some cases, as happened in Weyl's oral examinations, Hilbert, who seemed to have been somewhat allergic to oral examinations, was not present, but had asked Husserl to question Weyl not only in philosophy, but also in mathematics. (One could wonder whether the greatest mathematician of his time would have had so much trust and respect for the intellectual capacity and scientific knowledge of Wittgenstein, Russell, Schlick, Carnap, Quine, Putnam, Ryle, the poor but very vocal Neurath or any analytic philosopher as he had for Husserl. The answer is clearly "NO".) And when Husserl was already teaching in Freiburg and visited Göttingen, he used to meet his old friend Hilbert and his former student Born.

In fact, it is in *Logische Untersuchungen* –one of the really great works in the history of philosophy – that phenomenological analysis (not transcendental phenomenology) originates. But that is certainly not the greatest achievement of that work. The first volume of *Logische Untersuchungen* contains –in chapters I-IX – the most thorough and detailed refutation of psychologism to this day. The last chapter of that volume contains Husserl's philosophy of logic and mathematics, as well as important considerations in the preliminaries, for example, the important distinction for the philosophy of the sciences between the nexus of the researcher's thoughts, the objective ontological nexus of the things studied, and the also objective nexus of truths, as well as important insights about the nature of physical theories, the distinction between laws of lower and of higher level – which he called *hypotheses cum fundamento in re* –, the explanatory nature of physical theories and their underdetermination by experience, as well as the role of probability in physical science. In the main part of that chapter Husserl is concerned firstly with the distinction between laws that protect against formal nonsense, and the usual logical laws that protect against formal countersense (or contradiction) and guide derivations, thus, the distinction between what was later called the 'formation rules' and the 'transformation rules' –a distinction erroneously attributed to Carnap's *Logische Syntax der Sprache*, published thirty-four years later. Husserl developed a conception of logic as a syntactic-semantic theory that runs parallel to the formal ontological sister discipline usually called mathematics. Husserl conceived mathematics as a theory of structures, a sort of generalisation of Riemann's views on mathematical manifolds and a very strong anticipation of the views of the Bourbaki school of mathematicians. Mathematics was for Husserl a theory of structures. At the bottom of the mathematical building there were, to use some Bourbakian terminology, the mother structures based on different fundamental mathematical concepts, whereas the remaining structures were obtained either by specialization, or by combination, or by combination of specializations of the mother structures. Thus, Husserl was a mathematical Platonist, though a Platonist of structures in which objects had their place. He was not a logical Platonist, like Frege, nor was he a logicist or, more generally, a reductionist, since the notion of set was for him only one of the fundamental formal-ontological categories, at the side of the concept of relation, of that of number, of that of whole, and possibly others, hence, not the unique fundamental notion to which all other mathematical notions have to be reduced.

It is impossible to briefly expound here the richness of the second volume of Husserl's *Logische Untersuchungen* and their relevance for rigorous research in philosophy. It should just be pointed out that in the First Logical Investigation there is a discussion about the ideality of meanings, as well as Husserl's alternative semantics of sense and referent, – in Husserl's terminology: of meaning and objectuality –, including a thorough treatment of the problem posed by the so-called 'indexicals', and a very plausible solution. The second Logical Investigation is concerned with the problem of universals, and contains, among other things, a thorough critical assessment of the theories of abstraction of English empiricists. In the Third Logical Investigation there is a foundational work on wholes and parts, which could be divided into a synthetic *a priori* and an analytic treatment. The synthetic *a priori* treatment gives rise to novel definitions both of syntheticity *a priori* and analyticity. The analytic treatment serves as sketch for a future foundation of mereology. In the Fourth Logical Investigation Husserl applies his results of the former investigation to the problem of language with the objective of building a pure logical grammar. The Fifth Logical Investigation contains both a generalization to all intentional acts of the sense-referent distinction, as well as an anticipation of future epistemological developments. But probably the most important Husserlian conception of the second volume of *Logische Untersuchungen* is his theory of categorial (and, hence, also of mathematical intuition) developed in the second part of the Sixth Logical Investigation, a part suggestively baptized by Husserl as 'Sensibility and Understanding'. It is in this part that Husserl expounds his theory of categorial intuition, which has nothing mysterious, mystic or metaphysical, but is immediately grounded on sense perception. In fact, at the very ground level is Husserl's conception of sense perception, which is clearly different from those of all sorts of empiricists and positivists. For Husserl, in sense perception we not only perceive whole objects, but states of affairs, not only the chair, the book and the pencil, but the state of affairs that both the book and the pencil are on the table and, moreover, the pencil at the side of the book. Isolated sensations of colour, sense data, etc. are not experienced in sense perception, according to Husserl, but are constructions obtained when we analyse what is given in sense perception, and that is precisely states of affairs. Thus, Husserl could proclaim that phenomenologists are the true positivists, not Mach, Avenarius *et alia*.

But in the perception of states of affairs there are already categorial components, to which nothing physical corresponds. We clearly distinguish between the perception of the book on the chair from the perception of the book under the chair; and we distinguish between the perception of John and Peter at the door and that of John or Peter at the door. The 'on', the 'under', the 'and' and the 'or' have no sensible correlates in the pure sensible part of sense perception, but are categorial components already present in sense perception. The same occurs when we say that we perceive a set of students in a political demonstration. Nothing sensible corresponds to the 'set', nor to the relation of 'being taller than' when we perceive 'Charles and Peter' and say that we see that Charles is taller than Peter. Categorial intuition is in some sense embedded already in sense perception. That is the beginning of the hierarchy of categorial objectualities that can be easily built by forming relations between sets, sets of relations, and so forth up to any finite degree of complexity. Thus, originates the hierarchy of categorial objectualities. Finally, at any point in this hierarchy, we can introduce a process of formalization called by Husserl "categorial abstraction", by replacing concrete objects by variables. For example, we can formalize the statement 'Charles is taller than Peter' as 'x is taller than y' or even as '$x>y$'. Thus originates the whole hierarchy of mathematical objects, which are constituted at every finite level, and the corresponding statements about them. Therefore, mathematical intuition is for Husserl basically categorial intuition plus categorial abstraction (i.e. formalization).

It is, hence, not something casual that Gödel urged logicians to read precisely Husserl's exposition of categorial intuition in the Sixth Logical Investigation. It is also not casual that some of the greatest minds of the last century, very especially Hilbert, Weyl and Gödel, were convinced of Husserl's greatness as a philosopher, though lesser minds in the analytic philosophy circles have opted to completely ignore or to distort Husserl. The present book has as main objective to make once and for all clear that you cannot do rigorous philosophy while ignoring one of the really great philosophers in the history of mankind, the author of the seminal and monumental *Logische Untersuchungen*, and of many other of the most important philosophical works of the twentieth century – as, for example, *Ideen zu einer reinen Phänomenologie und phänomenologischen Philosophie I*,

Formale und transzendentale Logik and *Erfahrung und Urteil*, or even *Cartesianische Meditationen* or *Die Krisis der europäischen Wissenschaften und die transzendentale Phänomenologie*, which could have been the *opus magnum* of many other renowned philosophers.

The present book is divided into two somewhat unequal parts. The first part considers Husserl's philosophy from a more systematic standpoint, beginning with a paper of the present editor titled 'Husserl as Analytic Philosopher'. The paper considers Husserl's analyses –mostly in *Logische Untersuchungen* and related writings- of different philosophical issues usually treated by analytic philosophers, for example, the sense-referent distinction, the relation between logic and mathematics, the nature of physical theories and Husserl's relatively unknown response to Frege's 1906 letters in his lectures on *Alte und neue Logik* of 1908–1909.

The second paper, written by the distinguished Brazilian Husserl specialist Jairo J. da Silva, is concerned with Husserl's fine distinction in *Logische Untersuchungen* between analytic, synthetic *a priori* and synthetic *a posteriori* truths. It should be clear to the reader that Husserl's notion of analyticity as based on logical form is different from Frege's and from Carnap's, and that Husserl's notion of synthetic *a priori* is much more refined than Kant's and more difficult to refute. Nonetheless, da Silva considers attempts by Schlick and Putnam to get rid of those uncomfortable synthetic *a priori* truths by trying to render them as analytic. Finally, there is an attempt to modify Husserl's definition of analyticity to account for some presumed analytic statements like "bachelor=unmarried man".

The third paper, written by the German Husserl specialist Uwe Meixner, author of an important book on Husserl and Wittgenstein, is mostly concerned with issues in Husserl's transcendental phenomenology and their negative assessment by philosophers, like Ryle, strongly influenced by Wittgenstein's *Philosophical Investigations*. Meixner expounds Husserl's notions of intentionality and consciousness, and defends Husserl's views against the views of some prominent so-called philosophers of ordinary language, namely the late Wittgenstein, Gilbert Ryle, Daniel Dennett and others. In particular, Meixner discusses some renderings and criticisms of Ryle, inspired by Wittgenstein, of Husserl's analyses of consciousness, and defends Husserl from some Rylean criticisms as well as from Ryle's too frequent misunderstandings. Ryle himself had studied sometime with Husserl, though that is no guarantee for having correctly understood his views. In fact, it should be clear from the exposition that the Wittgensteinian-Rylean blindness to Husserl's views is based on the general prejudice of all Anglo-American empirical philosophy that only what I can relate to with my so-called five senses exists. Since Meixner's paper is not concerned solely with Husserl's views, but with what some influential analytic philosophers say about Husserl, it may serve particularly well as a transition to the second part of the book, in which Husserl is more directly confronted with analytic philosophers.

The second part of the book is concerned with Husserl's influence on philosophers or scientists usually considered as belonging to the analytic tradition. The first of those papers, written by the distinguished Husserlian scholar Claire Ortiz Hill, is naturally a study of Husserl and Frege, the presumed two founding fathers of the two most important philosophical trends of the twentieth century, analytic philosophy and phenomenology. But though it is true that Husserl is the conscious founder of transcendental phenomenology, it is also true that there is much more in Husserl's philosophical views than transcendental philosophy, as clearly seen from the fact that Husserl's opus magnum does not belong to the transcendental phenomenological tradition. In the case of Frege, there is no conscious founding of any philosophical school. Moreover, Frege has nothing to do with the empiricism that has permeated so-called analytic philosophy from Russell until the present, nor anything with the nominalist or semi-nominalist trends in the philosophy of mathematics that grow like mushrooms in the brains of many analytic philosophers. In fact, Frege had much more in common with the Husserl of the pre-transcendental period. Not only did they both, independently of each other and around 1890 arrived at the distinction between sense and referent, and faced the same difficulty with the so-called "indexicals", but both were intellectual grandsons of the rationalist Leibniz and both faced the necessity to clarify the relation between logic and mathematics. Ortiz Hill's paper is mostly concerned with Husserl's conception of functions and its comparison with Frege's related views.

The fifth paper and second of the second part was written by the young Husserlian scholar Carlo Ierna, and is concerned with the impact of the so-called Russell's Paradox – in reality Zermelo-Russell Paradox, since Zermelo discovered it first – on the circle around Husserl's teacher Brentano, and on Husserl's student Koyré, who tried to write a dissertation on that issue under Husserl's guidance, as well as Husserl's reflections motivated by Koyré.

The sixth paper, written by one of the foremost North-American Husserlian scholars, author of a standard book on Husserl's philosophy, and who has contributed the most to make Husserl known in the Anglo-American world, David Woodruff Smith, is a study of Husserl's relationship to Tarski, a relation that could be traced through Twardowski, Lesniewski, and from the latter to Ajdukiewicz and Tarski. In particular, Smith's very interesting paper traces a parallelism between Husserl's conception of intentionality and Tarski's conception of semantics. But when talking about Tarski's semantics, it seems inevitable to say a few words about Carnap's views on semantics. In this way Smith's very stimulating paper serves as a bridge to the final two papers of this collection.

The two last papers, the first of them by the distinguished Frege, Carnap and Husserl scholar Verena Mayer, and the second by the present editor, deal with the very delicate but important issue of Carnap's relation to Husserl. Most analytic philosophers do not know or try not to know that Carnap was Husserl's post-doctoral student during four semesters from 1923 to 1925. There were some extreme cases of blindness, ignorance or whatever, as that of Günther Patzig, who alleged that Carnap never met Husserl, while trying to render Carnap as a "born empiricist", a rendering very popular up to the 1990s. Then –as briefly mentioned above – a sort of "boom" among Carnapian scholars began to render the young Carnap either as a Kantian or a Neo-Kantian, a tendency that is still alive in Anglo-American and Austrian circles. That rendering of the young Carnap has been forcefully contested first by Verena Mayer in two pioneering papers, by Sahotra Sarkar in his excellent 'Husserl's Role in *Der Raum*' and by the editor of this collection in his 2008 book *The Young Carnap's Unknown Master* and in his paper 'On the Interpretation of the Young Carnap's Philosophy'. The three authors mentioned point out a very strong influence of Husserl on the young Carnap, an open one in *Der Raum* and an equally decisive but camouflaged influence in *Der logische Aufbau der Welt*. The two papers in this collection, one of them written in German – which being the language in which Kant, Husserl and Frege wrote, as well as many other important philosophers, is still the most important language for philosophy –, offer a definitive proof both of the thesis that Carnap's *Aufbau*, as it is usually called, is a book written under the main influence of Husserl and of the fact that Carnap's attempt at camouflaging that influence led him to commit plagiarism. Moreover, in other works of the early thirties Carnap continues to appropriate Husserl's conceptions without mentioning the source – that is the case of the distinction between two forms of nonsense in his famous paper of 1932 and the already mentioned distinction between formation rules and transformation rules in *Die logische Syntax der Sprache* –, and in his *Intellectual Autobiography*, instead of acknowledging his great debt to Husserl, Carnap tries to bury the unburied corpse of his crime. Prof Mayer's outstanding and definitive paper is more concerned with the plagiarism itself, whereas the present author's paper puts the emphasis on Carnap's attempt in the *Intellectual Autobiography* to bury the corpse.

The book contains three Appendices, the first one is a part of Husserl's until now unpublished manuscript, identified as A I 35 (α) and (β) on the Zermelo-Russell Paradox, part (α) dating from 1912 and part (β) from 1920, and edited with commentaries by Carlo Ierna and Dieter Lohmar. The second Appendix is a letter of Carnap to Jonas Cohn from 26th September 1925, in which Carnap acknowledges that he had tried to present his professorship's thesis – *Aufbau* – under Husserl's auspices but that Husserl had rejected him, and Carnap seems to hope that Cohn could intercede for him with Husserl. It is important to stress that when Carnap wrote such a letter he had already contacted Schlick and agreed with him to present his professorship's thesis under his auspices, what should leave no doubt that Carnap would have preferred Husserl to Schlick. The third Appendix is a commentary by Thomas Vongehr concerned with the relation between Husserl and Cohn, which at that moment were co-directors of the Psychological Institute of the University of Freiburg, thus, making clear the context of that especially important letter.

Finally, there are probably three important issues that are not covered by the present book, for which we apologize. One of those issues is very evident, namely, the relation between Husserl and Gödel. There was certainly no personal relationship between Husserl and Gödel, nor can one speak of Husserl's direct influence on the early development of Gödel's philosophical views. Nonetheless, when Gödel began to study carefully Husserl's work, he found it not only congenial with his rationalism and Platonism, but he also considered that it was following the footsteps of Husserl's phenomenology that we can arrive at a satisfactory account of mathematics. In fact, he considered Husserl, together with Plato and Leibniz, and possibly Kant as one of the great philosophers in the history of mankind, and was particularly fond of the usually ignored but extremely important Husserlian conception of categorial intuition. And that was certainly a very bold opinion in the context of the philosophical atmosphere that prevailed and prevails in the United States of America, polluted with severe amounts of empiricism and nominalism, as well as lacking a sufficient dosage of knowledge of the writings of foreign philosophers in their original language, especially – though not only –, German.

The second important issue not discussed in the present collection is the relation between Husserl and Hilbert. As already mentioned, this was a very strong personal and philosophical relation, and the extent of Husserl's influence on Hilbert is still to be determined. In fact, as already mentioned, Husserl had by far a better reception in the Klein-Hilbert mathematical circle than in the Philosophy Department at Göttingen, as attested, not only by the many students of Hilbert who also studied with Husserl, but also by the fact that, although Ernst Zermelo never was a student of Husserl – being then a young auxiliary professor ("Privatdozent") in mathematics –, he communicated his discovery of what is unjustly called the Russell Paradox both to Hilbert and Husserl.

Finally, we have omitted any consideration of the probable indirect relation between Husserl and the French school of the Bourbaki mathematicians. This is an issue that has received very little consideration, though as already mentioned, the similarities between Husserl's conception of mathematics and that of the Bourbaki school are considerable. Maybe the link to this relation is Jean Cavaillès, perhaps some less known French scholar. Hopefully, the new generation of Husserlian scholars will fill this gap, since it is very difficult to conceive those similarities as being merely casual.

Those three important issues and other related ones could very well provide material for a continuation of the present enterprise.

Part I: **Husserl and Analytic Philosophy:
A General Assessment**

Guillermo E. Rosado Haddock
Husserl as Analytic Philosopher

Abstract: Analytic philosophers tend to ostracize Husserl without ever having read him. In fact, very few scholars know that in a text from 1908–09 Husserl stated that analysis was the method of philosophy and that logic was 'first philosophy'. In fact, as Frege himself acknowledged, Husserl obtained the sense-reference distinction independently of him. The rest of the paper is concerned with Husserl's many contributions, ignored by analytic philosophers, to the philosophy of logic and mathematics, the philosophy of language, the epistemology of mathematics and even the philosophy of physical science.

§1 Introduction

Consider the following quotations:

> Introduction in this philosophical logic means at the same time introduction to philosophy properly. Since philosophical logic is the introductory discipline of philosophy, it is the first one in view of its nature in the series of philosophical disciplines, it is presupposition and foundation for all the other disciplines that can be called philosophical in a genuine sense. In order to use an Aristotelian expression…: it is "first philosophy", and by the way first philosophy in the most rigorous and authentic sense.[1]

> Our procedure will be purely analytic. We proceed from what is near to us, from what is evident to the beginner.[2]

> Our path being analytic proceeds from the composite and near to us to what is simple…. Every science grounds, and analytic grounding laws ought to belong in common to all sciences. Thus, let us go on analytically.[3]

---

[1] "Einführung in diese philosophische Logik bedeutet zugleich Einführung in die Philosophie selbst. Denn die philosophische Logik ist die Eingangsdisziplin der Philosophie, sie ist in der Reihe der philosophischen Disziplinen die ihrer Natur nach erste, sie ist Voraussetzung und Fundament für alle anderen Disziplinen, die im echten Sinn philosophisch heißen können. Um einen aristotelischen Ausdruck zu gebrauchen…: sie ist ‚Erste Philosophie', und zwar die Erste Philosophie im strengsten und eigentlichsten Sinn." *Alte und Neue Logik: Vorlesungen 1908/1909*, p. 3.

[2] "Unser Verfahren soll rein analytisch sein. Wir gehen von dem Nächstliegenden, von dem dem Anfänger Selbstverständlichen." *Alte und Neue Logik: Vorlesungen 1908/09*, p. 8.

[3] "Unser Weg als analytischer geht ja überhaupt vom Zusammengesetzten und Näherliegenden zum Einfachen…. Alle Wissenschaft begründet, und analytische Begründungsgesetze müssen zu

The above quotations are certainly not from Frege or from any acknowledged analytic philosopher. Nonetheless, they put logic – or philosophical logic – as the most fundamental philosophical discipline, as first philosophy, and analysis as the method of first philosophy. The quotations are from a little known text of Husserl, namely, his 1908–1909 lectures on ancient and new logic. The fact of the matter is that even that relatively late Husserl was concerned with some of the problems that concerned Gottlob Frege, the so-called 'father of analytic philosophy'. Thus, Husserl could very well have been considered one of the founding fathers of analytic philosophy. Of course, orthodox historians of analytic philosophy would immediately object that Husserl was no empiricist, though Frege himself had nothing to do with empiricism, being clearly a Platonist in the philosophy of mathematics and a rationalist all his life. Thus, if on the basis of not being a sort of empiricist or even nominalist you want to exclude Husserl from having been a sort of analytic philosopher, you would also have to exclude Frege.

In any case, it is interesting that the course on ancient and new logic from which those quotations were taken is from the winter semester of 1908–1909, thus, it was given more than one year after his course on "the idea of phenomenology", which is usually considered the official date of Husserl's transcendental phenomenological turn, and three years after his course on the phenomenology of internal time consciousness, which already dealt with issues central to his transcendental phenomenology. Those two sets of lectures, certainly, can be seen as a return to epistemology as first philosophy, and in its most radical Cartesian sense. Nonetheless, the fact of the matter is that the transcendental turn did not bring with it any essential changes either in Husserl's views on the nature and foundational role of logic or of mathematics, or in his explanation in the Sixth Logical Investigation of how we have access to logical and mathematical entities and truths. No discipline, not even epistemology, can violate the laws of logic or mathematics, though it can very well try to explain how we have access to such laws. In fact, in Husserl's philosophy there are two very different senses in which one can legitimately say – of course, without contradiction – that logic is first philosophy and that epistemology is also first philosophy. Leaving that issue aside, let us consider other Husserlian texts that can serve to confirm our thesis that Husserl can very well be considered, besides a phenomenologist, also an analytic philosopher.

---

aller Wissenschaft gemeinsam gehören. Nun gehen wir analytisch weiter." *Alte und Neue Logik: Vorlesungen 1908/09*, p. 40.

§2 Frege and Husserl on Sense and Referent

The best-known contribution of Gottlob Frege to analytic philosophy is the semantic distinction between sense and referent introduced by Frege for the first time in his 1891 paper "Funktion und Begriff"[4] and discussed extensively in his classic paper of analytic philosophy "Über Sinn und Bedeutung"[5] of 1892. However, there is a posthumously published text of Husserl, dating from 1890, in which the distinction between sense and referent is also made. Moreover, in his 1891 critical review of Ernst Schröder's *Vorlesungen über die Algebra der Logik I*[6], published in March of 1891, thus, two months after the publication of Frege's "Funktion und Begriff" – but sent to the publisher already in January –, Husserl makes use of that semantic distinction. Furthermore, in a letter to Husserl of May 1891 Frege acknowledges what hard-core analytic philosophers would never acknowledge, namely, that Husserl obtained the distinction independently of Frege. In fact, a few decades earlier Bolzano had almost obtained the fundamental semantic distinction.[7] But leaving the great Bolzano aside, it seems pertinent to quote Husserl once more.

> In the case of indirect signs it is necessary to distinguish that which the sign means from that which it designates. In the case of direct signs the two are the same. The meaning of a proper name, for example, consists precisely in that it names this determinate object. In the case of indirect signs, however, there are intermediaries between sign and thing, and the sign designates exactly by means of these intermediaries, and precisely because of this [fact] constitute the meaning.[8]
>
> Two signs are equivalent in case they designate in different manner the same object or objects of the same contour, be it by means of external or conceptual means, for example, a

---

4 'Funktion und Begriff' 1891, reprinted in his *Kleine Schriften*, edited by I. Angelelli 1967, revised edition 1990, pp. 125–142.
5 'Über Sinn und Bedeutung' 1892, reprinted in *Kleine Schriften*, edited by I. Angelelli, revised edition, pp. 143–162.
6 'Besprechung von E. Schröders *Vorlesungen über die Algebra der Logik 1*' 1891, reprinted in *Aufsätze und Rezensionen 1890–1910*, pp. 3–43.
7 See *Wissenschaftslehre I*, §25.
8 "Bei indirekten Zeichen ist es notwendig zu trennen dasjenige, was das Zeichen bedeutet und das, was es bezeichnet. Bei direkten Zeichen fällt beides zusammen. Die Bedeutung eines Eigennamens z. B. besteht darin, daß er eben diesen bestimmten Gegenstand benennt. Bei indirekten Zeichen hingegen bestehen Vermittlungen zwischen Zeichen und Sache, und das Zeichen bezeichnet die Sache gerade durch diese Vermittlungen, und eben darum machen sie die Bedeutung aus." 'Zur Logik der Zeichen', p. 343.

pair of names with the same meaning, like king and rex; William the third=the present German emperor, 2+3=7−2=√25.⁹

Meanwhile...the author identifies the meaning of a name with the representation of the object named by the name.... Moreover, he uses the term meaning equivocally, and [does] this in an already unacceptable level. In the above quotation, the incompatible and confusing explanations aside, what is pointed out to is the usual sense. But in another occasion what is really meant is the object named by the name.¹⁰

With the unclearness about the concept of meaning is, moreover, connected [the fact] that Schröder puts names of the sort of "round circle" as 'senseless" together with those with one or more meanings. Obviously, he confuses two different questions, namely, 1) whether a name has a meaning (a "sense"); and 2) whether an object corresponding to it exists or does not exist. Senseless names in a strict sense are names without meaning, pseudonames like Abracadabra. "Round circle", however, is a univocal general name to which, nonetheless, nothing really corresponds.¹¹

Although one could add here a pair of additional passages from 'Zur Logik der Zeichen' to make *ad nauseam* clear that Husserl obtained the sense-referent distinction independently of Frege, we prefer to include another quotation from Husserl's review of Schröder's book because it also serves to make clear that already in 1891, hence three years before Frege's late review of his *Philosophie der Arithmetik*, Husserl had already abandoned the mild psychologism of his youth

---

9 "Zwei Zeichen sind äquivalent, sofern sie denselben Gegenstand bzw. die Gegenstände eines und desselben Umkreises von Gegenständen in verschiedener Weise bezeichnen, sei es durch verschiedene äußerliche oder begriffliche Mittel, z.B. ein Paar gleichbedeutender Namen wie König und rex; Wilhelm III=gegenwärtiger deutscher Kaiser; 2+3=7−2= √25." 'Zur Logik der Zeichen', p. 344.
10 "Indessen...identifiziert der Verfasser die Bedeutung des Namens mit der Vorstellung des durch den Namen genannten Gegenstandes.... Überdies gebraucht er den Terminus Bedeutung selbst äquivok, und dies in einem schon unerträglichen Grade. Im obigen Zitat ist trotz der entgegengesetzten und irrigen Erklärungen auf den gewöhnlichen Sinn abgezielt. Ein andermal aber ist wirklich gemeint der durch den Namen genannten Gegenstand" 'Besprechung von E. Schröders *Vorlesungen über die Algebra der Logik I*', p. 11.
11 "Mit der Unklarheit über den Begriff der Bedeutung hängt es ferner zusammen, daß Schröder Namen der Art "rundes Viereck" als "unsinnige" den ein- und mehrsinnigen an die Seite stellt. Offenbar vermengt er hier zwei verschiedene Fragen, nämlich 1) ob einem Namen eine Bedeutung (ein "Sinn") zukomme; und 2) ob einem Namen entsprechend ein Gegenstand existiere oder nicht. Unsinnige Namen, in exaktem Sinne sind Namen ohne Bedeutung, Scheinnamen wie Abracadabra. "Rundes Viereck" aber ist ein univoker Gemeinname, dem jedoch in Wahrheit nichts entsprechen kann." 'Besprechung von E. Schröders *Vorlesungen über die Algebra der Logik I*', p. 12. In this last quotation one can see that Husserl's terminology differed from Frege', using 'Gegenstand' as the referent, but 'Sinn' and 'Bedeutung' as synonyms, as is usual in German.

book, and clearly distinguished the logical content of a statement –its meaning– from any psychological sort of content.

> That is why also Schröder's distinction between "logical" and "psychological" content of a judgement, or more exactly: of a statement, is unacceptable. The truly logical content of a statement is the judgement content, hence, that what it states.[12]

Interestingly enough, though orthodox analytic philosophers have never accepted that the discovery of the sense-referent distinction was independently made not only by their dear but never understood Frege but also by Husserl, the conscious founder of the phenomenological school, as already mentioned above, it was Frege himself who, after having received copies of Husserl's *Philosophie der Arithmetik* and of his critical review of Schröder, acknowledged in a letter dated 24 May 1891 that Husserl had arrived at the distinction independently of him.[13] In that letter, Frege discusses an important difference in the details, namely, that for him the referent of what he called a 'conceptual word' was the concept, whereas it seemed to him –and he was right– that for Husserl the referent of the conceptual word was the extension of the concept, whereas the concept itself was the sense of the conceptual word. Husserl could have asked Frege what was then the sense of the conceptual word and how can one distinguish it, on the one hand, from the concept and, on the other, from the conceptual word. Frege never answered that hypothetical question.

A much more important difference, not mentioned by Frege, concerns the referents of statements. As is well known, for Frege the referents of statements are truth-values, as discussed in great detail in his duly famous 'Über Sinn und Bedeutung'.[14] Although already at that moment Husserl would have rejected Frege's identification of the referents of statements with truth-values and would probably had identified the referents of statements somewhat vaguely with states of affairs, it took him almost a decade to gain complete clarity on this issue. In fact, even in the First Logical Investigation, in which he discusses these issues thoroughly and makes clear that statements refer to states of affairs[15], there is some inadequacy in the examples, which will disappear only

---

12 "Demgemäß ist auch die Schrödersche Unterscheidung zwischen "logischem" und "psychologischem" Gehalt eines Urteils, oder genauer: einer Aussage, nicht zu billigen. Der wahrhaft logische Gehalt einer Aussage ist ihr Urteilsgehalt, also das, was sie behauptet." 'Besprechung von E. Schröders *Vorlesungen über die Algebra der Logik I*', p. 25.
13 See his *Wissenschaftlicher Briefwechsel* 1974, pp. 94–98, especially p. 98.
14 'Über Sinn und Bedeutung' 1892, reprinted in I. Angelelli (ed.), *Kleine Schriften* 1967, revised edition 1990, pp. 143–162.
15 See *Logische Untersuchungen II*, U. I, §12. See also U. IV, §12.

in the Sixth Logical Investigation[16] with the introduction of the important and useful semantic distinction between states of affairs (the referents of statements) and situations of affairs (the foundations –or bases– of the states of affairs).[17] To understand this important distinction, let us consider the following inequalities: (i) 5+2<9–1, (ii) 4+3<9–1 and (iii) 9–1>4+3. According both to Frege and Husserl, the inequalities (i) and (ii) express different senses, though have the same truth-value. For Frege, that is all that counts, since he considers that the referents of statements are truth-values. For Husserl, however, though those statements have the same truth-value, they have much more in common than the truth-value: they refer to the same state of affairs, namely, that the number '7' is smaller than the number '8'. In fact, the statements (iv) '2 is a prime number', and (v) 'Paris is the capital of France in January 2015' have the same truth-value as (i), (ii) and (iii), but intuitively seem far less related to (i), to (ii) and even to (iii) than any of these three from each other. Leaving (iii) aside for a moment, one can say of (i) and (ii) that they have different senses, but refer to the same state of affairs, whereas (iv) and (v) refer to very different states of affairs, respectively, to the mathematical fact that the number '2' is a prime number and to the contingent fact that a certain city named 'Paris' is the capital in January 2015 of a certain country named 'France'.

The difference between (i) and (ii), on the one hand, and (iii) is more subtle. Let us consider the distinction between (ii) and (iii). They are certainly also very nearly related, but not in the same way that (i) and (ii). They are not obtained from each other by replacing a name with a different name having the same referent, as is the case not only of (i) and (ii), but also of Frege's well-known example (vi) 'The morning star is a planet' and (vii) 'The evening star is a planet'. Hence, contrary to what happens with the pairs of statements {(i), (ii)} and {(vi), (vii)}, (ii) and (iii) refer to different states of affairs, namely, in one case to the state of affairs that the number '7' is smaller than the number '8' and in the other case to the state of affairs that the number '8' is larger than the number '7'. Nonetheless, they are also very nearly related. Both inequalities have in common a sort of non-categorial proto-relation that serves as their base. That proto-relation is what Husserl called 'the situation of affairs'. In the same way in which states of affairs can be seen as equivalence classes of statements having different senses but referring to the same state of affairs, situations of affairs can be seen as equivalence classes of states of affairs. The statements (i), (ii) and (iii)

---

16 Ibid. U. VI, §48.
17 Husserl certainly had been dealing with this distinction without obtaining complete clarity for many years. See on this issue, e. g. his *Logik Vorlesungen 1896*, edited by Elisabeth Schuhmann, p. 95.

have the same situation of affairs as referential basis and, thus, the state of affairs referred to by (i) and (ii) and the state of affairs referred to by (iii) belong to the same equivalence class of states of affairs.[18]

It is certainly surprising how much valuable semantic analysis was hidden under the carpet by the founding father of so-called analytic philosophy and of contemporary logic, and even more astonishing how such a procedure was uncritically accepted by orthodox analytic philosophy. Nonetheless, the fact of the matter – acknowledged or not – is that only in propositional logic does one work with such a semantics like Frege's, for which the referents of statements are truth-values, and that is all that counts. Certainly that is not the case in first-order logic with its extremely rich semantics (classical model theory), nor in its extensions, or in philosophical logic or in any mathematical theory.

§3 On *Logische Untersuchungen*

The prejudices of orthodox analytic philosophers notwithstanding, Husserl's *opus magnum*, *Logische Untersuchungen*, has much more to say to analytic philosophy than to transcendental phenomenologists. For example, Husserl's refutation of psychologism in logic in the first nine chapters of the first volume of that work does not presuppose any phenomenological thesis, and is far superior to Frege's refutation of psychologism in logic in the Preface to the first volume of his *Grundgesetze der Arithmetik*[19] and to his earlier refutation of psychologism in mathematics in his *Die Grundlagen der Arithmetik*.[20] Not only is Husserl's refutation more detailed and better organized than Frege's, but it also contains a criticism of earlier anti-psychologistic conceptions of logic, like Kant's, who conceived logic as a normative discipline. Though Frege coincided with Husserl in conceiving logic as a theoretical science, his distancing from the normative conception was not as neat as Husserl's. In fact, some prominent Fregean scholars – like Hans Sluga[21] – have erroneously thought that Frege conceived logic as a normative discipline. Moreover, whereas Frege did not distinguish between the spe-

---

18 Of course, in a very trivial sense, truth-values can be seen as equivalence classes of situations of affairs. See on this issue, the present author's paper 'Remarks on Sense and Reference in Frege and Husserl', published in 1982 in *Kant-Studien*, and reprinted in the joint collection of papers with Claire Ortiz Hill, *Husserl or Frege?*, Open Court 2000, 2003.
19 See the Preface to *Grundgesetze der Arithmetik I* 1893, pp. XIV-XXV.
20 *Die Grundlagen der Arithmetik* 1884, Centenary Edition 1986. See parts I through III.
21 See, e.g. his *Gottlob Frege* 1980, as well as, for example, his paper 'Frege as a Rationalist', in M. Schirn (ed.) *Studien zu Frege I*, pp. 27–47.

cific relativism of logical psychologism and individual relativism, and both in his critique of mathematical psychologism in his philosophical masterpiece as of logical psychologism in the first volume of his logical treatise he passed from a sober criticism of the specific relativism of his adversaries to the construction of a caricature of such adversaries, ascribing to them a subjectivism –according to which each of us would be speaking about his subjective representations of numbers or of logical laws– that none of them had ever sustained.

The last chapter of the first volume of *Logische Untersuchungen* contains – besides very interesting views on scientific theories and, especially, on physical theories in its first sections –, beginning on §67, Husserl's mature philosophy of logic and mathematics, which Husserl conceived already in 1894–1895[22] and which survived any changes in his philosophical conceptions on other issues. Husserl's conception of logic and mathematics as being formal disciplines running parallel to one another, being logic basically syntactic and semantic, whereas mathematics is a sort of formal ontology, more specifically, a theory of manifolds, a sort of generalization of Riemann's conception of mathematical manifolds[23], and such that there are some (more than one) fundamental mathematical disciplines, being the remaining mathematical disciplines combinations of the fundamental disciplines, specializations of those disciplines or combinations of their specializations, is a clear anticipation of the conception of mathematics of the mid-twentieth century French school of mathematicians usually known as the Bourbaki school.[24]

Of the six 'logical investigations' of the second volume the first one is concerned with problems of semantics and philosophy of language, the second mostly with the traditional problem of universals, the third with problems of philosophical logic and ontology, including, among many other issues the first steps towards a formal theory of wholes and parts – a mereology, in later parlance –, and definitions of analyticity, syntheticity *a priori* and related notions, whereas the fourth one is concerned with logical grammar and linguistic universals. Only the last two investigations are of an epistemological flavor but, nonetheless, references to intuitions of essences are not frequent: the treatment is that of an analysis of knowledge. In the second part of the Sixth Logical Investigation – titled not casually 'Sensibility and Understanding' – Husserl's catego-

---

[22] See Husserl's *The Idea of Phenomenology*, M. Nijhoff 1975 pp. 35–36.
[23] See Riemann's duly famous monograph *Über die Hypothesen, welche der Geometrie zugrunde liegen* 1867, third edition, 1923, reprint, Chelsea 1973.
[24] See Nicholas Bourbaki, 'The Architecture of Mathematics', *American Mathematical Monthly* 57 1950, pp. 221–232.

rial intuition, which should be clearly distinguished from intuition of essence, is introduced as a clear alternative to Kant's conception of mathematical knowledge. Mathematical intuition is then conceived as categorial intuition plus formalization. It would take us too long to explain this almost completely ignored but extremely interesting Husserlian theory of categorial intuition and mathematical knowledge.[25]

A few words, however, should be said about some of the most interesting issues for analytic philosophers treated in *Logische Untersuchungen*.

§4 On Physical Theories

Husserl did not write much on physical theories, at least in comparison with other areas of knowledge. Nonetheless, his remarks on physical theories both in Chapter IV and, especially, in Chapter XI of the first volume of *Logische Untersuchungen* go so deep into the nature of physical theories that had many later authors read him carefully, they would not have wasted their time trying to develop a positivist approach to the philosophy of science. We cannot deal here with Husserl's views in detail and refer the reader to our paper 'Husserl's Conception of Physical Theories and Physical Geometry in the Time of the Prolegomena: A Comparison with Duhem's and Poincaré's Views'.[26] Thus, we can only mention here a few salient points.

Husserl distinguishes three sorts of nexus that are present in scientific activity.[27] Firstly, there is the subjective nexus of the mental activities of the scientist, a nexus that properly does not interest us much here, but which should be clearly differentiated from the two more important objective nexus. Secondly, in every science there is an objective ontological nexus. We do not have different sciences to study lions, dogs and elephants, but a single science, zoology, which studies all sorts of animals. Similarly, we do not have a discipline studying the history of countries below the equator and one studying the history of countries above the equator – or one studying world history before Christ and one studying world history after Christ –, but a single discipline, history, to study the history of each and every country, and as far into the past as feasible. In

---

[25] On this issue see the present author's paper 'Husserl's Epistemology of Mathematics and the Foundation of Platonism in Mathematics' 1987, reprinted in Hill & Rosado Haddock, *Husserl or Frege*, pp.121–139.
[26] Originally published in *Axiomathes* in 2012 and immediately thereafter as Chapter 6 of the authors' collection of papers *Against the Current*.
[27] See §62.

this same sense, physics –or its best-known subdiscipline: classical mechanics– is concerned with masses, forces, velocities and accelerations, not a special discipline (or subdiscipline) for each physical concept. There is, thus, an ontological connection between objects (or concepts) that is objective and serves as a base for the building of even the most primitive sciences. In fact, this ontological nexus is sufficient for the building of a science, and many sciences –e.g. history– have no other foundation than that given to them by the ontological nexus. Nonetheless, there is still a very different objective nexus, namely, the nexus of truths present only in the most developed sciences, especially, in those called by Husserl explanatory sciences, like logic, mathematics and (theoretical) physics. Thus, Newton's second law tells us that force equals mass times acceleration, establishing a perfectly definite relation between such concepts that, as already mentioned, are ontologically related and deserve to be treated by the same discipline. Other physical theories could have envisaged other sorts of definite relations, other presumed nexus of truths, between such same ontologically related concepts.

It should be clear that the nexus of truths is the most perfect of the three nexus, though it is present only in the more advanced sciences, like logic, mathematics and physical science. In these three disciplines, truths are obtained from other more fundamental truths by deduction, and Husserl calls those disciplines "explanatory sciences".[28] But whereas logic and mathematics are purely deductive and formal disciplines, the situation in the case of physical science is more complicated, since physical science is, after all, a science of (the most general aspects of) our physical world. Certainly, in physics as in other empirical sciences, like biology, there are low-level laws, more or less obtained from experience by some sort of induction. But that does not characterize physical science. Physical theories go far above the realm of induction by introducing – and that is what makes them special – *hypotheses cum fundamento in re*.[29] These are theoretical high-level laws thinly based on experience and introduced to explain the low-level laws obtained by a sort of induction, though they themselves are not obtained by any induction. In fact, as Husserl – and, less neatly though almost at the same time, Duhem – has emphatically argued, there exists an indefinite number of other possible *hypotheses cum fundamento in re* that could also do the same task of serving to derive the low-level law. This derivation of the low-level laws from the higher-level laws follows the path of the deductive-nomolog-

---

28 See §64.
29 See Chapter IV, §23 and Chapter XI, especially §§65–66.

ical or the probabilistic-nomological schemes of explanation of low-level laws.[30] Husserl obtained such schemes a few decades before their rediscovery by Hempel, Popper and others. Moreover, if the logical empiricists and even Popper had studied Husserl carefully, they would not have wasted their time discussing the empirical verification or falsification of hypotheses. They would have learned that although in the last instance physical theories have to respond to experience, it is not the case that there is such a direct relation between experience and the higher-level laws of physics as the logical empiricists envisaged. Carnap, in particular, who was so strongly influenced by Husserl's *Ideen zu einer reinen Phänomenologie und phänomenologischen Philosophie*[31] both in *Der Raum*[32] and in *Der logische Aufbau der Welt*[33], and –as mentioned in the next §– by Husserl's *Logische Untersuchungen* both when distinguishing two sorts of nonsense in 'Überwindung der Metaphysik durch logische Analyse der Sprache'[34] and when distinguishing between formation rules and transformation rules in *Logische Syntax der Sprache*[35], failed to learn from Husserl about the nature of physical theories.

§5 On Protecting against Nonsense

In §67 of the first volume of *Logische Untersuchungen* Husserl begins the exposition of his conception of logic, mathematics and their relationship. The theoretical building begins with a discussion of the meaning categories ("Bedeutungskategorien") and the formation of more and more complicated statements on the basis of the simpler ones by the iterative use of the propositional connectives. Husserl calls such laws of formation of complex statements by the iterated use of logical connectives "laws that protect against nonsense". In all further ex-

---

30 See Chapter XI, §§65–66 and 72.
31 *Ideen zu einer reinen Phänomenologie und phänomenologischen Philosophie I* 1913, Hua. III, 1950, revised edition, III(1), edited by Karl Schuhmann 1976.
32 *Der Raum* 1922, reprint 1991.
33 *Der logische Aufbau der Welt* 1928, second edition, 1961. See our book *The Young Carnap's Unknown Master* 2008, as well as our papers 'On the Interpretation of the Young Carnap's Philosophy', in *Against the Current* 2012, pp. 261–284, and 'The Old Husserl and the Young Carnap'.
34 'Überwindung der Metaphysik durch logische Analyse der Sprache' 1932, reprint in his *Scheinprobleme in der Philosophie und andere metaphysikkritische Abhandlungen* 2004, pp. 81–109.
35 *Logische Syntax der Sprache* 1934, expanded English version 1937.

positions of his views on logic and mathematics[36] these logical-grammatical laws constitute the basis of the system, and Husserl makes it perfectly clear that the level in which appear the logical laws properly, that is, the level of the laws that "protect against formal countersense" or contradiction and govern formal deduction is necessarily based on the logical-grammatical level. Briefly: the distinction between formally coherent sense and countersense is already a distinction in the realm of sense. In the Fourth Logical Investigation Husserl discusses once more the issue of the meaning categories and the laws protecting against nonsense.

This important distinction between the laws that protect against nonsense and the logical laws was not present in Frege. In fact, this distinction, which is now part of the logical folklore and is present in every rigorous textbook in logic, was introduced for the first time in the literature read by most analytic philosophers in Carnap's 1934 *Logische Syntax der Sprache* as the distinction between formation rules and transformation rules. But Carnap not only does not mention that Husserl had made the distinction thirty-four years before, but does not even include Husserl's *Logische Untersuchungen* in the bibliography. However, Carnap not only had studied with Husserl from 1923 to 1925[37], but he had also included *Logische Untersuchungen* in the bibliographies of his dissertation, *Der Raum,* and of *Der logische Aufbau der Welt.* Thus, one can assume that Carnap had read Husserl's *Logische Untersuchungen* and had learned the distinction between formation rules and transformation rules from Husserl.

Furthermore, the distinction between two different sorts of nonsense discussed in Carnap's 'Die Überwindung der Metaphysik durch logische Analyse der Sprache', namely, (i) that a statement is devoid of sense because it contains a word devoid of sense, and (ii) that a statement is devoid of sense because it combines words with sense in a way not allowed by the rules of logical grammar, is also present in Husserl's Fourth Logical Investigation, though once more Carnap does not give credit to Husserl in his 1932 paper, and does not even include *Logische Untersuchungen* in its bibliography.

---

36 See his 1929 *Formale und transzendentale Logik*, as well as his posthumously published *Einleitung in die Logik und Erkenntnistheorie: Vorlesungen 1906/1907* and *Logik und allgemeine Wissenschaftstheorie: Vorlesungen 1917/1918.*

37 See on this important historical issue both Karl Schuhmann's *Husserl-Chronik* 1977, p. 281, and Ludwig Landgrebe's letter to Husserl in the latter's *Briefwechsel IV*, p. 298, as well as the Carnap diaries.

§6 On Logic and Mathematics

In the exceptionally important Chapter XI of *Logische Untersuchungen I* Husserl also expounds for the first time his mature conception of logic and mathematics, arrived at about 1894–1895, a conception that – as already mentioned – will not suffer any essential transformation either with his transcendental phenomenological turn or with any other change of emphasis in his later philosophy. For Husserl, logic and mathematics are intimately related, though none of the two can be derived from the other, as Frege and the logicists believed. Logic is essentially a syntactic-semantic discipline, whereas mathematics is more ontologically committed. As already mentioned in §5, Husserl conceives logic as based on a logical-grammatical foundation constituted by what he called 'meaning categories' [Bedeutungskategorien], among them the concept of (an elementary) statement, together with rules for forming elementary statements and, more importantly, rules –he calls them 'laws'– for forming complex statements by the iterative composition of statements by means of the logical connectives. As mentioned above, Husserl calls these rules that guarantee the formation of well-formed complex statements of any degree of complexity on the basis of well-formed elementary statements 'laws that protect against nonsense'.

Once this sort of logical-grammatical grounding of logic is fixed, on a second level logic proper is constituted. It is constituted firstly as a syntactic theory, as the formal theory of deduction, a theory of formal consequence or, to put it negatively – as Husserl liked to do –, the theory of the laws that protect against formal countersense (or contradiction). In *Logische Untersuchungen* and some posthumously published works the distinction between this syntactic level and a semantic one are not clearly demarcated.[38] Nonetheless, in his definitive exposition of his logical views in *Formale und transzendentale Logik*[39], this second level of the logical building is extended by a semantic level obtained by the addition to the syntactic level of the concept of truth and related concepts. Any similarity with Carnap's distinction between syntax (and its rules of formation), logical syntax (and its rules of transformation) and semantics (with the introduction of the concept of truth and related concepts) is not a pure coincidence.

On the other hand, the building blocks of mathematics are what Husserl called the 'formal-ontological categories', that is, the fundamental mathematical concepts. Husserl, who not only was not a logicist but also not a set-theoreticist,

---
38 See *Einleitung in die Logik und Erkenntnistheorie*, based on lectures of 1906–1907, and his *Logik und allgemeine Wissenschaftstheorie*, based on lectures of 1917–1918.
39 *Formale und transzendentale Logik* 1929.

considered that the notion of set was only one of the formal-ontological categories. Relations, parts and wholes, ordinal numbers, and possibly others seem to have been considered by Husserl also as formal-ontological categories.[40] Such formal-ontological categories are the basis on which the fundamental theories of mathematics are built, as groups of axioms characterizing the different formal-ontological categories. The rest of the mathematical theories are obtained, (i) either by combination of the basic ones, (ii) or by specialization of one of the basic ones, (iii) or by combinations of specializations of the basic ones. The similarity with the Bourbakian conception of mathematics is obvious, though up to now the line of influence from Husserl to Bourbaki has not been traced.[41]

Husserl conceived mathematical theories as formal manifolds, and mathematics, in general, as a theory of manifolds. This theory of manifolds combined with logic – as the theory of formal deduction – to form a sort of Husserlian *mathesis universalis*. Thus, this *mathesis universalis* would include the whole domain of what can be formally studied, that is, the totality of the logical-mathematical. Finally, Husserl's conception is crowned by what Husserl called a 'theory of all formal theories', which from a sort of metamathematical perspective was supposed to be able to *a priori* apprehend all possible formal theories. This upper level of Husserl's conception of formal theories was perhaps somewhat ambitious, and Husserl seemed to postulate a sort of completeness of this theory of all theories though[42], as was common before Gödel and Tarski, he did not seem to clearly distinguish between semantic and syntactic completeness. In any case, Husserl's assertions have prompted a discussion among Husserlian scholars on whether Gödel's incompleteness results apply or not to Husserl's theory of all theories.[43] But even if it were not feasible in all its strength, that is, even if some of the tasks of its upper level remain as a sort of Kantian

---

40 See Husserl's different expositions of his views on logic and mathematics in *Logische Untersuchungen* and in his writings mentioned in the previous two footnotes.

41 It is, however, very probable that French mathematicians of the Bourbaki group heard about Husserl's theories from Jean Cavaillès or from some other French scholar interested in Husserl's views on logic and mathematics.

42 See *Formale und transzendentale Logik*, pp. 101–102.

43 For some of the most recent discussions on this issue see Ulrich Majer, 'Husserl and Hilbert on Completeness', *Synthese* 110, 1997, pp. 37–56, Jairo da Silva's papers 'The Many Senses of Completeness', *Manuscrito 23(2)*, 2000, pp. 41–60 and 'Husserl's Two Notions of Completeness, Husserl and Hilbert on Completeness and Imaginary Elements', *Synthese* 120, pp. 417–438, both reprinted in Claire Ortiz Hill and Jairo José da Silva, *The Road Not Taken*, College Publications 2013, and Stefania Centrone's *Logic and Philosophy of Mathematics in the Early Husserl*, Springer 2010.

idea, already Husserl's conceptions both of logic and, especially of mathematics as a theory of manifolds, and its union in the Husserlian *mathesis universalis* represent a great contribution to our understanding of the realm of formal theories.

§7 Husserl's Response to Frege's Letters of 1906

It seems pertinent to conclude this paper with an issue barely discussed even by Husserlian scholars. As is known from Frege's correspondence, Husserl and Frege exchanged letters in 1891 and fifteen years later in 1906. Of the letters exchanged in 1906 only Frege's letters are included in his *Wissenschaftlicher Briefwechsel*[44]. Husserl's letters seem to have been destroyed by bombings in the Second World War. Thus, the reader has only one side of the debate. However, precisely in his lectures on *Alte und Neue Logik*, dating from 1908–1909, Husserl returns to the issue of the 1906 exchange and clearly shows why he could not accept Frege's analyses.

In his letters to Husserl of 1906 Frege argued that logical equivalence is identical to having the same sense. Though Fregean scholars have not thought through what such unfortunate assertions of Frege mean, let us firstly point out that such an identification is incompatible with Frege's conception of having the same sense both in 'Über Sinn und Bedeutung' and in *Grundgesetze der Arithmetik I*. In this last work Frege underscores that statements like (a) '2+2=4' and (b) '2×2=4' do not express the same thought, since '2+2' and '2×2' do not have the same sense. Nonetheless, equations (a) and (b) are mathematically equivalent and, in virtue of Frege's logicism, they are also logically equivalent. In fact, according to Frege's official notion of sense, present in those two fundamental Fregean writings, only synonymous expressions, be it in the same language or in different ones, can be considered as having the same sense. Hence, the identification of logical equivalence with sameness of sense would make logical equivalence a rather uninteresting and unfruitful trivial notion. However, as we have emphasized in earlier writings[45], in the 1906 letters and in a passage of 'Der Gedanke'[46] Frege's notion of sense is certainly different and non-equivalent to the official one, in fact, it seems to approach his notion

---

44 Gottlob Frege, *Wissenschaftlicher Briefwechsel*, pp.101–107.
45 See, for example, our paper 'On Frege's Two Notions of Sense' 1986, reprint in Claire O. Hill and Guillermo E. Rosado Haddock, *Husserl or Frege* 2000, 2003, pp. 53–66.
46 'Der Gedanke' 1918, reprint in *Kleine Schriften*, edited by I. Angelelli, pp. 342–362.

of conceptual content from his *Begriffsschrift*.[47] But Frege's notion of conceptual content is a forerunner of Husserl's notion of a situation of affairs. Thus, it seems pertinent to examine what Husserl had to say about Frege's identification of logical equivalence with sameness of sense.

As Husserl puts it on p. 111 of his *Alte und Neue Logik*, it is an error to identify the sameness of meaning of two judgements with their being immediately derivable from each other. As Husserl puts it on p. 163 and elsewhere, having the same sense and being interderivable are not the same thing. In general, two statements can be interderivable without – in Frege's official terminology – expressing the same thought. In fact, on p. 272 Husserl characterizes logical equivalence similarly to one of Frege's not easily reconcilable characterizations of conceptual content in *Begriffsschrift*, while at the same time reiterating that logical equivalence does not coincide with sameness of sense. Husserl says[48]:

> Thus, with respect to the same collection of fundamental truths and the same terms M ought to follow, that is, be demonstrable, from N and N from M. Of course, M and N do not need to have the same terms.

Furthermore, on pp. 273–274 Husserl distinguished two sorts of logical equivalence both different from Frege's 1906 characterization – if we insist in understanding Frege's 'sense' as 'official sense' –, namely, one corresponding to the identity of state of affairs referred to by two statements expressing different thoughts, and which Husserl calls 'specifically logical equivalence', and a second one, which he calls 'content equivalence' – better: 'content logical equivalence'– of two statements expressing different thoughts and referring to different states of affairs, but having the same situation of affairs as referential basis. It is most surely the second of these two concepts, which is characterized in the quotation from p. 272 and which is more important for logic and mathematics.

It should finally be pointed out that in these lectures Husserl also goes on to reject –see p. 72 – Frege's Context Principle of *Die Grundlagen der Arithmetik* with respect to the referents[49], and throughout the whole lectures a very important

---

[47] See *Begriffsschrift* 1879, §3. In the preceding §2 he had already introduced the notion of judgeable content, which is a forerunner of his later official notion of thought, that is, the sense of statements. It should be clear to anyone not blind that the notions of conceptual content and of judgeable content are completely different.

[48] "Also mit Beziehung auf denselben Inbegriff von Grundwahrheiten und dieselben Termini soll M aus N und N aus M folgen bzw. beweisbar sein. Natürlich brauchen dabei M und N nicht dieselben Termini zu haben." *Alte und Neue Logik: Vorlesungen 1908/1909*, p. 272.

[49] In his later philosophy, both in 'Über Sinn und Bedeutung' and in *Grundgesetze der Arithmetik*, Frege also seems to clearly reject the Context Principle for the referents –if not also tacitly for

issue treated briefly in *Logische Untersuchungen*, namely Husserl's definitions of analyticity and syntheticity *a priori*, receives its due consideration. Husserl's definition of an analytic statement as one that can be completely formalized *salva veritate* is a refinement of Bolzano's, in contrast to those of Frege and Carnap, which are both refinements of Kant's two non-equivalent definitions of analyticity.[50]

§8 Appendix: Two Words on Husserl's *Philosophie der Arithmetik*

It is customary among analytic philosophers not to read Husserl and especially to completely ignore his youth work *Philosophie der Arithmetik I*, so strongly criticized by Frege in his very late review of 1894. The fact of the matter was that in his youth work – which was supposed to be only the first volume of a two volume work, of which the never completed second would be concerned with logical foundations of arithmetic – Husserl incurred in a mild psychologism, one that had little to do with Frege's exaggerations in his critical assessment. Thus, analytic philosophers did not benefit from reading Husserl's criticisms, among them, those of Frege's attempt to define the concept of number.

Much more importantly, analytic philosophers and logicians missed the opportunity of getting acquainted with Husserl's studies on arithmetical operations and, by the way, his anticipation by almost half a century of recursive function theory. Just recently Stefania Centrone, in an especially deep study of Husserl's early investigations on logic, arithmetic and the philosophy of mathematics[51] unearthed this important contribution to the history of logic. Of course, Frege missed the point completely, but many later authors sympathetic to Husserl, as the present author, also missed it. We cannot discuss even briefly this issue here and refer the reader to Centrone's book.

---

the senses. See on this issue the discussion in the present author's book *A Critical Introduction to the Philosophy of Gottlob Frege* and the references therein to Frege's texts.
50 See Kant's *Kritik der reinen Vernunft*, A7–8, B11–12, and A150–153, B190–193.
51 *Logic and Philosophy of Mathematics in the Early Husserl* 2010, §§1.16–1.18.2.

References

Bolzano, Bernard: *Grundlegung der Logik*, selected sections from volumes 1 and 2 of his *Wissenschaftslehre*, Meiner 1963, revised edition 1978.
Bourbaki, Nicholas: 'The Architecture of Mathematics', *American Mathematical Monthly 57* 1950, pp. 221–232.
Carnap, Rudolf: *Der Raum* 1922, reprint, Topos, Vaduz 1991.
Carnap, Rudolf: *Der logische Aufbau der Welt* 1928, second edition, Meiner, Hamburg 1961.
Carnap, Rudolf: 'Überwindung der Metaphysik durch logische Analyse der Sprache' 1932, reprint in Rudolf Carnap, *Scheinprobleme in der Philosophie und andere metaphysikkritische Schriften*, edited by Thomas Mormann, Meiner, Hamburg 2004, pp. 81–109.
Carnap, Rudolf: *Logische Syntax der Sprache* 1934, English revised edition, Routledge, London 1937.
Carnap, Rudolf: Tagebücher 1908–1935, in http://homepage.univie.ac.at/christian.damboeck/carnap_diaries_2015-2018/index.html
Centrone, Stefania: *Logic and Philosophy of Mathematics in the Early Husserl*, Springer 2010
Da Silva, Jairo J.: 'The Many Senses of Completeness', *Manuscrito 23(2)*, 2000, pp. 41–60, reprinted in Hill & Da Silva, *The Road Not Taken*, pp. 137–150.
Da Silva, Jairo J.: 'Husserl's Two Notions of Completeness, Husserl and Hilbert on Completeness and Imaginary Elements', *Synthese 120*, 2000, pp. 417–438, reprinted in Hill & Da Silva, *The Road Not Taken*, pp. 115–136.
Frege, Gottlob: *Begriffsschrift* 1879, reprint, Georg Olms, Hildesheim 1964.
Frege, Gottlob: *Die Grundlagen der Arithmetik* 1884, Centenary edition, edited and with an Introduction by Christian Thiel, Meiner, Hamburg 1986.
Frege, Gottlob: 'Funktion und Begriff' 1891, reprint in Gottlob Frege, *Kleine Schriften*, edited by I. Angelelli, second edition 1990, pp. 125–142.
Frege, Gottlob: 'Über Sinn und Bedeutung' 1892, reprint in Gottlob Frege, *Kleine Schriften*, edited by I. Angelelli, second edition 1990, pp. 143–162.
Frege, Gottlob: *Grundgesetze der Arithmetik I* 1893, reprint of the two volumes in one, Georg Olms, Hildesheim 1962.
Frege, Gottlob: 'Der Gedanke' 1918, reprint in *Kleine Schriften*, edited by I. Angelelli, second edition 1990, pp. 342–362.
Frege, Gottlob: *Kleine Schriften*, edited by I. Angelelli, 1967, second edition 1990.
Frege, Gottlob: *Wissenschaftlicher Briefwechsel*, Felix Meiner, Hamburg 1974.
Hill, Claire O. & Rosado Haddock, Guillermo E.: *Husserl or Frege: Meaning, Objectivity and Mathematics*, Open Court, Chicago et al. 2000, 2003.
Hill, Claire O. & Da Silva, Jairo J.: *The Road Not Taken*, College Publications, London 2013.
Husserl, Edmund: *Philosophie der Arithmetik I* 1891, Hua XII, M. Nijhoff 1970.
Husserl, Edmund: 'Besprechung von E. Schröders *Vorlesungen über die Algebra der Logik I*' 1891, reprint in Edmund Husserl, *Aufsätze und Rezensionen 1890–1910*, pp. 3–43.
Husserl, Edmund: *Logische Untersuchungen* (two volumes) 1900–1901, reprint, Hua XVIII 1975 & XIX 1984.
Husserl, Edmund: *Ideen zu einer reinen Phänomenologie und phänomenologischen Philosophie* 1913, Hua III, 1950, revised edition, M. Nijhoff, Den Haag 1976.

Husserl, Edmund: *Formale und transzendentale Logik* 1929, Hua. XVIII, M. Nijhoff, Den Haag 1974.
Husserl, Edmund: 'Zur Logik der Zeichen', Appendix B.I to Husserliana edition of *Philosophie der Arithmetik*, Hua XII, 1970, pp. 340–373.
Husserl, Edmund: *Introduction to the Logical Investigations*, M. Nijhoff, Den Haag 1975.
Husserl, Edmund: *Aufsätze und Rezensionen (1890–1910)*, Hua XXII, M. Nijhoff, Den Haag 1979.
Husserl, Edmund: *Einleitung in die Logik und Erkenntnistheorie*, Hua XXIV, M. Nijhoff, Den Haag 1984.
Husserl, Edmund: *Vorlesungen über Bedeutungslehre*, Hua XXVI, M. Nijhoff, Den Haag 1987.
Husserl, Edmund: *Briefwechsel* (ten vols.), Kluwer, Dordrecht 1994.
Husserl, Edmund: *Logik und allgemeine Wissenschaftstheorie*, Hua XXX, Kluwer, Dordrecht 1996.
Husserl, Edmund: *Logik Vorlesung 1896*, edited by Elisabeth Schuhmann, Kluwer, Dordrecht 2001.
Husserl, Edmund: *Alte und Neue Logik: Vorlesung 1908/09*, edited by Elisabeth Schuhmann, Kluwer, Dordrecht 2003.
Kant, Immanuel: *Kritik der reinen Vernunft* 1781, revised second edition 1787, reprint of both editions, edited by R. Schmidt, Meiner, Hamburg 1930, third edition 1990.
Majer, Ulrich: 'Husserl and Hilbert on Completeness: A Neglected Chapter in Early Twentieth Century Foundation of Mathematics', *Synthese 110*, 1997, pp. 37–56.
Riemann, Bernhard: 'Über die Hypothesen, welche der Geometrie zugrunde liegen' 1867, third edition, Berlin 1923, reprint, Chelsea, New York 1973.
Rosado Haddock, Guillermo E.: 'Remarks on Sense and Reference in Frege and Husserl' *Kant-Studien 73(4)* 1982, reprint in Hill & Rosado Haddock, pp. 23–40.
Rosado Haddock, Guillermo E.: 'On Frege's Two Notions of Sense' *History and Philosophy of Logic 7(1)* 1986, reprint in Hill & Rosado Haddock, pp. 53–66.
Rosado Haddock, Guillermo E.: 'Husserl's Epistemology of Mathematics and the Foundation of Platonism in Mathematics', *Husserl Studies 4(2)* 1987, reprint in Hill & Rosado Haddock, pp. 121–139.
Rosado Haddock, Guillermo E.: *A Critical Introduction to the Philosophy of Gottlob Frege*, Ashgate, Aldershot 2006.
Rosado Haddock, Guillermo E.: 'Husserl's Conception of Physical Theories and Physical Geometry in the Time of the Prolegomena', *Axiomathes 22* 2012, reprint in *Against the Current*, pp. 183–214.
Rosado Haddock, Guillermo E.: 'On the Interpretation of the Young Carnap's Philosophy', in *Against the Current*, pp. 261–284.
Rosado Haddock, Guillermo E.: *Against the Current*, Ontos, Frankfurt 2012.
Rosado Haddock, Guillermo E.: 'The Old Husserl and the Young Carnap' (this volume).
Schirn, Matthias (ed.): *Studien zu Frege* (3 vols.), Frommann-Holzboog, Stuttgart-Bad Cannstatt 1976.
Schuhmann, Karl: *Husserl-Chronik*, M. Nijhoff, Den Haag 1977.
Sluga, Hans: 'Frege as a Rationalist', in M. Schirn (ed.), *Studien zu Frege I*, Frommann-Holzboog, Stuttgart-Bad Cannstatt 1976, pp. 27–47.
Sluga, Hans: *Gottlob Frege*, Routledge, London 1980.

Jairo José da Silva
The Analytic/Synthetic Dichotomy

Husserl and the Analytic Tradition

Abstract: The concept of synthetic *a priori* truth is central in Husserl's phenomenology. The fact that there are truths that are not analytic, or purely formal, but not empirical either, or so Husserl thought, opens a domain for an *a priori* science whose task is precisely that of investigating such truths, or better, the grounds where they are rooted. However, the existence of synthetic *a priori* truths is explicitly and emphatically denied in the analytic philosophical tradition. One can say that this is indeed its most fundamental tenet. Unsurprisingly, Husserl has been explicitly criticized by Schlick, who believed that such truths are in fact analytic, that is, true by virtue of meaning. I here analyze both Husserl's views on the matter and Schlick's criticism, showing that Schlick's purported demonstration of the analyticity of supposedly phenomenological synthetic *a priori* truths implicitly presupposes certain phenomenological truths. So, the fact that these presuppositions are true cannot, short of circularity, rest on matters of meaning. In other words, meaning, to the extent that it is based essentially on how words are actually used, depends on *a priori* determinations of possible experience, which is precisely what synthetic *a priori* truths, as Husserl conceives them, do.

§1 Introduction

Both the analytic/synthetic and the a priori/a posteriori distinctions apply to truth-bearers, thoughts, judgments, propositions, assertions, and the like (which I will call *truths*, indistinctively). Analytic and synthetic have to do, broadly speaking, with what makes truths true, and a priori and a posteriori with how truths can be known or justified. In the simplest possible formulation, an *a priori* truth is one that *can* be known independently of (empirical) experience, an *a posteriori* truth is one that cannot.[1] The distinction analytic/synthetic cannot be so easily drawn and has been a matter of much debate. On a first approach, one could say that analytic truths are *explicative* and synthetic truths

---

[1] One could consider other types of experience, but here experience will always mean *empirical* experience, unless explicitly stated otherwise.

ampliative; that is, by knowing an analytic truth one only knows what is implicit in knowledge one already has, whereas by knowing a synthetic truth one adds to one's stock of knowledge. These ideas can, if we allow for terminological differences, be traced back to Descartes, Hume, Leibniz and Kant. For Kant, a truth (he would say a *judgment*) is analytic if the *idea* expressed by the predicate is contained in the *idea* expressed by the subject; by asserting an analytic truth one only explains what is contained in the idea of the subject and this is what makes it true. In certain philosophical circles, however, obsessed with the threat of psychologism, where the simple mention of the word "idea" sends a red alert, the distinction is usually phrased in terms of *meaning*. Assertions – no longer ideas, thoughts and the like, but their linguistic expressions – are analytic, so the characterization goes, if they are true by virtue of logic and what their terms *mean*, and synthetic if logic and meaning are not enough to secure truth.

This apparently innocent rephrasing is in fact a momentous change of perspective, which has important philosophical consequences. Note how easily Quine makes this move in his well-known essay "Two Dogmas of Empiricism":

> [...] Kant's intent, evident more from the use he makes of the notion of analyticity than from his definition of it, can be restated thus: a statement is analytic when it is true by virtue of meanings and independently of fact.

According to Quine, he is only interpreting Kant's intentions, "evident from the use he makes of the notion of analyticity". But,of course, he is doing much more than that; the "linguistic turn" is *entirely* contained in this "interpretation". There is a change of focus, from *judgments as acts* to assertions, i.e. linguistic expressions of judgments (considered either noetically as acts or noematically as the objective content of judgment-acts), from meaning-giving acts emanating from *subjects* – to which the notion of "idea" makes implicit reference – to *objective* meanings dissociated from subjectivity. In his approach to the problem of semantic analytic statements (statements that are true by virtue of synonymy), for example, Quine (op. cit.) takes for granted that meanings are *objectively* given entities. His problem is only to determine how meanings can be *grasped* and identity among them established; his focus is on *objective* conditions for synonymy, such as definitions, interchangeability *salva veritate*, or semantic rules, while completely ignoring meaning-giving *acts*, the very source of meaning.

The reason is that Quine and the entire analytic philosophical tradition believe that indulging in analyses of *subjective* acts (by reflecting on them, for example) is to indulge with psychologism; questions as to *how* meaning is created are, they think, psychological questions irrelevant for philosophy. A quote from

Dummett's *Truth and other Enigmas* is symptomatic of this disposition. For him, one of the basic tenets of analytic philosophy, as Frege clearly stated, he says, is that "the goal of philosophy is the analysis of the structure of *thought* [*but*] that the study of *thought* is to be sharply distinguished from the study of the psychological process of *thinking* and [...] that the only method for analyzing thought consists in the analysis of *language*" (p. 458). For Husserl, on the other hand, thought cannot be dissociated from thinking, considered however as an *intentional* act of sense-giving, not a *psychological* act, and the study of thoughts has both an object-oriented noematic and a transcendental-subjective noetic dimension. Objectivity in particular *is not given but constituted*, and meanings, albeit objective, are intentional constructs that can be analyzed in second-order acts of *reflection* on meaning-bestowing acts. Quine obliterates the subject; Husserl places it at the center of his considerations. More about this later.

Whereas analytic philosophers tend to draw the analytic/synthetic distinction in terms of truth due to *logic* or *meaning* (analytic truths) and truth due to *facts* (synthetic truths), throwing all analytic truths together in the category of a priori truths and all synthetic truths together in that of a posteriori truths, with no room for synthetic a priori truths, for Husserl, on the other hand, a priori truths are necessary truths of *essence* and are either analytic or synthetic depending on whether the essences in question are formal-logical or material-ontological, respectively. Formal-ontological categories are formal-logical and differ from material-ontological categories in scope, the totality of objects for the formal-ontological and proper subdomains of the domain of all objects for the material-ontological. As Benoist puts it (Benoist 1999: 98), in Husserl, the analytic a priori appears as the limit of the synthetic a priori. A posteriori truths, those that can be known only by experience, are, for Husserl, *factual* and *contingent*, not like a priori truths *essential* and *necessary*, and are all synthetic.

As is clear, there is a distinct cleavage between analytic philosophers and Husserl on this matter; for the former the class of synthetic a priori truths is empty, for the latter, as for Kant, it is not. The central issue is whether *original* knowledge can be obtained by means others than experience. Kant thought that mathematics and theoretical physics were living testimonies that synthetic a priori knowledge exists. For him, Tales' angular theorem – the internal angles of any triangle add to two right angles – and the principle of causality – no physical phenomenon without a physical cause –, for example, were synthetic a priori truths. The idea of triangle does not contain the idea that the sum of internal angles is equal to two right angles, nor the idea of physical phenomenon contains the idea of cause. Since the truths of mathematics or the principle of causality are obviously not truths of experience, voilà, they must be synthetic a priori. Logical positivists, on the other hand, made their entire epistemology rest on the "dogma" that there are only two sources of knowledge, logic and experience; if things can be known by logic only they are analytic and a priori, if experience is required they are synthetic and a posteriori, there is no room for synthetic a priori knowledge, no room for a *tertium*. Kant, Husserl and the entire phenomenological tradition disagree; for them, there is a tertium, *transcendental* knowledge. I believe I am not too far off the mark by saying that it is the possibility of a form of knowledge that does not depend on experience, but is not only a matter of logic, the *pomme* fuelling the *discorde* between phenomenologists and analytic philosophers.

In this essay I want to present and discuss Husserl's treatment of the problem of analytic and synthetic a priori truths, confronting it with the analytic approach. For Husserl, there is an analytic a priori and a synthetic a priori, the first being *formal*, the second, *material*. Jacques English, the translator of Husserl into French, says that the first a priori is *subjective*, having to do with the transcendental conditions for perceiving, thinking and reasoning *in general*, the second, objective, having to do with the transcendental conditions for perceiving, thinking and reasoning about *particular* categories of objects (English 2009: 24). The possibility of synthetic a priori knowledge, for Husserl, rests on the fact that ontological categories harbor transcendental presuppositions associated with their intentional positing that can be known a priori by categorial intuition. Synthetic a priori knowledge is *eidetic* knowledge, that is, knowledge of laws of essence pertaining to material-ontological (as opposed to formal-ontological) categories. According to Husserl, eidetic sciences (sciences of *essences*, not facts), can be either formal (constituting the *mathesis universalis*), divided in formal logic and formal ontology, or material, such as, for example, physical geometry (*Ideas I* §8 note 1). In order to appreciate these things better a quick overview of his conception of formal logic is in order.

§2 Husserl's logic

According to Husserl, formal logic (in the broad sense of a *mathesis universalis*) comprises two disciplines, apophantic logic and formal ontology. The former has to do with assertions, the latter with objects (things which assertion are about, things about which one is saying something) considered in complete generality, objects merely as such. Logic, for Husserl, is the meta-science of science; science is a system of truths; truths are assertions about objects; so, logic must be equally concerned with assertions (apophanses) and objects, considered, however, simply as things-about-which. Despite superficial similarities, apophantic logic and formal ontology cannot be identified with, respectively, syntax and semantics in the sense of modern logic.[2] Syntax is the part of logic whose objects are assertions independently of any particular interpretation, semantics with assertions with semantic content, assertions referring to *particular* domains of objects. Syntax belongs to what Husserl calls formal apophantics. But there is more to formal logic than apophantic logic, there is also formal ontology. To apophantic categories – subject, predicate, etc. – there correspond in strict parallelism formal ontological categories – object, property, etc. *Particular* domains of objects, on the other hand, are not matters of concern for formal logic, but *regional ontologies*. For Husserl, synthetic a priori truths are a priori truths of regional ontologies whereas analytic truths are a priori truths of formal logic. The distinction analytic-synthetic corresponds exactly to the formal-material one; analytic truths are formal truths referring to both apophantic and formal ontological categories; synthetic truths are material truths concerning *material* (regional) ontological categories. Synthetic *a priori* truths are *necessary* material truths, synthetic a posteriori truths are *contingent* material truths.

For Husserl, the first task of formal logic is to establish the formal categories of science, those by which objects are categorized regardless of what they are, i.e. the formal ontological categories, and those by which thinking and asserting are possible, i.e. the apophantic categories. The establishment of the system of categories of formal logic requires, as a complement, a sort of categorial "grammar", the system of all necessary truths pertaining to them. These are, for Husserl, by definition, the analytic *laws*. Analytic laws concern logical categories exclusively (of both formal apophantics and formal ontology); the linguistic expression of analytic laws must, therefore, contain only names of logical categories and variables (for objects, properties, relations, etc.), nothing more.

Since, for example, the categories of number and class are formal ontological categories, arithmetic and the theory of classes are analytic. This deserves some comments. For Frege, the analyticity of arithmetic requires the restatement of arithmetical judgments in terms of logical concepts and the logical reduction of so rephrased arithmetical judgments, via proofs within a specific logical context, to logical axioms – an immense endeavor. For Husserl, on the other hand, the analyticity of arithmetic is manifest, it is so by simply being a *conceptual* science whose object is a formal-logical concept. By examining the concept of number directly in conceptual intuition and extracting the necessary truths pertaining to it, or indirectly, by deriving the logical consequences of its definition, the

---

[2] In *Formal and Transcendental Logic*, Husserl adds to apophantics a third level, concerned with the concept of truth and related concepts. This clearly shows that what we would call today semantics belongs, for Husserl, to apophantic logic, not formal ontology (I thank the editor of this volume, G. Rosado Haddock, to have brought this to my attention).

mathematician is *ipso facto* doing logic. The *logical status* of the concept of number suffices to grant arithmetic its analytic character. Synthetic a priori truths are also conceptual truths, the difference is that the concepts in question are *not* logical concepts. It is important, however, to notice that Husserl is *not* a reductionist in the modern sense of the term; he is not proposing, as Frege did, that arithmetic be reduced to logic nor that all formal ontological categories be reduced to that of set.[3]

Material domains (such as, for instance, empirical reality, space, color, etc.) have their truths too, both a priori and a posteriori. *Material* or *synthetic a priori* truths concerning a *particular* ontological domain are truths that objects *must necessarily satisfy* so as to be objects of *that* domain. For example, perceptual objects must necessarily be objects immersed in the flux of time; objects of visual perception must necessarily be colored. Another way of saying this is that synthetic a priori truths are *necessary conceptual truths regarding material concepts*.

What Husserl sees as truths of *essence* (necessary conceptual truths), analytic philosophers operating within the linguistic turn regard as truths concerning the *meaning* of concept-names. Whereas the fact that colors cannot exist without colored objects, for example, is for Husserl an *essential* feature of color-*concepts*, for analytic philosophers, it is part of the *meaning* of color-*words*. Since for the latter truths of meaning are analytic by the very definition of analyticity, Husserlian synthetic a priori truths are, for them, merely explicative analytic truths devoid of relevant cognitive content.

The anti-essentialism of analytic philosophers is evident, for example, in Quine's "Two Dogmas of Empiricism". "Meaning", he says, "is what essence becomes when it is divorced from the object of reference and wedded to the word". Would Husserl agree with this identification? Must one know the essence of a concept in order to define its name? And vice-versa, is to know what a name means sufficient to know the essence of the concept that the name names? I believe he would not; he would point out, I think, to the phenomenological difference between the meaning of a name, whose sole task is to allow the *identification* of what the name names, and digging into the essence of the thing named. In order to know the essence, or *clarify* a concept, he would say, it does not suffice to be able to *distinguish* it from other concepts, i.e. to know what its name means. A mathematical definition, for example, exhausts the meaning of a concept-name, but to *clarify the essence of the concept more* is required than drawing logical consequences from the definition. Definitions have to do with the *evi-*

---

[3] The fact that Husserl was not a reductionist was brought to my attention by the editor of this collection, G. Rosado Haddock.

dence of distinction, and do not necessarily reach the *evidence of clarity*. For one to grasp meanings it suffices to reflect on *meaning giving* acts; for essences to be grasped one may have to investigate the concept *directly* in conceptual intuition. In short, Husserl would strongly disagree that truths of essence merely disclose the meaning of *words*. I will come back to this later.

§3 Definitions

Some explicit definitions from Husserl's *Logical Investigations* are in order. According to him, "analytic laws are unconditionally universal propositions, which are accordingly free from all explicit or implicit assertions of individual existence; they include none but formal concepts, and if we go back to such as primitive, they contain only formal categories" (3rd LI, §12). By *analytic laws*, then, Husserl means analytic truths concerning formal categories, i.e. the *necessary, universal* truths of formal logic. "This is an analytic law: it is built up exclusively out of formal-logical categories and categorial forms" (3rd LI, §12). For example, "no non-X is an X", which expresses a fundamental truth concerning the concept of negation.

"We may define *analytically necessary propositions* as propositions whose truth is completely independent of the peculiar content of their objects [...] and of any possible existential assertion" (3rd LI, §12). "The specification of laws", Husserl says, "always yields necessary connections: specifications of analytic laws therefore yield analytically necessary connections. What are called 'analytic propositions' are in general *analytically necessary connections*" (3rd LI, §12). In short, *analytic necessities* are specifications of analytic laws. For example, "no unmarried [non-married] man is married", which is an instantiation of the analytic law mentioned above, "X" being substituted by "married man".

The formal abstraction of an analytic necessity must then be an analytic law. For example, "no non-X is an X", the formalization of "no non-married man is a married man", is indeed an analytic law. An analytic necessity is true and *remains true under formal abstraction*, i.e. the substitution of the particular material (i.e. non-formal) concepts that occur in it by concept-variables. The fact that formal abstraction preserves truth indicates that the truth in question is indeed the specification of an analytic law. A *necessary but not universal* law, on the contrary, that is, a necessary law "which includes material concepts, so as not to permit of a formalization of these concepts *salva veritate* [...] is a *synthetic a priori* law (3rd LI, §12). Analogously, Husserl defines *synthetic necessities* as specifications of synthetic a priori laws (3rd LI, §11). For example, "this red which I have in front of me now is not green", which specifies the synthetic a priori law that says that no two different colors can appear to a viewer as covering simultaneously the same regions of space all over. In short, *necessary* assertions are *a priori* and can be either universal or particular. Necessary and universal logical truths and necessary truths containing particular semantic content that allow formal abstraction *salve veritate* are analytic (*syntactic* and *semantic* analytic, respectively); necessary, but particular truths, which do not allow unrestricted formal abstraction *salve veritate*, are synthetic.[4]

But things are not so simple; formal abstraction can sometimes transform an assertion many would see as an analytic necessity into an assertion-form (or formal assertion) that is not even in general true. Let's consider, for example, the assertion S = no bachelor is a married man. Obviously, S is not an analytic law; it does not involve only logical concepts. But it is, obviously, a necessary truth, and so must be either an analytic necessity, i.e. the instantiation of an analytic law, or a synthetic a priori truth. According to Husserl's criterion, S is an analytic necessity if its formal abstraction, that is, the substitution of its material content by variables turn out to be an analytic law. But if "bachelor" and "married man" are substituted by, respectively, concept-variables X and Y, S becomes "no X is Y", which not only is not an analytic law but is not even true in general (for instance, if X and Y are instantiated by, respectively, "man" and "mortal").

So the question imposes itself, how Husserl sees cases such as these? The unproblematic way out would be to classify assertions such as S as *synthetic* a priori. Theodorou 2015 (p. 247), for instance, thinks that this is as Husserl himself sees the matter, for he says: "Phenomenology considered as analytic *only* the truths of Formal Apophantics and Formal Ontology [*emphasis added*]". But, he adds, "[...] there are also necessary connections among the possible contents of intuition, but that must be acknowledged as a priori *synthetic* (e.g. 'all bodies are extended', 'the same surface cannot be blue and green all over at the same time', etc.). Those that remain are just a posteriori synthetic ('gold is a yellow metal', etc.)." Since according to Husserl's criterion S is not analytic, then it must be synthetic a priori. The reason I find this solution unsatisfactory is that whereas the truth of "no surface can be colored in two different colors all over simultaneously", for instance, like all Husserl's synthetic a priori truths, rests on conceptual necessity and demands conceptual intuition in order to be known, that of "no bachelor is married", analogously to all semantic analytic truths of the same sort, rests on mere *synonymy* and can be known by simply knowing what "bachelor" means. The former expresses a truth of *essence*, the

---

[4] Essentially the same characterizations are given in *Ideas I*, §9, and *Formal and Transcendental Logic*, §55.

latter a *linguistic* or "grammatical" truth. Although Husserl certainly does *not* think that meaning is the reason why the assertion "no surface can be colored in two different colors all over simultaneously" is true, he would maybe think so in the case of "no bachelor is married". Although Husserl does not, as far as I know, treat this issue explicitly, I believe that he would make a distinction between truths of meaning, on the one hand, which have to do with *words* and *linguistic* meaning from, on the other, truths of *essence*, which have to do with *concepts* and *conceptual* meaning. The former he would, I believe, take as purely formal, and so analytic; the latter as material, and so synthetic. I will come back to this below.

§4 Analytic truths

Let's now focus our attention on Husserl's notion of analyticity. As we have seen, for him, an analytic truth is true due to its logical form, not its material content, and can be either an analytic law or an analytic necessity, i.e. the specification of an analytic law. I also advanced the view that Husserl would probably agree that truths of meaning should *also* count as analytic necessities. But before arguing for this view, let me dedicate some lines to a particular class of analytic laws, arithmetical truths.

Analytic laws, as Husserl emphasized, are *universal* truths which do not involve presuppositions of existence or, still, universal truths regarding logical categories. Since arithmetical concepts are formal ontological, hence logical concepts, arithmetical laws in particular are analytic. But what about *particular* truths such as 5+7=12, which obviously presuppose the existence of the objects 5, 7 and 12? I believe, having in mind the treatment of numbers in Husserl's first major philosophical work, *Philosophy of Arithmetic* (1891), that he also saw truths as that as *universal* truths, in which however numbers appear as logical (formal-ontological) categories, *not* themselves objects-about-which. In other words, 5+7=12 is *not* an assertion about numbers, but about unspecified objects in which 5, 7 and 12 appear as *predicates*. Let me explain. For Husserl, numbers are higher-order abstract objects or, more specifically, non-independent *forms* attached to well-determined collections of objects of whatever type. Any well-determined (finite) collection of things, no matter what they are or whether they are assembled under a well-determined concept or gathered and taken as a unity in combined intentional acts of collecting and unifying, have a determinate (finite) number associated with it which "measures" the quantity of its members. *Numbers are logical forms* and two collections have the *same* number if they are equinumerous, i.e. if there is a 1–1 correspondence between them. Given two collections X and Y, whose numbers are, respectively n and m (I denote this by writing $n(X)$ and $m(Y)$), the sum $n+m$ is, *by definition*, the number of the *disjoint* union $X\hat{\ }Y$. The assertion 5+7=12 can then be rewritten thus: $(X)(Y)(Z)(5(X)\ \&\ 7(Y)\ \&\ Z = X\hat{\ }Y \to 12(Z))$, a *necessary universal* truth about *arbitrary* collections of *objects*. Arithmetic is part of formal ontology to the extent that it is a theory of a particular class of abstract formal-ontological categories, namely, numbers; these categories apply to arbitrary collections of objects and do *not* involve presuppositions of existence. So, even *particular* assertions about *numbers* are disguised *general* assertions about *classes of objects* where numbers appear as logical categories.

Let's now consider in more details the notion of analytic necessity. As I have already noticed, if we take Husserl's definition to the letter, truths which we tend to see as analytic turn out to be synthetic, as S, "no bachelor is married", exemplifies. The judgment S', "no unmarried man is married", is of course an instance of the logical law "no non-X is an X", and is true regardless of what "married man" or "to be married" mean. S follows from S' by simply substituting in it "unmarried man" by the *synonymous* term "bachelor", identical with it in meaning. S' is an analytic necessity, i.e. the specification of a logical law, but what about S? Is it a material or a formal truth? In the first case, it would be synthetic a priori; in the second, analytic. Does our knowledge that "bachelor" *means* "unmarried man" is *material* knowledge? Husserl does not, to my knowledge, discuss this issue explicitly, but I believe he would not see the knowledge of the meaning of words as material knowledge. If this were indeed so, one could assemble logical laws and instantiations of logical laws together as *syntactic* analyticities and analytic truths involving synonymy in a category of itself, the *semantic* analyticities.

As we have already seen, if we apply Husserl's criterion for analytic necessities, namely, formal abstraction of analytic necessities should be logical laws, "no bachelor is married" turns out *not* to be an analytic necessity, for its formal abstraction "no X is a Y" is not even in general true. The problem, of course, is that there are hidden meaning relations between the *terms* "married man" and "bachelor" (identity of meaning in this case) which formal abstraction completely obliterates. If we take the reasonable point of view that formal abstraction cannot ignore meaning relations among relevant terms, then these relations must be rendered explicit *before* formal abstraction is carried out. Logical form manifests itself only when different variables stand for meaning independent terms. Since "bachelor" is *equivalent in meaning* to "unmarried man", the assertion "no bachelor is married" can be rephrased, *without change of meaning*, as "no unmarried man is a married man", which is an instantiation of the analytic law "no non-X is an X", so, an analytic necessity. Husserl's criterion of analytic necessity can then be generalized thus: *an assertion is an analytic necessity if it admits a meaning equivalent syntactic variant whose formal abstraction is a logical law.*

A reader of Quine would feel uneasy at this point, because he believes to know that meaning analyses are difficult, tend to turn in circles and often cannot get anything definite. Is identity of meaning based on synonymy or the other way around? Can definitions settle the matter? Semantic rules maybe? What if these things are not available? Are meanings in general well-defined entities bearing definite logical relations with one another?

Although meanings are, from both perspectives, objective entities, the analytic philosopher and the phenomenologist do not have equivalent conceptions of what objectivity is. In the analytic tradition objectivity is *given*, in the phenomenological tradition it is *constituted*. Whereas the phenomenologist asks how objective meanings come to be, the analytic philosopher is mostly interested on how one comes in possession of them. Meanings are well-determined entities "out there" somewhere, the analytic philosopher believes, the problem is how one grasps them. Explicit definitions is a way. Although definitions can sometimes be, he concedes, ways of creating meanings *ex nihilo*, in which case to examine definitions is the best way to clarify meanings, more often definitions are only ways, and not always completely successful ways of *grasping* meanings that already exist "out there". In these cases, better try something else. But, as Quine emphasized, hopes of success are slim.

Consider again Quine's assertion that "meaning is what essence becomes when it is divorced from the object of reference and wedded to the word". In an objectivist and essentialist perspective, essences *belong* to things and are what they are; if meanings are to words what essences are to the objects the words name, then for the meaning of conceptual terms to be determined one must inquire the essence of concepts. If this is so, attributing meaning to words goes hand-in-hand with "capturing" the essence of what these words denote. In an objectivist but non-essentialist approach, on the other hand, as Quine says, "definitions reporting selected instances of synonymy come [...] as reports upon usage". Instead of definitions determining synonymy, it is synonymy-in-use that finds its way into definitions. Meaning, then, boils down to usage, becoming notoriously fluid and indeterminate.

Although approaching the issue from a different perspective Husserl too must cope with the indeterminacy of meaning. Although fully objective, Husserl thinks, meanings do not exist without being brought into existence. For him, words are infused with meaning by meaning-conferring acts (sounds or written symbols are *expressions* only if they are *infused with meaning*, which requires specific intentional acts or experiences: "[t]hese acts we shall call the *mean-*

ing-conferring acts or the *meaning-intentions*" – 1st *LI*, §9). As intentional acts, they require a subject who performs the acts, the *intentional subject*. The meaning-constituting subjectivity, however, is not an individual. Individuals may, of course, use words, or better, sounds resembling words, without meaning them (meaningless blabbing), but they cannot give them arbitrary meanings and still participate in the linguistic community; language usage and linguistic meanings are communitarian affairs. The meaning-conferring intentional subject is, in the case of language (but not only), the entire *linguistic community*, spread in space and time; the constituting subjectivity has a *historical* dimension. Although meaning-constitution does not necessarily finds its way into explicit definitions, semantic rules and the like, meanings are *displayed* in meaningful communication and can be accessed by inquiring meaning-intentions in communication.

But given their *historical* dimension, meanings may fluctuate depending on time, place, or context, and may not be completely determinate at a given moment and situation. *Meanings*, in short, although completely objective, *are dynamical entities* and communication, even if for all purposes meaningful, often admit some degree of indeterminateness and vagueness. Attempts to explicitly bring out the "implicit" meaning of words may fail; synonymy may not, in some cases, be a *matter of fact*. The status of assertions that depends on the establishment of synonymy must, then, be left undecided.

Meanings do not float in the air, being merely "grasped" in meaningful thought, in Frege's colorful but utterly incomprehensible metaphor. Meanings are *created*, and can be brought to consciousness by unpacking meaning-given acts. Is this enough to settle synonymy among any given terms? Certainly not, but failure at this cannot be credited to a failure of the method of meaning clarification, but to meaning indeterminacy itself. Be as it may, *clarity as to meanings* must be an ideal of science. In logic, however, this ideal must be fulfilled; one must be clear about what the categories of thinking are and what is a priori true of them. All analytic *laws* must be clearly and exhaustively displayed. *Syntactic* analytic necessity is, consequently, straightforwardly decidable, but *semantic* analytic necessity, that which involves synonymy, may sometimes not be so.

In conclusion: In order for analytic necessities to be recognized as such one must need *first* to render meaning relations among relevant terms explicit, which can be done by reflecting on meaning given-acts. This, however, is not always guaranteed to succeed due to meaning indeterminacy. I don't want to suggest that Husserl himself would see matters thus, maybe he would prefer to take semantic a priori necessities as *synthetic* necessities. I only offer this as an alternative view, which however can be coherently formulated within a phenomenological perspective.

§5 Synthetic a priori truths

Consider the following assertion S = no surface can be simultaneously red and green all over. This is, of course, true, but why? Consider, for simplicity, that the two colors are monochromatic red and green. For a surface to be colored *simultaneously* in red and green *all over* it is necessary that *each point* of the surface, no matter how minuscule, extensionless in the limit, reflects light of *two* well-defined but *different* frequencies *simultaneously*, which are perceived respectively as a well-defined red *and* a well-defined green, not a third color (like the distinct perception, for instance, of all the notes of a chord individually and simultaneously). The *fact* that this does not happen is a *physiological fact* concerning color perception in humans. So, one may argue, since the truth of S depends on how the world is, S is a synthetic *a posteriori* truth.

But although S is an empirical truth one does *not* need empirical experience (or science) to know that it is true, unlike more pedestrian synthetic a posteriori truths like "pure water boils at 100^0 C at sea level". All one needs is *imagination*. By trying to conjure in imagination a red-and-green perception one soon realizes two things, namely, that this is impossible and that this impossibility is *not* due to one's limited imagination. What then? The answer Husserl offers is that this *Gedankenexperiment* gives us access to an *essential* aspect of the phenomenon of color perception, namely, that no extension can be simultaneously colored in red and green, or for that matter any two different colors, all over. Impossibility of imagining is impossibility of being. Husserl says:[5]

> Whenever therefore the word 'can' occurs in conjunction with the pregnant use of 'think', there is a reference, not to subjective necessity, i.e. to the subjective incapacity-to-represent-things-otherwise, but to the objectively-ideal necessity of an inability-to-be-otherwise.

Husserl calls *imaginative variation* this process of bringing *essential legalities* into consciousness or, in other words, intuiting essences. By going beyond the *pure phenomenon*, by scientific reconstructions of the given, for example, one can reduce phenomenological to scientific legalities, but by so doing one has already passed beyond phenomenology. The *phenomenological* synthetic a priori

---

5 3rd LI, §7.

relies solely on *phenomenological* legalities discernible in presupposition-free intuition.

If one *cannot imagine* a surface that is simultaneously red and green all over, then such a surface *cannot be*, for the impossibility one experiences is one of essence, not accident. The content red *necessarily excludes* in intuition the content green. Given that this impossibility is not purely *formal*, for "red" is not identical *in meaning* (or extension) with "not green", it must be *material*. Since *S* is *not* equivalent in meaning to "no surface can be simultaneously red and non-red all over", *S* is *not* an analytic truth (an analytic necessity in Husserl's terminology).

Husserl draws a distinction between empirical and a priori essential laws, the latter are, he says, "a priori necessities, grounded in pure essence" (3rd *LI*, §4), the former, a posteriori matters of fact. The truth of "no two different colors can color an extension simultaneously all over" is granted in the essence of the concept "color", brought to consciousness by *imaginative variation*; it is by trying to cover an arbitrary extension with two arbitrary colors in *imagination*, and failing for no circumstantial reason, that the *essential impossibility* of the task presents itself clearly in consciousness.

Free variation in imagination, Husserl says, is "a variation that is free, though not excluded by a law rooted in the content's essence" (3rd LI, §5). Let me explain. A content (e. g. color) is what it is, not what the subject wants it to be; it has an essence of its own. In order to find out what it (its essence) is the subject tries (in imagination) *to make it be something else.* If he cannot, then that which the subject tried to force the content to be *cannot be*; the subject has thus brought to consciousness an aspect of the essence of the content. Metaphorically, imaginative variation is like making a mental map of a room by walking freely around the room with the eyes shut and being forced to change the direction of motion due to things in the way (it is also a technique children often apply, albeit unintendedly; by acting freely until stopped by parental authority they learn what can and cannot be done).

For Husserl, a priori laws are *constitutive* of the domain of sense, they *determine* what has and does not have sense. They are not merely "grammatical" laws, based on usage, for the meaningful use of words. Assertions, Husserl thinks, can have, or lack, sense in two different ways, formal and material; it has formal (or syntactic) sense if it conforms to essential laws concerning formal-logical (apophantic and formal-ontological) categories and material (or semantic) sense if it conforms to essential laws regarding material categories (such as color, space, etc.). So, formal sense is regulated by analytic laws, material sense by synthetic a priori laws. Material a priori laws have to do with "the concepts or propositions which have content"; formal a priori laws with "purely formal concepts and propositions, which lack all 'matter' or 'content'". (3ʳᵈ LI, §11). Material a priori laws concern material-ontological concepts to the same extent that formal a priori laws concern formal-logical concepts.

The robustness of Husserl's notion of synthetic a priori depends on one single thing, namely, that material-ontological concepts, *as the intentional constructs they are*, display *essential* characters that were *attached to them in their intentional positing*. Analytic thinkers, however, like Schlick, for example, who abhor essences and have no dealings with intentional constitution think that essence-talk is too metaphysical to be taken seriously, but can be reduced to meaning-talk. Let's consider an example in detail.

In his "Reds, Greens, and Logical Analysis" Putnam presents what *he* calls a logical-philosophical analysis of phenomenological assertions of the type of S. "A philosophic analysis " he says, "merely presents one out of many possible *reconstructions of a group of concepts; the aim of the analysis is to develop the theory of these concepts*; and anyone who feels that his meaning for the concepts has not been clarified is invited to develop his own explication, and to discover how an alternative interpretation of the concepts would affect the theory" (p. 212, *emphasis added*). This is worth notice, for Putnam philosophical analyses involve conceptual *reconstruction*, a task *he* identifies with the clarification of the meaning of concept-words as, we may infer, *ordinarily* used. Instead of using Husserl's conceptual intuition, the meaning of words is inferred from the way they are used.

Putnam takes as primitive the notion of *indistinguishability with respect to color*, *Ind* in notation; a relation between *objects*. *Ind* is supposed to be symmetric and reflexive (but not transitive because of the paradox of the continuum). The binary relation *Ex*, also among objects, is defined thus: $Ex(x, y) = (z)$ (Ind $[z,x] \equiv$ Ind $[z,y]$), i.e. two objects x and y have *exactly the same color* if for any object z, x is color-indistinguishable from z if and only if y is too. Now, x has color F, in symbols $F(x)$, if there is some object A which is color indistinguishable from x; i.e. to have color F means to have the color of A, the color-sample. Hence, two objects x and y have *exactly the same color* if, for any color-sample z, x is color-indistinguishable from z if and only if y is too.

F is a (shade of) color, in symbols $Col(F)$, means $\exists y\, (x)\, [F(x) \equiv Ex(x, y)]$, i.e. there is an object y such that, for all objects x, x has F if, and only if, x and y have exactly the same color. In other words, F is a (shade of) color if, and only if, there is an object which has color F – the F-sample – and to have color F means to have exactly the same color as the F-sample.

Putnam claims to have shown, *on the basis of logic only*, that:

$(F)(G)(x)(Col(F) \wedge Col(G) \wedge F \neq G \to \neg\, (F(x) \wedge G(x)))$, i.e. no object can be simultaneously colored with two different colors all over. The reasoning is more or less like this: for an object x to have two *different colors* F and G all over there must be two *different objects* A and B such that A has color F, B has color G, $Ex(x, A)$, and $Ex(x, B)$. By reflexivity and symmetry of Ex, A and B must be color-indistinguishable; so, $F = G$, contra hypothesis. So, according to Putnam, the assertion that no object can have two different colors simultaneously all over is an analytic proposition, i.e. true by virtue of what the concepts *mean*. It is, in other words, a semantic a priori analytic truth.

Suppose, however, that *there is*, as a matter of *fact*, an object A which has *both* colors F and G all over simultaneously. Then A can be *both* an F-sample *and* a G-sample. The above *reductio ad absurdum* could no longer be carried through. Putnam's "argument" begs the question for it presupposes what it is supposed to show, namely, that there is *no* object that has two different colors all over simultaneously. Putnam is saying that if one *defines* "red" as the color of one of the objects in class A and "green" as the color of one of the objects in class B, and assume by definition, convention or fact that $A \cap B$ is empty, to say that nothing can be simultaneously red and green all over is simply to repeat that $A \cap B$ is empty, a logical consequence of the definition. And, he concludes, if you do not like this, it is up to you to fix this definition. My objection is that the problem is not with the definition, but the supposition that samples of different *colors must be* different *objects*. Why *must* they? This implicitly presupposes an *essential legality* working on the backstage, namely, that no single object can be simultaneously colored in two different colors all over.

Putnam recognizes this, for he says: "[...] by 'that shade of red' and 'that shade of green' anyone speaking standard English *must mean* 'exactly the same color as A' and 'exactly the same color as B' where A and B *must be so chosen or imagined as to be distinguishable in color*. But if 'that shade of red' and 'that shade of green' are always the colors of objects which are distinguishable in color, then it is not a cause for wonder that 'Nothing is that shade of red all over and also that shade of green all over at the same time' is always true, no matter who asserts it" (p. 211, *emphasis added*). But why *must* A and B be taken to be *different objects*, one may ask, isn't enough that they have *different colors?* The answer, of course, is that they *cannot be imagined* to be the same object. Putnam's reconstruction, if correct, only shows that a *law of essence* is *behind* the meaning of color words, imposing a *"must"* to usage. Whereas Putnam prefers to say that "nothing is that shade of red all over and also that shade of green all over at the same time" is analytic because it is true by virtue of *meaning*, Husserl goes to the crux of the matter, choosing to see it as synthetic a priori because it is true by virtue of the *essence* of a material concept. Putnam passes lightly by a "must" which Husserl takes very seriously.

§6 Conclusion

Anti-metaphysical prejudices and empiricist parti-pris set the tone for the analytical approach to analyticity and a prioricity. The dogmas are that empirical concepts are extracted fully formed from experience and knowable only through experience and that non-empirical knowledge, if not simply logical, is merely "grammatical", i.e. knowledge of the meaning of words. These things come out clearly in Quine's classical, if overrated paper "Two Dogmas of Empiricism", where analytic and synthetic truth are characterized as, respectively, truth "grounded in meanings independently of matters of fact" and truth "grounded in fact". Analytic truths, consequently, are knowable by knowing either logic or what words mean, hence a priori; synthetic truths are knowable through experience, hence a posteriori. No room for synthetic a priori truths.

Husserl, on the other hand, believed that even empirical concepts are *intentionally constituted*, i.e. *given a sense* that does *not* come entirely from empirical experience. A good example is the concept of physical space; some of its features are, of course, extracted from experience, but some are not, and there is something to be learned a priori about space.[6] The *essential* notes of a concept are those that are *necessarily* attached to it, i.e. the notes that any object *must* display in order to fall under the concept. These notes are part of the *intentional meaning* associated with the concept. Empirical concepts can, of course, have contingent notes too, which experience alone can disclose. They, however, are matters of mere fact, not necessity.

For Husserl, analytic truths are formal truths, all others are synthetic. But not all synthetic truths are a posteriori, since knowing the intentional sense attached to concepts, even empirical concepts, is not a matter of experience, but conceptual intuition. Husserl sees a tripartition of truths where analytic philosophers see only a bipartition: analytic, synthetic a priori and synthetic a posteriori. Analytic truths are knowable by categorial intuition of logical categories, synthetic a priori truths by categorial intuition of material-ontological categories, and synthetic a posteriori truths by experience.

Analytic philosophers such as Putnam and Quine think that analytic truths are true by virtue of logic (or meaning), but curiously do not care so much about logical knowledge *itself* and how it can be *justified*. For Husserl, on the other hand, analytic truths are essential truths related to logical categories, both apo-

---

6 The great mathematician and physicist Hermann Weyl, for example, who was influenced by Husserl's phenomenology, thought that experience is required only for specifying *which* among the metrics that are *a priori* possible is *in fact* the space metric.

phantic and formal ontological, and are known by conceptual intuition. As any concept, logical concepts also have their intentional senses, which conceptual intuition can bring out. For Husserl, *logical laws express the intentional meaning of logical concepts.*[7]

Whereas Husserl presupposes that there are two ways of knowing (empirical) truths, namely, experience (i.e. empirical perception) and categorial intuition, analytic philosophers believe that empirical truths can be known only by experience. Husserl's eidetic knowledge (which is *transcendental* knowledge) is reduced to "grammatical" knowledge, knowledge of what words mean. But, as Quine came close to admitting, meaning is not dissociated from essence and truths of meaning may hide truths of essence. But for analytic philosophers in general, the essence of concepts *completely* dissolves into the meaning of the words which denote them. But, to the extent that meanings reduce to usage (the meaning is in the use) one has a problem. If the laws of a conceptual "grammar" are indeed laws, if they are *regulative*, if a *"must"* is involved, they cannot be mere reports of usage. If laws *regulate* usage, not merely *describe* it, and meaning is in the use, then there must be something of *essential* in the laws of meaning. This was, I believe, shown in my discussion of Putnam's "reconstruction" of the meaning of color words.

As for analyticity I believe that Quine is closer to Husserl than one might suspect. For instance, both agree on what characterizes *logical* truths, namely, logical form independent of material content. Quine says in "Two Dogmas of Empiricism":

> [...] the relevant feature of this example [*no unmarried man is married*] is that it is not merely true as it stands, but remains true under any and all reinterpretations of 'man' and 'married.' If we suppose a prior inventory of *logical* particles, comprising 'no,' 'un-' 'if,' 'then,' 'and,' etc., then in general a logical truth is a statement which is true and remains true under all reinterpretations of its components other than the logical particles.

If my phenomenologically oriented approach to semantic analyticities were acceptable to Husserl, he would, like Quine, probably also fail in providing a universal criterion of *decision* for semantic analytic truths (of the "no bachelor is married" type, whose truth depends on the meaning of words), due to indeterminateness of meaning intentions rather than, as for Quine, difficulties in accessing meanings.

---

7 So, there is a transcendental dimension to formal logic in which logical laws are justified, i.e. clarified.

Quine believed that a theory of meaning could be conceived as a theory of synonymy. He says (ibid.):

> Once the theory of meaning is sharply separated from the theory of reference, it is a short step to recognizing as the business of the theory of meaning simply the synonymy of linguistic forms and the analyticity of statements; meanings themselves, as obscure intermediary entities, may well be abandoned.

But synonymy, he thought, is not prior and independent of analyticity. He says (ibid.):

> Analyticity at first seemed most naturally definable by appeal to a realm of meanings. On refinement, the appeal to meanings gave way to an appeal to synonymy or definition. But definition turned out to be a will-o'-the-wisp, and synonymy turned out to be best understood only by dint of a prior appeal to analyticity itself. So we are back at the problem of analyticity.

He, then, throws his hands up and concludes, that "for all its *a priori* reasonableness, a boundary between analytic and synthetic statement simply has not been drawn". Husserl, I believe, although also facing *practical* unfeasibility to sort out truths due to word-meaning from truths due to conceptual-(intentional) meaning, he would still see a conceptual difference between both types of truth. But, as I said before, it is possible that Husserl would throw semantic analyticities in the bag with synthetic a priori truths. In any case, Husserl maintains firmly in place the dichotomy analytic/synthetic that Quine wants to abandon. But, more importantly, he also upholds, against general analytic ideology, the notion of synthetic a priori truth and the associated notion of transcendental knowledge. This is enough to carve an abyss between him and the analytic philosophic tradition.

References

Benoist, Jocelyn: *L'a priori conceptual. Bolzano, Husserl, Schlick.* Paris: Vrin, 1999.
Dummett, Michael: *Truth and other Enigmas.* Cambridge, Mass.: Harvard University Press, 1978.
English, Jacques: *Le vocabulaire de Husserl.* Paris: Ellipses, 2009.
Husserl, Edmund: *Philosophie der Arithmetik.* Halle: Pfeffer, 1891.
Husserl, Edmund: *Logical Investigations* (vol. I and II). Trans. J. N. Findlay, London & New York: Routledge, 2001.
Husserl, Edmund: *Ideas, General Introduction to Pure Phenomenology (Ideas I)* New York: Colliers, 1962.
Husserl, Edmund: *Formal and Transcendental Logic.* The Hague: M, Nijhoof, 1969.

Putnam, Hilary: 'Reds, Greens and Logical Analysis', *Philosophical Review* 65: 206–17, 1956.
Quine, Willard Van Orman: 'Two Dogmas of Empiricism', *Philosophical Review* 60: 20–43, 1951.
Schlick, Moritz: Is there a factual a priori? Trans of "Gibt es ein materiales Apriori?" (1930), in H. Feigl & W. S. Sellars (eds.), *Readings in Philosophical Analyses*, New York: Appleton-Century-Crofts, 1949: 277–285.
Theodorou, Panos: 'Kant's Analyticity: A Historico-Phenomenological Revisiting and Restatement (For All)', *Kant Studies Online (KSO)* 2015: 204–250.

Uwe Meixner
Husserl's Classical Conception of Intentionality – and Its Enemies

Abstract: This paper aims to display and explicate in what sense Husserl accepts the thesis (some philosophers call "inseparatism") that there is no intentionality without phenomenology, and in what sense he rejects the thesis that intentionality can only work via representations. It also aims to show that Husserl is not obviously wrong in that "yes" and in that "no". A further aim of this essay is to defend Husserlian phenomenal intentionality (and therewith, to a considerable extent, phenomenal intentionality *tout court*) against the anti-mentalistic and anti-realist criticism raised by the Wittgensteinians (and by Wittgenstein himself), that is, by philosophers who have, in effect, a functionalist (hence anti-phenomenal and anti-Phenomenological) conception of intentionality.

> "Also ‚Bewußtsein von etwas' ist ein sehr
> Selbstverständliches und doch zugleich höchst
> Unverständliches."* (*Id1*, §87, 201)

§1 Introduction

In Chapter 30 of *The Oxford Handbook of the Philosophy of Mind*, "Phenomenology, Intentionality, and the Unity of the Mind", the three authors proclaim and defend the thesis of *inseparatism:*

> [P]henomenology and intentionality are inseparable. [...] In some sense: No phenomenology without intentionality, and no intentionality without phenomenology (ibid., 514).

By the word "phenomenology", the authors do not mean *Husserlian phenomenology*, or (in short) *Phenomenology*; they mean

---

* In English: "Thus, 'consciousness of something' is a very obvious thing and yet, at the same time, a thing supremely hard to understand." The pun contained in the German sentence ("Selbstverständliches" – "Unverständliches") is untranslatable. – A general note on the references and quotations in this paper can be found at its end, in front of the Bibliography.

the feature of conscious experience that makes conscious experience conscious: its phenomenology. Its phenomenology is the something it is like to have or undergo an experience (ibid., 513).

To use the word metaphorically in *this* sense is today normal philosophical jargon, yet slightly absurd, like saying "biology" and meaning *animals and plants*, or "astronomy" and meaning *the stars*. Nevertheless, *Husserl* would have, with qualifications, agreed to the second part of the thesis of inseparatism (the first part he would have, with qualifications, rejected: see *Id1*, §36, 74–75; §84, 187). For Husserl, too, there is "no intentionality without phenomenology" (though he certainly would not have put it this way). Implicitly presupposed in the cited chapter of the *Handbook* (see ibid., 513), there is, however, another inseparatist thesis, one that Husserl would *not* have agreed to, one that he did, in fact, reject (whereas the authors of the cited chapter merely distance themselves from *some* versions of that other thesis: see ibid., 524–525); it is the thesis that there is no intentionality without *representations*, that intentionality can only work *via* representations.

Husserl's "yes" to (part of) the first inseparatist thesis, and "no" to this second, are among the things that the present essay aims to display and explicate; it also aims to show that Husserl is not obviously wrong in that "yes" and in that "no". Another aim of this essay is to defend *Husserlian phenomenal intentionality* (and therewith, to a considerable extent, phenomenal intentionality *tout court*) against the anti-*mentalistic* and anti-*intentional-realist* criticism raised by the Wittgensteinians (and by Wittgenstein himself): by philosophers who have, in effect, a *functionalist* (hence anti-phenomenal and anti-Phenomenological) conception of intentionality.

§2 A prologue: *epoché*

How plausible one is going to find Husserl's views on intentionality may well depend on the extent one has managed to go through a certain cognitive procedure. The procedure is not a thought experiment, for it does not require one to suppose or to imagine anything. In a way, it requires one *to abstain* from believing in certain things one normally believes in – *in a way*, for the procedure does not require one to give up any of the beliefs one has, let alone to put other beliefs in their places. In fact, the procedure requires one to change nothing in one's consciousness – *except* to adopt a reflexive stance towards it (which, of course, is bound to modify it to a certain degree, but that can't be helped) and *to abstain*, while maintaining this reflexive stance, from *living in* those of one's beliefs which are such that they include belief in the existence or non-existence of objects "out there in objective reality". Husserl would also say: the procedure requires one *to bracket* [*einklammern*] such beliefs, and that is perhaps the best way to express, in one word, the procedure's two-sided intention: *that* one's beliefs that include belief in the existence or non-existence of objects "out there in objective reality" are still there, as one's beliefs, but *that*, at the same time, one is not *living in* them but rather is seeing them from above (so to speak), observing them from a detached point of view.

The procedure just described is the basic phenomenological method of *epoché* (as Husserl called it, appropriating a term of ancient scepticism for his own – entirely non-sceptical – purposes). *Epoché* serves the purpose of securing the phenomena of one's consciousness – the "Erlebnisse" (there is no precise equivalent in English for "Erlebnisse", "experiences" being the relatively best translation of the term, though it would better fit the German "Erfahrungen") – for one's inspection *without any loss* (though, certainly, in a somewhat modified form) and to free, at the same time, one's inspecting glance from any (often quite unexamined) presuppositions about objective reality. In Phenomenology, one wants to see the phenomena of one's consciousness – the "Erlebnisse" – in their purity. Curiously, to the extent we manage to do *epoché*, current theories of intentionality, each one of which is heavily dependent upon presuppositions about objective reality, will fade to the status of being *just theory* (though we may happen to *believe* in one of them), whereas what Husserl calls "intentionality" – this intrinsic structural element of the Phenomena [*Erlebnisse*] themselves – will seem far from being *just theory*, but will stand out in its purity and undeniable actuality. And then current theories of intentionality, which usually presume that intentionality, properly understood, is a part of nature and which usually are obsessed with naturalizing it physico-causally, may well seem to be more or less missing the point.

§3 Ryle (and Wittgenstein) versus Husserl

The ultimate source of a large part of the current mainstream in intentionality theory is the philosophy of Ludwig Wittgenstein. At the end of Part I of the *Philosophical Investigations*, the abysmal difference between Wittgenstein's and Husserl's views on intentionality is evident with complete finality:

> 'When I teach someone the formation of the series …. I surely mean him to write …. at the hundredth place.' – Quite right; you mean it. And evidently without necessarily even thinking of it. This shows you how different the grammar of the verb 'to mean' is from that of the

verb 'to think'. And nothing is more wrong-headed than calling meaning a mental activity! Unless, that is, one is setting out to produce confusion. (One might as well speak of an activity of butter when it rises in price, and if no problems are produced by this it is harmless.) (*PhI* I, §693, 172^e; tr. modified)

For highlighting the radical opposition of this to Husserl's views, it suffices to point out that, for Husserl, *occurrent mental intentionality* – the intrinsic intentionality of subjective experiences [*Erlebnisse*], the intentionality of "thinking": of *consciousness* – is *the basis* of *all* intending/meaning *an object* (in the widest sense), and that intentional experiences were often called "Akte [acts]" by Husserl.

But one can only wonder at the discrepancy between, on the one hand, Wittgenstein's emphatic conviction that the grammar (or logic) of meaning (meaning *an object*) is fundamentally different from that of thinking, and, on the other hand, the utter weakness of his reasons for holding this. *True:* one can mean/intend something without thinking of, or about, it. This happens all the time, and cannot be denied even if we look exclusively at *occurrent, non-dispositional intending*. After all, one all the time *perceives* – i.e., perceptually intends – objects one does not think of, *if* "to think of" is to mean something more specific than "to be conscious of" ("to be conscious" is, however, the best rendering of Descartes' "cogitare" in his *Meditations on First Philosophy:* in view of Meditation II, §8, and Meditation III, §1). And if we also look at *non-occurrent, dispositional intending*, then the two kinds of intending – occurrent and dispositional – provide in collaboration (so to speak) the stock example for intending without thinking: one is now (dispositionally) believing (that is, *dispositionally* doxastically intending) thousands of propositions none of which one is now (occurrently) thinking of (since one is *not occurrently* intending those propositions, but only dispositionally). And when I teach someone the formation of a number-series, I (dispositionally) mean/intend the correct (numerical) filling of *each* of its many, usually infinitely many places – yet I (occurrently) think of the filling of only a very few of those places (say, the first three or four). But do these *trivial* facts *show* that the grammar of meaning/intending is *fundamentally* different – *categorially* different – from that of thinking, as Wittgenstein believes? They do not. Though intending, in its intentionality-use, is *not always* thinking-of, *not* even if "to think of" is generalized – as it is by Descartes – beyond its normal meaning and is semantically assimilated to "to be conscious of" (for intending is sometimes dispositional, whereas thinking-of never is), still thinking-of is *always* intending: whoever thinks of, or about, something (in a certain mode: e.g., specifically or non-specifically, non-verbally or verbally) intends and means (*in that same mode*), while thinking, what is being thought of in the thinking. Now, is the (so-called) *grammar* of "mammal" fundamentally different from the *grammar* of "dog"? The answer is: emphatically no (or else I don't know what Wittgenstein means by "grammar" in the above quotation). But then: *neither* is the grammar of "to mean/intend" fundamentally different from the grammar of "to think of"; for these two verbs stand in the same logical relationship to each other as the nouns "mammal" and "dog": their instances of truthful application constitute a necessary genus-species relation. Of course: "to mean it" does not mean *to think of it* – as Wittgenstein reminds himself and his readers in *PhI* I, §692, 172/172^e. But this, again, is a *trivial* truth, just as trivial as the truth that "mammal" does not mean *dog*; in neither of the two cases the difference in meaning amounts to a difference in "grammar".

As there is no justification for Wittgenstein's conviction that the grammar of "to mean/intend" is fundamentally different from the grammar of "to think", so there is no justification for Wittgenstein's further conviction that to call meaning/ intending a mental activity is as absurd as to call the increase of the price of butter an activity of butter. Rather, at least to the extent that thinking-of is a mental activity (it always is), intending/meaning must be a mental activity, too: because thinking-of is a species, and intending/meaning a (necessary) genus of that species.

But, doubtless, intending/meaning is not always a mental *activity*; merely consider that meaning/intending is often *dispositional*. Yet, in those cases where intending/meaning is not an activity, it is still a *mental* disposition – which will manifest itself under the right circumstances in the right *mental* occurrences. However, one can count on it, Wittgenstein would not have been happy with this reasonable solution. Ultimately, the problem with the classification of intending/meaning as a *mental activity* was for Wittgenstein *not* so much the *activity*-component in that classification; the problem for him was the component of *mentalness* – in the sense in which "mental" is normally understood, which sense essentially involves *inwardness* and *subjectivity*.

The same diagnosis is true of Gilbert Ryle, who, indeed, made a large-scale effort in *The Concept of Mind* to replace the "official" talk (in psychology and philosophy) of *mental activities and occurrences* ("ghostly", "occult", and ultimately *non-existent* for Ryle) by the talk of *mental dispositions*. But the dispositions that Ryle had in mind were certainly not *mental* in the normal sense of the word; rather, *mentalness* in this normal sense – essentially involving *inwardness* and *subjectivity* (and implying *non-physicalness*) – was anathema to Ryle (along with "the Ghost in the Machine"):

> [R1] One of the central negative motives of this book [*The Concept of Mind*] is to show that 'mental' does not denote a status, such that one can sensibly ask of a given thing or event whether it is mental or physical, 'in the mind' or 'in the outside world' (*CoM*, 199).

The so-called "mental" dispositions – and abilities, liabilities, inclinations; powers; capacities and tendencies (all of these words are used by Ryle in affirmative descriptive connection with "mind" or "mental": see *CoM*, 199; 245; 125) – that Ryle *did* allow and advocate were, in fact, more or less complex *behavioural* dispositions (respectively, *behavioural* abilities, liabilities, etc). *Given* the normal primary sense of "mental", such dispositions [R2] "to do and undergo certain sorts of things [...] in the ordinary world" (*CoM*, 199) can be called "mental" (or "of the mind") only in a rather secondary, remotely analogical sense of the word. But, needless to say to readers of *The Concept of Mind*, the normal primary sense of "mental" was for Ryle – likely under the influence of Wittgenstein – not a philosophically correct sense, because of the element of *privacy and subjectivity* in that sense.

The epistemological worries connected with *subjectivity* take a special direction when it comes to *intentionality*; for intentionality is often *intersubjective*, or *objective* (so to speak). Accordingly, Wittgenstein remarks about an attempt to explain *intersubjective* linguistic intentionality by *subjective* linguistic intentionality:

> Only let us take this assumption seriously! – Then we see that it is not able to explain *intention*.
>
> For if it is like this: that the possible uses of a word float before us in half-shades as we say or hear it – if it is like this, then this simply holds for *us*. But we communicate with other people without knowing whether they have these experiences too (*PhI* II, vi, 181ᵉ; tr. modified).

Note, in contrast, that it is Husserl's plan to explain intersubjective, or objective, intentionality on the basis of *subjective* (or *mental*) intentionality, and ultimately on the basis of its *non-dispositional* (or *occurrent*, or *manifest*) form, as found in intentional consciousness, in intentional experience. Accordingly, I shall call the intentionality found therein, as interpreted by Husserl, *Husserlian basic intentionality*. For Husserl, the indicated plan for intentionality explanation is the only viable plan for explaining *cognition*. This emerges (among other things) from the following passage:

> [H1] It is clear: only if we resolve to set all prejudices aside and to identify experience [Erfahrung] or intuition [Anschauung] [simply] with self-evidence [Evidenz], with cognition in the salient sense; and only if we embrace the fact that this extended 'experience' is nothing else but the having of the intended/meant itself exactly as it is intended/meant – only then

we can seriously plan to understand cognition [Erkennen]; that is, to understand how not only the world of simple non-conceptual experience, but also the logical objectivity, and thus the objectivity of any kind and level with all its real and ideal forms, can have meaning [Sinn] and warrantable being for us. Consciousness in itself, in its essential forms, creates meaning/intending [Sinn] and, in the forms of self-evidence, possible and true meaning/intending [that is: intending of *what is possible*, of *what is true*], as the form of a possible fulfilment of unfulfilled intentions of thinking, of a fulfilment in the form of the giving-itself-as-itself [Selbstgebung], respectively, in a form 'measuring up' to such a form (*EPh1*, §19, 138).

Thus, Husserlian basic intentionality, or in other words: *Husserlian phenomenal intentionality*, is indeed *fundamental* for Husserl.

Daniel Dennett – *no* friend of phenomenal intentionality (Husserlian or other) – believes that "[m]ost of Husserl's topics can be found in *The Concept of Mind* by anybody who knows what they are, but in these pages you will find no talk of *intentionality*, no *noemata* – and no talk of *qualia* either, I am happy to report" ("Re-introducing *The Concept of Mind*", xiv; note that "qualia" is not a term of Husserl's, but could easily be given a place in Phenomenology: qualia are the aspects of hyletic content). Dennett attributes the absence of those terms in *The Concept of Mind* to Ryle's "distrust of philosophical jargon" (ibid.). Dennett is right on both accounts – *if* one does not subsume too many of Husserl's topic under Dennett's "Husserl's topics", and *if* "distrust of philosophical jargon" is read as "distrust of *what for him, Ryle, was* philosophical jargon"[1].

How utterly *different* Ryle's views are from Husserl's may already be suspected (or known); yet in order to highlight the truly abysmal difference between the two philosophers, I offer an analysis of the following passage:

> [R4] Epistemologists have sometimes confessed to finding the supposed cognitive activities of seeing, hearing and inferring oddly elusive. If I descry a hawk, I find the hawk but I do not find my seeing of the hawk. My seeing of the hawk seems to be a queerly transparent sort of process, transparent in that while a hawk is detected, nothing else is detected answering to the verb in 'see a hawk'. But the mystery dissolves when we realise that 'see', 'descry' and 'find' are not process words, experience words or activity words. They do not stand for perplexingly undetectable actions or reactions [...]. The reason why I cannot

---

1 Here goes Ryle inveighing (with some amount of truth and yet *deeply unjustly*) against the way Husserl wrote: [R3] "When Husserl inherited in the early years of this century his master's [Brentano's] '*Messiasbewusstsein*' he lost what humour he had ever possessed as well as nearly all his original clarity and vigour of style. [...] Deaf to the language of others, he found that the appropriate expressions for his own discoveries required an independent mint, and he accordingly coined a vast jargon of his own which subserves, apparently, the ends neither of brevity nor of perspicuity" ("Review of Marvin Farber: 'The Foundations of Phenomenology' ", 222–223).

catch myself seeing or deducing is that these verbs are of the wrong type to complete the phrase 'catch myself ....' The questions 'What are you doing?' and 'What was he undergoing?' cannot be answered by 'seeing', 'concluding', or 'checkmating' (*CoM*, 152).

Thus, Ryle would surely have agreed with Wittgenstein that "nothing is more wrong-headed than calling meaning [i.e., intending] a mental activity" – considering that seeing, hearing, inferring, descrying, finding, deducing, concluding, and checkmating are without exception specific forms of meaning/intending *something*, that is: specific forms of *intentionality* (though very different such forms). Unfortunately (or fortunately for Husserl), what Ryle says in R4 is just a collection of falsehoods. *Firstly*, whatever the epistemologists that Ryle has in mind, and Ryle himself, may confess to, there is no such thing as cognitive activities – or more generally speaking: processes in consciousness – appearing (or seeming) to be "transparent".[2] As long as I do not explicitly adopt the reflexive stance towards my own conscious activities or processes, I do not explicitly notice them – and thus *they do not appear to me to be transparent*; but as soon as I explicitly adopt that stance, I explicitly notice them, and notice them as being in no way elusive or easily overlooked – and thus, also in this other case (covering what the first case left open), *they do not appear to me to be transparent* (and as it is with me, so it is with others, I trust; one merely needs to adopt the reflexive stance). *Secondly*, conscious processes do not merely *not appear to be* transparent, they *are not* transparent (for if they were transparent, then they would appear to be transparent[3]); if I direct my attention at them (and I can do so at most points of my conscious life), then they neither seem *nor are* in any way un-

---

[2] The idea of the *transparency* or *diaphaneity* of consciousness is still extant (for example, according to Bennett & Hacker in *The Philosophical Foundations of Neuroscience*, 193, "mental images, like thoughts, *are all message and no medium*") and is perhaps even more present today than it has ever been before (many Anglo-American philosophers are under the influence of Gilbert Harman and others). The idea is false none the less. Consider the following quotation from Michael Tye's *Consciousness and Persons*, 24: "Visual experiences are transparent to their subjects. We are not introspectively aware of our visual experiences any more than we are perceptually aware of transparent sheets of glass. If we try to focus on our experiences, we 'see' right through them to the world outside." Inexplicably, Tye completely ignores the indicators of non-transparency: the perspectival organization of the visual field and the resulting familiar – in fact, omnipresent – illusions (e.g., that the full moon is as big as a silver dollar); the limitedness of the visual field which, strangely, is without visible limits; jumping pictures (occurring when you switch rapidly between closing one eye and then the other); the visual experience that occurs when you cross your eyes; the contrast between foreground and background, between what is in the focus of attention and what is not, between the blurring and sharpening of vision (occurring when you take off your glasses and put them back on).
[3] The inverse of this is also true.

noticeable. *Thirdly*, conscious processes, and specifically the "cognitive activities" Ryle is talking about, *are* detectable – I merely need to adopt the reflexive stance towards them in order to detect them – and they are, therefore, *existent processes* (contrary to Ryle's fairly transparent suggestion of their non-existence). *Fourthly*, contrary to what Ryle is asserting with such confidence, "see", "descry" and "find" *are*, in fact, process words, experience words, or activity words (and so are "hear", "infer", "deduce", "conclude", "checkmate"): they require for their truthful application – and most conspicuously in the first-person case (and *no less* for "I find ...." and "I checkmate ...." than for "I see ...." and "I hear ....") – the occurrence of experiential episodes *in* (or rather *with*) the relevant subject, though these episodes of conscious activity may, of course, be very short. *Fifthly*, contrary to what Ryle believes about himself, *I* (at least) can very well catch myself *seeing* or *deducing* (and this is not as uncommon as it may seem): I suddenly notice that I am seeing – not a scarecrow but – a man who looks like a scarecrow. And even while I am saying "It wasn't the gardener, it was the butler", I suddenly notice that I am deducing that it was the butler from (1) *the fact* that it wasn't the gardener *and* (2) from *the assumption* that it must have been either the gardener or the butler. *Sixthly*, contrary to what Ryle believes, the questions "What are you doing?" and "What was he undergoing?" can of course be answered by "seeing", "concluding", or "checkmating". Gertrude asks: "What are you doing here, sitting all alone by yourself on the parapet?" – Possible answers: "Just *looking* [and therefore *seeing*]"; "I am just now *concluding* that, all things considered, I should not go to Wittenberg". Looking at an on-going game of chess, a child asks: "What are you doing?" – Possible answer: "I am *checkmating* him" (and simultaneously I make the move that checkmates him).

If, as Ryle would have it (*contrary* to Husserl), we could only see (and *find*) a hawk, but could not at the same time experience (and *find*) our seeing it; if we could only hear a cry, but could not at the same time experience our hearing it; if we could only infer that there are infinitely many primes, but could not at the same time experience our inferring this; then it is *conceivable*, though hardly probable, that even in this case we could and would continue to use the first-person present-tense *intentionality way of speaking:* "I see a hawk", "I hear a cry", "I infer that there are infinitely many primes". Under Rylean premises, such utterances simply come out of our mouths, we know not why; and under Rylean premises, there remains *the task of explaining* why they do come out of our mouths. The Rylean premises – to be honest about them and put aside all language-critical paraphernalia (which, as a rule, do not work anyway) – simply amount to *the premise, the prejudice* that conscious processes (in the traditional sense: as episodes of subjectivity, episodes of the inward mental life) are undetectable and, in fact, non-existent (or, though existent, totally irrelevant, hence dispensable). Ryle did not get far with the mentioned task of explanation (cf. "Phenomenology vs. 'The Concept of Mind' ", 195–196); but his student Daniel Dennett – who is certainly no less outspoken than his teacher about *that task's premise* (i.e., the non-existence of consciousness; see "On the Absence of Phenomenology", 95) – applied himself to it with particular enthusiasm, calling the result of his efforts, *weirdly*, an "explanation of consciousness" (cf. Dennett, *Consciousness Explained*).

For a *first-hand* recognition of *Husserlian basic intentionality* – that is: for a recognition, resulting from what Husserl calls "Evidenz",[4] of the manner of intentionality that Husserl discerns in intentional phenomenal consciousness[5] – *reflexive* (inner, introspective) *perception* is necessary, *and* the acknowledgement of such perception. Therefore, since neither Wittgenstein nor the Wittgensteinians (consider as representative the very prominent ones: Ryle, Dennett, and Bennett & Hacker[6]) acknowledge reflexive perception,[7] there is *no* first-hand recognition of Husserlian basic intentionality by Wittgenstein and the Wittgensteinians – and without any first-hand recognition of it, a *second-hand* recognition will not be forthcoming either. Indeed, leaving the intellectual honesty of Wittgenstein and the Wittgensteinians undisputed, one must speak of *their blindness* for Husserlian basic intentionality, which is a consequence of their blindness for phenomenal consciousness. This blindness is not constitutional: they can – or could – reflexively perceive as satisfactorily as Husserl or anybody else. Their blindness is an outcome of *philosophical prejudice*. The great prejudgment – only thinly disguised by language criticism, often markedly arbitrary and highhanded (see the Wittgenstein-inspired pontifical decrees of

---

[4] The best, though not perfect, rendering in English of Husserl's "Evidenz" is "self-evidence" (see H1). The best, though not perfect, rendering in English of Husserl's "Anschauung" is "intuition" (see again H1). The translations are not perfect, for both *Evidenz* and *Anschauung* have a distinctly *perceptual* dimension (for Husserl, and quite generally for every speaker of German) that is not present in *self-evidence* and *intuition*.

[5] There was a time when it would have been otiose to modify, even occasionally, the words "consciousness" or "experience" by the word "phenomenal". Not so in *our* time.

[6] These three (or four) thinkers – *different* though they are from each other – have been inspired in important ways by Wittgenstein's anti-Cartesian philosophy, which gives them certain family resemblances [Familienähnlichkeiten], as Wittgenstein would say (see *PhI* I, §67). This is why I call them "Wittgensteinians". For more on the Wittgensteinian enmity to Husserl's positions (for the most part it is implicit) than is written about in this essay, see my recent book *Defending Husserl*.

[7] See *PhI* I, §§ 412–413, 416–418; *CoM*, 164–166, 205–207; "On the Absence of Phenomenology", 95; *The Philosophical Foundations of Neuroscience*, 88, 91–92, 96–97.

Bennett & Hacker on what is, and what is not, *philosophically correct* English in *The Philosophical Foundations of Neuroscience*[8]) – is that there is *no such thing* as phenomenal consciousness, *no such thing* as the inward, subjective mental life and its intentionality.

But, as far as Ryle is concerned, the rejection of *Husserlian basic intentionality* can be found even without anti-Cartesian and anti-introspectionist premises, namely, in Ryle's article "Phenomenology" from 1932.[9] What Ryle offers in that article is, as a matter of fact, much more interesting than mere anti-Cartesianism and anti-introspectionism. According to Ryle, for Husserl – [R5a] "to employ a misleading expression of which Husserl is fond" (ibid., 173) – [R5b] "*the object of an intentional experience,* treated as such, is just the intrinsic meaning or sense of the experience" (ibid.; italics mine). Well, yes, this is for Husserl precisely the truth of the matter. But why is the italicized expression in R5b deemed "misleading" in R5a? Ryle:

> [R6] He [Husserl] *should* hold (I believe) that what we miscall 'the object or content of an act of consciousness' is really the specific character or nature of that act, so that the intentionality of an act is not a relation between it and something else, but merely a property of it so specific as to be a differentia or in some cases an individualizing description of it. He does in fact, however, continue to speak as if every intentional act is related, though related by an internal relation, to a *genuine subject of attributes* (ibid., 175; second italics mine).

This quotation still gives no answer to the question just asked. (Did Husserl really not know *what* he was saying?) And why is the idea of basic intentionality that is described and attributed to Husserl by R5a, R5b, and R6, deemed *wrong* by Ryle? I shall come back to this question and its answer in due course; for the time being, I merely note that the quotation in R6 proposes *an alternative*, which Ryle believes correct, to what he thinks Husserl erroneously thinks is the correct way of describing basic intentionality. It is also true: R6 – like R5b – manages to state Husserl's opinion correctly (though somewhat indirectly: in what it says, in its second sentence, is Husserl's continued *way of speaking*). This is not the case with other Rylean reports on Husserl's opinions, as we shall see.

Husserl *does* hold that the intentional objects of, say, (outer) perceptions are *genuine subjects of attributes* (to which perceptions *are* internally – or *intrinsically-essentially* – related in the intentionality way). But intentional objects are gen-

---

[8] Characteristically, Husserl is not mentioned even once in the entire book (461 pages thick).
[9] For clear indications of Ryle's *relative* friendliness in that article towards phenomenal consciousness and introspection (considering what came *later*), see ibid., 176–177.

uine subjects of attributes for Husserl certainly not in such a manner that, given *any* attribute F, either F or non-F can be truthfully attributed to them:

> [H2] There is nothing that *the tree simpliciter* [*der Baum schlechthin*], the thing in nature, is less [identical to] than this *perceived tree as such* [dieses *Baumwahrgenommene als solches*], which, as perceptual intent [Wahrnehmungssinn], belongs inseparably to the perception. The tree simpliciter can burn down, dissolve itself into its chemical elements, and so on. But the intent – intent of *this* perception, something necessarily belonging to its essence – cannot burn down, it has no chemical elements, no powers [Kräfte], no real properties (*Id1*, §89, 205).[10]

We may be certain: *this* perceived tree as such – the intentional object of *this* perception – is, for Husserl, not only *not combustible*, but also *not incombustible* (or else it would have *a power*, contrary to what is stated in H2). Yet, this does not impugn the ontological status which the perceived tree as such has in Husserl's eyes: that of being *a genuine subject of attributes*; after all, it is for Husserl an *individual item*, no less *individual* than the perception itself. *Note* that if an item X fails to fulfil the condition presented immediately before H2, then this fact alone cannot by itself exclude X from the class of genuine subjects of attributes. Otherwise there would be *no* genuine subjects of attributes. This is so because for *every* item – hence even for each *individual item*, even for each actually existing material object – an attribute can be found which is such that neither itself nor its negation can be truthfully attributed to it (thus, each actually existing material object is neither divisible by 3 nor non-divisible by 3, just as, conversely, every natural number is neither orbiting the sun nor non-orbiting it).

---

10 This quotation should not mislead one into thinking that when Husserls says [H3] "It is [...] an error in principle to believe that perception [...] cannot get at the thing itself" (*Id1*, §43, 89), he only means to assert this, say, of *the perceived tree as such*, not also of *the tree simpliciter*. Husserl, as a matter of fact, misleadingly overstates (in the perspective of phenomenological reduction: of *epoché*) the distinction he wishes to make between the two when he says in H2 that there is nothing that *the tree simpliciter* is less (identical to) than *the perceived tree as such* (see also Husserl's all too strong *further* separative remarks in *Id1*, §89, 205). In fact, *the tree simpliciter* (or in other Husserlian words: *the actual/"real" tree*) is after all – *if* it exists, and *only if* it exists – *identical*, for Husserl, to *the perceived tree as such*. It is only that the epistemic distance to the latter is much shorter – being *zero* – than the one to the former, which distance, for Husserl, is unforeseeably long (*if* a *definitive and ultimate* determination regarding the tree simpliciter, in particular, regarding its existence, is to be arrived at). Consider, as an analogy, the relationship between *the sequence 7777 in the decimal development of* π and *the sequence 7777*: the former – *if* it exists, and *only if* it exists – is identical to the latter; but the epistemic distance to the latter is zero, whereas the one to the former is unforeseeably long (but existent and finite if the sequence 7777 in the decimal development of π *exists*).

Note also, in this connection, that the expression "real properties [reale Eigenschaften]" has a special meaning for Husserl: in Husserl's sense, it is not synonymous with "actual attributes" but, in effect, with "causal dispositions of real things [things *simpliciter*]". (In support of this interpretation, see *Id2*, §15, 45, 47–48.) Thus, when Husserl asserts in H2 that the perceived tree as such has "no real properties", he is *not* saying that it has no actual attributes.

The intentional objects of (outer) perceptions, though *inseparable* from the perceptions, are, for Husserl, not only *individuals* and, therefore, genuine subjects of attributes, they are also *(numerically) identically recurrent individuals* in temporally separate perceptions, and in such perceptions *re-identifiable individuals*;[11] in other words, they are *individuals of recurrence* in temporally separate perceptions, not *individuals of occurrence* like the perceptions themselves, which cannot *identically recur*, recur as numerically the same item, and hence cannot be *perceptually re-identified* (in their case: re-identified in temporally separate *reflexive perceptions*). It is an immediate consequence of this that the intentional objects of (outer, non-reflexive) perceptions, though *inseparable* from the perceptions, cannot be in any real sense *parts – pieces* [Stücke] or *aspects* [Momente] – of their perceptions, as Husserl inculcates (and not only for *perceptions* and *their* intentional objects):

[H4] [T]he object appearing in the manifold of the experiences and intended in it as existing [seinsgemeinter] is, vis-à-vis these experiences, non-real [irreell]; it is not a real aspect [reelles Moment] of them, for it is identically the same object in immanently temporally separated experiences ($\Phi\Psi$, §41, 207–208).

[H5] [H]ere it is first of all necessary to describe faithfully what is here the immediately perceived, purely following the meaning-content [Sinn] that belongs to the perception itself. It is necessary to realize that it [i.e., the immediately perceived] is not a complex of sensual data that belong to the perception in question as real pieces [reelle Bestandstücke], hence come into being with it and disappear with it, but that it is nothing other than, for example, this table here, only at one time coming to be perceived from this side, and then from that side, and becoming, in the further progress of perceptions that synthetically unify themselves, ever more richly, ever more multiformly seen. But it is always itself, this table (the synthetic unity, one and the same object in consciousness), that progressively displays [vorweist] and warrants [ausweist] its content of being and confirms its actual there-being – presupposing only that the occurrence of disharmony does not force us to cross out, so to speak, its there-being and to say: it was a mere illusion. What any conceivable confirmation or warrant of actuality warrants here is, therefore, as I said, the synthetic unity, had in conscious perception with the consciousness character of being-there-itself, and is nothing

---

11 As A. D. Smith notes: "[W]hen Husserl writes about an experience's object being inseparable from that experience, he is definitely not talking about a mere *kind* of object, but an individual, identifiable and re-identifiable object" ("Husserl and Externalism", 322).

other than the *external item itself*, the thing-in-space itself; it is from the start the transcendent item itself.[12] If not, where, supposedly, does knowledge of it ever come from? (*EPh1*, §17, 118–119)

And this is what Ryle has to say about the issues that are addressed by H4 and H5:

[R7] Husserl […] denies that what an act is 'of' is essentially contained in or adjoined to the act. 'Contents' are not real parts of mental functioning. Introspection cannot find them. (This is proved by the fact that two acts of different dates can have the same object.) ("Phenomenology", 175).

[R8] The theory of intentionality [Husserl's] is an attempt not to repudiate, but to modify, elaborate and reform the 'idea' epistemology [deriving from Descartes and Locke] (ibid., 174).

[R9] [Husserl holds that] all that I can *know* about the world is what I can know about my fallible cognizings of the world and my resultant practical and emotional attitudes towards it. And if this were true, Husserl would, I think, have established some sort of primacy for phenomenology (ibid., 177).

But Husserl did not maintain, and what he maintained does not entail, the view Ryle attributes to him in R9. *That view* is a consequence of what Ryle calls " 'idea' epistemology" in R8, in other words: a consequence of *mental representationalism*, which involves the assumption [R10] "that what I am aware of when I am aware of something must always be an 'idea'" (ibid., 174), that is: a *mental representation* (as one says in more recent times than Locke's). But, contrary to what Ryle (in effect) asserts in R8, Husserl did not maintain, and what he maintained does not entail, a sophisticated version of mental representationalism. That Husserl had no sympathies for mental representationalism and its consequence: *the locking-in of the mind* (lifelong prison with no hope to get out), is sufficiently evident from H3 (see footnote 10) and H5. Even at the time Ryle wrote "Phenomenology", he ought to have known from Husserl's published works (notably the *Logical Investigations* and *Ideas I*) that Husserl was *not* a sympathizer with, let alone a modernizer of, Lockean (or Cartesian) representationalism. It is true that the conscious mind is an epistemological and ontological *first principle* for Husserl; for him, as Ryle says, [R11] "[n]ot merely was the theory of Mind [qua Phenomenology] logically prior to all the other branches of theory, but Mind became the source or home of all existence" ("Review of Marvin Farber: 'The Foundations of Phenomenology'", 221). But this – Husserl's idealism – does not entail a modernized version of Lockean representationalism; rather,

---

12 Compare H3 and the subsequent comment, both in footnote 10.

it is *incompatible* with any non-otiose form of mental representationalism about the physical world, since *non-otiose* mental representationalism about the physical world requires *realism* (*without* realism, the cognition of the physical *via* mental representations of the physical seems a perfectly superfluous detour) and realism is logically incompatible with idealism.

But how can one embrace Husserl's theory of intentionality – in particular, his theory of basic intentionality – without also embracing his idealism? This may seem a question exceedingly difficult to answer. I hold that Husserl's theory of intentionality is, in fact, compatible with an unorthodox form of realism: *direct realism* (which must not be confused with naïve realism); but for reasons of limitations of space I cannot here go into this matter. In any case, Ryle's unquestioning adherence to realism in combination with a fixed idea of what realism under broadly Cartesian premises (i. e., Husserl's premises) *must* be like is likely to be one of the factors responsible for Ryle's *confusion* in reporting on Husserl's philosophy, which confusion is exhibited by R8 and R9, *and* in no less degree also by R7. *True:* for Husserl, as Ryle says in R7, "'contents' are not real parts of mental functioning", *and true:* in a sense Husserl denies, as Ryle says, "that what an act is 'of' is essentially contained in or adjoined to the act". Husserl *does* deny (with good reason, I think) the *real in-being* of the intentional object in the intentional experience [Erlebnis], that is: its being *in* the latter as a real part – *piece* or *aspect* – of it: see H4 and H5 (and see also, interestingly, *Id1*, §90, 207–208, where Husserl denies the real in-being of the intentional object in the intentional experience precisely because it would lead to the absurd doubling of *realities* one observes in mental representationalism[13]). However, Ryle would have done well to point out that *in another sense* Husserl *also affirms* "that what an act is 'of' is essentially contained in or adjoined to the act": see the *inseparably belonging* and *necessarily belonging* that are spoken of in H2, and consider the force of the "*eo ipso*" in the following:

> [H6] If this experience is present in its psychical, concrete fullness, then *eo ipso* the intentional 'relation to an object' is consummated [vollzogen], *eo ipso* an object is 'intentionally present' (*V.LU*, §11, 32; cf. *LU²21*-subtext, 386).[14]

---

13 One may well wonder: had Ryle not read §§ 90 and 43 of *Id1* when he made a mental representationalist out of Husserl?
14 And compare the following quotation, which – being from the second, 1913-edition of Husserl's *Logical Investigations* – presents a later version of the quotation in H6, a version that is *explicit* regarding the *essentiality* of the intentional object for the intentional experience: [H6a] "If this experience is present, then *eo ipso* – this, I emphasize, is due to its own *essence* – the intentional 'relation to an object' is consummated, *eo ipso* an object is 'intentionally present'" (*LU²21*, V. LU, §11, 386). And just as explicit in the same regard is the following quotation

Ryle apparently did not take notice of *that other sense* (of the in-being of the intentional object in the intentional experience). At least, he does not mention it. On the other hand, Ryle's correctly ascribing to Husserl the view that intentionality is an *internal relation* – see R6 – suggests that *that other sense* touched at least the fringes of Ryle's mind. If he *did* take notice of it, then presumably he did not mention it because he believed that the Husserlian conception of basic intentionality as an inner relation of intentional experiences to intentional objects *qua genuine subjects of attributes* – is untenable *even if* intentionality may be taken to be an internal relation that is *not* a specification of the *having-as-a-real-part* relation for experiences. We have not yet seen Ryle's reasons for believing this. But before I get to them, note how very puzzling Ryle's further remarks in R7 are: "Introspection cannot find them [i.e., the intentional 'contents' of mental acts]. (This is proved by the fact that two acts of different date can have the same object.)" But of course introspection can "find them"! It must presumably remain forever unknown to us what made Ryle ascribe the opposite view to Husserl. For the fact mentioned parenthetically in R7, though indeed a fact, does not *prove* that opposite view – and certainly does not prove it for Husserl. Quite the contrary: that "two acts of different dates can have the same object" is proven true for Husserl (and others) by *introspection* (involving retrospection) *finding the same object* "in" two acts of different dates.

But introspectively finding *the same object* "in" temporally separate mental acts A and B presupposes introspectively finding *the object* "in" A – and *how* is even this latter feat possible? In this way: *by* looking introspectively at the intentional experience, I also look introspectively at the content of that experience, its object, which is essentially implied by the experience and inseparable from it (though not a *piece* or *aspect* of it). If I perceive a tree, I may pay no attention to my perception of the tree; but if I concurrently pay attention to my perception of the tree, that is, if I *explicitly* perceive that perception (thus doing introspec-

---

from a lecture of 1907: [H6b] "Perceiving this bank or perceiving that house, and so on, or bringing to mind such perceiving, I find that the statement: this perception is a perception of a bank, that perception is a perception of a house, and so on, expresses something that belongs to the essence of the respective perceptions and cannot be separated from them. If we consider [...] other *cogitationes*, other pure phenomena, then we also find such among them that we, without counting them as perceptions, find nevertheless to be the same as perceptions in the following respect: relatedness to an object belongs to their essence, too; for example, a bringing to mind, in fantasy, of a bank, of a house etc, a bringing to mind of a picture of a house, a thinking of a house, and so on. Even without entering into an essence-investigation of these natures of pure phenomena, we have self-evident knowledge of the fact that here, too, the objectualness [Gegenständlichkeit] which is expressed by the little word *of* (fantasy of a house, etc) is something that is essential to them" (*DuR*, §4, 14).

tion *par excellence*), then the tree perceived "in" the perceived perception has of course not suddenly disappeared "from" the perception: the perception has not turned suddenly "meaningless".[15] The tree is still "there", and I may inspect it together with its perception, learning from that inspection precisely in which manner the tree is presented by its perception. And if I do such introspective inspection, then I do the work that is basic for Phenomenology.

§4 Rylean Husserl and non-Rylean Husserl

Sometimes Husserl came rather close to holding what Ryle says in R6 that he, Husserl, *should* hold:

> [H7] Though speaking of a *relation [Beziehung]* is not going to be avoidable here, still those [linguistic] expressions must be avoided that positively invite the misinterpretation of the relationship [Verhältnisses] as a relationship that is psychologically real [i.e., real according to the findings and presuppositions of the natural science of psychology], or pertains to the real content [i.e., the pieces or aspects] of the experience. [...] [O]nly one item is present, the intentional experience, whose essential descriptive character is, precisely, the referential [bezügliche] intention. According to its [the intention's] specific particularization, it fully and solely amounts to the having-in-mind [Vorstellen] of this object, or the making of judgments about it, etc (*LU²21*, V. LU, §11, 385–386; with some differences also in *V.LU*, 31–32).

In this quotation, Husserl shows himself somewhat dissatisfied with the designation "relation [Beziehung]" for basic intentionality, and avoids a decidedly relational description of it. In fact, the two misinterpretations of (basic) intentionality that Husserl speaks about in *LU²21* immediately before the passage in H7 may even give one the idea that Husserl is, in effect, rejecting *any* (truly) relational conception of basic intentionality. Yet, immediately following the passage from *LU²21* in H7, we have in *LU²21* the statement contained in H6a (in footnote 14), and this latter statement – a modified version of the H6-statement – rather persuasively suggests (and even more so the passage in H6b, also in footnote 14) that basic intentionality is for Husserl *after all* a *relation* to a *genuine subject*

---

[15] Perhaps Ryle is regarding introspection as a sort of abstractive procedure, analogous to the one that is in operation when, in contrast to one's normal way of perceiving written words of one's mother tongue, one is looking exclusively at the graphic appearances of them, abstracting from what they mean. But even if introspection *can* be done in a meaning/intent-abstracting manner, it certainly *need not* be done in that manner.

of attributes, albeit an *internal* relation. However, a few lines further down in *LU²21*, we find Husserl saying the following:

> [H8] And of course such an experience can be given in consciousness, with its particular intention, without the object existing, perhaps even without it being capable of existing; the object is intended/meant, that is, the intending of it is experience [Erlebnis]; but it is then [i.e., in the case of non-existence] only intended, as supposedly existing [vermeint], and is, in truth, nothing (*ibid.*, 386; verbatim in *V.LU*, 32).

This, again, suggests that Husserl advocates a non-relational view of basic intentionality, a view rather in accordance with Ryle's ideas in R6, and the impression is strengthened further on in the text:

> [H9] That the object is a 'merely intentional' one does, of course, not mean that it *exists*, but only in the *intentio* (hence as its real part), or that there exists in it some shadow of the object; but it means: the intention, the '*meaning*'/intending an object which is such-and-such exists,[16] but *not* the object (*LU²21*, V. LU, §21, supplement, 439; verbatim in *V.LU*, 80, disregarding insignificant differences).

Should we, therefore, conclude that for Husserl there is, in the end, *no* intentional object as a genuine subject of attributes that is intrinsic to an intentional experience, but, properly speaking, merely the intentional experience's (the *act's*) intrinsic *intending*, which, in Ryle's words (see R6), is "merely a property of it so specific as to be a differentia or in some cases an individualizing description of it" – an intending that attains its object, *if* it attains its object, quite *outside* of the intentional experience itself?

If this is Husserl's position in *LU²21* and earlier (the picture is not entirely clear since Husserl seems to waver somewhat: see H6a, H6b, and H6), it is certainly not his position in *Id1* and later, notwithstanding the fact that *Id1* and *LU²21* were both published *in the same year:* 1913. In *Id1* Husserl distinguishes – but *note:* he does not distinguish in *V.LU* and *LU²21* (see *V.LU*, §21, supplement,

---

16 In a footnote, Husserl adds: [H9a] "This [i.e., that the meaning/intending an object which is such-and-such exists] does not straightaway say, to emphasize it again, that one is attentive to it [i.e., the meant/intended object], perhaps even thematically concerned with it, although such-like, too, is included in our general talk of meaning/intending" (*LU²21*, V. LU, §21, supplement, 439; the footnote is not in *V.LU*). Husserl here implicitly distinguishes between *explicit* meaning/intending and *implicit* meaning/intending (meaning/intending *simpliciter* covering both modes) – and at the same time demonstrates implicitly (and presumably unintentionally) how tenacious is an understanding of the expressions "intentional object [intentionaler Gegenstand]" and "meant/intended object [gemeinter Gegenstand]" according to which these expressions *are not* mere façons de parler.

79–80, and *LU²21*, 439) – between, on the one hand, the object *simpliciter*, the actual/"real" object,[17] the object *in nature* (or, as I shall also say, the object *in the world*) and, on the other hand, the meant/intended object *as such* (see *Id1*, §89, 205, in particular H2, and *Id1*, §90, 207–208). The meant/intended object as such (for example, the perceived tree as such; cf. H2) *exists*, and exists as a *genuine subject of attributes, along with* the intentional experience to which it intrinsically belongs (i.e., it exists *as an intentional object*); but the corresponding object simpliciter (for example, the tree simpliciter; cf. H2) may well *not exist* even though the intentional experience and its essentially implied intentional object *exist*, and exist entirely unscathed by the non-existence of the object simpliciter. But *if* the corresponding object simpliciter does exist (or in other words: *if* the meant/intended object as such exists not only as an intentional object, but also *as an object in the world: if* it is "actual"), then the object simpliciter is, for Husserl, *no other object* than the meant/intended object as such; that much emerges from H5 and is presupposed by H3. This *conditional* identification of the object simpliciter with the intended/meant object as such (Husserl's explicit formulation of this idea can be found in *EPh1*, §17, 117) is the joint product of Husserl's rejection, throughout his career, of mental representationalism *and* of the new direction his thought took with *Id1*.

Thus, if we look at the position Husserl has in *Id1* and later, it is true that the intentional objects of consciousness are for Husserl genuine subjects of attributes to which intentional experiences are internally (intrinsically-essentially) related: basic intentionality is, then, an internal relation for Husserl, and a relation directed at genuine subjects of attributes.[18] "And what's *wrong* with that?" one

---

[17] I have put scare-quotes around the word "real" in "the *actual/real* object" (already in footnote 10) for the following reason: *On the one hand*, "real", as normally understood, is a prima facie correct rendering of Husserl's "wirklich" in "der wirkliche Gegenstand", "das wirkliche Objekt", just like "actual" is, and it is a rendering that carries, considerably less elusively than "actual", the connotation of *non-mentalness* and *extra-mentalness* (in addition to the core content *possible-but-not-merely-possible*) – a connotation not unwanted, in fact: *essential*, in the present context. *But on the other hand*, "real" has a special technical meaning for Husserl (the word "thinglike" could be used for expressing it) that, already in its core, is non-identical to the meaning of "actual" (see *Id2*, §17, 54, and *Id1*, §152, 354). Thus, Husserl himself, when speaking *Phenomenologically*, would not have used "real" instead of "wirklich". Hence the scare-quotes.
[18] That intentional objects are genuine subjects of attributes to which intentional experiences are intentionally related – *precisely this* (and not more) can be truthfully asserted, if understood in a certain way, *even if* one adopts the Rylean position that is ascribable to Husserl in *LU²21* and earlier. But the crucial differences between that position and the position that Husserl has in *Id1* are the following: (1) according to the former, but not the latter position, intentional experiences *can fail* (and in fact many of them do fail) to be intentionally related to an intentional object (since there is no actual/"real" object that corresponds to their intention); (2) according to

may wish to ask Ryle in consideration of what he says in R6. I finally get to Ryle's reasons *against* interpreting talk of *the object of an intentional experience* (according to Ryle, *misleading* talk: cf. R5a, b, and R6) as being talk of a *genuine subject of attributes* to which an intentional experience is *internally* related (cf. R6) – which interpretation is, to have a brief designation for it, *the Id1-intentionality-view*. This view, which we must regard as Husserl's *definitive* view on basic intentionality (definitively defining *Husserlian basic intentionality*), is called "erroneous" by Ryle ("Phenomenology", 175) – and here is *why*: Ryle, in effect, believes that that view is either *non-Meinongian and (hopelessly) unclear* (Scylla), or *Meinongian and inconsistent* (Charybdis):

Scylla:
[R12] [A]s Husserl seems, anyhow latterly, to reject Platonic or Meinongian subsistence theories, it becomes very hard to see in what sense he holds that 'intentional objects' really are genuine objects or subjects of attributes at all ("Phenomenology", 175).

Charybdis:
[R13] [T]he phrase 'the object of Jones' desire or fancy', e.g., is not necessarily a referentially used 'the'-phrase […] For there is nothing of which we can say truly or even falsely '*that* is the object of Jones' desire or fancy'. We can indeed state which attributes Jones is imagining something to be characterized by or what are the features of his situation, the absence or alteration of which Jones desiderates. But these statements will not require us to employ descriptive phrases referring to queer non-actual objects. Such references could not be made, for they would be self-contradictory (ibid.).

As in every Scylla-and-Charybdis argumentation, it is also in the present instance of one the decisive question whether its two monstrous alternatives are all the relevant *still open* – i.e., not already definitively excluded – alternatives. Might the *Id1*-intentionality-view not also be *non-Meinongian and clear (and consistent)*? Or *Meinongian and consistent (and clear)*? Let me *first* consider the chances – of not being definitively excludable – of the *second* of these two non-monstrous alternatives.

The *Id1*-intentionality-view *in Meinongian perspective* is the *Id1*-intentionality-view *combined* (1) with Meinong's assumptions *that some objects do not exist* and *that existence is actuality* (for references, see footnote 19), and (2) with the readiness to employ non-existent objects in the description of intentionality. Ryle believes (as I understand R13) that for many instances of inten-

---

the former, but not to the latter position, if an intentional experience *is* intentionally related to an intentional object (since there is an *actual/"real"* object – therefore: a genuine subject of attributes – that corresponds to its intention), then that relationship *is not internal* to the intentional experience itself.

tional experience (in particular, of the desiring or fancying kind, and we might also consider the hallucinating kind) the *Id1*-intentionality-view *in Meinongian perspective* requires us, when we try to implement it in describing those experiences, to refer to non-actual objects, which referring, however, is self-contradictory, according to Ryle, and therefore impossible. Ryle is right with respect to what the *Id1*-intentionality-view *in Meinongian perspective* requires us to do here; but what he finally concludes – namely, the impossibility of doing what it requires us to do – is questionable. For obtaining that conclusion, Ryle relies (unquestioningly) on the assumption of the identity, or at least the necessary co-extensiveness, of existence and actuality *and* on the assumption that (successful) reference necessarily requires the existence of what is, allegedly, being referred to. Ryle can be regarded to be implicitly arguing in R13, on the basis of those two implicitly made assumptions, against the possibility of reference to the non-actual, and therefore also against the *Id1*-intentionality-view *in Meinongian perspective*. As follows:

> Suppose one refers to a non-actual X. This entails that X *exists* (for reference necessarily requires existence). But the supposition that X is non-actual has the further necessary consequence that X *does not exist* (for actuality is identical to, or at least necessarily coextensive with, existence).

But it is entirely reasonable to hold against this attempted *reductio* of reference to the non-actual that existence and actuality *are not* the same, are not even coextensive; after all, the state of affairs that London is flooded by a tsunami is a state of affairs, and of course an *existent* state of affairs, but, fortunately, not an actual (or *obtaining*) one. And *even if* actuality and existence were the same – and it must be admitted that many, perhaps most, people cannot help identifying them and that, indeed, Meinong himself identified them – it is still entirely reasonable to hold against Ryle's attempted *reductio* that reference *does not* necessarily require existence; for of course one can refer to *the non-existent* (the non-existent being nothing other than *the non-actual* if existence and actuality *are* the same). Let me give an example, one that, in fact, emerges from R13 itself – assuming for the sake of the argument, as Meinong assumes, that actuality and existence are the same. Somebody asks: "*What* is it that Jones desires most?" Answer: "He most desires travelling to the moon. *That* is the object of Jones' strongest desire." Contrary to what is implied by what Ryle tells us (see R13), the person who gives this answer can reasonably be taken to be making a statement that is true or false *of something* – even in case Jones never in fact travels to the moon, which not unlikely outcome renders the state of affairs of Jones' travelling to the moon (perpetually) *non-actual*, that is, *non-existent* (assuming identity of actuality and existence). For if Jones never travels to the moon, then the phrase "the object of Jones' strongest desire" can *none the less* be reasonably taken to be used referentially in the above-described brief dialogue, namely, to refer to *the state of affairs of Jones' travelling to the moon*, which, if Jones never travels to the moon, is an object (of Jones' desire) that is (perpetually) *non-actual* and (assuming identity of actuality and existence) *non-existent*.

It is safe to conclude that the *Id1*-intentionality-view *in Meinongian perspective* is *consistent* (and clear). It is also safe to presume that only a small minority of philosophers will find such a perspective attractive (in spite of Meinongianism having found able defenders). "The prejudice in favour of the actual" that Meinong noted in 1904 ("On Object Theory", 485)[19] is still alive and flourishing, although *today*, when non-actual objects are being commented on, the frequency of discriminatory epithets – like "queer" (see R13), "fleshless", "other-worldly" (for the latter two, see *CoM*, 245) – is somewhat lower (it seems to me) than it was in Ryle's times.

How fortunate, then, that Husserl, in having the *Id1*-intentionality-view, is not committed to a Meinongian perspective and, in fact, does not adopt a Meinongian perspective! This is correctly noted by Ryle in R12; but, contrary to what Ryle believes, having the *Id1*-intentionality-view *in non-Meinongian perspective* does not render it *unclear*, so as to make true what Ryle also says in R12: that "it becomes very hard to see in what sense he [Husserl] holds that 'intentional objects' really are genuine objects or subjects of attributes at all". The *Id1*-intentionality-view can be – and *is* in Husserl's hands – *non-Meinongian and clear* (and consistent). This is best seen when we consider an example: a visual experience of a golden mountain, which is, however, a hallucination. As a preliminary, I note (*a*) that Husserl, unlike Meinong (see footnote 19), does not identify existence and actuality, but uses "actual [wirklich]" (*not* always, but when he employs the word to characterize *the not-merely-intentional*) to express *exis-*

---

19 A few pages further on, Meinong speaks of the "just now touched on prejudice in favour of existence" ("On Object Theory", 489). Thus: the prejudice in favour of existence *is*, for Meinong, the prejudice in favour of the actual. This indicates that Meinong belongs with those who identify existence and actuality (as does Ryle). But Meinong is debarred (or perhaps saved) from joining the vast multitude of *the orthodox* – the host of the *actualists* – by his heterodox belief that *some objects do not exist* (for the notorious paradoxical formulation of this belief – a formulation that Meinong meant merely playfully, and not as the formulation of a substantial paradox – see "On Object Theory", 490). Note that by his asserting that some objects do not exist, Meinong did not mean to assert that some objects are *nothing*, that is: not identical with anything (not even with themselves). He merely meant to say that *some objects*, though they are each *something* (that is, identical with something), *are not actual*.

tent-as-an-object-in-the-world, which is a concept that exceeds both the concept *existent* and the concept *possible-but-not-merely-possible* (*we* may also use "real" for expressing that Husserlian concept, though this option is closed to Husserl himself: see footnote 17); and (*b*) that Husserl, unlike Meinong (see footnote 19), does not believe that there are non-existent objects or anything non-existent. (Husserl, therefore, is neither an actualist nor a Meinongian.)

According to the *Id1*-intentionality-view *in Meinongian perspective*, the just-mentioned visual experience (and via the experience also the subject of it) is internally intentionally related to a golden mountain, but to a non-existent golden mountain. In contrast, according to the *Id1*-intentionality-view *in Husserl's non-Meinongian perspective*, the visual experience is *not* internally or otherwise intentionally related to anything non-existent (for there is no such thing). Rather, what is true according to that view, in that perspective, is this: the visual experience is, qua *this* visual experience, internally intentionally related to something that exists *as an intentional object*, namely, to *this* (visually experienced) golden mountain (*as such*, that is: *as visually experienced*), a genuine subject of attributes;[20] but the visual experience, being a hallucination, is *not* intentionally related to any golden mountain that exists *as an object in the world* (or as one also says: to an "actual" or "real" golden mountain). It follows that the (*visually experienced*) golden mountain (*as such*), though existing as an intentional object, does not exist *as an object in the world*. But this does not imply that Husserl is on Meinongian tracks after all, as little as being on Meinongian tracks is implied by saying that a horse exists *as a horse*, but does not exist *as a dog* – for it does not follow from this that the horse is a non-existent object. Regarding the object which, according to *Id1*, *corresponds to* (and *is not* – as it would be according to V.LU, 79–80, $LU^2 21$, 439 – *unconditionally identical to*)[21] the *visually experienced* golden mountain *as such*, namely, the golden mountain *simpliciter*, the actual/"real" golden mountain, the golden mountain *in nature* (or *in the world*) – regarding this "object" (but, you may ask, why the scare-quotes?), the thing to be said according to the *Id1*-intentionality-view *in Husserl's non-Meinongian perspective* is this (given the hallucinatory nature of the experience considered): it is neither an existent object *nor* a non-existent object (hence the scare-quotes!); it is for Husserl, in his later *Id1*-guise no less than in his earlier $LU^2 21$-guise, [H10] "not at all [überhaupt nicht]" ($LU^2 21$, V.LU, 387; verbatim in

---

20 If it were not a genuine subject of attributes, it would be impossible that it be identical with the actual golden mountain, which, however, is possible and would be the case if the golden mountain existed as an object in the world.

21 But *neither* should "corresponds to" here be taken to imply a *duality of objects*.

V.LU, 32), "nothing [nichts]" (see H8, the end of the quotation).²² And Husserl would also say: *it does not exist*. That Husserl would use this latter way of speaking – the simple predication of simple non-existence – is shown by the end of the quotation in H9, and that he would use it specifically and explicitly with respect to the object *simpliciter*, in contrast to the intentional object *as such*, is shown by *Id1*, §90, 207. But "the golden mountain simpliciter does not exist" does not mean for Husserl: the golden mountain simpliciter is an object *and* does not exist. This latter, precisely, is what that sentence would mean for *Meinong*, on the basis of his property-conception of existence and, derivatively, non-existence, which conception has that sentence *entail* that some object does not exist, and very naturally leads (by the conjunction of several true statements of singular non-existence, each understood to be about yet another object) to the tenet that some, indeed *many objects* do not exist. (Thus, Meinong is speaking of *the many*, which share *one and the same:* non-existence.) In contrast, the meaning that *Husserl* attaches to "the golden mountain simpliciter does not exist" is that the "the golden mountain simpliciter" – this designator – has *no referent*, or what is for this designator (with this sense) saying the same thing: no referent *among the objects in the world*. (Consequently, "the golden mountain simpliciter does not *exist*" and "the golden mountain simpliciter does not *exist as an object in the world*" are, in their Husserlian interpretation, logically equivalent.)

Husserl would not have needed Ryle to tell him that a 'the'-phrase "is not necessarily a referentially used 'the'-phrase" (cf. R13); for he would have asserted (as true) the statement "the golden mountain *simpliciter* does not exist [or in view of H10: is *not at all*, is *nothing*]" precisely because the 'the'-phrase "the golden mountain *simpliciter*" had in his eyes *no referent*, and thus, since that 'the'-phrase has indeed no referent (as everyone knows), he would have used

---

22 The difference at this point between *Id1* and *LU²21* is this: in the latter, but *not* in the former, the *nothingness* of the actual object is transferred to the intentional object – due to the *unconditional* identity of them that is assumed in *V.LU* and *LU²21*, but *not* in *Id1*. Thus, Husserl would say in *LU²21* that the had-in-mind golden mountain is *nothing*, just as the actual golden mountain is *nothing*; all that exists is the *intention* (see H9). *Not so* in *Id1*. – The emphaticalness of the earlier, unconditional identification of intentional and actual object is truly remarkable and well worth quoting: [H10a] "One only needs to say it, and everybody must acknowledge it: *that the intentional object of the having-in-mind [der Vorstellung] is the same object as its actual and, if applicable, its outer object, and that it is absurd to distinguish between the two*" (*V.LU*, §21, supplement, 79; verbatim in *LU²21*, 439, disregarding insignificant differences). In the German original, the italicized passage is printed spaced out, and the words "derselbe [the same]" and "widersinnig [absurd]" are, *in addition* to being printed spaced out, *italicized* (already). Husserl's emphasis could hardly be greater.

it non-referentially and would have known that he is doing so. Accordingly, Husserl would not have inferred from the statement "the golden mountain simpliciter does not exist" the (literally understood) statement "something does not exist" (and compare the behaviour of the negated existence-predicate in modern *free logic*).

On the other hand, given that a golden mountain is visually experienced by him, Husserl would have asserted (as true) "the visually experienced golden mountain *as such* exists" precisely because the 'the'-phrase "the visually experienced golden mountain *as such*" had in his eyes *a referent* (in, or relative to, the situation), or what is for this designator (with this sense) saying the same thing: a referent *among the intentional objects*. (Consequently, "the visually experienced golden mountain as such *exists*" and "the visually experienced golden mountain as such *exists as an intentional object*" are, in their Husserlian interpretation, logically equivalent.)

It may be helpful to give a schematic description of the *Id1*-intentionality-view (always taken now in Husserl's own, *non-Meinongian* perspective, which, qua Husserl's perspective, is also *non-representationalist*[23]), to the extent that this view has here been examined:

> (1.) Suppose you have an intentional experience, P. P is internally (intrinsically-essentially) related to a genuine subject of attributes: P's intentional object, O [e.g., the experienced tree as such]. O cannot fail to exist as long as P itself exists.
>
> (2.) Existence, for O, means existence *as an intentional object*. But if O not only exists – i.e., exists as an intentional object – but also exists *as an object in the world*, then *the object that in the world corresponds to O*[24] [e.g., the tree simpliciter, the actual tree] is simply O. If, however, O does not exist as an object in the world, then *the object that in the world corresponds to O* is not O, but *nothing*, that is: the just formulated (italicized) 'the'-phrase does not refer to anything.
>
> (3.) Existence, for the object that in the world corresponds to O, means existence *as an object in the world*. But if the object that in the world corresponds to O exists – i.e., exists as

---

23 That is, basic intentionality is taken by Husserl to be directed, in consciousness, *immediately* at the intentional object itself, which, in turn, is taken to be *in no sense* a representation (mental or other) – *unless*, of course, we are dealing with *representational consciousness* (e.g., perceiving a picture, symbol, etc).

24 Since the expression "corresponds to" *does* suggest a *duality* of objects (of intentional objects and the objects "out there"), I herewith explicitly warn against connecting this idea with it; it is as un-Husserlian as can be. Instead of "the object that in the world corresponds to O [i.e., to the intentional object of P]" one can simply say, entirely avoiding the notion of correspondence, "the object that exists in the world and is identical to O", but must firmly keep in mind that this latter definite description need not have a referent, let alone one that is identical to O, the intentional object of P. However, the notion of correspondence – due to its unspecific nature (very different in this respect from the notion of identity) – *does* have its advantages in the present context.

an object in the world – then the object that in the world corresponds to O is simply O (cf. footnote 10). If, however, the object that in the world corresponds to O does not exist – i.e., does not exist as an object in the world – then the object that in the world corresponds to O is not O, but *nothing*.

(4.) Given P, it is self-evident that O *exists – exists as an intentional object*. But it may take unforeseeably long to find out definitively whether or not O *exists as an object in the world*, and unforeseeably long to find out definitively whether or not the object that in the world corresponds to O *exists* (cf. footnote 10). (Note that according to (2.) and (3.) O exists as an object in the world if, and only if, the object that in the world corresponds to O exists.)

(5.) The nature of the correspondence between O and the object that in the world corresponds to O is such that – according to a systematic ambiguity – one and the same singular term may be meant to refer to the one, but may also be meant to refer to the other. For example, if O is the experienced golden mountain as such, then "the golden mountain" may be meant to refer to O, and if it is meant to refer to O, then *the golden mountain* exists (for then "the golden mountain" refers to O, and O exists); but instead it may be meant to refer to the object that in the world corresponds to O, and if it is meant to refer thus, then *the golden mountain* does not exist (for then "the golden mountain" refers, in fact, to nothing – assuming, of course, that there is no such thing as a real golden mountain).

(6.) The nature of the correspondence between O and the object that in the world corresponds to O is also such that it can be said that the object that in the world corresponds to O is, like O, an intentional object of P.[25] If the object that in the world corresponds to O exists, one can even say that P is *intentionally related* to the object that in the world corresponds to O (for then that object is simply O, according to (3.)).[26] This is not possible if the object that in the world corresponds to O does not exist; in that case, calling "it" an intentional object of P is a *mere façon de parler* (and any relation to it is impossible); for in that case all we really have to do with is this: P's intending – in intending O (*projected* to be appropriately recurring in *further* experiences) – an object that in the world corresponds to O, though there is no such thing.

Obviously, this schematic description of the *Id1*-intentionality-view firmly belongs with what is often called the "East Coast interpretation" of Husserlian intentionality (it comes, so to speak, from the *extreme* "East Coast"). It has no truck with the "West Coast interpretation": there is no need in it for Fregean senses, and it is not a mediator-theory of intentionality (cf. David Woodruff Smith's

---

[25] Note that Husserl in at least one place speaks of the had-in-mind or thought object simpliciter [vorgestellten oder gedachten Objekt-schlechthin] of a having-in-mind [Vorstellung] *besides* its had-in-mind object as such [sein Vorgestelltes als solches]: see *Id1*, §90, 207.

[26] Note that an – in some sense – external description of a *relatum* in an internal relationship does not turn that relationship into an external one. *Smaller-than* between numbers is an *internal relation*, and 7 is *intrinsically-essentially* smaller than 8; these truths are not abolished by the fact that 8 can be arithmetico-externally described as "the number of the planets".

and Ronald McIntyre's influential book *Husserl and Intentionality*). It is simply true to Husserl.

One may well wonder why Husserl moved from his rather Rylean non-Meinongian LU^221-intentionality-view to his still non-Meinongian, but essentially *non-Rylean Id1*-intentionality-view – the view that has just been described (but only in a schematic way, and far from completely). But doubtless it has to do with – is itself an aspect of – Husserl's strengthening of the ontological significance of consciousness in *Id1*, a strengthening that prominently concerns the subject of consciousness (the ego) and the objects of consciousness (the objects of basic intentionality), to the point that consciousness, for Husserl, came to carry within itself – as emerging in it – *the world*. Very likely, Husserl tended in this direction from the very beginning of his mature philosophy; this is suggested by his famous remark that

> [H11] [t]he first breakthrough of this universal a-priori-correlation of object of experience and modes of givenness [Gegebenheitsweisen] (while working on my 'Logical Investigations', roughly in the year 1898) shook me so deeply that since then my entire life-work has been ruled by this task of working out systematically this a-priori-correlation (*Crisis*, §48, 169fn).

Quite possibly, all that prevented Husserl from adopting the *Id1*-intentionality-view *even before Id1* was the philosophically accidental circumstance that before *Id1* he did not see as clearly as he did in *Id1* how an intentional object can be taken to be *in* consciousness *without* also taking it, absurdly, to be a real part – an *aspect* [Moment] or *piece* [Stück] – of (the process of) consciousness. A striking indication of the existence of that accidental circumstance can be read out of the quotation in H9. When Husserl says in this LU^221-quotation (also to be found in *V.LU*) that "the object is a 'merely intentional one' does, of course, not mean that it *exists*, but only in the *intentio* (hence as its real part)", he obviously repudiates the interpretation of "X is a merely intentional object" as "X is an object existing merely in the *intentio*" *because* he takes the latter to entail "X is a real part of the *intentio* [therefore, of the intentional experience]": *see* the parenthetical explanatory phrase "hence as its real part". Even in *V.LU* and LU^221 Husserl seems to have sometimes known better than to assume the inevitability of *that* entailment, as is indicated by the *V.LU*-quotation in H6 and its LU^221-version in H6a. But his state of insight was certainly unstable. By and large, *before Id1*, being a real part of the intentional experience seemed to Husserl the only conceivable way of existing *in*, and of existing *merely in*, the intentional experience[27] – a way, however, that is *not viable* for intentional objects (since such objects are *identical* in temporally separated experiences). Thus, *before Id1*, it seemed to Husserl that there is no way for a merely intentional object to be *in* the intentional experience; and, of course, there is also no way for a merely intentional object to be *outside* of it: [H13] "But neither is he [Jupiter] *extra mentem*, he is not at all" (*LU²21*, V. LU, §11, 387; verbatim in *V.LU*, 32; the first quotation in H10 are the three last words of the quotation in H13). For Husserl in *LU²21*, talk of "a merely intentional object" is in the Rylean way a mere façon de parler, for there is, in fact, *nothing* there to speak of, not even a shadow (see H9; for Husserl's interpretation of non-existence as *nothingness*, see the end of H8). And yet, at the same time it is also true for Husserl in *LU²21* that [H14] "[f]or consciousness, what is given is essentially the same, whether the had-in-mind object exists, or is fictitious and perhaps even absurd" (*ibid.*; verbatim in *V.LU*, 32, disregarding insignificant differences). What is given – the had-in-mind object, the object that is *eo ipso* "intentionally present" when the intentional experience is present (see H6, H6a) – is essentially the same whether that object exists or not? This manner of speaking certainly does not fit well with Husserl's *Ryleanism (avant la lettre)* in *LU²21*. It even sounds Meinongian. The conflict is resolved in Husserl's very own non-Meinongian and non-representationalist way in *Id1*, where he could *consistently* say, and only a few lines apart, the following two things (for the way to say them *consistently*, see the propositions (1.) – (6.)):

> [H15a] I perceive the thing, the object of nature, the tree there in the garden; this, and no other item, is the actual object of the perceiving 'intention'. A second, immanent tree, or an 'inner picture' of the actual tree, of the tree standing out there before me, is not given [to consciousness] in any manner, and to suppose the like hypothetically only leads to absurdity (*Id1*, §90, 207–208).
>
> [H15b] And thus we ask quite generally [...]: what is it that 'lies' self-evidently in the whole 'reduced' phenomenon [that is: the phenomenon considered without employing *any* assumptions regarding *outward* existence, existence *in the world*]? Well then, there lies in

---

[27] In *Id1*, Husserl no longer concludes being *a real part of* the intentional experience from being *in* the intentional experience: [H12] "It is only too tempting to say: in the experience the intention is given with its intentional object, which, as such, belongs inseparably to it, hence *really* inheres in the intention itself" (*Id1*, §90, 207). In this quotation, what Husserl is no longer attached to (though attached to in *LU²21*) is *merely* the inferential transition marked by the occurrence of "hence [in German: also]". What comes before the "hence", Husserl is still attached to (as the further context shows). Thus, Husserl was, at bottom, attached in *LU²21*, *and remains attached in Id1*, to the idea that the intentional object is *inseparable* from the intention and the intentional experience itself.

the perception also this: that it has its noematic sense, its 'perceived as such', 'this flowering tree there in space' – understood with the quotation marks – [that is: the object taken without employing *any* assumptions regarding *outward* existence, existence *in the world*] precisely the *correlate* belonging to the essence of the phenomenologically reduced perception (*Id1*, §90, 209).

There are many open questions, of course. In the rational elucidation of how an object with its properties is *itself in the mind*, it is only the first step to say that an object – the object itself – is, as intentional object, in the mind *not* as a real part, but in the sense of an experience being intrinsically-essentially related to it, it being inseparable from it. Whether one speaks of *constitution* (as Husserl did) or of *intrinsic grasp* (as a direct realist would), a true understanding of the matter can only be reached by *describing the details* of how an object *as intentional object*, and, as may be the case, also *as real object for the mind*,[28] arises from (or is captured in) the correlative experiential modes of givenness [Gegebenheitsweisen]. This description was the task to which Husserl dedicated the, by far, greatest part of his life-work (cf. H11). A self-respecting philosophy of mind cannot afford to ignore it.[29]

Note on the references and quotations

In all cases of books and articles originally published in German, references are to editions that contain the original German text. For references to Husserl, the editions in the Husserliana series have been used – with one exception: a separate edition of the original Fifth Logical Investigation of 1901 (but the matching bibliographical data from the Husserliana volume that contains the original Fifth Logical Investigation *as a subtext* have also been provided).

All references are by title or by a short italicized label that is indicative of title; the labels can each be found in square brackets at the end of the corresponding bibliographical entry. Often, in addition to page-numbers, paragraph-numbers have been provided. Paragraph-numbers are either standard – as in the case of Wittgenstein – or make it easier for readers to find a quotation

---

[28] Since Husserl is an idealist, *a real object for the mind* is, for him, simply *a real object* (or in *his* diction: an actual object, an object *simpliciter*). Whether an object is *real for the mind* (or in idealist interpretation: *real*) is, usually, not the matter of one experience alone, but emerges only in the long, and intersubjective, course of experience.

[29] I would like to thank Michael Wallner from the University of Graz, Austria, for his perceptive and inspiring comments on an earlier version of this paper.

(if they use a book-edition that is different from the one I used). Purely non-English titles have been translated into English by me, sometimes in abbreviated form (see, in the Bibliography, the titles inserted in square brackets). The translated titles are sometimes used in the paper for the general mention of a work; but in the case of Meinong, the translated title is also used for specific – page-indicating – reference to a German-language edition.

All translations of quotations from Meinong or Husserl into English are my own translations. In the case of Wittgenstein, Anscombe's (original) translation has, in places, been modified by me in order to achieve a greater semantic nearness to the German original.

I always represent *by italics* the typographic devices of emphasis in quotations (in particular, double-spacing between letters). The devices are always already present in the originals – unless otherwise indicated. Square brackets are used in this paper, among other things, for insertions in quotations: insertions of interpretative remarks, of hard-to-translate German expressions right beside their translations, etc.

Bibliography

Bennett, M. R., and Hacker, P. M. S.: *Philosophical Foundations of Neuroscience*, Malden, MA/Oxford/Victoria (Australia): Blackwell 2003.

Dennett, Daniel C.: *Consciousness Explained*, Boston/New York/London: Little, Brown and Company 1991.

Dennett, Daniel C.: On the Absence of Phenomenology, in: *Body, Mind, and Method*, edited by D. F. Gustafson and B. L. Tapscott, Dordrecht/Boston/London: Reidel 1979, 93–113.

Dennett, Daniel C.: Re-introducing *The Concept of Mind*, in: Ryle, Gilbert, *The Concept of Mind. With an Introduction by Daniel C. Dennett*, Chicago: University of Chicago Press 2002, vii-xvii.

Descartes, René: *Meditationes de Prima Philosophia – Meditationen über die Erste Philosophie* [Meditations on First Philosophy], Latin and German, translated and edited by G. Schmidt, Stuttgart: Reclam 1986.

Graham, George; Horgan, Terence; Tienson, John: Phenomenology, Intentionality, and the Unity of the Mind, in: *The Oxford Handbook of Philosophy of Mind*, edited by B. P. McLaughlin et al., Oxford: Clarendon Press 2009, 512–537.

Harman, Gilbert: The Intrinsic Quality of Experience, in: *The Nature of Consciousness: Philosophical Debates*, edited by N. Block, O. Flanagan, and G. Güzeldere, Cambridge, MA: The MIT Press 1997, 663–676.

Husserl, Edmund: *V. (Fünfte) Logische Untersuchung* [Fifth Logical Investigation], as presented in the first edition of the Second Part of the *Logische Untersuchungen* [1901], edited by E. Ströker, Hamburg: Meiner 1988. [*V.LU*]

Husserl, Edmund: *Logische Untersuchungen: Zweiter Band, I. Teil* [Logical Investigations: Second Volume, First Part] [1913], edited by U. Panzer (Hua XIX/1), containing also, as a subtext, the original text of the first edition of the Second Part of the *Logische Untersuchungen* (but without the Sixth Logical Investigation), The Hague: Nijhoff 1984. [*LU²21; LU²21*-subtext]

Husserl, Edmund: *Ding und Raum* [Thing and Space]: *Vorlesungen 1907*, edited by U. Claesges (Hua XVI), The Hague: Nijhoff 1973. [*DuR*]

Husserl, Edmund: *Ideen zu einer reinen Phänomenologie und phänomenologischen Philosophie: Erstes Buch* [Ideas Pertaining to a Pure Phenomenology and to a Phenomenological Philosophy: First Book; Ideas I] [1913], edited by K. Schuhmann (Hua III/1), The Hague: Nijhoff 1976. [*Id1*]

Husserl, Edmund: *Ideen zu einer reinen Phänomenologie und phänomenologischen Philosophie: Zweites Buch* [Ideas Pertaining to a Pure Phenomenology and to a Phenomenological Philosophy: Second Book] [1912–1928], edited by M. Biemel (Hua IV), The Hague: Nijhoff 1952. [*Id2*]

Husserl, Edmund: *Erste Philosophie (1923/24): Erster Teil, Kritische Ideengeschichte* [First Philosophy I], edited by R. Boehm (Hua VII), The Hague: Nijhoff 1965. [*EPh1*]

Husserl, Edmund: *Phänomenologische Psychologie* [Phenomenological Psychology]: *Vorlesungen Sommersemester 1925*, edited by W. Biemel (Hua IX), second, corrected impression, The Hague: Nijhoff 1968. [*ΦΨ*]

Husserl, Edmund: *Die Krisis der europäischen Wissenschaften und die transzendentale Phänomenologie* [The Crisis of the European Sciences and Transcendental Phenomenology] [1935–1938], edited by W. Biemel (Hua VI), The Hague: Nijhoff 1976. [*Crisis*]

Meinong, Alexius: Über Gegenstandstheorie [On Object Theory] [1904], in: *Abhandlungen zur Erkenntnistheorie und Gegenstandstheorie*, edited by R. Haller, R. Kindinger, R. M. Chisholm, Graz: Akademische Druck- u. Verlagsanstalt 1971, 481–530.

Meixner, Uwe: *Defending Husserl. A Plea in the Case of Wittgenstein & Company versus Phenomenology*, Berlin: De Gruyter 2014.

Ryle, Gilbert: *The Concept of Mind* [1949]. *With an Introduction by Daniel C. Dennett*, Chicago: The University of Chicago Press 2002. [*CoM*]

Ryle, Gilbert: Phenomenology [1932], in: *Collected Papers*, vol. I (Critical Essays), London: Hutchinson 1971, 167–178.

Ryle, Gilbert: Review of Marvin Farber: 'The Foundations of Phenomenology' [1946], in: *Collected Papers*, vol. I, 215–224.

Ryle, Gilbert: Phenomenology versus 'The Concept of Mind' [1962], in: *Collected Papers*, vol. I, 179–196.

Smith, A. D. (Arthur David): Husserl and Externalism, *Synthese* 160 (3) (2008), 313–333.

Smith, David Woodruff, and McIntyre, Ronald: *Husserl and Intentionality*, Dordrecht: Reidel 1982.

Tye, Michael: *Consciousness and Persons*, Cambridge, MA: MIT Press 2003.

Wittgenstein, Ludwig: *Philosophical Investigations – Philosophische Untersuchungen*, German and English, translated by G. E. M. Anscombe, edited by G. E. M. Anscombe and R. Rhees, New York: Macmillan 1953. [*PhI*]

Part II: Husserl and some Analytic Philosophers

Claire Ortiz Hill
Husserl and Frege on Functions

Abstract: Groundwork is laid for answering questions as to how to situate Husserl's theory of functions in relation to Frege's. I examine Husserl's ideas about analyticity and mathematics, logic and mathematics, formalization, calculating with concepts and propositions, the foundations of arithmetic and extensions, to show that, although he knew, studied and lauded Frege's ideas about functions and concepts, each philosopher approached the issue from different angles, Seduced by the sirens of transcendental phenomenology, Husserl did not pursue the issues, implications, and consequences of his ideas about functions. I ask whether doing so could provide new insight into, or even solutions to, the problems involving functions that beset Frege, Russell and have beset their successors

§1 Introduction

In 1918, Edmund Husserl wrote in a letter to Hermann Weyl that he had accorded his theory of functional judgments a very important role in the courses he had taught over the past twenty years. He in fact had discussed a theory of functional judgments at length in his lecture course *Logic and General Theory of Science, Lectures 1917/18* (a work which unhappily has not found the attention it deserves from philosophers of any stripe), where he linked it to what mathematicians call a function, something that without having arrived at the full descriptive analysis of the kinds of judgment concerned, the sharp-witted Frege, had had the merit of recognizing in his article "Function and Concept" (Husserl 1917/18, §40b). Reporting on R. Heilner's *System der Logik im Sinne eines allgemeinen Organon der menschlichen Erkenntnis* in 1903, Husserl had written that "the manner in which the author... seeks to interrelate the concepts of judgment and concept, on the one hand, and the concept of function, on the other, recalls the work–probably unknown to him, and for that matter incomparably more valuable–of the ingenious mathematician G. Frege, *Funktion und Begriff* (Jena, 1891), which unhappily has not found the attention it deserves from professional logicians" (Husserl 1903, 247).

In his 1891 correspondence with Gottlob Frege, Husserl alluded to that article (Frege 1980a, 64), a copy of which Frege himself had sent him and on which Husserl marked passages and wrote comments in the margins, thus leaving a valuable record of his keen interest in the work. His copies of the article, of Frege's related articles "On Concept and Object", "On Sense and Meaning", "On Formal Theories of Arithmetic", his *Begriffsschrift* and other writings, with Husserl's marks and comments can be examined in the Husserl Archives in Leuven, Belgium.

These facts are interesting and thought-provoking in their own right, but they are all the more so because of the important role that Frege's ideas about functions played in his work and went on to acquire in mainstream logic and analytic philosophy. Indeed, the preeminent Frege scholar Michael Dummett– whom William Demopoulos, for one, considers "to have set an intellectual standard to which most all philosophers of his generation aspire" (Demopoulos 1995, xi; Hill 2002b)–even went so far as to suggest that the "metaphor which is really important... is that whereby Frege speaks of concepts (properties) and relations in analogy with mathematical functions: it is by the appropriateness or inappropriateness of this analogy that Frege's account stands or falls" (Dummett 1956, 296). In notes dated 1906, Frege himself wrote that he regarded the result of his work as being almost entirely tied up with his concept-script and his recognition of the true nature of concepts and functions (Frege 1906, 184).

Moreover, Bertrand Russell identified Frege's use of functions in the *Basic Laws of Arithmetic* (Frege 1893) as leading to the contradictions (Frege 1980a, 130–31) that finally led him to abandon his logic, that had what David Hilbert once said had had a "downright catastrophic effect in the world of mathematics" (Hilbert 1925, 375), and that Russell and Alfred North Whitehead expended a great deal of labor to solve in *Principia Mathematica* (Russell & Whitehead 1927, vii, 1). Moreover, it is highly questionable whether the logical issues surrounding Frege's use of functions have been sufficiently confronted and the problems uprooted even today (Hill 1997b; Hill 1997c).

Given the important nature of these considerations, intriguing questions arise as to how we are to understand and situate Husserl's little-known theory of functions in relation to Frege's well-known theory of the same and whether Husserl's theory can be connected up with these larger issues in ways that might prove of some interest to us today. Here, I wish to lay some groundwork for determining answers to those questions. I do so in conjunction with a look at Husserl's insufficiently explored, but intimately intertwined, ideas about analyticity and mathematics, logic and mathematics, formalization, calculating with concepts and propositions, the foundations of arithmetic, extensions....

§2 Analyticity and Mathematics

According to Michael Dummett, "Frege's statement and detailed exposition of the logicist thesis that arithmetical statements are analytic and can be explained in purely logical terms and derived from purely logical principles" was one of his "basic contributions" to the philosophy of mathematics" in *The Foundations of Arithmetic* (Dummett 1981, 631). For Dummett, it was in turning to the actual process of trying to formalize arithmetic that Frege

> hit upon the famous conception, which has been used to characterize the so-called 'logicist' school of philosophers of mathematics, that arithmetic could, and to give a correct interpretation of it, should, be so analyzed as to employ for it no primitive notions or axioms peculiar to it.... Thus all arithmetical statements are expressible, when properly analysed, by using only notions belonging to logic, and, when provable, can be proved from purely logical principles. (Dummett 1981, xxxvi)

Frege himself did not seem to be thinking that the idea was original to himself when he wrote that, "Nowadays, it seems, more and more supporters are being won by the view that arithmetic is a further development of logic; that a more rigorous establishment of arithmetical laws reduces them to purely logical laws and to such laws alone. I too am of this opinion...". (Frege 1891, 30)

Like Frege, Husserl was a mathematician by training, but unlike him (or Russell, Whitehead and other makers of analytic philosophy, for that matter), he was long on intimate terms with the greatest and most innovative mathematicians of his time. From 1877 to 1881, he studied under Karl Weierstrass in Berlin, where he was also influenced by Leopold Kronecker, whose special field was the philosophy of mathematics and who is thought to have "sown the first seeds of philosophical understanding" in Husserl. He subsequently prepared his doctoral thesis in mathematics on the calculus of variations under the direction of Leo Königsberger, who had studied under Weierstrass. He then served as Weierstrass' assistant. From 1886 to 1901, he was a colleague and close friend of the creator of set theory Georg Cantor, then at the height of his creative powers. From 1901 to 1916, he was a member of the great mathematician David Hilbert's brilliant circle at the University of Göttingen (Schuhmann, 7; Osborn 1934, 12–15; M. Husserl 1988; Hill 1997a; Hill 2002a).

In a sense quite different from Frege's ideas, and more akin to ideas about axiomatization that Hilbert would espouse, Husserl came embrace the thesis that arithmetical statements were analytic, explicable in purely logical terms, and derivable from purely logical principles (Hill 2010a). Reflecting on the evolution of his thought years later in *Formal and Transcendental Logic*, Husserl would explain that the sole purpose of his war against logical psychologism had been the "supremely important one of making the specific *province* of analytic logic visible in its purity and ideal particularity" (Husserl 1929, §67). He had come to see arithmetic truths as being analytic, as grounded in meanings independently of matters of fact (Husserl 1975, 42–43). For him, pure arithmetic, pure mathematics, pure logic were a priori disciplines entirely grounded in conceptual essentialities, where truth was nothing other than the analysis of essences or concepts. Pure mathematics as pure arithmetic investigated what was grounded in the essence of number. Pure mathematical laws were laws of essence (Husserl 1906/07 §14).

On one of the only pages that Husserl ever explicitly retracted of his critique of Frege (Husserl 1900–01, 179n.) in his quickly disavowed *Philosophy of Arithmetic* of 1891, Husserl had characterized Frege's ideal as "a founding of arithmetic on a sequence of formal definitions, out of which all the theorems of that science could be deduced purely syllogistically" and said that it was not necessary to show why he could not share Frege's view because all the investigations he had engaged in up to that point had presented nothing but arguments to refute it (Husserl 1891, 124).

In the 1890s, Husserl in fact began teaching his students that the whole of arithmetic belonged within the scope of a sufficiently broadly understood logic, that the entire theory of cardinal and ordinal numbers was no more than a piece of formal logic, and the same was true of all of pure formal mathematics, of all of analysis, number theory, function theory, etc. According to him, all these fields were purely logical because their basic concepts express reasoning forms that are free of any cognitive content and could not be had through sensory abstraction. No epistemological reflection is required. If 19th century mathematicians had adopted the deductive theories of traditional syllogistic logic and gradually developed a mathesis of propositional, conceptual, and relational meanings in the spirit of the only proper mathematical method, he contended, they were only laying hold of a field that was their own to begin with. He stressed that with formal mathematics one does not actually enter into any essentially new domain, but one deals with pure concept-truths whose conceptual matter is inseparably linked to the original matter of the logic of meaning (Husserl 1896, 241, 271–72; Husserl 1902/03b, 19, 34; Husserl 1906/07, §15; Husserl 1917/18, §§46b, 50).

From 1896 on, Husserl repeatedly explicitly attributed the idea that he had come to endorse that pure arithmetic was basically no more than a branch of logic that had developed very early through independent treatment to Frege's teacher Hermann Lotze. He was very explicit about this. For instance, in his Logic course of 1896, he told students that they would "have to befriend Lotze's initially indeed disconcerting conception that arithmetic is only a relatively independent and from time memorial particularly highly developed piece of logic" (Husserl 1896, 271–72, see also page 241). In his course on general theory of knowledge, he taught that the "whole of pure mathematics is, as Leibniz already saw, and as in recent times Lotze has repeatedly stated with respect to arithmetic, nothing but a piece of pure logic that under the fortuitous historical circumstances that led to the development of logic in Greece did not develop within the context of logic, but completely outside of it". (Husserl 1902/03a, 43)

In his Logic course of 1902/03, Husserl taught his students that Lotze had "stated that pure arithmetic was fundamentally nothing more than a thriving branch of logic that had developed further independently, and very early, for independent treatment .... Hence, not only arithmetic, but the whole of pure Mathematics... would essentially be one with pure logic...". (Husserl 1902/03b, 19). He further stated that he had already said that,

> in recent times Lotze had said that Arithmetic was an independently developed branch of Logic.... And one will really contrast set habitual ways of thinking with such views to the point of having to decide to recognize the essential unity of pure mathematics and pure logic. I beg you not to be frightened.... If one ascends to a purely theoretical and a priori discipline having reference to what I have called logical categories, therefore to all the concepts that determine the objective meaning of science in general and are inseparable from it, then it is clear without further ado that all of pure mathematics belongs in this sphere, that all purely mathematical disciplines, aside from the syllogistics traditionally dealt with in logic, are encompassed by pure logic as naturally conceived. According to my arguments, all concepts belong in pure logic that are not to be assigned to a particular science limited to particular domains of objects, but to all sciences in general and are necessarily common to them, all concepts, therefore, that have this reference to objects in general in the most universal way.... All such concepts belong in pure logic. The concept of cardinal number is such a concept, and every numerically determined cardinal number belongs among these concepts. One is something in general. Anything, no matter what it is, can be posited as one.... And all numbers are built upon units.... (Husserl 1902/03b, 34–35).

Later, in *Introduction to Logic and Theory of Knowledge*, he wrote that when Lotze had said of arithmetic that it was no more than an independently developed branch of pure logic, he had doubtlessly seen what was right, and that what had kept logicians from joining them up until now had been the lack of an intrinsic understanding of the essence of logic (Husserl 1906/07, §15). Much later, in *Formal and Transcendental Logic*, he would explain that logic and mathematics had only originally developed as separate fields because it had taken so long to elevate any particular branch of mathematics to the status of a purely formal discipline free of any reference to particular objects. Until that had been accomplished the important internal connections obtaining between the two fields had been destined to remain hidden (Husserl 1929, Chapter 2).

Specifically, Husserl taught that pure number theory was a science that unfolds the meaning of the idea number and arithmetic in a systematic theory of the laws unfolding the meaning of cardinal number, itself the answer to the question: "How many?" Since each and every thing can be counted as one, to conceive (*konzipieren*) the concept of number, or any arbitrarily defined number, we only need the concept of something in general. One is something in general. Anything can be counted as one and out of the units all cardinal numbers built (Husserl 1902/03b, 33–43, 49). One pear and one man, one apple and one pear, one apple and one apple all have the form "one and one…". (Husserl 1896, 102; Hill 2010a)

Lastly, because Husserl's thought has been almost exclusively associated with his transcendental phenomenology, it really needs to be interpolated here, that he did his best to hammer into people's minds a sense of the proper relationship between it and formal logic and mathematics. He maintained that, while theoretical disciplines have a systemic form that belongs to formal logic itself and must be constructed a priori within formal logic itself as part of the overall system of forms of deductive systems that are possible a priori, not all sciences are theoretical disciplines like mathematical physics, pure geometry, or pure arithmetic whose systemic principles are purely analytical. Sciences, he said, such as psychology, history, the critique of reason and, notably, phenomenology require one to go beyond the analytico-logical model. When they are formalized and one asks what binds the propositional forms into a single system form, one finds oneself facing nothing more than the empty general truth that there is an infinite number of propositions connected in objective ways that are compatible with one another in that they do not contradict each other analytically (Husserl 1917/18, §54; Husserl 1929, §35a).

In particular, Husserl emphasized, transcendental phenomenology has no dealings with formal logic and formal mathematics, none with geometry as a priori theory of space, none with a priori real ontology of any kind. The natural sciences of physical and mental nature, the mathematical sciences, logic, including formal logic, the sciences of value, ethics are not phenomenology. The special interest of transcendental phenomenology does not lie in the theoretical concepts and laws to which the sciences are subject. It does not aim at objective being and laying down truths for objective being, consequently, is not an objective science. What is objective belongs precisely to objective science, and what objective science still lacks for completion is its affair to obtain and its affair alone. The interest of transcendental phenomenology aims rather at consciousness as consciousness of objects. It is phenomenology of the constituting consciousness, and consequently not a single objective axiom, meaning one relating to objects that are not consciousness, belongs in it, no a priori proposition as truth for objects, as something belonging in the objective science of these objects, or of objects in general in formal universality. The axioms of geometry do not belong in phenomenology, because phenomenology is not a theory of the essences of shapes, of spatial objects. Essence-propositions about objects do not belong in the phenomenology of knowledge, insofar are they are objective truths and as truths have their place in a truth-system in general (Husserl 1906/07, Appendices III-V; Hill 2013b).

§3 Calculating with Concepts and Propositions

Frege first set out his ideas about functions in his *Begriffsschrift, a formula language, modeled upon that of arithmetic for pure thought*, where he explained that arithmetic had been the point of departure for the train of thought that had led him to the ideography he outlined there (Frege 1879, 8). In that work, Frege described the encounter with the inadequacy of language that had led him to conceive of the idea of an ideography. He had concluded that the most reliable way of carrying out a proof was to follow pure logic in disregarding the particular characteristics of objects and depending exclusively upon those laws upon which all knowledge rests. When it came to determining whether the judgments of arithmetic belonged among judgments for which the proof could be carried out purely by means of logic or among those needing to be supported by facts of experience, he realized that he would first have to determine how much one could prove in arithmetic solely by means of inferences with the sole support of laws of thought transcending all particulars. He found that he had to do everything he could to keep the chain of inferences free of gaps and anything intuitive from slipping in unnoticed and that language did not adequately achieve this in the strictest possible way. Hence an ideography was needed. He further reasoned that if one of the tasks of philosophy was to break the domination of the word over the human mind by laying bare misconceptions concerning the relations between concepts that often almost inevitably arise through the use of language and thus by freeing thought from what only the means of expression of ordinary language fetter it, his ideography could eventually prove to be a useful tool for the philosopher (Frege 1879, 5–7).

Now, few people realize that Husserl too was committed to the idea of a formal language for calculating with concepts and propositions. In his late work *Formal and Transcendental Logic*, he explained how the formalization of large tracts of mathematics in the 19th century had brought the parallels existing between its structures and those of logic to the fore, and by thus laying bare the deep, significant connections obtaining between the two fields, had raised profound new questions about the deep underlying connections existing between the two fields. In particular, developments in formalization had unmasked the close relationships between the propositions of logic and number statements thus making it possible for logicians to develop a genuine logical calculus that would enable them to calculate with propositions in the way mathematicians did with numbers, quantities and the like. (Husserl 1929, Chapter 2)

Husserl taught that only the completely unfounded prejudice that the essence of the mathematical lies in number and quantity could explain the rejection of the new mathematical theory of conceptual and propositional inferences. But, what is mathematical in the procedure of arithmetic, he protested, does not hinge upon our having to do with numbers in them. The essence of the mathematical does not lie in being quantitatively determinable, but in establishing a purely apodictic foundation of the truths of a field from apodictic principles. It is a matter of a rigorously scientific, a priori theory that builds from the bottom up and derives the manifold of possible inferences from the axiomatic foundations a priori in a rigorously deductive way (Husserl 1896, 272–73; Husserl 1902/03b, 231–32; Husserl 1906/07, Appendix B VII).

In his logic course of 1896, he was already teaching that there was nothing at all extraordinary about the idea of calculating with concepts and propositions, because the formal discipline of propositions in general and of concepts in general was a mathematical discipline of precisely the same nature, and used the same methods, as familiar mathematical disciplines such as arithmetic. Arithmetic, he told students, was the most marvelous tool devised for purposes of deduction; it was the science in which the deductive relations were analyzed most carefully (Husserl 1896, 250, 271–72). The idea of judgments having the form, for example, "All a are b", or "Something is a", and so forth, he later told students in *Logic and General Theory of Science* is mathematically precisely analogous to the idea of cardinal number, for instance one and one (Husserl 1917/18, §27a).

Husserl taught students that to be rigorously carried out purely deductive theory requires the very same algebraic method everywhere (Husserl 1917/18, §§19a, c), that every purely formal procedure that proceeds strictly deductively can be presented in algebraic forms and when this occurs scientific thinking first wins a free overview of all possibilities of deductive reasoning and the sovereign mastery of all possible problems and ways of solving them that is the prerequisite for the most exact and most universal solution of problems of the field concerned (Husserl 1896, 272–73; Husserl 1902/03b, 37).

In his courses on *Introduction to Logic and Theory of Knowledge* and *Logic and General Theory of Science*, Husserl taught that there was the second level of pure logic (in between subject-predicate logic (apophantic logic) and the highest level, that of manifolds). On this second level, it was a matter of an expanded, completely developed analytics in which one proceeds in a purely formal manner because every single concept used is analytic. One calculates, reasons deductively, with concepts and propositions. Signs and rules of calculation suffice because each procedure is purely logical. One manipulates signs, which acquire their meaning in the game through the rules of the game. One may proceed mechanically in this way and the result will prove accurate and justified. On this second level of pure logic, Husserl located the basic concepts of mathematics, the theory of cardinal numbers, the theory of ordinals, set theory, mathematical physics, formal pure logic, pure geometry, geometry as *a priori* theory of space, the axioms of geometry as a theory of the essences of shapes, of spatial objects, but also the pure theory of meaning and being, *a priori* real ontology of any kind (thing, change, etc.), ontology of nature, ontology of minds, natural scientific ontology, the sciences of value, pure ethics, the logic of morality, the ontology of ethical personalities, axiology or the pure logic of values, pure esthetics, ontology of values, the logic of the ideal state or the ideal world government as a system of cooperating ideal nation states, or the science of the ideal state, the ideal of a valuable existence, objective axioms (relating to *a priori* propositions as truth for objects, as something belonging in the objective science of these objects, or of objects in general in formal universality), essence-propositions about objects insofar are they are objective truths and as truths have their place in a truth-system in general (Husserl 1906/07, §§18–19, 434–35; Husserl 1917/18, Chapter 11; Hill 2013b). Here, Husserl's ideas are obviously closer to those of formalists than to Frege's ideas. However, a proper discussion of this would take us too far afield. I have looked at it in my *Husserl and Hilbert on Completeness* (Hill 1995) and "Husserl on Axiomatization and Arithmetic" (Hill 2010a).

In *Logic and General Theory of Science*, Husserl taught that constructing actual deductive theories was the business of mathematicians who were the technical experts most qualified in deductive theory. To philosophers, he assigned the task of undertaking complementary reflections on the essence and meaning of the governing basic concepts and basic laws. He thought that mathematizing logicians had done well to recognize the essential likeness between the formal mathematical disciplines and the disciplines of logical validity and to have brought them to a higher level of technical perfection by applying the same, completely appropriate, algebraic methods to them, thus expanding the scope of the exact mathematical disciplines to include these new disciplines. However, he complained, they were still confused about the nature and meaning of these disciplines, about the content of the main basic concepts. He lamented the fact that the idea of a theory of forms of meanings as a discipline prior to the disciplines of logical validity was still completely beyond their horizons. He further attempted a more precise characterization of the disciplines of formal logic, the essential problems, boundaries, and reciprocal relationships of which, he maintained, the dominant logic hardly had a hint (Husserl 1917/18, §19a, d).

In doing so, he was fulfilling a promise made in a note at the end of the Fourth Logical Investigation of the second edition of the *Logical Investigations*. There he had lamented the fact that logic still lacked a prime foundation, a scientifically rigorous, phenomenologically elucidated distinction between primitive meaning elements and structures and essence-laws germane to knowledge, because logicians had never scientifically formulated a purely logical theory of forms. He maintained that that was why the many theories of concept or of judgment had yielded so few tenable results (Husserl 1900/01, 528 n. 3). He concluded §13 of the Fourth Logical Investigation of that edition stating that he hoped that the much improved study of the theory of forms of meanings that he had hinted at in a note at the end of §13 of the first edition of that work, and that he had expounded in his lecture courses at the University of Göttingen since 1901, would be made available to a wider public (Husserl 1900/01, 522). According to Ursula Panzer's introduction to *Logic and General Theory of Knowledge* that more thorough presentation of the theory of forms of meanings was published for the first time in that work (Husserl 1917/18, XXVII and n. 2).

§4 Husserl on Functions

Husserl's keen interest in functions dated back to his years as Weierstrass' student. He said that it had been his teacher's thoroughgoing, systematic, treatment *ab initio* of the theory of analytic functions that had inspired him to inquire deeply into the principles of arithmetic, that Weierstrass' scrupulous manner of submitting the foundations of analytic functions to close scrutiny had awoken in him an interest in seeking radical foundations for mathematics (Jourdain, 295–96; Schuhmann, 7). However, though Husserl studied mathematical functions as a philosopher, something which Stefania Centrone has investigated in "Functions in Frege, Bolzano and Husserl" (Centrone 2010a) and *Logic and Philosophy of Mathematics in the Early Husserl* (Centrone 2010b), in the allusions to Frege's theory of function and concept of interest to us here, Husserl was not referring to mathematical functions per se. His thoughts, like Frege's, were formulated within the context of his theory of judgments and concepts.

In the letter to Weyl mentioned above, Husserl wrote that for 20 years a central part of his lectures had been the theory of functional judgments, of judgments with empty places, and the distinguishing of the different modes of this empty something. He also mentioned having dealt extensively with implementation of the fundamental distinctions between factual and formal ways of judgment, between proposition form and proposition (or judgment), proof- and theory-form and theory and the objective correlates associated with them. He added that his concept of complete manifolds dating from the beginning of the 1890s had also proved especially fruitful (Husserl 1918, 287f., cited Husserl 1917/18, XXIII n. 1).

All these subjects are pursued in *Logic and General Theory of Science*, where, in particular, Husserl spelled out for his students how they might convince themselves that there was something in logic that was akin to what mathematicians had in mind when they talk of functions. He told them that an analysis of judgments could persuade them beyond a shadow of a doubt that something that looks like a complete proposition and is stated grammatically as a complete proposition, but is not in fact a proposition lurks in every universal or particular judgment. (Husserl 1917/18, §§32c; 40b).

To demonstrate his conviction, he pointed out that it was obvious that corresponding exactly to every universal judgment, for example, "An A generally is p", is a particular judgment that differs from it only in that the generality has been changed into particularity. Comparing the two judgments, he argued, one finds that they obviously have a content in common, a propositional "An A is p" that usually leaves open whether it is the content of a universal or a particular generality.

In paraphrases such as "That an A is p holds generally", "...holds in special cases", that common content and the different characterizations of it come more distinctly to the fore. What should be meant there, he reasoned, is "an a in general" and not "a certain a". As an example of what he meant, he proposed, "A triangle in general has as the sum of its angles two right angles". The "in general", he maintained, could be understood either universally, in which case one readily says "every triangle, completely generally—or in the plural, all triangles". But, he pointed out, what is intended in propositions of such a form can also be different. To illustrate this, he pointed out that it is known from general theorems that in application to a given figure a vertex moves to infinity. However, there may be several vertices in the figure, and several may actually move to infinity. But, we are only certain that "in general one" moves to infinity. Stating this, we again encounter the verbal form of generality, the fact that, in general, a vertex moves to infinity, but the "in general" does not then mean universal generality. We cannot then instead say, every, all. We can but propose paraphrases, such as "There is one that moves to infinity", or "The fact that in general a vertex..., is certain, holds". In those cases, it is clear that the "one" does not have the sense of "a certain", that on the contrary, the latter can never be affected in an equivalent way by such paraphrasing. A distinction must therefore be made between two kinds of generality. Besides universal generality, there must be particular generality (Husserl 1917/18, §32c).

It is apparent, he further reasoned, that, by their essence, the predicates "holds generally", "holds universally", "holds in individual cases" only make sense for specific contents of this kind and not for actual, complete propositions. In the statement, "An equilateral triangle is generally equiangular", for example, the "is" expresses the fact that equiangularity is generally attributable to an equilateral triangle. However, there is no definite subject there, and the words "an equilateral triangle" figuring in the subject position obviously function completely differently than an ordinary noun phrase does, for example, as when "this...", or "a certain..." is stated. Yet, there is a marked inclination to paraphrase the statement as, "The fact that an equilateral triangle is equiangular is in general the case, holds generally, and in the particular case as well". "That a triangle is obtuse-angled in general occurs". We further realize, he maintained, that such paraphrases are just that and that every paraphrase not only changes the words, but also the meaning. The new forms exhibit arrangements of the meaning that are not actually present in the original judgment, "An a generally is b". In them, the subject is "that a triangle is obtuse-angled", "that an a is a P", and as predicate we have, "that holds generally", "holds universally and in the particular case". So, only equivalence obtains, not identity (Husserl 1917/18, §32c).

Looking at the paraphrasing in conjunction with an understanding of the remarkable manner in which the generality affects the entire makeup of the judgment, Husserl continued, we find a layering predicatively unfolded in paraphrasing forms of speech in the meaning running through the entire syntax. If we judge, "S is p", "Socrates is a philosopher", we are judging on one layer. We have a nominal basic positing, "Socrates!", and the predicate is posited on it. However, if we judge "Humans generally—or a human generally—rank(s) among mammals", then the double layering finds expression in the paraphrase. The fact that a human is a mammal holds completely universally, is so generally. That a triangle is obtuse-angled holds in particular cases. The propositional thought "An a is b" is lower layer in a curious way, and this layer is characterized as a whole in a twofold manner by the "being valid generally".

If we ask what figures in the subject position in the propositional thought "An a is b", which in a curious way, on one occasion, bears the universal, on another, the particular generality-trait, then on the surface it is a complete proposition, "An a is b", which holds generally. But, that cannot be. The meaning of an actual proposition is complete in such a way that, with respect to its empty places, it is either a particular or a universal proposition, or even, when the empty places are *quidam*-places, is a proposition determined in this regard. The curious constructions extractable from the content of particular and universal judgments are not at all different from such substrata of particular or universal judgments, or parts of such substrata. It is only the analysis of these judgments themselves that is new, only the knowledge that figuring in them are forms of this sort characterized in one case by the mode of validity of particularity and of universality in the other (Husserl 1917/18, §32c).

It was those curious formations that, inspired by the language of mathematics, Husserl called propositional functions. It was apparent to him that when mathematicians speak of "functions" they had precisely such meaning-forms in mind. To illustrate this, he took the function $x + 3$. As a function of whole numbers, he explained, $x + 3$ only says "any whole number + 3", but it does so in such a way that the "any" leaves it open as to whether a particular or universal mode of judgment is to be made with the expression (Husserl 1917/18, §32c). As another example, he gave "A human being is mortal" is a function or propositional function that is featured nominally when we state, "That a human being is mortal is valid generally". We cannot state general validity of the judgment. The judgment "A human being in general is mortal" or "Every human being is mortal" is a general judgment and a valid judgment, but upon close inspection, it makes no sense to say that it is valid in every case. In contrast, is this simple proposition-form "A human being is mortal" with the empty place "a" holds in every case. It always yields a valid proposition, where we may also put particular humans in the empty place, "An A is something" (Husserl 1917/18, 40b). He stressed that the concept of function is not just to be understood in relationship to propositions, that one may as well speak, for example, of nominal functions such as "an a", "an a and a b" (Husserl 1917/18, §32c).

The empty places, Husserl continued, are what mathematicians call arguments. Many empty places can occur in a judgment, so that the same judgment can have several places, or terms, of universality and several of particularity. These places can be pure empty places as, for example, "Something or other is red", in which a nominal something figures in the subject position and is the bearer of a particular function, or universal as, for example, "Everything is red". However, as a rule, the "something" is specified by a letter of the alphabet, as in the arithmetic example, $a + b = b + a$, where two terms function universally and are determined as the numbers a and b. Argument places are specifically nominal forms. He stated as a principle that every nominal position in a judgment-form can become an argument place and take on the generality-forms in relation to it. Arguments or generality positions, terms of universality and particularity also occur in predication since nouns can occur there in many different ways. Everything formal, he stressed, is exclusively composed of terms of this kind (Husserl 1917/18 §§26b, 32c).

Husserl considered that his analyses showed that all judgments were either functional or definite. As an example of the former, he proposed, "There are numbers smaller than an arbitrary number n", as examples of the latter, "Bismarck was the greatest statesman of the 19th century" and "Plato was the student of Socrates", which result from filling the empty places with definite values and so do not contain arguments. Functional judgments have empty places, arguments, which could be naturally classified in terms of universality and particularity. Functions are pure functions when they do not in general contain any definite terms and positings. They are mathematical functions when they contain only purely logical forms and concepts. In a statement such as "a lion has escaped", he explained, the indefiniteness lies in the little word "a". A lion is a definite something, but indefiniteness is still present there. In comparison, in the statement "Our Kaiser is in Breslau" everything is determined. There is no empty place (Husserl 1917/18, §§§26a, 32e, 40b-e).

Husserl considered the empty something to be of the greatest importance for the theory of meaning and all of formal logic. As what is specifically mathematical in the mathesis, specifically formal in formal logic, absolute emptiness of content was for him the hallmark of the formal logical. He saw it as occupying a remarkable middle position between form and stuff. A form such as "A is b" is thought of as being logically universal in such a way that the A and b are presented as "something or other" through one syntactical category or another. In its full indeterminacy, the "something or other" is determinable as everything and anything and so plays a role everywhere, has its place in every realm of thought. In every field of knowledge, thinking as determining continuously proceeds from what is tentative and incompletely determined to further determining. "Something is A", "Something that is A—or an A—is then further determined as B", and so forth. "Something" plays an overriding role in the theory of forms, is omnipresent, because everything stated there remains indeterminate with respect to any material individuation connected with special fields of knowledge and because everywhere the sole determinate thing is the form. In contrast what is definite, for example, "blue", "soft", "rectangle" does not have any place in formal logic. A theory of forms of meanings has no more to do with them, with their factual differences and the differences they require for meanings to be built out of them than a theory of validity of meanings has to do with the truths pertaining to "blue things", "rectangles" (Husserl 1917/18 §26b). In §§26a-b, 40b-45a, and Appendix XIII of *Logic and General Theory of Science*, Husserl pursues his ideas about functional propositions at length, something which certainly merits further study in its own right, but which would take us far too afield here.

§5 Frege on Functions, Husserl's Comments

As part of his efforts to contribute to breaking the pernicious sway of the word over the human mind, in his *Begriffsschrift*, Frege began advocating replacing the usual analysis of statements into subject and predicate by analysis in terms of what mathematicians call functions and arguments. He hoped that logicians would not allow themselves "to be frightened by an initial impression of strangeness" and would assent to innovations that he had been "driven" to make "by a necessity inherent in the subject matter itself" and that were justified by the fact that logic had "always followed ordinary language and grammar too closely". He was in particular persuaded that his replacement of the concepts subject and predicate by those of function and argument would "stand the test of time" (Frege 1879, 7).

Still intent upon breaking the sway of language over the human mind, in 1906, Frege complained to Husserl that logicians were still clinging too closely to language and grammar while their main task was to free themselves from language and to simplify it. In particular, he told Husserl that we should "tidy up logic by throwing out subject and predicate" (Frege 1980a, 68). That was the year, as mentioned in the introduction, in which Frege had written that what he regarded as the result of his work was almost entirely connected with his concept-script and the recognition of the true nature of concept and function, with construing a concept as a function, a relation as a function of two arguments, and the incompleteness of both concepts and functions (Frege 1906, 184).

As Husserl would later do in *Logic and General Theory of Science*, Frege defined functions as what remained common throughout different variations of a judgment. In §9 of the *Begriffsschrift*, he provided examples of what he meant:
1) "Hydrogen is lighter than carbon dioxide".
2) "The center of mass of the solar system has no acceleration if internal forces alone act on the solar systems".
3) "Cato killed Cato".

Such expressions, he explained, break down into two components: on the one hand, a stable component representing the totality of the relations, which he called the function; on the other, the words replaceable by others denoting the object that stands in those relations, which he called the arguments of the function. In the first example, substituting the word "oxygen" for the word 'hydrogen' in his formula language would yield "Oxygen is lighter than carbon dioxide", while substituting the word "nitrogen" for the word "hydrogen" would yield "Nitrogen is lighter than carbon dioxide". In that case, "...is lighter than carbon dioxide" would be the function and "hydrogen", "oxygen", and "nitrogen", the arguments. There could also be cases of two or more arguments. For example, if "carbon dioxide" is removed, giving the invariant, stable part, the function as "...is lighter than...". In the second example, "solar system" occurs twice. So this could be considered as a function of the argument "solar system" in different ways depending on whether "solar system" is replaced by something else in one or another, or both, of its occurrences. In the third statement, "to kill Cato" is the function, if "Cato" is taken to be replaceable the first time it occurs. "To be killed by Cato" is the function, if "Cato" is taken as replaceable the second time it occurs. "To kill oneself" is the function, if Cato is taken to be replaceable both times it occurs. He summed up his theory with these words,

> If in an expression, whose content need not be capable of becoming a judgment, a simple or a compound sign has one or more occurrences and if we regard that sign as replaceable in all or some of these occurrences by something else (but everywhere by the same thing), then we call the part that remains invariant in the expression a function, and the replaceable part the argument of the function. (Frege 1879, §9)

Frege symbolized the form of the one-argument function as $\Phi(A)$, where A was to represent the argument and $\Phi(\ )$ the function. It was to read, "A has the property Φ". He used $\Psi(A, B)$ to symbolize the form of the two-argument function. There $\Psi(\ ,\ )$ is the function and A and B the arguments and is to read "B stands in the relation Ψ to A", or "B is a result of an application of the procedure Ψ to the object A". He cautioned that in general $\Psi(A, B)$ differs from $\Psi(B, A)$. He maintained that since "Φ" figures in the expression "$\Phi(A)$" and is replaceable by other signs, for example Ψ or X, expressing other functions of the same argument, $\Phi(A)$ could also be seen as a function of the argument Φ. He considered that that made it especially clear that his conception of functions was much broader than the concept in analysis that had served as his guide (Frege 1879, §§9–10).

Mathematical expressions, Frege later explained in "Function and Object", the work Husserl cited favorably, can be split into two dissimilar parts, an argument that is a whole complete in itself and the function that is incomplete, in need of an argument to go together with it to make up a complete whole (Frege 1891, 24–25, 31–32). On his copy of that article, Husserl marked the passage where Frege had affirmed, "I am concerned to show that the argument does not belong with a function, but goes together with the function to make up a complete whole; for a function by itself must be called incomplete, in need of supplementation, or unfilled.¹ And in this respect functions differ fundamentally from numbers" (Frege 1891, 24).

Frege went on to say that, just like equations or inequalities or expressions in Analysis, statements in general could also be imagined to be split up into two parts, one complete in itself and the other in need of supplementation or unfilled. He used the statement "Caesar conquered Gaul", divided into "Caesar" and "conquered Gaul", to illustrate his point. According to his analysis, "Caesar" is the argument and the unfilled part "conquered Gaul". Husserl underlined the word "meaning" where Frege had written that in a sentence like "Caesar conquered Gaul" he called the meaning (*Bedeutung*) of the unfilled portion the function and Caesar the argument (Frege 1891, 31).

Turning to concepts, Frege argued that they, like functions, need supplementation and completion. Concept-words are unfilled. They contain a gap that is intended to receive a proper name. They have to have something to fall under them and therefore cannot exist on their own. Concepts are predicative, the meanings of grammatical predicates. When we say "This leaf is green", we are saying that something falls under a concept meant by the grammatical predicate. For Frege, the predicable nature of concepts was conferred upon them by the particular kind of incompleteness and dependency they exhibit with respect to objects (Frege 1891, 30; Frege 1892, 43–44, 48, 50). In reply to the question as to what, once he had admitted objects without restriction as arguments and values of functions, it was that he was calling an object, Frege answered that an "object is anything that is not a function, so that an expression for it does not bring any empty place" (Frege 1891, 32). Husserl underlined the word "object" in that answer.

Alongside Frege's statement that we "give the name 'the value of a function for an argument' to the result of completing the function with the argument", Husserl commented that the definition was unclear and that value should surely be distinguished from truth value (Frege 1891, 25). And next to Frege's statement that the value of our function was a truth value, Husserl noted that this was

---

1 In Frege's special vocabulary, functions, concepts, predicates were *ungesättigt*, which has usually been translated as 'unsaturated'. Here I translate *ungesättigt* as 'unfilled', which I find clearer in meaning and more natural. According to my *Random House College Dictionary*, 'to saturate' means 1. to cause (a substance) to unite with the greatest possible amount of another substance through solution, chemical combination, or the like. 2. to charge to the utmost, as with magnetism. 3. to soak, impregnate, or imbue thoroughly or completely. 4. to destroy (a target) completely with many bombs or missiles. 5. to furnish (a market) with goods to the point of oversupply. None of these meanings speak to Frege's concerns. I have also modified the published translations.

again not completely clear, that each value of a function was necessarily true or false, existing or not existing (Frege 1891, 28). Husserl also marked the passage where Frege had written, "We thus see how closely that which is called a concept in logic is connected with what we call a function. Indeed, we may say at once: a concept is a function whose value is always a truth-value" (Frege 1891, 30). Then Husserl asked in the margins whether or not he could not speak of the truth or falsehood, meaning the existence of the capital of the number 4, whether he could not say that there was no capital of the number 4, as it appears that absurd concepts would not reckoned as concepts (Frege 1891, 31–32). Next to Frege's comment that for any argument x for which '$x+1$' is meaningless (*bedeutungslos*), the function $x + 1 = 10$ would have no value and thus no truth value either, so that the concept: 'what gives the result 10 when increased by 1' would have no sharp boundaries, Husserl importantly objected that the function does not, however, do this to concepts first, but delimits their logical use. The call to work with possible concepts is generally justified, but impossible concepts are also concepts. There we find the ambiguity again. Having a value, he protested, surely does not mean having a truth value. Each function has *eo ipso* a value, or this not being the case, then value and truth value collapse together (Frege 1891, 33; Hill 2003).

Frege further considered that a sentence could be dissected and rearranged in various ways, so that what in one case figured as the incomplete element could in another be the filled or complete part. Function-argument analysis, he maintained, respected this fact in a way that subject-predicate analysis could not and so might offer a clear, flexible, and effective way of manipulating expressions that was compatible with his ideas about logic and mathematics. Husserl marked Frege's sentence, "Language has means of presenting now one, now another, part of the thought as the subject" and underlined the word "language" (Frege 1892, 49). He also marked Frege's note to his claim that a concept could be converted into an object. In that note, Frege had written that in "the sentence 'this rose is red': The grammatical predicate 'is red' belongs to the subject 'this rose.' Here the words 'The grammatical predicate 'is red' are not a grammatical predicate, but a subject. By the very act of explicitly calling it a predicate, we deprive it of this property" (Frege 1892, 46 n. †).

And, Frege was famously aware that with respect to what is called a function in Analysis, we come up against an obstacle that "is grounded in the matter itself and in the nature of our language" (Frege 1892, 55). Functions do, he found, and sometimes have to, take other functions as their arguments. When they do, however, he insisted, they differ fundamentally from functions whose arguments are objects and cannot be anything else, he insisted. Just "as functions are fundamentally different from objects, so also functions whose arguments are and must be functions are fundamentally different from functions whose arguments are objects and cannot be anything else". He called the latter first-level functions and the former second-level functions and distinguished between first-level and second-level concepts in the same way (Frege 1891, 38).

On his copy of "On Concept and Object", Husserl marked the paragraph in which Frege wrote that with his distinction between concept and object he had got hold of a distinction of the highest importance (Frege 1892, 54). He also marked the statement that a "concept is the meaning (*Bedeutung*) of a predicate; an object is something that can never be the total meaning (*Bedeutung*) of a predicate, but can be the meaning (*Bedeutung*) of the subject" (Frege 1892, 48). On one of the first pages of "Function and Concept", Husserl had written that the object of a concept would be something hard to express, but is easily represented in arithmetical notation (Frege 1891, 24). He marked the sentence: "The relation of an object to a first-level concept that it falls under is different from the (admittedly similar) relation of a first-level to a second-level concept" (Frege 1892, 50), as well as Frege's declaration that the concept must always be distinguished from the object, even in cases like that of the concept word "Venus", where just one object falls under the concept. "Venus", Frege had stressed, could never be a proper predicate, although it can form part of a predicate. "The meaning of this word is thus something that can never occur as a concept, but only as an object" (Frege 1892, 44). Husserl also marked Frege's conclusion that what the example showed "holds good generally; the behaviour of the concept is essentially predicative, even where something is being said about it; consequently it can be replaced there only by another concept, never by an object. Thus what is being said concerning a concept does not suit an object" (Frege 1892, 50). In addition, he marked the line where Frege had written in the paragraph before: "I do not want to say it is false to say concerning an object what is said here concerning a concept; I want to say that is impossible, it is senseless to do so" (Frege 1892, 50). Here Husserl tellingly underlined the word 'senseless' on his personal copy.

Yet, even as Frege wrote of those inviolable differences in "Function and Concept" and "On Concept and Object", he was developing the logical system of *Basic Laws of Arithmetic I* (Frege 1893) where, to avoid sterility of false or nonsensical conclusions (Frege 1884, §§66–67), he decreed Basic Law V to mandate that the generality of an identity could always be transformed into an identity of courses of values and conversely an identity of courses of values could always be transformed into the generality of an identity. By this, he meant that if it is true that $(x) F(x) = G(x)$, then those two functions have the same extension and functions having the same extension are identical (Frege 1893, §§9, 21). He knew that what he wished to achieve by his law was forbidden by the basic difference between first and second level relations, but he temporarily convinced himself that, though an actual proof could scarcely be furnished, and an unprovable law would have to be assumed, a transformation might take place in which concepts correspond to extensions of concepts. As he explained in a passage that Husserl marked in "Function and Concept", "Graphs of functions are objects, whereas functions themselves are not... Extensions of concepts likewise are objects, although concepts themselves are not" (Frege 1891, 32; Hill 2004). Husserl tellingly put a question mark where Frege had written that the possibility of regarding an equivalence (*Gleichung*) holding generally between values of functions as an equivalence (*Gleichung*) between graphs is not demonstrable and must be taken to be a fundamental law of logic (Frege 1891, 26).

§6 Bertrand Russell Copes with Frege's Contradiction-Producing Use of Functions

By decreeing that a function could take another function as an object, Frege authorized himself to do what he believed must not be done. As a consequence, he suffered the contradiction about the class of all classes that are not members of themselves. So it was that in 1903, Bertrand Russell, who in 1919 professed to believe that he was the first person ever to have read Frege's *Begriffsschrift* more than twenty years after its publication (Russell 1919, 25), wrote to Frege,

> On functions in particular (sect. 9 of your *Conceptual Notation*) I have been led independently to the same views even in detail. I have encountered a difficulty only on one point. You assert (p. 17) that a function could also constitute the indefinite element. This is what I used to believe, but this view now seems to me to be dubious because of the following contradiction: Let *w* be the predicate of being a predicate, which cannot be predicated of itself. Can *w* be predicated of itself? From either answer follows its contradictory. We must therefore conclude that *w* is not a predicate. (Frege 1980a, 130–31)

True to his convictions that the fundamental differences between predicates and objects were inviolable and founded in the deep nature of the matter, Frege replied to Russell that "A predicate is predicated of itself" did not seem exact to him and that one should rather say "A concept is predicated of its own extension". A predicate, he explained, was as a rule a first-level function, which requires an object as argument and cannot therefore have itself as argument (Frege 1980a, 132–33). The problem, he said, had already been dealt with in "On Concept and Object". It was "only an apparent one occasioned by the inexactness of the linguistic expression" (Frege 1980a, 141). Nevertheless, once he tested the validity of the chain of inferences leading up to the contradiction, Frege concluded that the transformation effected by his law about extensions was false (Frege 1980a, 132).

In the subsequent years, Russell multiplied his efforts to avoid the contradictions derivable in Frege's logic. He invented the theory of types, devised the technique for analyzing away classes and one for making incomplete symbols obey the same formal rules of identity as symbols directly representing objects, and so on, all of which has been studied extensively by many philosophers, not to mention by myself, for example, in my *Rethinking Identity and Metaphysics* (Hill 1997b, or Hill 1997c, Hill 2004).

However, Russell ultimately came to realize that evading the contradictions would mean having to come to terms with problems intimately involving the identity and formal equivalence of functions. And that called for a new tactic. In particular, he found himself facing the following predicament: The contradictions had taught him that there was a hierarchy of logical types. If contradiction producing vicious circle fallacies were to be avoided, functions would have to be divided into types, and all talk of functions would then necessarily be limited to some one type, which would make statements about all functions true with a given argument, or all properties of some given object, meaningless. Yet, he saw that it was "not difficult to show that the various functions which can take a given object a as argument are not all of one type", and, even "that the functions which can take a given argument are of an infinite series of types". By various technical devices we could, he once reminded readers, "construct a variable which would run through the first n of these types, where n is finite, but we cannot construct a variable which will run through them all, and, if we could, that mere fact would at once generate a new type of function with the same arguments, and would set the whole process going again". So whatever selection of functions one made there would always be other functions. which would not be included in the selection (Russell 1919, 189–90).

However, Russell believed that for mathematics to be possible it was necessary to have some statements that would usually be equivalent to what we have in mind when we inaccurately speak of all properties of x. It was therefore necessary to find a method of reducing the order of a propositional function without changing the truth or falsehood of its values (Russell & Whitehead 1927, 166; Russell 1956, 80). So to cope with contradictions arising from necessary talk of all properties, or all functions, he invented the axiom of reducibility, a specially designed axiom that would be "equivalent to the assumption that 'any combination or disjunction of predicates is equivalent to a single predicate'" (Russell 1973, 250; Russell & Whitehead 1927, 58–59) and would provide a way of dealing with any function of a particular argument by means of some formally equivalent function of a particular type. It would thus yield most of the results that would otherwise require recourse to the problematical notions of all functions or all properties and so legitimize a great mass of reasoning apparently dependent on such notions (Russell & Whitehead 1927, 56).

The axiom seemed to Russell to embody everything that was really essential in his theory of classes (Russell 1919, 191; Russell & Whitehead 1927, 58, 166–67; Russell 1956, 82). "By the help of the axiom of reducibility", he maintained, "we find that the usual properties of classes result. For example, two formally equivalent functions determine the same class, and conversely, two functions which determine the same class are formally equivalent" (Russell 1973, 248–49). It seemed to him "that the sole purpose which classes serve, and one main reason which makes them linguistically convenient, is that they provide a method of reducing the order of a propositional function" (Russell & Whitehead 1927, 166). Classes were producing contradictions. They should be expunged and replaced with this axiom (Russell & Whitehead 1927, 166–67; Russell 1956, 82; Russell 1919, 191).

Russell leaned on the axiom of reducibility at every crucial point in his definition of classes in *Principia Mathematica* (Russell & Whitehead 1927, 75–81). He was conscious that many of the proofs of *Principia Mathematica* "become fallacious when the axiom of reducibility is not assumed, and in some cases new proofs can only be obtained with considerable labour" (Russell & Whitehead 1927, xliii). He called it "only convenient, not necessary" and a "defect" (Russell 1919, 192–93). "This axiom", he confessed, "has a purely pragmatic justification: it leads to the desired results, and to no others. But clearly it is not the sort of axiom with which we can rest content" (Russell & Whitehead 1927, xiv).

In the second edition of *Principia Mathematica*, Russell assumed "that a function can only enter into a proposition through its values", an assumption that he deemed "amounts to saying that mathematics is essentially extensional rather than intensional". He believed that his use of the assumption could "be validated by definition, even if the assumption is not universally true". He considered that, "This assumption is fundamental.... It has its difficulties, but for the moment we ignore them. It takes the place, not quite adequately of the axiom of reducibility" (Russell & Whitehead 1927, xxix and n., Appendix C). But the deep problems inherent in Frege's use of functions survived Russell's campaign to extirpate them with the stroke of a pen (Hill 1997b). And Russell concluded that the "solution of the contradictions... seemed to be only possible by adopting theories which might be true but were not beautiful" and that the "splendid certainty" he had "always hope to find in mathematics had become lost in a bewildering maze" (Russell 1959, 155–57; Hill 2015).

§7 Husserl and Extensions

As for Husserl, his theories about functions never could have had led him to have anything at all to do with extensions, which did not tempt him in the least.[2] Perhaps, he was influenced by the review of Frege's *Foundations of Arithmetic* in which his future colleague and friend Georg Cantor had written that it was unfortunate that Frege had taken extensions of concepts as the foundation of the number because the extension of a concept was generally something quantitatively completely undetermined (Frege 1885; Hill 1994). In any case, on pages of his critique of Frege in *Philosophy of Arithmetic* that he never retracted, Husserl explicitly criticized Frege's recourse to extensions. There he wrote that he had not been able to find that Frege's method "represents an enrichment of logic. Its results are of a type that can only make us wonder how anyone could even provisionally take them to be correct. In fact, what this method allows us to define are not the intensions[3] of the concepts..., but their *extensions*". He went on to explain what he meant by that, concluding that further "commentary is surely pointless. We note, however, that all the definitions become correct statements if the concepts to be defined are replaced by their extensions. Correct but certainly entirely obvious". In a note to that comment, Husserl remarked that "*Frege* himself seems to have sensed the questionable status of this definition, since he says in a note to it: 'I think that simply 'concept' could be said in place of 'extension of the concept''" and then went on to reflect on the implications of that (Husserl 1891, 128 and n. 14).

Husserl in fact expressed grave doubts about extensional logic all throughout his career. His antipathy is evident in several articles of the period (ex. Husserl 1994, 92–114, 115–20, 121–30, 135–38, 443–51), in which he was intent upon laying bare the "the follies of extensional logic" (Husserl 1994, 199) and showing "that the *total* formal basis upon which the class calculus rests is valid for the relationships between conceptual objects" and that one could solve logical problems without "the detour through classes" (Husserl 1994, 109), which he considered to be "totally superfluous" (Husserl 1994, 123). How-

---

[2] Once again, a proper discussion of this subject cannot be integrated into this essay. I refer readers to my papers on the subject, for example, "Varied Sorrows of Logical Abstraction" (Hill 1997c), "Frege Attacks Husserl and Cantor" (Hill 1994), "Husserl's *Mannigfaltigkeitslehre*" (Hill 2000), "Tackling Three of Frege's Problems: Edmund Husserl on Sets and Manifolds" (Hill, 2002c), "Reference and Paradox" (Hill 2004), "Husserl and Hilbert on Completeness" (Hill 1995).
[3] Here Dallas Willard has translated "*Inhalten*" by contents. I believe the proper translation is "intension".

ever, there he was not principally criticizing Frege's ideas, but those of Boole, de Morgan, Jevons, Schröder and others, which Frege also criticized.

Later, in *Logic and General Theory of Knowledge*, Husserl argued against the traditional talk of extensions of concepts according to which the totality of objects that are to be subsumed under each valid universal-concept are to belong to it as its extension. He taught that no pure concept had anything like an extension and that it was nonsense to say that for every concept a distinction was to be made between intension and extension (Husserl 1917/18, §39). Indeed as evinced by the remarks he wrote on Frege's "Function and Concept" cited above, Husserl believed that there were extensionless concepts, that impossible concepts, imaginary, absurd concepts were also concepts. It was precisely the search to justify the use of apparently meaningless signs in calculations or in deductive thought that had led him to develop his theory of manifolds as the third and highest level of pure logic. He considered that that his theory of complete manifolds was the key to the only possible solution to the as yet unclarified problem as to how in the realm of numbers, impossible, non-existent, meaningless concepts might be dealt with as real ones (Husserl 1900–01, *Prolegomena* § 70; Hill 2000; Hill 2002c). As seen above, he stressed that pure logic was a purely formal discipline free of any reference to particular objects. He considered the empty something to be of the greatest importance for the theory of meaning and all of formal logic. For him, absolute emptiness of content was what was specifically formal in formal logic, the hallmark of the formal logical

In contrast, the use of signs or combinations of signs without reference was at the heart of Frege's dispute with formalists who, he considered, only manipulated signs without any regard for what those signs might stand for. In formal theories of arithmetic, Frege maintained, there is only talk of signs that neither have nor are meant to refer to objects. But, Frege insisted, "logic is not concerned with how thoughts, regardless of truth value, follow from thoughts", but "the laws of logic are first and foremost laws in the realm of reference ... we have to throw aside proper names that do not designate or name an object...." Indeed, Frege had to have objects because that was the way he had designed his logic. "Only in the case of objects can there be any question of identity (equality)", he held (Frege 1979, 182, 120). And he had put identity statements at the very heart of his project to provide foundations for the theorems of arithmetic (Frege 1884, x, §§55–67, 106; Frege 1979, 122; also Frege 1885, Frege 1891, 22–23, 32–33; Frege 1903, 162–213; Hill 2004).

Late in his life, Husserl was still denouncing extensional logic as naive, risky, doubtful and the source of many a contradiction requiring every kind of artful device to make it safe for use in reasoning (Husserl 1929, §§23b, 26c), something which it is high time readers of *Principia Mathematica* fess up to.

Conclusion

The foregoing discussion of Husserl's and Frege's ideas about functions has shown that both philosophers, in principle, saw eye to eye about the analyticity of mathematics. They both strove to open the way to a new era in logic. They both advocated the adoption of a propositional calculus. They both thought that their theories could be applied to elucidate the foundations of arithmetic. And, most importantly in terms of the aims of this essay, they both saw how according what mathematicians call functions a place in logic could play a key role to achieving their goals and defined functions and arguments in a comparable manner.

However, I hope to have shown that, although Husserl significantly uncritically praised Frege's thoughts about functions and concepts, a comparison of their ideas about them reveals that each man approached the issues involved in that rapprochement from different angles. Although they basically had the same ideas about what functions were, they had entirely different ideas about the role they might play in formal logic. Husserl never tried to transform subject-predicate propositions in which numbers figure as dependent properties into propositions about self-sufficient objects, something studied in my essay "The Strange Worlds of Actual Consciousness and the Purely Logical" (Hill 2013b) and he never invented a law mandating that that could be done. Reflection upon the broadest universality of the concepts number and set, and also upon the concepts unit and element determining them, showed Husserl that the theory of sets and that of the theory of cardinal numbers related to any object whatsoever with a formal universality and were derivative formations of the concept of anything-whatsoever, that their fundamental concepts were syntactical formations of the empty something, that the theory of cardinal numbers dealt with numbers as differentiations of forms of sets and set theory with sets as made up of any objects whatsoever that are taken together (Husserl 1929 §§24, 27a). In contrast to Russell's belief that "without a single object to represent an extension, Mathematics crumbles" (Russell 1903, §489), Husserl believed that essential thing in mathematics was not the objects, but its method that naturally flows into a purely symbolic, hence calculational, technique (Husserl 1906/07, §19a; Hill 2013a; Hill 2015)

As part of his project to break the sway of language over the human mind, Frege chose to analyze judgments in terms of functions and arguments rather than in terms of subjects and predicates. Most decisively, in theorizing about the foundations of arithmetic, he put identity statements at the heart of his project to provide foundations for the theorems of arithmetic, which eventually led him to violate what he considered to be inviolable differences between functions and arguments, concepts and objects, by appealing against his better judgment to the extensions that led to the contradictions that Russell publicized and strove to evade. Husserl's theory that arithmetic could be derived from an analysis of the concept of 'how many' was of a completely different order.

Seduced by the siren of transcendental phenomenology, Husserl unfortunately did not pursue the issues, implications, and consequences of his ideas about functions as far as he might have had he not decided to follow transcendental phenomenology whenever it led him. As seen above, he confessed to Weyl that despite of all the work he had devoted to the theory of functional judgments, of judgments with empty places, and to distinguishing the different modes of the empty something, as well as to implementing the fundamental distinctions between formal and factual ways of judgment, between proposition form and proposition or judgment, proof- and theory-form and theory and the objective correlates associated with them, to his concept of complete manifolds, he had not found the time and peace of mind to pursue that train of thought completely to the end, because it had had to be more important to him to develop his ideas about transcendental phenomenology (Husserl 1918, 287f., cited Husserl 1917/18, XXIII n. 1). To Georg Misch he wrote that he had lost all the interest that formal logic and all real ontology had held for him in the face of a systematic grounding of a theory of transcendental subjectivity (cited Husserl 1917/18, XXIII, n. 4).

It is unlikely that, had they been pursued, Husserl's ideas about functions, logic, philosophy and the foundations of arithmetic could have ever generated all the hullabaloo and rigmarole Frege's have, but could they have provided new insight into, or even solutions to, the unsolved problems that beset Frege, Russell and have beset their successors up until our times? That is something that we should be asking ourselves today. What is needed is a sufficient number of philosophers who are genuinely interested in finding solutions to the unsolved problems involved in the philosophical issues that have been the stuff of analytic philosophy and are capable of overcoming pride and prejudice to pursue Husserl's ideas about the very ideas that went into the making of that school of philosophy.

References

Cantor, Georg 1885, "Rezension von Freges *Grundlagen der Arithmetik*", *Deutsche Literaturzeitung* 6, 1885, 728–29, also in his *Gesammelte Abhandlungen*, E. Zermelo (ed.), Berlin, Springer, 1932, 440–41.
Centrone, Stefania 2010a, "Functions in Frege, Bolzano and Husserl", *History and Philosophy of Logic* 31, November, 315–36
Centrone, Stefania 2010b, *Logic and Philosophy of Mathematics in the Early Husserl*, Dordrecht, Springer.
Demopoulos, William (ed.) 1995, *Frege's Philosophy of Mathematics*, Cambridge, Harvard University Press.
Dummett, Michael 1956, "Note: Frege on Functions", *The Philosophical Review* 65, 229–30. Also in Klemke (ed.), 295–97.
Dummett, Michael 1981, *Frege, Philosophy of Language*, London, Duckworth, 2nd ed. rev.
Frege, Gottlob 1879, "Begriffsschrift, a formula language, modeled upon that of arithmetic, for pure thought", in van Heijenoort (ed.), 5–82.
Frege, Gottlob 1884, *The Foundations of Arithmetic*, Oxford, Blackwell, 2nd rev. ed., 1986.
Frege, Gottlob, 1885, "On Formal Theories of Arithmetic", *Collected Papers on Mathematics, Logic, and Philosophy*, B. McGuinness (ed.), Blackwell, Oxford, 1984, 112–21.
Frege, Gottlob 1891, "Function and Concept", in Frege 1980b, 21–41.
Frege, Gottlob 1892, "On Concept and Object", in Frege 1980b, 42–55.
Frege, Gottlob 1892–1895 ["Comments on Sense and Meaning"], in Frege 1979, 118–25.
Frege, Gottlob 1893, *Basic Laws of Arithmetic*, Berkeley, University of California Press, 1964.
Frege, Gottlob 1903, "Frege Against the Formalists", *Grundgesetze der Arithmetik*, vol. ii, Sections 86–137, in Frege 1980b, 162–213.
Frege, Gottlob 1906, "What May I Regard as the Result of my Work?" in Frege 1979, 184.
Frege, Gottlob 1979, *Posthumous Writings*, Oxford, Blackwell.
Frege, Gottlob. 1980a, *Philosophical and Mathematical Correspondence*, Oxford, Blackwell.
Frege, Gottlob 1980b, *Translations from the Philosophical Writings*, P. Geach & M. Black (eds.), Oxford, Blackwell, 3rd ed. (1952).
Hilbert, David 1925, "On the Infinite", in van Heijenoort (ed.), 367–92.
Hill, Claire Ortiz 1994, "Frege Attacks Husserl and Cantor", *The Monist* 77 (3), 347–57. Anthologized in Hill & Rosado Haddock.
Hill, Claire Ortiz 1995, "Husserl and Hilbert on Completeness", in *From Dedekind to Gödel, Essays on the Development of the Foundations of Mathematics*, J. Hintikka (ed.), Dordrecht, Kluwer, 143–63. Anthologized in Hill & Rosado Haddock.
Hill, Claire Ortiz 1997a, "Did Georg Cantor Influence Edmund Husserl?" *Synthese* 113, October, 145–70. Anthologized in Hill & Rosado Haddock.
Hill, Claire Ortiz 1997b, *Rethinking Identity and Metaphysics, On the Foundations of Analytic Philosophy*, New Haven CT, Yale University Press.
Hill, Claire Ortiz 1997c, "The Varied Sorrows of Logical Abstraction", 10th Anniversary Issue of *Axiomathes*, Centro Studi per la Filsofia Mitteleuropa, Trento, Italy, 53–82. Anthologized in Hill & Rosado Haddock.
Hill, Claire Ortiz 2000, "Husserl's *Mannigfaltigkeitslehre*", Anthologized in Hill & Rosado Haddock.

Hill, Claire Ortiz 2002a, "On Husserl's Mathematical Apprenticeship and Philosophy of Mathematics", *Phenomenology World Wide*, Anna-Teresa Tymieniecka (ed.), Dordrecht, Kluwer, 76–92. Anthologized in Hill & da Silva.

Hill, Claire Ortiz 2002b, "Review of W. Demopoulos' *Frege's Philosophy of Mathematics* and W. W. Tait's *Early Analytic Philosophy, Frege, Russell, Wittgenstein, Essays in Honor of Leonard Linsky*", *Synthese* 133, 441–452.

Hill, Claire Ortiz 2002c, "Tackling Three of Frege's Problems: Edmund Husserl on Sets and Manifolds", *Axiomathes* 13, 79–104. Anthologized in Hill & da Silva.

Hill, Claire Ortiz 2003, "Incomplete Symbols, Dependent Meanings, and Paradox", in *Husserl's Logical Investigations*, Daniel O. Dahlstrom (ed.), Dordrecht, Kluwer, 69–93. Anthologized in Hill & da Silva.

Hill, Claire Ortiz 2004, "Reference and Paradox", *Synthese*, 138,2, January, 207–32. Anthologized in Hill & da Silva.

Hill, Claire Ortiz 2010a, "Husserl on Axiomatization and Arithmetic", *Phenomenology and Mathematics*, Mirja Hartimo (ed.), Dordrecht, Springer, 47–71. Anthologized in Hill & da Silva.

Hill, Claire Ortiz 2010b, "On Fundamental Differences Between Dependent and Independent Meanings", *Axiomathes, An International Journal in Ontology and Cognitive Systems* 20: 2–3, online since May 29, 2010, 313–32 (DOI 10.1007/s10516–010–9104–1). Anthologized in Hill & da Silva.

Hill, Claire Ortiz 2013a, "Husserlian Sets or Fregean Sets?" *Notae Philosophicae Scientiae Formalis*, vol. 2, n. 1, p. 22–32, May.
http://gcfcf.com.br/pt/files/2013/07/Hill-Claire-Ortiz-NPSF-vol.2-n.1.pdf

Hill, Claire Ortiz 2013b, "The Strange Worlds of Actual Consciousness and the Purely Logical", *New Yearbook for Phenomenology and Phenomenological Philosophy*, Abingdon, Routledge, Burt Hopkins (ed.), vol. XIII, 62–83.

Hill, Claire Ortiz 2015, "Husserl's Way Out of Frege's Jungle", in *Objects and Pseudo-Objects Ontological Deserts and Jungles from Brentano to Carnap*, Bruno Leclercq, Sébastien Richard and Denis Seron (eds.), Berlin, de Gruyter, 183–96.

Hill, Claire Ortiz & G. E. Rosado Haddock 2000, *Husserl or Frege? Meaning, Objectivity, and Mathematics*, Chicago, Open Court.

Hill, Claire Ortiz & Jairo José da Silva 2013, *The Road Not Taken, On Husserl's Philosophy of Logic and Mathematics*, London, College Publications.

Husserl, Edmund 1891, *Philosophy of Arithmetic, Psychological and Logical Investigations with Supplementary Texts from 1887–1901*, tr. Dallas Willard, Dordrecht: Kluwer, 2003.

Husserl, Edmund 1896, *Logik, Vorlesung 1896*, Dordrecht, Kluwer, 2001.

Husserl, Edmund 1900–01, *Logical Investigations*, London, Routledge & Kegan Paul, 1970.

Husserl, Edmund 1902/03a, *Allgemeine Erkenntnistheorie, Vorlesung 1902/03*, Elisabeth Schuhmann (ed.), Dordrecht, Kluwer, 2001.

Husserl, Edmund 1902/03b, *Logik, Vorlesung 1902/03*, Elisabeth Schuhmann (ed.), Dordrecht, Kluwer, 2001.

Husserl, Edmund 1903, "A Report on German Writings in Logic from the Years 1895–1899, Third Article", in Husserl 1994, Dordrecht, Kluwer, 246–59.

Husserl, Edmund 1906/07, *Introduction to Logic and Theory of Knowledge*, Springer, 2008.

Husserl, Edmund 1917/18, *Logik und allgemeine Wissenschaftstheorie, Vorlesungen 1917/18, mit ergänzenden Texten aus der ersten Fassung 1910/11*, Ursula Panzer (ed.) (Hua XXX),

Dordrecht, Kluwer, 1996. The English translation, *Logic and General Theory of Science*, is forthcoming Springer Verlag.
Husserl, Edmund 1918, "Brief an Hermann Weyl 10.4.1918", *Briefwechsel*, vol. VII, *Wissenschaftlerkorrespondenz*, Dordrecht, Kluwer, 287f.). Cited Husserl 1917/18, XXIII n. 1.
Husserl, Edmund 1929, *Formal and Transcendental Logic*, The Hague, Martinus Nijhoff, 1969.
Husserl, Edmund 1975, *Introduction to the Logical Investigations: A Draft of a Preface to the Logical Investigations (1913)*, The Hague, Martinus Nijhoff.
Husserl, Edmund 1994, *Early Writings in the Philosophy of Logic and Mathematics*, Dordrecht, Kluwer.
Husserl, Malvine 1988, "Skizze eines Lebensbildes von E. Husserl", *Husserl Studies* 5, 105–25.
Jourdain, P. 1991, "The Development of the Theory of Transfinite Numbers", *Selected Essays on the History of Set Theory and Logic*, Bologna, CLUEB.
Klemke, E. D. (ed.) 1968, *Essays on Gottlob Frege*, Urbana IL, University of Illinois Press.
Osborn, Andrew 1934, *Edmund Husserl and his Logical Investigations*, Cambridge, Cambridge University Press. 2nd ed., 1949.
Russell, Bertrand 1903, *Principles of Mathematics*, New York, Norton.
Russell, Bertrand 1919, *Introduction to Mathematical Philosophy*, London, Allen and Unwin.
Russell, Bertrand 1956, *Logic and Knowledge*, London, Allen and Unwin.
Russell, Bertrand 1959, *My Philosophical Development*, London, Unwin Paperbacks, 1985.
Russell, Bertrand 1973, *Essays in Analysis*, D. Lackey (ed.), London, Allen and Unwin.
Russell, Bertrand & Alfred North Whitehead 1927, *Principia Mathematica to *56*, Cambridge, Cambridge University Press, 2nd ed. (1964).
Schuhmann, Karl 1977, *Husserl-Chronik*, The Hague, Martinus Nijhoff.
van Heijenoort, Jean (ed.) 1967, *From Frege to Gödel. A Source Book in Mathematical Logic, 1879–1931*, Cambridge, Harvard University Press.

Carlo Ierna
The Reception of Russell's Paradox in Early Phenomenology and the School of Brentano: The Case of Husserl's Manuscript A I 35α

Abstract: Edmund Husserl's engagement with Bertrand Russell's paradox stands in a continuum of reciprocal reception and discussions about impossible objects in the School of Brentano.[1] Against this broader context, we will focus on Husserl's discussion of Russell's paradox in his manuscript A I 35α from 1912.[2] This highly interesting and revealing manuscript has unfortunately remained unpublished, which probably explains the scant attention it has received.[3] I will examine Husserl's approach in A I 35α by relating it to earlier discussions of relevant topics in his manuscripts and the broader historical context of the School of Brentano and early phenomenology.

§1 Husserl's Background in the Brentanist Philosophy of Mathematics

As is increasingly well-known, Husserl began his academic career as a formally trained mathematician, having studied with Karl Weierstrass and Leopold Kronecker in Berlin and obtained his doctorate in mathematics with Weierstrass's former pupil Leo Königsberger in Vienna. After studying philosophy with Franz Brentano and Carl Stumpf and writing his first works on the philosophy of mathematics and logic, Husserl became a colleague and friend of Georg Can-

---

[1] These of course prominently involved Alexius Meinong and Kazimierz Twardowski. Husserl himself also looked into the Meinong-Russell debates around 1907, see Varga 2016.
[2] I'd like to thank the director of the Husserl-Archives Leuven, Ullrich Melle, for the generously conceded permission to quote the manuscript in this article and publish it in the present volume. I'd also like to thank Dieter Lohmar from the Husserl-Archives Cologne for his support and collaboration in the collation and interpretation of the manuscript.
[3] With the notable exception of Haddock and Hill who over the years have repeatedly drawn attention to this manuscript, i.a. in Hill 2002, Haddock 2006; 2010. While the first discussion of the manuscript can be found in Haddock's unpublished 1973 dissertation, the first publication discussing A I 35 in some detail (though mostly its second part from the 1920s) was Schmit 1981, 114–117.

tor in Halle and later of David Hilbert, Ernst Zermelo, and Felix Klein in Göttingen.⁴ Not only would the philosophy of mathematics and logic remain a life-long interest for Husserl, encompassing nearly six decades from his dissertation to his last works, but this background is highly relevant to his philosophical development as well.⁵ However, what is only recently coming more and more to light is the contribution to Husserl's early philosophy of mathematics from the School of Brentano itself.⁶ The formative influences on Husserl's early philosophy cannot be neatly separated into a philosophical source in Brentano and a mathematical source in Weierstrass.⁷ Growing evidence indicates that a Brentanist philosophy of mathematics was already in place when Husserl started to work on his habilitation essay *On the Concept of Number*. Hence, Husserl's early writings contain an elaboration of issues already under discussion in the School of Brentano.⁸ This background then informs his reception and discussion of the important mathematical debates of his age. Moreover, in many cases there are parallel developments and discussions by and among the other members of the School of Brentano. Particularly with respect to Russell, Meinong has mostly been considered among the main interlocutors from the School of Brentano.⁹ In this contribution I will try to show how, with respect to Russell's Paradox, there was a wider reception and discussion in the School of Brentano and among the early phenomenologists, and then focus on Husserl's discussion in A I 35α.

§2 The Reception of Russell's Paradox in Göttingen

One of the central question surrounding A I 35α, is the reason why Husserl would turn to Russell's paradox specifically at this point in time, in 1912, i.e. a decade after the well-known exchange between Russell and Frege? There are some quite

---

4 A more technical discussion of Husserl's early philosophy of mathematics can be found in Centrone 2010. For a more historical approach to this early period, see Ierna 2005; 2006.
5 Regarding the relevance of his early work on mathematics for the later development of phenomenology, see Hartimo 2006 and Haddock 2006.
6 See Ierna 2011a, 2015.
7 The idea of Husserl creatively combining Weierstrass' mathematics and Brentano's philosophy into a new philosophy of mathematics is the mainstream view, see i.a. Miller 1982, 4; Haddock 1997, 127; Hartimo 2006, 319; Centrone 2010, 5.
8 See Ierna 2016.
9 See e.g. Russell's repeated discussion of Meinong in Russell 1904, 1905a, 1905b, 1907.

relevant antecedents that we need to take into account here, that might contribute to an explanation for the discussion in A I 35α. Let us first consider the closest proximal "cause": Alexandre Koyré's dissertation proposal.

According to Zambelli[10], Koyré arrived in Göttingen in the Winter Semester of 1908–1909. He studied phenomenology and philosophy of mathematics, i.a. attending Hilbert's lectures on the foundations of mathematics in the SS 1910. Hence, he formed an important connection between the two circles of phenomenologists and mathematicians.[11] Moreover, Zermelo was also still close to Husserl[12] and had interacted with both circles up to 1910, when he transferred to Zürich. Given that he had discovered "Russell's" paradox independently and was working on a new axiomatization of set theory[13] to avoid it, during the early 1900s the issue of the paradoxes of set theory understandably was the topic of frequent discussions.[14] This was the context in which Hans Lipps arrived in 1911, becoming likewise immediately immersed in the discussions about the logic of mathematics.[15]

During this time Koyré and Lipps both developed a specific interest in the paradoxes, both ancient and modern. Indeed, Adolf Reinach had discussed Zeno's paradoxes and the liar paradox in his 1910 lectures (and then again in 1914), possibly stimulated by Zermelo and the similarity of the set theoretical paradox with the liar paradox.[16] These lectures and the ensuing discussions in the Göttingen Philosophical Society had a lasting influence on Lipps and Koyré, who dedicated their later works on this topic to the memory of Reinach.[17] Around 1911, under the influence of Reinach, Koyré wrote the manuscript titled

---

10 Zambelli 1999, 210: "Koyré gehörte von WS 1908–09 bis 1912 und noch einmal im SS 1913 der Schule Husserls an". A more recent and extensive account of "The History Between Koyré and Husserl" can be found in Parker (2016). I'd like to thank Burt Hopkins for making me aware of this work and Rodney Parker for kindly sending me a draft of his article.
11 Schuhmann 1987, 152f.
12 After studying in Berlin with Weierstrass' student Knoblauch, Zermelo had attended lectures by Cantor and Husserl in Halle during one semester in 1890/91. After returning to Berlin, Zermelo wrote his dissertation on the same topic as Husserl had done a decade earlier in 1882: "*Untersuchungen zur Variations-Rechnung*", the calculus of variations. This shared background and personal history might contribute to explain why Zermelo would be interested in Husserl's work, not only during their time in Göttingen, but also later in Freiburg (even though he lost interest in transcendental phenomenology soon). Ebbinghaus & Peckhaus 2007, 7–8, 139, 147.
13 Zermelo 1908.
14 Schuhmann 1987, 152.
15 Schuhmann 1977, 158.
16 Schuhmann & Smith 1989, 775.
17 Schuhmann & Smith 1989, 776; Schuhmann 1987, 153.

Insolubilia, meant as a first draft for a dissertation.[18] Due to the fact that Reinach was a *Privatdozent* and could not supervise dissertations, Koyré then sent the materials to Husserl in early 1912.[19]

What was Husserl's position in all this? Husserl himself had witnessed the debates of the mathematical community in Göttingen about the paradoxes first hand, shortly after arriving there from Halle. Indeed, besides attending and giving lectures in Hilbert's mathematical seminar, he also had private discussions about mathematical topics with i.a. Zermelo. To this we owe the now well-known fragment in which Husserl annotated an "oral communication of Zermelo"[20] in which we find expressed for the first time in writing the set-theoretical paradox now commonly attributed to Russell. Indeed, we find the same formulation of the oral communication also repeated in A I 35.

Husserl had continued to lecture on logic and mathematics throughout his permanence in Göttingen: *Logic and Theory of Knowledge* in the WS 1901/02, *Logic* in the WS 1902/03, *Theory of Judgment* as well as a seminar on "*Philosophical Exercises as an Introduction to the Main Problems of the Philosophy of Mathematics*" in the SS 1905, *Introduction to Logic and the Critique of Knowledge* in the WS 1906/07, a seminar with "*Discussions on Fundamental Questions of Logic and Critique of Reason*" in the WS 1907/08, *Old and New Logic* in the WS 1908/09, and then *Logic as Theory of Knowledge* in the WS 1910/11, which Koyré repeatedly quotes, and which discussed i.a. sets, numbers, universality, etc.[21] Yet, we find no discussion at all of Russell's or the ancient paradoxes.[22] I conjecture therefore, that despite the lively discussions of such topics among his student and colleagues, including Reinach and Zermelo, Husserl did not engage personally with these topics, until confronted with Koyré's dissertation proposal. This makes it

---

18 The extant materials make it difficult to assess the respective weight of the influences of Husserl and Reinach. It is certain that Koyré's early works, and particularly his dissertation, were influenced by both. Yet, given that the dissertation manuscript does not address phenomenology directly, it is not clear in how far Koyré would have been more aligned with Reinach's realism or Husserl's transcendentalism. For a more detailed discussion about this issue, see Parker (2016): "To suggest that Reinach had more of an influence over Koyré's intellectual development than Husserl would be an exaggeration."
19 Schuhmann 1987, 154.
20 "Notiz einer mündlichen Mitteilung Zermelos an Husserl" from 16 April 1902, Hua XXII, Beilage II, p. 399.
21 The 1910 version of these lectures are partially published in Husserliana XXX.
22 Zeno is mentioned by name in an example, but not discussed, in *Alte und Neue Logik* 1908–09, Husserliana Materialien VI, 125 f.. There is a discussion of the paradoxes of the impossibility of movement and change in Zeno in the lectures on *Erkenntnistheorie und Hauptpunkte der Metaphysik*, from 1898/1899, Husserliana Materialien III, 250.

all the more relevant and interesting to analyze A I 35 in depth: why engage with Russell's paradox now and why in these terms?

As is well known, Husserl rejected Koyré's thesis proposal, although it is not entirely clear what the exact reasons for the rejection were.[23] In a letter to Conrad dated on "Spring 1912" Reinach reports the following:

> I have not said anything about Koyré's affair, because I essentially agree with you, and because I do not believe I can do anything about it. It seems likely to me that Husserl mainly took into account matters of personality. Of course, entirely objective ones. Husserl does really consider Koyré as arrogant and somewhat immature – which is perfectly understandable based on his somewhat primitive psychology. He will have decided "for Koyré's own sake", not to allow him to obtain his doctorate just yet. The whole uncomfortable affair makes me feel very sorry for Koyré.[24]

The conjecture that Koyré's dissertation manuscript was the main reason that prompted Husserl to engage with Russell's paradox in 1912 is strengthened by the explicit reference to a discussion with Koyré in A I 35 page 16b. Indeed, the very "title" on the cover of A I 35 echoes the title of Koyré's dissertation manuscript, which bore "*Insolubilia*" as title and "*Die Antinomien der Mengenlehre*" as title of its second part.[25] According to Zambelli the manuscript of *Insolubilia* also bears some annotations by Husserl.[26] However, much more importantly in the present context, Schuhmann observes that:

> The pages 5 to 17 of the manuscript A I 35 of the Husserl Archives are kept in an envelope dated "march 7, 1912" bearing the title "Die Paradoxien. Die Insolubilia. Insbesondere auch die Paradoxien der Mengenlehre". These are clearly extracts from Koyré's manuscripts. Page 15b of the manuscript refers to a "discussion with Koyré" on the concept of set.[27]

---

23 According to Parker (2016) it is not likely that Koyré was the victim of any "infighting" among phenomenologists in Göttingen: "There is no good reason to believe that Husserl would have attempted to hold back Koyré's career as a result of disagreements over the nature and aims of phenomenology or departmental politics."
24 See Schuhmann 1987, 154–155 for a french translation of the letter.
25 See Koyré 1912, p. 323.
26 Koyré 1912, 323 n.
27 Schuhmann 1987, p. 165, n. 51: "Les feuillets 5 à 17 du ms. A I 35 des Archives Husserl se trouvent dans une enveloppe datée "7 mars 1912" portant Je titre "Die Paradoxien. Die Insolubilia. Insbesondere auch die Paradoxien der Mengenlehre". Il s'agit donc manifestement des extraits des manuscrits de Koyré. La page 15b du manuscrit fait allusion à un "entretien avec Koyré" sur le concept d'ensemble." Actually the mention of the discussion with Koyré is to be found on page 16b of the manuscript.

We will analyze this claim in more detail later on. The discussions about these topics in the phenomenological circle of Göttingen would then continue in lectures and in publications, from Reinach's continued interest for the foundations of mathematics in his seminars e. g. on the concept of number in 1913 and again *Über das Wesen der Bewegung*, on Zeno's paradoxes and movement, in 1914, to Lipps' 1917 "*Das Paradoxon des Zeno*", Koyré's 1922 "*Bemerkungen zu den Zenonischen Paradoxen*", Lipps' 1923 "*Bemerkungen zu der Paradoxie des Lügners*", etc.

§3 Russell's Paradox in the School of Brentano

There is still a missing link in this discussion, since it is not entirely obvious what the relation between the ancient paradoxes and the modern set theoretical paradoxes would be. What was the connection for Koyré and Lipps? Reinach had after all explicitly rejected a purely formal-mathematical solution to Zeno's paradox of movement and change in his lectures.[28] First of all, Russell himself discussed the classical paradoxes that were referred to as "*Insolubilia*" in scholastic literature, e.g. the liar, together with Richard's and Burali-Forti's paradoxes in his 1906 "*Les paradoxes de la logique*". Here Russell aimed to show how the application of his logical techniques could yield a solution to both kinds of paradoxes, by avoiding the vicious circles implied in them. Koyré, in his later article on "The Liar" would then reminisce, somewhat poetically:

> The paradox of the Liar, it seems, was popular among the Greeks. In the Middle Ages its popularity did not wane; medieval logicians unfailingly mention it, and propose solutions for the "insoluble" sophism. Slowly, it was put aside and was asleep when, in our times, Lord Russell noticed that its logical structure was identical with that of the mathematical paradoxes which he discovered (344)

This establishes a connection between the reflexivity of the liar and Russell's paradox. On the other hand, as proceeds from Koyré's 1922 "*Bemerkungen zu den Zenonischen Paradoxen*", the idea of infinite divisibility can be connected to the modern discussions in Bolzano and Cantor about infinity and the basic definitions and axioms of set theory, and thence into the foundations of mathematics.

---

28 See Reinach *Sämmtliche Werke* 555. While this text is based on the 1914 lectures, it is likely he would have presented the same arguments in the earlier lecture course.

Much more immediately than this, however, we see that one of the main sources for establishing the connection between the ancient and the modern paradoxes is Benno Urbach's 1910 article "*Über das Wesen der logischen Paradoxa*". In Koyré's dissertation manuscript Urbach is referred to quite often and Koyré even notes that:

> The same paradoxes were discussed in a work by Dr. B. Urbach. This work coincides with our own in important respects, though in the most important one our opinions differ.[29]

Indeed, they both address the same three ancient paradoxes of the court (Evathlus), the crocodile, and the liar, though in a different order. According to Zambelli, the editor of Koyré's manuscript, Koyré used Urbach also as a source to indirectly reference earlier discussions of the ancient paradoxes, such as the discussion of the paradox of the court in Fries and the discussion of Savonarola's approach to the *insolubilia* in Bolzano.[30] Indeed, Urbach reports a lengthy citation from Fries to introduce the paradox (Urbach 1910, 91)[31] and the passage about Savonarola in Bolzano's *Wissenschaftslehre* that Koyré refers to can be found also quoted in full in Urbach (1910, 89). Moreover, in a few notes Koyré explicitly engages with Urbach's position, discussing whether the existence of a relation presupposes or implies the existence of its foundations (Koyré 1912, 331, n. 14–15).

Interestingly, Urbach adds in a lengthy endnote that his article was actually originally co-written with Hugo Bergmann. Both had been students of Anton Marty in Prag and were in correspondence with Brentano. Urbach thanks Bergmann extensively for their discussions about the foundations of mathematics, and regrets that Bergmann decided to withdraw from their publication. Urbach notes that "around 1 1/2 years ago Dr. Bergmann told me about Russell's paradox and stimulated me to look for a solution." (Urbach 1910, 108) Given that the note is from August 1910, this would point to the period around February 1909 for the original stimulus coming from Bergmann. Precisely at that time Bergmann had been in correspondence with Brentano about these topics.[32] During 1908 they discussed the works of Poincaré, Couturat, the foundations of mathematics

---

29 Koyré 1912, 326, n. 6: "Die selben Paradoxien wurden in einer Arbeit von Dr. B. Urbach besprochen. Diese Arbeit trifft mit <der> unseren in manchen wichtigen Puncten zusammen, obwohl gerade in den für mich wichtigsten wir verschiedener Meinungen sind."
30 Koyré 1912, p. 326, n. 7: "*Attraverso il già citato articolo di Urbach, Koyré dipende da Jakob Friedrich Fries*".
31 Likewise Koyré reports Fries opinion that the mother would be at an advantage here (1912, 329), which can likewise be found in Urbach (1910, 95, n. 1).
32 See Bergmann 1946.

and the axioms of geometry. In the closing of his letter of December 21, 1908, Brentano advises Bergmann to look up the works of Russell, as an opponent of Poincaré who seemed to have affinity with Brentano's position.[33] Apparently in his next letter, as we may desume from Brentano's answer on January 6, 1909, Bergmann had inquired about Brentano's opinion about Bergmann's own proposal for a solution to Russell's paradox.[34] Brentano only briefly discusses the paradox in his letter, remarking on the ambiguities in the concept of "Class" as employed by Russell. However, in an unpublished letter from February 21, 1909 he then sent a much more extensive commentary to Bergmann, a treatise on Russell's paradox in its own right.[35] This matches exactly with the date recalled by Urbach, so we might suppose an indirect influence of Brentano's analysis on Bergmann and Urbach's article.[36] This is further confirmed when Urbach discusses the first attempt at a solution of the paradox tried by "the author", without specifying whether he means himself or Bergmann. This first attempted solution matches a proposal by Bergmann criticized by Brentano in his unpublished letter, which Bergmann acknowledged in his answer, and is then also rejected in the article.[37] From Bergmann's reaction to Brentano's own

---

[33] Brentano in Bergmann 1946, 122: "Maybe you have in your library the philosophical-mathematical works by Russell, the opponent of Poincaré; he endeavors, I am told, to integrate the various axioms. Vailati once remarked that Russell would be close to my views." (*"Vielleicht haben Sie in Ihrer Bibliothek die philosophisch-mathematischen Arbeiten von Russell, des Antagonisten von Poincaré; er mueht sich, hoere ich, die saemtlichen Axiome zusammenzustellen. Vailati aeusserte einmal, Russell beruehre sich mit meinen Ansichten."*)

[34] Brentano in Bergmann 1946, 122: "Regarding Russell's paradox, I would be interested in hearing in what sense you think you might have the solution." (*"Was das Russell'sche Paradoxon betrifft, so wuerde es mich interessiert haben, zu hoeren, in welcher Weise Sie die Loesung zu besitzen vermeinen."*)

[35] I'd like to thank Hynek Janousek from the Academy of Sciences of the Czech Republic for sending me an index to the transcriptions made by Oskar Kraus of Brentano's manuscripts, where I discovered the existence of the letter and the treatise, and for making the text of the transcription available to me. The treatise was originally dictated by Brentano to his son Giovanni and then Kraus prepared a typescript, also adding notes with a view to edit it. However, as far as I have been able to determine, the text remains unpublished.

[36] Bergmann had also written a book on *Das Philosophische Werk Bernard Bolzanos*, published in 1909, in which he makes extensive comparisons between Bolzano and Russell. While the 200 page book contains a lengthy 50 page appendix on Bolzano's contributions to the philosophical foundation of mathematics, there is no discussion of any paradoxes. Bergmann does however reference some works that address them, such as Schönfließ' article, and at least mentions Zeno (p. 152).

[37] Urbach 1910, 101–103.

proposal for a solution, it is clear that the solution advanced in Urbach and Bergmann's article was at least partially inspired by Brentano.

What is the relevance of all this for the content of Husserl's manuscript A I 35? Since Husserl reacts to Koyré, and Koyré's discussion is based for a significant part on Urbach's article, co-authored with Bergmann, who had been discussing precisely these topics with Brentano after the latter actually pointed him in the direction of a solution for Russell's paradox, this entire chain of events, readings, and reactions did certainly contribute to the choice of authors, examples, and arguments that ended up in A I 35. Of course there is a much broader background to take into account, including the well-known article by Grelling and Nelson (1908), the axiomatic solution proposed by Zermelo (1908), Hilbert's ongoing efforts, etc. But if we consider, narrowly, the sources that are actually quoted and used, the path sketched above is quite relevant to take into account. Besides his direct engagement with Koyré's dissertation manuscript, Husserl's background in the School of Brentano is highly relevant to understand why Husserl would discuss the paradox at all in 1912 in A I 35, and why he would frame his discussion in a certain way.

Given the topic and the timing of the text, a technical mathematical topic discussed in 1912 shortly before the publication of the *Ideas I*, it is quite surprising that there is no extensive formal treatment of the paradox and barely any actual phenomenology involved. Beyond the introduction and reproduction of Russell's and Richard's paradoxes and Zermelo's and Schönfließ' accounts, there are few mathematical formulae or arguments to be found, and besides appeals to the essence of sets and quantities, there is hardly any transcendental phenomenology. Instead, the terminology and concepts involved are much more strongly reminiscent of Husserl's earlier approach to these matters, going back to the famous *Doppelvortrag* Husserl held in Hilbert's seminar in 1901 and even further back to the 1890s. The central problem of the paradox, the set of all sets that does and doesn't contain itself, is treated for the most part as an impossible object. This immediately shifts the focus from the mathematical definition and construction of the set to its conceptualization and ontological status. Regardless how we obtained the set and what the implications would be for the foundations of mathematics and set-theory, as an impossible object it can be treated conceptually like e.g. the square circle: an object with contradicting properties. The question whether such an object is admissible in mathematics moves the problem closer to the topic of Husserl's *Doppelvortrag* (Schuhmann & Schuhmann 2001) and the related manuscripts on "The Transition through the Impossible and the Completeness of a System of Axioms" (see Ierna 2011b).

§4 Husserl on Koyré on Russell's Paradox

Bearing in mind that Schuhmann suggested that pages 5–17 of the manuscript would be excerpts from Koyré's *Insolubilia*, we will now look at the manuscript itself in detail. This portion of A I 35 begins with a discussion of objects whose properties may change through time, in such a way that an object could even be the bearer of contradictory properties (5a):

> The thing has its duration and has determinations for different parts of the duration [...] that the thing has changing properties means that it has different ones in different stretches of duration, indeed such as are incompatible in the same stretch.

However, Husserl argues that ideal objects and their properties do not have a duration in time ("*ein idealer Gegenstand [hat] keine Zeitdauer*"). Empirical objects can have e.g. many colors in their different parts, or can be first liquid and then solid at different times. Husserl underscores that the identity of the thing is not affected by the changes in its determinations: it is the same thing that has different, incompatible properties at different times (5b).[38] For instance, a man may have youthful characteristics when young, and elderly ones when old, but it is nevertheless the same man (9b).

In (affirmative) categorial judgments, of the form "S is P", as well as in relational judgments the being of the subject and the property or the being of the two relata is presupposed (6a). Normally we mean "the real object in nature" ("*das reale Objekt in der Naturwirklichkeit*"), but sometimes we mean an intentional object as such, e.g. a fiction or product of the imagination. For instance, we might compare the actual emperor and a fictional emperor. For Husserl, the being of the intentional object as such, lies in its possibility ("*das Sein des Intentionalen liegt in seiner Möglichkeit*"). In order to be part of a relational judgment, an intentional object merely needs to be logically possible, i.e. non-contradictory. Then what about imaginary objects with contradictory properties, i.e. logically impossible objects?

> A round square is something thought, but contradictory thought as such. It cannot stand in any relations, it is nothing, it is impossible. We may say that "a round square" would be a supposition [*Vermeintheit*][39]; but it is only a mental supposition [*Denkvermeintes*] that can-

---

[38] Also see Reinach *Sämmtliche Werke* 568: "Wenn sich ein Ding verändert oder sich bewegt, so ist es immer dasselbe Ding, was in verschiedenen Zuständen oder an verschiedenen Orten sich befindet."
[39] See Cairns 1973, 124

not be turned into a fulfillable intuition as something "possible". Mental suppositions as such (thought meanings [*Denk-bedeutungen*]), can be put in relation to others as objects. In that case I merely compare the logical meanings, I relate "concepts" and "judgements". (6b)

This is strongly reminiscent of the distinction between proper and improper presentations. Already in the *Philosophy of Arithmetic* Husserl had connected the Brentanian account of proper and symbolic presentations to Meinong's account of direct and indirect presentations.[40]

> A symbolic or improper presentation is, as the name already says, a presentation through signs. When content is not given directly to us as what it is, but only indirectly through signs that characterize it unambiguously, we have, instead of a proper presentation, a symbolic presentation of it. (Husserl, 1891, p. 215; 1970, p. 193; 2003, p. 205)

Meinong clarified that indirect presentations through relative determinations and attributes would be akin to mathematical operations that remain "indicated" [*angezeigt*] without being "executed" (1882, pp. 656–658). This would also be the case with impossible objects. We cannot genuinely combine "roundness" and "squareness" into a unitary whole, but can only keep them side by side. Hence, what we can do, is judge about the signs, which is why Husserl talks about the possibility of relating "concepts" and "judgements" in quotes. While a contradictory object cannot exist, we can say that relations to such a "mental supposition" or assumption may obtain, i.e. we are allowed to judge that "a round square is round".[41]

What now, he then asks, about the relations a thing might have to itself? (9b) To answer this question, Husserl here reflects on the notion of relation as applicable to individual objects and to essences (10a). He analyzes essential relations and connections (*Wesensrelation und Wesensverbindung*). Husserl emphatically denies that the same essence could occupy both the positions of the relata:

> A relation, a connection of essences to a whole essence presupposes a plurality of essences, originally two essences. One and the same essence cannot appear as foundation and correlate [*Grundglied und Gegenglied*] (as part and as whole) in a relation or connection! A rela-

---

[40] Husserl profusely thanks Brentano for the "deeper understanding" of the significance of improper presenting and the awareness of the importance of the distinction between proper and improper presenting, but also refers to Meinong's 1882 *Hume Studien II* in the very same note. See Ierna 2009a for the ensuing controversy.

[41] See Ierna 2011b, pp. 220f., 222, 224.

tional judgment, i.e. a relational proposition, that would have the same essence (the same concept) as subject and as predicate, would be countersensical [*widersinnig*]. (10b)⁴²

Husserl then carefully distinguishes the cases where an object would be the bearer of multiple essences, e.g. at different times. In this case, there would be no difficulties. We can compare e.g. the age of a man when he is older and when he is younger, i.e. we compare him to himself at different times: "*Derselbe Mensch ist älter als er selbst: nämlich derselbe im Alter älter als derselbe in der Jugend.*" (10b)⁴³

Yet if we do not specify such a respect of comparison, according to which essence an object is related to itself, reflexive relations entail a certain vagueness ("*eine Unbestimmtheit des Sinnes*", 11a).⁴⁴ Such an empty variable must always be determined in the same way, and it is precisely when it is not, that paradoxes arise: "*Allerlei Paradoxien erwachsen daraus, daß man das unbestimmte nicht im selben Sinn nimmt, und so auch die Insolubilia.*"

According to Husserl, the confusion is due to the fact that in the formulation of the paradox a predicate that is not reflexive, is taken to nevertheless apply to itself too, hence shifting the meaning: "A name cannot name itself, that is a countersense. A proposition cannot posit itself."⁴⁵ Husserl argues that in logical generality of course "word" is a word just like "name" is a name for a certain kind of word, and hence applies to itself. However, we have to pay attention to how it is used in the context of a specific individual proposition. In an indi-

---

42 Compare Koyré 1912, 330: "It belongs to the essence of a relation that it has at least two foundations." ("*es gehört zum Wesen einer Relation, dass sie zum mindesten zwei Fundamente haben muss.*")

43 Compare Koyré 1912, 332: "A man might have completely changed, an old man is wholly different from the youngster he once was, and yet we say: it is the same person, the same man." ("*Der Mensch kann sich ganz verändert haben, ein Greis ist von dem kleinen Knaben, der er war ganz und gar verschieden – und trotzdem sagen wir: es ist die selbe Person, der selbe Mensch.*")

44 Compare Koyré 1912, 332: "The whole argumentation, however, relies on a certain vagueness, connected to the concept of identity, a confusion, or at least insufficiently sharp distinction between two wholly different matters, i.e. the mere numerical identity, which I will henceforth call sameness, and strict logical identity." ("*Die ganze Argumentation beruht jedoch auf einer Unklarheit, die dem Begriffe der Identität anhaftet, auf einer Vermengung, oder zum mindesten nicht genügend scharfen Trennung von zwei gänzlich verschiedenen Sachen. Nämlich, der bloss numerischen Identität – die ich weiter unten nur mit dem Ausdruck Dasselbigkeit bezeichnen werde – und der eigentlichen logischen Identität.*") Also see Reinach *Sämmtliche Werke* 569 on the difference between "*Selbigkeit*" and "*Identität*".

45 11b: "*Ein Name kann nicht sich selbst nennen, das ist ein Widersinn. Ein Satz sich nicht selbst setzen.*"

vidual occurrence, where it applies to something specifically named, the name "name" cannot at the same time act as a variable referencing the specifically named and itself in logical generality. In other words, we have to distinguish different orders or levels of meaning: "When I say ⟨"⟩the name name⟨"⟩, then I have a new name, which is different from the name "name", a name of second order, etc."[46] The same applies to propositions.

This first criticism of the way in which the paradoxes, including Russell's paradox, are formulated is close to the first immediate reaction Frege himself gave when confronted with Russell's letter. Russell wrote:

> Let w be the predicate : to be a predicate that cannot be predicated of itself. Can w be predicated of itself? From each answer its opposite follows. Therefore we must conclude that w is not a predicate. Likewise there is no class (as a totality) of those classes, which, each taken as a totality, do not belong to themselves. From this I conclude that under certain circumstances a definable collection [[Menge]] does not form a totality.[47]

And Frege's first reaction was to make the formulation more precise by pointing out the different levels or orders of the terms involved:

> Incidentally, it seems to me that the expression "a predicate is predicated of itself" is not exact. A predicate is as a rule a first-level function, and this function requires an object as argument and cannot have itself as argument (subject).[48]

Husserl, however, connects this directly to his earlier argument about essential relations: the meaning and the meant have to be distinguished.[49] If we don't, we will produce a meaningless statement, since it would not be well-formed: "A statement that has itself as subject is not a statement, it is nothing at all." (11b *"Eine Aussage, die sich selbst zum Subjekt hat, ist keine Aussage, ist überhaupt nichts."*)[50] These are two essences that are put in relation and we cannot

---

46 11b: *"Sage ich, ⟨"⟩der Name Name⟨"⟩, so habe ich einen neuen Namen, der von dem Namen "Namen" verschieden ist, ein Name zweiter Stufe, usw."*
47 Heijenoort 1967, 125.
48 Heijenoort 1967, 128.
49 12a: *"Wie alle Wesensrelationen, so setzen die zwischen Namen und Genanntem, Aussagen und Ausgesagtem, verschiedene Termini voraus."*
50 Compare Koyré 1912, 337: "'I lie' is neither true nor false, which does not endanger the validity of logic in the least. It simply is not a proposition." (*"'Ich lüge' ist weder wahr noch falsch – was die Gültigkeit der Logik nicht im mindesten berührt. Es ist eben kein Satz."*). As Koyré points out, this is also the solution that can be traced back to Savonarola, and that he probably found through Urbach and Bolzano.

have identically the same essence in both positions (12a). This then points to the correct approach to the paradoxes: "The solution of the paradoxes consists in identifying the shifts in meaning that cause us to overlook the countersense and make it difficult, when we have the feeling that there is one, to point out where it is exactly."[51]

For Husserl it is crucial in the context of the logical and mathematical paradoxes, including Russell's, to provide an analysis of the essence "set" (*Menge*) and the essential relations it entails, such as the relation to the elements it contains: "An essential relation excludes that the two members of the relation would be identical. Hence, a set that contains itself as element is countersensical." (12b)

The text of A I 35 then carries on with an analysis of the essence of a manifold, of definiteness, and the role of axioms in defining the essence of the fundamental concepts and objects involved (13a-b). Up to this point we have noticed similarities to the structure and text of Koyré's *Insolubilia*, but a careful examination of the two manuscripts does not directly suggest that Husserl would have only made literal excerpts from Koyré. Husserl is rather developing his own reflections, prompted by the problems addressed in Koyré's dissertation proposal. There are some paraphrases, which Husserl then comments and elaborates upon in his own words. However, it does seem very likely, also given the choices and order of the topics discussed, that the manuscript originated as reaction to Koyré. This becomes increasingly clear in the next few pages.

On page 14 of A I 35 Husserl starts with a few phrases taken quite directly from Koyré's *Insolubilia*:

> The set P of all objects at all.
> It contains itself as an element.
> It is the biggest possible: and yet there can be no biggest number.
> The set of all its subsets is again an object, and hence contained in it as subset.[52]

Consider Koyré's third section titled: "*Die Menge aller Gegenstände.*" ("The set of all objects")

---

51 12a: "*Die Lösung der Paradoxien besteht aber in der Nachweisung der Sinnverschiebungen, die es machen, dass man den Widersinn eben nicht gleich merkt, und nicht angeben kann, wenn man ihn durchfühlt, wo er liegt.*"
52 "*Die Menge aller Gegenstände überhaupt P. Sie enthält sich selbst als Element. Sie ist die größtmögliche: und doch soll es keine größtmögliche Anzahl geben. Die Menge aller ihrer Untermengen ist selbst wieder ein Gegenstand, also in ihr enthalten als Untermenge.*"

This set has the most interesting properties. First of all it contains itself as element, since it is an object itself. Secondly, it is obviously the biggest possible – the number of its elements is hence the biggest number, which contradicts the well-known proposition that there is no such number. The set of its subsets is again itself one of its subsets, etc.[53]

Here it seems clear that Husserl is directly summarizing the main points of Koyré's text. Husserl then proceeds with an analysis of the concept of set, specifically in which cases we can say that to a general concept there corresponds a well-defined extension containing the objects that have the property expressed by the concept. According to both Husserl (14a) and Koyré (345f.) we run into problems both with negatively defined sets, i.e. sets that would contain all objects that lack a property, as well as with the totality of all objects itself ("*Allheit*").

For Husserl we can actually only assign an extension to genus concepts, not to all general concepts, since only in the case of a well-ordered genus we can provide a complete partition in disjoint sets, i.e. its species (15b). He acknowledges both finite and infinite cases: "Thus the number of numbers [...] is an "infinite number"; every single number [...] either 2 or 3 or 4 "etc.", and this is a complete disjunction." (16a). This is possible because one can provide an a priori definition of number, based on the essence of number, that determines how the series of numbers is generated.[54] The problem remains, of course, in which cases exactly it is possible to proceed in this way, so that we can tell whether or not the concepts have an extension that is completely disjoint.

Here we also find the explicit reference to a discussion with Koyré on these topics, which indeed echoes the formulations in the text of the *Insolubilia*:

---

53 Koyré 1912, 345: "*Diese Menge hat die interessantesten Eigenschaften. Erstens enthält sie sich selbst als Element, da sie auch ein Gegenstand ist. Zweitens ist sie offenbar die Grösstmögliche – die Anzahl ihrer Elemente ist somit die grösste Zahl, was dem bekannten Satz widerspricht, dass es eine solche nicht gibt. Die Menge ihrer Untermengen ist selbst eine ihrer Untermengen etc.*" Koyré then calls the set of all objects "P" further down the page.
54 This is very close to Husserl's position at the time of the *Philosophie der Arithmetik*, e.g. in "*Zur Lehre vom Inbegriff*", Hua XII, 398, Hua CW X, 373: "The series of natural numbers secures the exhaustive classification of the entire domain of finite numbers. [...] Through this classification it is simultaneously demonstrated that the concept of the finite number divides itself up into an infinite number of species concepts, which come together in their entirety to form an ordered manifold in which each member is followed by one member in univocal determination and only one member has none before it.
This order [...] arises, rather, from the pure concepts, through immediate and mediate Evidence, and consequently is apriori."

After the discussion with Koyré it seems to me that a further usable concept of set should still be possible and initially necessary for the mathematician. It would appear that Koyré's concept of set entails that a class-concept such as "the totality of all A" is acceptable if the individual judgment "there is an A" (where "an" is a positive concept) is true. "Something that is not A", yields no acceptable concept since with the negation we would introduce "paradoxical sets", that would relate to themselves. Though I need to think about this some more.[55]

On the following pages of A I 35 we do then find shorter excerpts and paraphrases of central paragraphs in Koyré's text. The pages 17a-b parallel *Insolubilia* 343–344, including the formulation of Russell's paradox, Schönfließ' argument, and Richard's paradox. Based on these pages, it is easy to see how Schuhmann might have taken all the notes together from 5–17 to represent little more than excerpts. Yet, a closer look shows that only these latter pages substantially consist of extracts from Koyré's dissertation manuscript, while the preceding portion does contain for the most part Husserl's own comments on Koyré's text, with some quotes and paraphrases.

Hence, this 1912 portion of A I 35 does not represent a spontaneous and original engagement with Russell's paradox by Husserl. The manuscript is not an unfinished treatise or a collection of thematically united research notes on the set-theoretical paradoxes proceeding from Husserl's own interest in the matter. This certainly changes the status afforded to the manuscript in the literature up to now. Therefore, I have instead attempted here to trace its origin philologically and place it in its appropriate context of the more widespread discussion of the ancient and modern paradoxes in the School of Brentano (Brentano, Urbach, Bergmann) and early phenomenology (Reinach, Lipps, Koyré).

Moreover, also beyond these initial pages dealing with Koyré's dissertation manuscript, we find further stray leaves of notes, such as 19a-b, which echoes almost literally a page contained in Husserl's 1908–09 logic lectures, but probably is from an even earlier date, perhaps going back to 1902–03.[56] Page 24 reports Zermelo's formulation of the paradox, 25 is a mere annotation, 26 repeats a summarized version of Russell's paradox following Koyré's text in *Insolubilia* (343), and 27–28 consists in translated excerpts and summarizing notes from Russell's 1911 article "*L'importance Philosophique de la Logistique*". All of these are indeed related to the problem of the set theoretical paradoxes, but

---

55 Koyré 1912 actually speaks of "*Pseudo-Mengen*", pseudo-sets.
56 See Husserliana Materialien VI, xix, 195 n. The page in the 1908–09 lectures can be found between two pages taken from the 1902–03 lectures. The text in *Husserliana Materialien* mentions a "blind" emperor of France, but I suppose this might be a typo or a misreading of "blond".

do not yield a coherent, autonomous position by Husserl.[57] The most original contribution to this end would be his short analysis of sets (*Mengen*) on pages 20–22.

§5 Husserl's Set Theory: Higher Order Objects and their Mereology

A I 35, 20–21 contains a discussion of the concepts of set and subset.[58] The fundamental questions Husserl asks is whether a set can be its own subset or element. Again, one of Husserl's first moves is to look at the levels of the meaning and order of "set": a set can only contain itself as element if it is a set of sets ("*Gelten könnte das natürlich nur von Mengen von Mengen*"). A first order set that only would contain concrete individuals cannot at the same time contain a second order element like itself. While this is very much in line with his earlier comments to Koyré, Husserl now provides a novel argument, expressed in two curious ways: one that sounds quite constructivist, one that sounds quite *Gestaltic*. The first version:

> It belongs to the purpose of speaking of a collection, of a multiplicity, ... that one should construct something new from thought-objects, that is determined by the given ones, but only arises through the construction. It would contradict this thought that the result of the construction would appear among the objects.[59]

---

[57] I agree with the assessment of Schmit (1981, 114) that the manuscript does not contain "an encompassing analysis of the origin of the crisis in the foundations or a systematic elaboration of an alternative approach to its solution", though it is not really an "*Entwurf*" (115) of anything either and many of the quoted passages actually go back to Koyré, as we have shown above.

[58] While one might argue, as I myself have done elsewhere (Ierna 2005, 11; 2007, 55), that "set" would not always be the most correct translation of *Menge* in Husserl, in the context of this topic I think it is appropriate enough to use "set" and "subset" as translations for *Menge* and *Teilmenge*.

[59] "*Zur Intention der Rede von einem Inbegriff, einer Vielheit ... gehört, daß aus Denkobjekten ein neues gebildet werden soll, das durch die vorgegebenen bestimmt ist, aber erst durch die Bildung erwächst. Es widerspricht diesem Gedanken, dass unter den Objekten das Resultat der Bildung vorkommen könnte.*" The talk of "*Denkobjecten*" might invite accusations of psychologism, but this was actually a quite common way to describe sets and their elements among mathematicians, particularly in the school of Weierstrass, e.g. Cantor (1895): "*Unter einer "Menge" verstehen wir jede Zusammenfassung M von bestimmten wohlunterschiedenen Objekten m unsrer Anschauung oder unseres Denkens (welche die "Elemente" von M genannt werden) zu einem Ganzen.*" See also Ierna 2006, §1.1.

Something very much like this can be found already in Husserl's earliest writings on the philosophy of mathematics. For instance, Husserl in 1890 speaks of *"Zahlbildung"* according to a given *"Bildungsgesetz"* when he means the symbolic construction of higher numbers, beyond the sphere of those authentically given (Husserl 2005, 298 ff.) and we find similar formulations in his *Über den Begriff der Zahl* and the *Philosophie der Arithmetik:*[60] "One is therefore entirely justified in referring to sets and numbers as results of processes and, in so far as our volition is involved, as results of activities, of "operations" of collecting resp. counting" (Husserl 1887, 24). What he said about collections (*Inbegriffe*) in the 1890s is very similar to what he is stating here with regard to sets. Since they are the results of mental activities, they cannot appear at the same level as the elements they are being built out of. This leads into the second version of the argument, the *Gestaltic* one:

> I would say: it belongs to the idea of the set to be a unity, so to say a whole, which encompasses certain "elements" as parts, but in such a way that it is something new in relation to these elements, which is only constructed through them. A whole cannot be its own part, a multiplicity not its own element, ⟨element⟩ of its own unity. (20b)

What makes me think of *Gestalten* in this passage is the high similarity to the way Christian von Ehrenfels had introduced this concept in his original 1890 article: "something novel in relation to this sum [of elements]" (Ehrenfels 1890, tr. Smith 1988, 83). A set, similarly, would be something more than the mere existence of its members, i.e. it is what brings the members together, either in the concrete act, or as the unifying criterion. A whole, in this sense, is more than the mere sum of its parts, but includes the mereological relations of the parts to the whole and to one another as parts of this specific whole.

> All mathematical-logical operations that can be performed with sets, depend on the fact that sets can be considered as a kind of whole, as new unities, constructions, that are something new in relation to their founding units, so that new constructions can be built on these constructions as their units, etc. (20b)

Here the "new unity" is characterized even more explicitly as a "founded content", to use Meinong's term for Ehrenfels' *Gestalt*. Given that Husserl very probably was the first one to use the term "*Gestalt*" in January 1890[61] and to discuss,

---

[60] In this early period Husserl was probably mostly inspired in this respect by Bolzano's *Paradoxien des Unendlichen*. See Ierna 2006, 46.
[61] See Husserl 2005, and Ierna 2009b.

as he indeed claimed, objects of higher order in the *Philosophie der Arithmetik*, it is not entirely surprising to see him indirectly appeal to his own earlier positions.[62] Yet, again, this makes the 1912 text less novel and original as an engagement with the crisis in the foundations. A reformulation rather than a revision of his views in the 1890s, even in this new context, does not really represent a creative new approach to the set theoretical paradoxes. Husserl's conclusion that "It does not follow from the fact that I can speak of all sets that the totality of sets [*Allheit der Mengen*] would itself be a set." is quite right, but also not very original as a solution to Russell's Paradox. After all, from the formal-mathematical point of view, Zermelo had already argued in his famous 1908 article that the domain of all objects itself could not be a set, and hence Russell's paradox could not arise.[63] And from the point of view of *Gestalten* and object-theory, Ernst Mally had given an extensive and detailed analysis of sets as higher order objects in his 1904 "*Untersuchungen zur Gegenstandstheorie des Messens*" (esp. §14). As we saw above, also Koyré had pointed out that the set of all sets leads to a countersense, while the set of e.g. all tables, or all red things does not. Koyré also explicitly indicated two problematic properties of the set of all sets: 1) that it would be the largest possible, and the number of its elements hence also the largest possible, which is impossible since there is no largest number, and 2) that the set of all sets would contain its power set as subset ("*Die Menge ihrer Untermengen ist selbst eine ihrer Untermengen.*" Koyré 1912, 345), which implies that it would actually be its own power set, which violates Cantor's and Zermelo's proofs that sets and their power sets have different cardinalities. This is the problem Husserl tries to analyze in a more formal fashion on pages 22a,b. He starts with the set "which contains all its subsets as elements", i.e. a set that is effectively its own power set. Now consider what happens when we take away one of its elements, i.e. one of its subsets: the resulting set either has or does not have the property of being its own power set. Of course both options lead to contradiction, prompting the conclusion that there can be no such set containing all its subsets as elements. Husserl however does not explicitly link his conclusion to Russell's paradox and the entire formulation and symbolism is much closer to the works of his fellow Weierstrassians Cantor and Zermelo instead.

---

[62] Also consider Koyré (1912, 351): "*Husserl hat in seiner* Philosophie der Arithmetik *eine Analyse dieser Gebilde gegeben. Wir möchten bloss darauf hinweisen, dass bei allen Aggregaten irgend welche Gestaltqualitäten, welche in den Elementen fundi<e>rt sind die zusammenfassende und vereinigende Function spielen, so dass man hier in einem gewissen Sinne schon von Ganzen sprechen könnte.*"

[63] On the other hand, Zermelo would simply say that "every set is determined by its elements" (1908, 263) and leave it at that, without remarking on a process of construction.

§6 Concluding remarks

The analysis I presented above of Husserl's manuscript A I 35 remains confined to its first part, generally indicated with "α", from 1912. This part of the manuscript, as we have seen, consists of an extensive reaction to and commentary upon Koyré's dissertation manuscript as well as various notes and excerpts. The material does not suggest that it was written and assembled with a view towards a publication, as is the case with other sets of research notes. The second part, from 1920 with some later annotations, is a quite different matter and falls outside the scope of the present discussion. While the first part from 1912 might not yield a spontaneous and original engagement of Husserl with Russell's paradox, it yet remains a highly interesting document. Thanks to A I 35 we can reconstruct the dynamics of the reception and discussion of Russell's paradox and the crisis in the foundations of mathematics in the broader contexts of the School of Brentano and the early phenomenological circle in Göttingen. Even though Husserl's text is a reaction to someone else, following the topics and structure of a secondary text, and not an autonomous treatise, the views and positions espoused are his own. It is crucial, however, to keep distinct the excerpts and paraphrases on the one hand, and Husserl's own reactions on the other. This is rendered possible thanks to Zambelli's publication of Koyré's dissertation materials and the publication of A I 35α in this volume.

Bibliography

Bergmann, Hugo, 1909, *Das philosophische Werk Bernard Bolzanos mit Benutzung ungedruckter Quellen kritisch untersucht. Nebst einem Anhange: Bolzanos Beiträge zur philosophischen Grundlegung der Mathematik* (Halle an der Saale: Max Niemeyer).

Bergmann, Hugo, 1946, "Briefe Franz Brentanos an Hugo Bergmann" in *Philosophy and Phenomenological Research* 7 (1), 83–158.

Cairns, Dorion, 1973, *Guide for translating Husserl*, Phaenomenologica 55 (The Hague: Nijhoff).

Cantor, Georg, 1895, "Beiträge zur Begründung der transfiniten Mengenlehre" in *Mathematische Annalen* 46/4, 481–512.

Centrone, Stefania, 2010, *Logic and Philosophy of Mathematics in the Early Husserl* (Dordrecht: Springer).

Ebbinghaus, Heinz-Dieter & Peckhaus, Volker, 2007, *Ernst Zermelo: An Approach to His Life and Work* (Dordrecht: Springer).

Ehrenfels, Christian von, 1890, "Über 'Gestaltqualitäten'", in *Vierteljahrsschrift für wissenschaftliche Philosophie*, 14, 249–292.

Grelling, Kurt and Nelson, Leonard, 1908, "Bemerkungen zu den Paradoxieen von Russell und Burali-Forti," *Abhandlungen der Fries'schen Schule*, n. s. 2, no. 3, 301–334.

Haddock, Guillermo Rosado, 1997, "Husserl's Relevance for the Philosophy and Foundations of Mathematics" in *Axiomathes* No. 1–3, 125–142.
Haddock, Guillermo Rosado, 2006, "Husserl's Philosophy of Mathematics: its Origin and Relevance" in *Husserl Studies* 22, 193–222.
Haddock, Guillermo Rosado, 2010, "Platonism, Phenomenology, and Interderivability", in Hartimo, Mirja (ed.) *Phenomenology and Mathematics*, Phaenomenologica 195 (Dordrecht: Springer).
Hartimo, Mirja, 2006, "Mathematical Roots of Phenomenology: Husserl and the Concept of Number", in *History and Philosophy of Logic* 27, 319–337.
Hill, Claire Ortiz, 2002, "Tackling three of Frege's Problems: Edmund Husserl on Sets and Manifolds" in *Axiomathes* 13, 79–104.
Heijenoort, Jean van, 1967, *From Frege to Gödel: A Source Book in Mathematical Logic, 1879–1931*, Harvard University Press.
Husserl, Edmund, 1887, *Über den Begriff der Zahl. Psychologische Analysen*. Heynemann'sche Buchdruckerei (F. Beyer).
Husserl, Edmund, 1891, *Philosophie der Arithmetik. Psychologische und Logische Untersuchungen*, C.E.M. Pfeffer (Robert Stricker), Halle.
Husserl, Edmund, 1970, *Philosophie der Arithmetik. Mit ergänzenden Texten* (1890–1901), L. Eley (ed.), Husserliana XII, Nijhoff, Den Haag.
Husserl, Edmund, 1979, *Aufsätze und Rezensionen (1890–1910)*, Bernhard Rang (ed.), Husserliana XXII.
Husserl, Edmund, 1996, *Logik und allgemeine Wissenschaftstheorie. Vorlesungen Wintersemester 1917/18. Mit ergänzenden Texten aus der ersten Fassung von 1910/11*, edited by Ursula Panzer, Husserliana XXX.
Husserl, Edmund, 2001, *Allgemeine Erkenntnistheorie. Vorlesung 1902/03*, Elisabeth Schuhmann (ed.), Husserliana Materialien III (Dordrecht: Kluwer).
Husserl, Edmund, 2003, *Philosophy of Arithmetic*, trans. by Dallas Willard, *Husserliana Edmund Husserl Collected Works* X (Dordrecht: Kluwer).
Husserl, Edmund, 2003, *Alte und neue Logik. Vorlesung 1908/09*, Elisabeth Schuhmann (ed.), Husserliana Materialien VI (Dordrecht: Kluwer).
Husserl, Edmund, 2005, "Vorlesung Über den Begriff der Zahl (WS 1889/90)" / "Lecture on the Concept of Number (WS 1889/90)", Ierna, Carlo (ed. & trans.), in *The New Yearbook for Phenomenology and Phenomenological Philosophy* V.
Ierna, Carlo, 2005, "The Beginnings of Husserl's Philosophy (Part 1: From *Über den Begriff der Zahl* to *Philosophie der Arithmetik*)" in *The New Yearbook for Phenomenology and Phenomenological Philosophy* V, 1–56.
Ierna, Carlo, 2006, "The Beginnings of Husserl's Philosophy (Part 2: Philosophical and Mathematical Background)" in *The New Yearbook for Phenomenology and Phenomenological Philosophy* VI, 23–71.
Ierna, Carlo, 2007, "Review of Dallas Willard" in *Husserl-Studies*.
Ierna, Carlo, 2009a, "Relations in the Early Works of Meinong and Husserl", in *Meinong Studies* 3.
Ierna, Carlo, 2009b, "Husserl et Stumpf sur la Gestalt et la fusion" in *Philosophiques* 36/2, 489–510.
Ierna, Carlo, 2011a, "Brentano and Mathematics", in *Revue Roumaine de Philosophie* 55/1, 149–167.

Ierna, Carlo, 2011b, "Der Durchgang durch das Unmögliche. An Unpublished Manuscript from the Husserl-Archives", in *Husserl-Studies* 27/3, 217–226.
Ierna, Carlo, 2015, "Carl Stumpf's Philosophy of Mathematics", in Fisette, Denis & Martinelli, Riccardo (eds.), *Philosophy from an Empirical Standpoint: Essays on Carl Stumpf* (Amsterdam: Rodopi).
Ierna, Carlo, 2016, "The Brentanist Philosophy of Mathematics in Edmund Husserl's Early Works" in *Essays on Husserl's Logic and Philosophy of Mathematics*, ed. Stefania Centrone, Synthese Library (Berlin: Springer, forthcoming).
Koyré, Alexandre, 1912, *Insolubilia*, Zambelli, Paola (ed.), in *Giornale Critico della Filosofia Italiana* 19 (3), 323–354 (1999).
Koyré, Alexandre, 1922, "Bemerkungen zu den Zenonischen Paradoxen" in *Jahrbuch für Philosophie und Phänomenologische Forschung* V, 603–628.
Koyré, Alexandre, 1946, "The Liar", in *Philosophy and Phenomenological Research*, Vol. 6, No. 3, 344–362.
Lipps, Hans, 1923, "Bemerkungen zu der Paradoxie des Lügners" in *Kant-Studien*, 28, 335–339.
Mally, Ernst, 1904, "Untersuchungen zur Gegenstandstheorie des Messens", in *Untersuchungen zur Gegenstandstheorie und Psychologie*, vol. 3, Meinong, Alexius (ed.), Leipzig: Barth, 121–262.
Meinong, Alexius, 1882, "Hume Studien II: Zur Relationstheorie", in *Sitzungsbereiche der phil.-hist. Classe der kais. Akademie der Wissenschaften* CI:II, 573–752.
Miller, J. P., 1982, *Numbers in Presence and Absence*, Phaenomenologica 90, Nijhoff, Den Haag.
Parker, Rodney, 2016, "The History between Koyré and Husserl", in Pisano, Agassi, and Drozdova (eds.) *Hypotheses and Perspectives within History and Philosophy of Science. Homage to Alexandre Koyré 1964–2014*, Springer (forthcoming).
Russell, Bertrand, 1904, "Meinong's Theory of Complexes and Assumptions", in *Mind* 13, 204–219, 336–354, 509–524.
Russell, Bertrand, 1905a, "On Denoting", in *Mind* 14, 479–493.
Russell, Bertrand, 1905b, "Review of Meinong's Untersuchungen zur Gegenstandstheorie und Psychologie", in *Mind* 14, 530–538.
Russell, Bertrand, 1907, "Review of Meinong's Über die Stellung der Gegenstandstheorie im System der Wissenschaften", in *Mind* 16, 436–439.
Russell, Bertrand, 1911, "L'importance Philosophique de la Logistique" in *Revue de Métaphysique et de Morale* 19 (3), 281–291.
Schmit, Roger, 1981, *Husserl's Philosophie der Mathematik. Platonistische und konstruktivistische Momente in Husserls Mathematikbegriff* (Bonn: Bouvier).
Schuhmann, Karl, 1977, *Husserl-Chronik (Denk- und Lebensweg Edmund Husserls)*, Husserliana Dokumente I (Den Haag: Nijhoff).
Schuhmann, Karl, 1987, "Koyré et les phénoménologues allemands", in *History and Technology: An International Journal*, 4:1–4, 149–167.
Schuhmann, Karl, and Smith, Barry, 1989, *Adolf Reinach, Sämtliche Werke. Textkritische Ausgabe in 2 Bänden*. (Philosophia Resources Library), München, Hamden, Wien: Philosophia.
Schuhmann, Elisabeth & Schuhmann, Karl, 2001 "Husserls Manuskripte zu seinem Göttinger Doppelvortrag von 1901", in *Husserl Studies* 17/2, 87–123.

Smith, Barry (ed.), 1988, *Foundations of Gestalt Theory.* Munich and Vienna: Philosophia.
Urbach, Benno, 1910, "Über das Wesen der logischen Paradoxa", in *Zeitschrift für Philosophie und philosophische Kritik* 140, 81–108.
Varga, Peter Andras, 2016, "The Non-Existing Object Revisited: Meinong as the Link between Husserl and Russell?" in David, Marian & Antonelli, Mauro (eds.), *Existence, Fiction, Assumption: Meinongian Themes and the History of Austrian Philosophy,* De Gruyter, 27–58.
Zambelli, Paola, 1999, "Alexandre Koyré im "Mekka der Mathematik"," in *Ntm International Journal of History and Ethics of Natural Sciences, Technology & Medicine* 7 (1), 208–230.
Zermelo, Ernst, 1908, "Untersuchungen über die Grundlagen der Mengenlehre", *Mathematische Annalen* 65, 261–281.

David Woodruff Smith
Husserl and Tarski: the Semantic Conception of Intentionality and Truth

Abstract: Here I want to consider an overarching conception of "semantics" in the form of a "semantic" conception of intentionality in relation to truth. That "semantic" conception can be seen as articulated in quite different ways, respectively, in Husserl's phenomenological theory of intentionality and in Tarski's metamathematical theory of truth. There are historical links between Husserl and Tarski. But my emphasis here will be on the intuitive conception of how thought or language is "semantically" directed at appropriate objects or structures in the world: *intentionality* by any other name. That basic vision animates both Husserl's model of intentionality *per se* and Tarski's subsequent model of truth in formalized languages. In that light we may see Tarski's theory of truth as a "mathematization" of Husserl's theory of intentionality – that is, for intentionality in forms of thought expressible in certain forms of language. Along the way I want to elaborate on an interpretation of Husserl's methodology of epoché (for phenomenology) vis-à-vis Tarski's methodology of metalanguage (for formal semantics). Distinguishing levels of language as in Tarski's famous theory of truth, we can see what is involved in Husserl's distinguishing levels of consciousness in the practice of epoché. From this perspective, what is revolutionary in Husserl's approach to phenomenology suggests what is philosophically revolutionary in Tarski's approach to truth – and vice versa.

In prior essays I have explored ways in which Edmund Husserl's theory of intentionality and Alfred Tarski's theory of truth might be synthesized, with each model extending into the terrain of the other. Here I want to consider an overarching conception of "semantics" in the form of a "semantic" conception of intentionality in relation to truth. That "semantic" conception can be seen as articulated in quite different ways, respectively, in Husserl's phenomenological theory of intentionality and in Tarski's metamathematical theory of truth. There are historical links between Husserl and Tarski, though the very idea of such links may seem surprising in today's world of philosophy. For Tarski produced technical proofs in mathematical logic, a context within which he developed his mathematical theory of truth in formalized languages. By contrast, Husserl had moved from his early work in mathematics, and then philosophy of arithmetic, into his work on intentionality and phenomenology, in the "new science" of consciousness, motivated by his anti-psychologistic philosophy of logic and mathematics.

My emphasis here will be on the intuitive conception of how thought or language is "semantically" directed at appropriate objects or structures in the world: *intentionality* by any other name. That basic vision animates both Husserl's model of intentionality per se and Tarski's subsequent model of truth in formalized languages. In that light we may see Tarski's theory of truth as a "mathematization" of Husserl's theory of intentionality – that is, for intentionality in forms of thought expressible in certain forms of language.

Along the way I want to elaborate on an interpretation of Husserl's methodology of epoché (for phenomenology) vis-à-vis Tarski's methodology of metalanguage (for formal semantics). Distinguishing levels of language as in Tarski's famous theory of truth, we can see what is involved in Husserl's distinguishing levels of consciousness in the practice of epoché. From this perspective, what is revolutionary in Husserl's approach to phenomenology suggests what is philosophically revolutionary in Tarski's approach to truth – and vice versa. (See Lynch ed. 2001 on problems in the theory of truth.)

We might say Husserl was a mathematically trained philosopher who launched the discipline of phenomenology, while Tarski was a philosophically trained mathematician who launched the discipline of formal semantics in logic. There was a time when logic and phenomenology were kindred spirits, and in that spirit we pursue the semantic approach to intentionality and truth. (On some of these background issues see Smith 2002, 2002a, 2005, 2013, 2016.)

§1 On "Semantics" in Husserl and Tarski

Let us set the scene by noting basic structures of Husserl's theory of intentionality and Tarski's theory of truth. I'll assume broad familiarity with these theories as we proceed. My discussion will weave back and forth between aspects of the two theories.

§1.1 Husserl's "logic", or semantics, of language and consciousness

Husserl's theory of intentionality works with a basic distinction among act, content, and object of consciousness. An *act* of consciousness is a conscious intentional experience, such as seeing something, thinking something, etc. The *content* of such an act is a *meaning* with a certain form or structure, such as seeing "that pelican gliding over waves" or thinking "Tarski was born in Poland". The *object* of an act of consciousness is that toward which the act is *intentionally* directed, say, the gliding pelican or Tarski's birth. On Husserl's basic theory, the act is directed toward its object (if such exists) *by virtue of its content*, and the content itself is an "ideal" (nonspatiotemporal) meaning.

From today's perspective we may call Husserl's theory *semantic* because it concerns the *intentional relation* between act and object, where the relation is mediated by *meaning-content*, and where the relation is successful or *veridical* insofar as the "intended" object *satisfies* the meaning-content. This retrospective view is informed by Tarski's "semantic" conception of truth featuring specified *truth-conditions* for a sentence in a given language. Yet the outlines of this view are well developed in Husserl's own writing. Indeed, Husserl set out his theory of the intentionality of consciousness explicitly in relation to what we today call a semantic theory of sense and reference for language.

Husserl's basic theory of intentionality was launched in his *Logical Investigations* (1900 – 01) and ramified in his later works including *Ideas* I (1913). Importantly, this theory developed out of Husserl's early work in mathematics and his rejection of psychologistic views of meaning in logic and mathematics. The theory evolved in Husserl's later "transcendental" phenomenology, featuring "transcendental" aspects of "noematic content". Husserl's theory of intentionality has been interpreted in various ways, especially where the concept of "noema" came to the fore in *Ideas* I. In any case, for present purposes I'll assume a basic interpretation that features the role of meanings in mediating intentional relations to objects in the world. Husserl's relatively late *Formal and Transcendental Logic* (1929) shows Husserl still concerned with "logical" issues informed by his theory of intentionality. That "logical" perspective is central to his "semantic" conception of intentionality, though Husserl did not have the terminology of "semantics", which developed in later logical theory owing largely to Tarski. (My interpretation along these lines is detailed in Smith 2013. Alternative readings of Husserl are discussed therein; the book ends with a formulation of a strong doctrine of meaning entities, Husserl's "noematic" meanings.)

Dagfinn Føllesdal has long stressed the parallel between Husserl's model of act-content-object, in the phenomenological theory of intentionality, and Frege's model of expression-sense-reference, in the logical theory of reference-and-truth in language. This parallel sharply defines a *semantic* conception of intentionality and truth. Here I explore such a semantic conception in the light of Tarski's conception of semantics, which developed after Frege's work in logic and largely after Husserl's work in logic and phenomenology. (See Dreyfus ed. 1982 for essays on Husserl and Frege on intentionality and reference, including Føllesdal's classic 1969 essay, "Husserl's Notion of Noema". Semantic aspects of Husserl's theory of intentionality are further studied in Smith and McIntyre 1982 and in Smith 2013. Further studies of relations between Husserl and Frege are pursued in Hill and Rosado Haddock 2000.)

§1.2 Husserl's conception of "pure logic"

Husserl's conception of "pure logic" in the Prolegomena to the *Logical Investigations* was explicitly a model for how *language, thought,* and *world* are correlated. And that pattern of correlation is precisely what would later be called "semantics" for the more limited system correlating language and world (via sense or meaning on some views).

A simple example of the correlation, in Husserl's scheme, will focus our perspective. Consider the *sentence* "Tarski was born in Poland". This sentence expresses a *proposition:* the proposition that Tarski was born in Poland, which Husserl takes to be an ideal *meaning* (a *Satz*, a propositional form of *Sinn*). We may cite that proposition by using angle brackets as a style of quotation marks (not dissimilar to a graphic style of quotation marks in German print). Then we say the sentence "Tarski was born in Poland" expresses the proposition <Tarski was born in Poland>. Following Bolzano, Husserl assumed propositions are ideal meaning entities, an ontology contrary to psychologistic reductions of logic to mental activities. Further, for Husserl, the proposition <Tarski was born in Poland> presents, or "intends" or is directed toward, the *state of affairs* that Tarski was born in Poland. Where the constituents of the proposition are concepts of Tarski and of Poland, the constituents of the state of affairs are the human being Tarski and the nation Poland. We may cite the state of affairs by using square brackets. Then we say the proposition <Tarski was born in Poland> is directed toward the state of affairs [Tarski was born in Poland].

In Husserl's ontology, a state of affairs is a concrete "fact" in the world, in this case formed (as noted) from the individual Tarski, the social-geographic entity Poland, and the relation of birth-in-a-place. Now, when I think that Tarski was born in Poland, my *act of thinking* includes as its *content* the proposition <Tarski was born in Poland>, and the act is directed via that proposition toward its *object*, which is the state of affairs [Tarski was born in Poland]. And if I utter the sentence "Tarski was born in Poland", then my *speech act* expresses the content of my act-of-thinking, viz. the proposition <Tarski was born in Poland>, and so my vocal assertion is directed toward the state of affairs [Tarski was born in Poland].

The structure of correlation just mapped out assumes a rich ontology of acts-of-consciousness, ideal meaning-contents of consciousness, acts-of-expression, and concrete states of affairs in the world. Accordingly, in Husserl's semantics, in his scheme of "pure logic", we would then define *truth* within the pattern of correlations recited: The sentence uttered – in a speech act expressing the meaning-content of an underlying act-of-thinking – is *true* if and only if its propositional content is veridically correlated with (or satisfied by) an appropriate state of affairs in the speaker's surrounding world.

Husserl called "pure logic", in his conception, "the theory of theories". Tarski called "metalogic", in his conception, "the deductive science of deductive sciences", or "metamathematics". The similarity in idioms is not coincidental, as we shall see.

§1.3 From Husserl to Tarski

In a Husserlian system of "logical" correlations as sketched above, does it seem unduly loquacious or even redundant to keep reciting the words "Tarski was born in Poland", albeit within different symbolic schemes (with double quotes, angle brackets, square brackets)? Well, Husserl's logical correlations assume specified *categories* of language, thought (or consciousness), meaning, and world, and types of relations among things at these levels. The distinct levels of language, thought, meaning, and world we mark as above by styles of quotation marks; these orthographic marks keep straight where we are in the semantics.

Indeed, Tarski's formal theory of truth works in close detail with categories of expression in a formal language. If we say:

"Tarski was born in Poland" is true if and only if Tarski was born in Poland,

then we need to correlate the *words in quotation* with appropriate *things in the world*. And accordingly, quotation is crucial in correlating categories of expression with categories of things in the world. Interestingly, Tarski's formal theory of truth begins with roots in Husserl's philosophical milieu and, as noted below, with a nod explicitly to Husserl's conception of semantic categories in Husserl's *Logical Investigations*.

Franz Brentano's students in Vienna included three thinkers of note to the present study: Kasimir Twardowski, Edmund Husserl, and Alexius Meinong. In *On the Content and Object of Presentations* [*Vorstellungen*] (1894/1977), Twardowski drew a distinction among act, content, and object. In his *Logical Investigations* (1900 – 01/2001) Husserl noted Twardowski's distinction, briefly criticized Twardowski's notion of "content", and developed a detailed logical conception of "content" as ideal meaning. Meinong also assumed a notion of "content" but focused on a complex scheme of "objects" (potential objects of consciousness), featuring objects "beyond being" that included merely possible objects and even impossible objects (see my reconstruction in Smith 1975). Twarkowski returned from his studies in Vienna to Poland, where he was influential in the Polish school of logic: from which Tarski came (a student of the philosopher-logician Tadeusz Kotarbinski), settling after World War II in the University of California, Berkeley, where his students included prominent mathematical logicians (notably Dana Scott and Solomon Feferman, who taught at Stanford in mathematics and philosophy, and Richard Montague, who taught at UCLA in philosophy). Tarski's background is noteworthy here because we can see the "semantic" perspective developing on the heels of the Brentano school's work on intentionality. And Tarski referenced Husserl's *Logical Investigations* not least in his seminal formal work on truth (Tarski 1983/1956/1936), noting Husserl's concept of categories. Indeed, Husserl posited specific formal categories at the different levels of language, consciousness, meaning, and world, and the correlations among these categories virtually define "semantics". (See Betti 2011 on Twardowski's role in Vienna and Warsaw. See Feferman and Feferman 2004 on Tarski's training in Poland and subsequent work, and compare Carnap 1963 on Tarski's role in bringing semantics into logic. On my reconstruction of Husserl's categorial system, see Smith 2013, and compare Smith 2002 on how structures in Husserl's ontology may be joined with structures in Tarski's truth theory.)

Tarski's technique in devising his formal theory of truth allows the parsimonious semantic theorist to stop short of positing either propositions, as ideal or abstract meaning entities, or states of affairs, as structured "facts" beyond objects with properties. For Tarski's recursive definition of "is true" arguably demonstrates how sentences with complex syntactic structures are rendered true, according to details of their truth-conditions, by appropriate objects and sets of objects. The devil is in the famous details regarding "satisfaction" of open sentences with variables, in virtue of which a more complex sentence is rendered "true". Arguing from Tarskian details, Donald Davidson championed Tarski's theory of truth as affording all we need in a theory of meaning without positing either "propositions" or "facts" (see Davidson 1984/1967).

Nonetheless, where the ontology of propositions and states of affairs enters the story, Husserl's scheme of correlations in pure logic shows where these entities would play their roles in a less parsimonious theory of truth. For the record, I believe that in the long run we cannot make do without both propositions and states of affairs as well as their respective constituents. In any case, Tarski's mathematical constructions in truth theory and model theory provide instructive details that show the way if we want to posit propositions and states of affairs for reasons of ontology. Such is the metaphilosophical perspective of the present essay. (Compare Smith 2002 on how to fit Husserl's notion of "manifolds", or structured wholes, into a Tarskian model of truth.)

§1.4 Tarski's formal theory of truth

Tarski's theory of truth emerged in the early 1930s with a formal theory of truth for a well-defined formal language. The formal theory appeared in a long essay, "The Concept of Truth in Formalized Languages", nicknamed "the *Wahrheitsbegriff*", from the 1936 German translation of the original 1933 Polish version. (See Tarski 1983/1936/1933.) This essay joined other seminal work in mathematical logic appearing in the 1930s, not least Kurt Gödel's ground-breaking theorems on the incompleteness of certain axiomatic theories. Gödel's incompleteness results assume a distinction between proof and truth: there are provably sentences in a given theory that are unprovable yet must be true. And so the scene was set, as it were, for a formal theory of truth (as opposed to provability – or, if you like, "verifiability" in a deductive system).

Subsequently, Tarski presented his theory of truth in a more intuitive form, applicable to ordinary language, in an essay, "The Semantic Conception of Truth and the Foundations of Semantics" (1944) (reprinted as 2001/1944). A central principle in Tarski's theory is the convention T, cast as follows:

(T) The sentence "p" is true if and only if p.

This formula T is a schema to be applied (we assume) to a range of English sentences "p". Here "p" is a sentence in a given *object language*, a part of English wherein (we may assume) "p" is talking about various things in the world. The sentence T is then a sentence in a *metalanguage* for that object language, where T is talking about the sentence "p" as part of the object language. Importantly, in Tarski's theory, the same sentence "p" occurs in the object language and again within quotation marks in the metalanguage. That is, one part of English includes "p", but another, higher-order part of English includes T.

The clause following "if and only if" in T specifies, in the metalanguage, the conditions under which "p" would be true in the object language: that is, the *truth-conditions* of "p". In this way, we may say, T articulates the *meaning* of "p". However, Tarski himself did not speak directly of "meaning", but rather of the *structure of relations* between elementary expressions in the object language and appropriate things in the world. In that way T articulates the *semantics* of "p" as an expression in the object language.

Following Tarski's famous example, we may specify the truth-conditions for the simple English sentence, "snow is white", as follows:

the sentence "snow is white" is true if and only if snow is white.

Thus, if S is the sentence "snow is white" in the *object language* part of basic English, we specify the truth-conditions for S as follows in the *metalanguage* part of English:

(S*)   "snow is white" in English is true if and only if snow is white.

Here we see that in the complex sentence S*, the expression "snow is white" occurs twice. In the first occurrence it is enclosed by quotation marks, forming a *name* of the English sentence S; in the second occurrence, following "if and only if", the sentence S simply states a condition of snow in the world. Thus, the metalinguistic sentence S* formulates the conditions *in the world* under which S, as a sentence of English, would be true: the truth-conditions of S as formulated in S*.

In this simple example, the metalanguage including S* is an extension of a more limited part of everyday English including S, and that extension includes a specification of basic grammar or syntax for the English sentence "snow is white". Now, the technical significance of Tarski's formal theory of truth is not apparent yet in the above simplification. Tarski developed a technique for specifying truth-conditions not only for simple subject-predicate sentences ("snow is white", "Tarski was Polish"), nor only for truth-functional forms of sentences (formed with the sentential connections "and", "or", "not", "if ... then"), but notably for quantified sentences, e. g., "all Polish logicians are gifted", "some Polish logicians read Husserl". Thus, the latter sentence is parsed as "for some x, x is a Polish logician and x read Husserl"; on Tarski's analysis, this sentence is *true* if and only if the open sentence "x is a Polish logician and x read Husserl" is *satisfied* by an assignment of objects to the variable "x" – here is a basic relation to the world of objects that serve to make true the quantified sentence. Well, the details of Tarski's formal construction of his theory are beyond the scope of our study here, but we need to appreciate how the metalanguage must talk about *expressions in the object language*, even as expressions in the object language talk instead about *things in the world*, objects that *make true* sentences in the object language. Thus, we move between object and meta-language depending on our concerns: with the world or with language about the world. Tarski's theory of truth has been interpreted in various ways, but for present purposes I'll assume a realist (non-"deflationist") reading of Tarski's convention (T). (See Lynch ed. 2001 on varying approaches to truth including Tarski's.)

§1.5 Husserl vis-à-vis Tarski

To foreshadow a leading theme in this essay: In the practice of epoché, in Husserlian phenomenology, we move between (i) mundane consciousness of *things in the world around us* and (ii) reflective consciousness of *our consciousness of those things*. For Husserl, the relation between consciousness and world is mediated by meaning, and similarly the relation between language and world is mediated by meaning. Here we see the "semantic" conception of intentionality in phenomenology and the corresponding "semantic" conception of truth in logical theory. For Tarski, the meaning of a sentence is modeled in the formulation of its truth-conditions for the sentence. Possible-worlds semantics would develop in later decades, in the work of philosophically minded logicians including Jaakko Hintikka and Saul Kripke. And Husserl's theory of intentionality has been presented accordingly in relation to possible-worlds semantics (see Smith and McIntyre 1982.)

Husserl and Tarski differed significantly in their ontological assumptions. Like others in the Austrian tradition, Husserl assumed the existence of both propositions (*Sätze*) and states of affairs (*Sachverhalten*), where (say) the sentence "snow is white" expresses the proposition <snow is white>, an ideal meaning-entity which presents the concrete state of affairs that snow is white. Like others in the Polish school of logic and philosophy, Tarski held to a nominalist ontology. We may see the meaning of the sentence "snow is white" as cashed out, per Tarski, in its truth-conditions (as Donald Davidson famously argued: see Davidson 1984/1967). Ultimately, these truth-conditions are detailed in set-theoretic, model-theoretic terms – comfortably nominalist insofar as sets and their members are treated formally as individuals (though sets are abstract individuals). However, possible worlds semantics takes set-theoretic "models" as modeling possible situations or sates of affairs, widening the ontology of truth-conditions. In any case, ontology aside, if we look to the distinction between language and metalanguage in Tarski's theory of truth, we should see a kindred distinction in Husserl's phenomenology between consciousness-of-objects and phenomenological reflection on such consciousness.

In his posthumous *Crisis – The Crisis of European Sciences and Transcendental Phenomenology* (1935–1938) – Husserl worried about the "mathematization" of nature: we lose sight of how our mathematical model of space-time is an abstraction from our everyday experience of things in space and time, as the way we experience things in nature seems to be covered over or even replaced by our mathematical model of the essence of spatiotemporal things. In the present study we might well see Tarski's mathematical model of truth as indeed a mathematical abstraction from our everyday experience of truth in veridical consciousness. In that spirit we may see Tarski's metalogical or metamathematical methodology – whence cometh logical "semantics" – as a formal elaboration on Husserl's methodology of "bracketing".

The rhetoric in Tarski's essay, "The Semantic Conception of Truth and the Foundations of Semantics" (Tarski 2001/1944), is striking. Tarski was much exercised to articulate how a formal theory of truth in a formalized language can serve not only mathematical logic, but also the ancient liar paradox ("this sentence is false", which is true if and only if false). Around the corner lies everyday language, beyond the bounds of a rigorous mathematical theory of truth. Everyday experience – in "veridical" perception or in "true" thought – is still further beyond the bounds of a mathematical "semantics". Yet Husserl had his own vision of what counts as "rigorous science" ("*strenge Wissenschaft*") (Husserl 1965/1911): mathematical precision is one kind of rigor, phenomenological perspicuity – in "intuition" – is another.

How might "semantics" be conceived, then, so as to apply to formal language, to everyday language, and to everyday experience?

§2 The Rise of Semantics in Logic and in Phenomenology

My central conceit here is that Husserl and Tarski worked in very different ways within a basic picture of how thought or its expression in language is directed toward things in the world – where *semantics* is the theory of these patterns of directedness toward the world.

In Husserl we find a *semantic* conception of *intentionality* in phenomenology: consciousness is (typically) a consciousness *of* something and is so "directed" toward an appropriate object or state of affairs in the world, directed by virtue of an appropriate content or sense (*Sinn*). In Tarski we find a *semantic* conception of *truth* in logic: a sentence in a well-formed language is true if and only if appropriate conditions in the world are satisfied, and so the truth-conditions of the sentence define what the sentence means or represents.

Where Frege spoke of "sense" (*Sinn*) and "thought(s)" (*Gedanke*), Husserl spoke of sense (*Sinn*) and (following Bolzano) "proposition(s)" (*Satz*) – and ultimately of "noema" or "noematic content" (*noematischer Inhalt*). Husserl addressed truth within his theory of intentionality: appraising how an act-of-thinking is directed via a proposition (*Satz*) toward an appropriate state of affairs (*Sachverhalt*) in the world – where a proposition is a particular *logical form* of sense (*Sinn*) that may serve as the "content" of an intentional act of thinking.

Subsequently, Tarski spoke of a "semantic conception" of truth, where a sentence's meaning is in effect delineated in terms of its truth-conditions. Accordingly, I propose, we may see a Tarskian account of truth-conditions as constraining a Husserlian account of the intentional correlation between a proposition and appropriate forms of entities in the world.

My task, then, is to outline the ways in which "semantics" is articulated in the respective systems of the two thinkers: for Husserl, in logic and phenomenology; for Tarski, in mathematical logic, with an eye to everyday language. This perspective allows us to see foundational motivations for Husserl's phenomenological program and for Tarski's metalogical program.

The semantic view of intentionality places Husserl's method of *epoché* in an illuminating perspective. What's the big deal about epoché? Why was it so difficult for early 20th century philosophers to see what was revolutionary in Husserl's phenomenology? Well, we need to understand the experiential shift from our familiar focus on *objects* in the world around us to the *meaning* or *sense* they have for us – even as meaning does its work incognito in the background.

Husserl's "breakthrough" to phenomenology was articulated in his *Logical Investigations* (1900 – 01). What was new and groundbreaking in that work? Fundamentally we should see: Husserl's theory of *intentionality*, his model of the structure <act-content-object> (if we may present it so). Arguably, this structure allows consciousness to break through the veil of appearances, the "phenomena", to the objects themselves, the objects in the world that "appear" in consciousness. The relation of intentionality is fundamentally semantic: relating act, "noematic" content or sense (*Sinn*), and object. Husserl's revolutionary technique of epoché, featured in his *Ideas* I (1913) as a "transcendental" perspective, consisted in "bracketing" the existence of objects in the surrounding world in order to focus on our "pure" consciousness of such objects via noematic contents. This technique, I emphasize, is made possible only on the ground of his basic "semantic" theory of intentionality. Until we clearly distinguish act, content, and object of intentionality, Husserl assumed, we cannot see how to focus properly on act and content – and thus begin to practice the "new science" of phenomenology. We shall return to the significance of this semantic model of intentionality for Husserl's "transcendental" phenomenology and for his method of *epoché* or "bracketing".

Similarly, the semantic view of truth places Tarski's method of *metalanguage* in an illuminating perspective. What was revolutionary in Tarski's metalogic? Well, we need to understand the logical shift from our familiar "object" language about things in the world around us to a "metalanguage" about the ways our object-language sentences are related to things in the world – a logical structure displayed in a Tarskian formulation of the truth-conditions for basic forms of sentences in our object-language. The pattern of semantic relations constrains the meaning of sentences in the object-language.

Until Tarski, the new logic launched by Frege, in connection with the new mathematics of set theory, was a system of "logistic" focused on formal structures of language and their role in rules of inference in that language. In today's idiom early logic was primarily concerned with these aspects of syntax, affording well-defined systems of logical inference. Tarski's theory of truth, however, provided an explicit model for the relations between expressions and objects in the world; the truth-conditions for a form of sentence were thereby grounded in relations between language and world. Echoing Husserl in effect, Tarski's breakthrough to semantics in logic took the form of showing how the truth of a sentence depends on the assignments of objects to terms (and variables) in the formally specified language in which the sentence is written. Within the details of Tarski's theory of truth we see how language breaks through the veil of syntax and reaches out to things in the world: semantics is thereby adjoined to syntax in mathematical logic.

Already in the *Logical Investigations* (1900 – 01) Husserl distinguished different areas within "pure logic", where formal proofs are one thing and truth is another. The "logic of consequence" (*Konsequenzlogik*) analyzes forms of proof within a formal axiomatic system, whereas the "logic of truth" (*Wahrheitslogik*) analyzes correlations between sentences or the propositions they express and states of affairs in the world that make them true. Today, following Tarski's lead, logicians take proof theory as part of syntax and truth theory as part of semantics. (See the final chapter of Husserl's "Prolegomena to Pure Logic", launching the *Logical Investigations*, and see Tieszen 2005, Ch. 1, pp. 24 – 34, on Husserl's distinctions among levels of logic in Husserl's system of metalogic.)

In the practice of phenomenology we need to appreciate the way things are *presented in our conscious experience:* we need to take a *metalevel* perspective on our own experiences. In the practice of logic we need to appreciate the way things *appear in the truth-conditions* of our sentences. The mode of presentation of an entity in language is codified in an ideal meaning. Bernard Bolzano called this sort of meaning a *Vorstellung an sich*, a content presenting an individual object, or a *Satz an sich*, or proposition, a content presenting what Husserl would call a state of affairs, or *Sachverhalt*. Frege spoke subsequently of a *Sinn* ("sense") or a *Gedanke* ("thought"). We speak of a "proposition" presenting a "state of affairs" or "situation". How a meaning presents or represents something becomes the heart of Husserl's theory of intentionality. And so Husserl spoke of a *Sinn* (sense) or a *Satz* (proposition), a *Satz* presenting a *Sachverhalt* (state of affairs).

For Frege the logician, a *Sinn* embodies an *"Art des Gegebensein"*, a way of being given (to consciousness), a sense expressible in language. For Husserl the phenomenologist, a *Sinn* embodies the way an object of consciousness is "given" or "meant" (*gemeint*) in consciousness, a sense expressible in language. In a nutshell, semantics defines the relation between consciousness or language, sense, and object.

If semantics lives on the road between logic and phenomenology, that road is a two-way street. Logic brings logical form to phenomenology. In the same breath, phenomenology brings phenomenological form to logic.

§3 Semantic Perspectives from Kantian "Phenomena" to Husserlian Intentionality

The term "semantics" has an interesting history for the present study. Husserl spoke of "logic" but did not use "semantics" as a term of art (nor was there such a German term in his day). Tarski used the term "semantics" in his account of truth in logic (as in the title of Tarski 1944/2001), and in his wake (through Carnap and onward) logical theory came to distinguish "syntax", "semantics", and "pragmatics". In retrospect, however, the basic concepts of semantics took shape in different logical systems, from Frege to Husserl to Tarski to Carnap and on into model theory and possible worlds semantics in Hintikka and Kripke.

A perceptive account of the development of semantics is detailed by J. Alberto Coffa in *The Semantic Tradition from Kant to Carnap / To the Vienna Station* (1991). Michael Friedman (1999) has also pursued Kantian themes in Carnap's logical empiricism. Husserl's role in the development of mathematical logical theory – not least his relations with Georg Cantor, David Hilbert, and Herman Weyl – has been duly observed, but some historical links warrant close attention in the present study. Carnap attended Husserl's lectures in 1923–24 and 1925. Carnap's iconic work *Der logische Aufbau der Welt*, or *The Logical Structure of the World*, appeared in 1928. As Friedman notes, Carnap called his project *Konstitutionstheorie*, or theory of "constitution" (see Friedman 1999, Chapter 5, pp. 89–113). The term *"Aufbau"* appears in the title of Carnap's book, but it is not used as a technical term in the body of the work. Carnap's technical term is *"Konstitution"*, a term prominent in Husserl's *Ideas* I (1913) and used in neo-Kantian debates in Germany. Unfortunately, the English translation of the *Aufbau* translates *"Konstitution"* as "construction", losing completely the Husserlian legacy. For Husserl, the "constitution" of an object consists not in a structure *constructing* the object, as where a natural object is built up from sense-data (phenomenalism); rather, the "constitution" of an object consists in a structure of meanings that hang together, presenting the object with different aspects. In fact, Carnap's footnotes throughout the *Aufbau* explicitly track similar notions in Husserl's *Ideas* I (1913), which Carnap would have encountered in detail in Husserl's lectures. Carnap focused on "constitution" in formal terms, in the syntax of the new logic. His approach he called "methodological solipsism" (p. 102): instead of talking about things in themselves we are to talk about forms of language in which we ostensibly talk about worldly things, thereby eschewing "metaphysics" in favor of logical formulations understood only as if about the things in themselves.

Of course, Carnap is remembered as a strong advocate of logical empiricism, or logical positivism, resolutely opposed to "metaphysics" on empiricist grounds. However, a deeper register in Carnap's voice is resonant with Kantian themes, as Friedman has shown, but even more resoundingly, I would argue, with Husserlian phenomenology. In very recent "metametaphysical" debates, a Carnapian approach of "semantic ascent" approaches issues of metaphysics indirectly through conceptual-linguistic structures. This is the approach in Amie Thomasson (2015), *Ontology Made Easy*. Thomasson's perspective is not anti-realist or anti-metaphysical, yet she uses "semantic ascent" as a "cognitive shift" in a way that is akin to Husserlian epoché while assuming the world is there to be known and referred to as best we can.

Now, Husserl adopted the Kantian term "transcendental idealism", following his so-called "transcendental turn" around 1907. This "turn" brought the method of epoché or "bracketing" into Husserl's own evolving conception of phenomenology as "transcendental". But what is meant by "transcendental" and by "transcendental idealism"? As interpretations of Kant's "critical" philosophy vary widely, so too do interpretations of Husserl's "transcendental" phenomenology. For my purposes here, I should like to focus on the role of ideal meaning – Sinn, Satz, noema – as the "transcendental" structure of intentionality. I assume that Husserl's theory of noema (Sinn) and object allows the phenomenologist to move back and forth – in the practice of epoché – between objects of consciousness and the meanings through which they are "intended". This practice assumes a "semantic" conception of intentionality according to the present study. (See Smith 2013 on different interpretations of Husserl's "transcendental idealism".)

In the perceptive interpetations of Coffa and Friedman, a driving issue for logical theory after Kant – in Bolzano, Frege, Husserl, and Carnap – is how meaning figures in grounding analytic truths and/or synthetic a priori truths: whether by logical form (Bolzano) or by fundamental concepts (Kant's conceptual "categories of the understanding"). Kant's account of analyticity gave way to Bolzano's account of logical truth (Quine has offered a similar account), and Carnap's *Aufbau*. However, Tarski's semantic conception of truth shifted the philosophical lens of logic in a direction arguably contrary to a Kantian perspective.

In 1935 Tarski and Carnap met in Vienna, and Carnap later reported on their discussion:

> When Tarski told me for the first time that he had constructed a definition of truth, I assumed that he had in mind a syntactical definition of logical truth or provability. I was surprised when he said that he meant truth in the customary sense, including contingent factual truth. Since I was thinking only in terms of a syntactical metalanguage, I wondered how it was possible to state the truth-condition for a simple sentence like "this table is black". Tarski replied: "This is simple; the sentence 'this table is black' is true if and only if this table is black". (Carnap 1963, p. 60 on semantics. Compare Feferman and Feferman 2004, pp. 95 f.)

Tarski's example, in Carnap's recollection, is interesting from a phenomenological perspective. For the use of "this table" would normally rest on perceptual experience of the table, and the content of an experience of seeing the table at hand "intends" a concrete object before the speaker on that occasion. Indeed, Husserl explicitly addressed this feature of semantics for demonstrative pronouns used in expression of the content of perception. (See Husserl 2001/1900–01, Investigation VI, §§4–6.) Logical or analytic truth is not at hand. Though Carnap would go on to use "formal mode" versions of semantics (as in Carnap 1942), he credited Tarski with bringing semantics to logic beyond syntax. And in our present study that is equivalent to bringing intentionality to the table.

Kant's concern for "intuition" (*Anschauung*) notwithstanding, Husserl's theory of perceptual "intuition" shifts to the correlation between internal and external aspects of intentionality, between content and object of consciousness. Arguably, Kantian and neo-Kantian concerns with "phenomena" do not yet move us beyond meanings or concepts or language to things themselves in the surrounding world. But Husserl's model of intentionality requires just that move: from act through sense to objects in the world around us – specifically, where experience is successful or "veridical", as we say with allusion to truth. Such is the essence of intentionality on Husserl's theory.

Husserl's conception of "pure logic" featured the "logic of truth" (*Wahrheitslogik*) grounded in the structure of <act-Sinn-object>. That *semantic* structure wove through Husserl's conception of phenomenology from his "logical" orientation through his "transcendental" turn and into his late "life-world" pivot: from the *Logical Investigations* (1900–01) through *Ideas* I (1913) into *Formal and Transcendental Logic* (1929) and on into the *Crisis* (1935–38). Husserl's semantic model of intentionality thus moved beyond "syntactic" structures – whether Kant's "phenomena" or Carnap's "logical syntax of language" – and into the realm of truth, where veridical intentionality reaches into the world. (See Tieszen 2005 for a detailed study of the complexities in Husserl's treatment of logical notions of truth, analytic truth, synthetic truth, "definite" mathematical theories and correlated "definite manifolds", incompleteness of formal theories, and how Husserl's system of logic and phenomenology prefigured emerging conceptions of metalogic or metamathematics.)

§4 Husserl's Semantic Conception of Intentionality

In order to appreciate Husserl's "semantic" conception of intentionality, we need to see his theory of intentionality within a philosophical system that integrates phenomenology with logic – and with ontology and epistemology. That is in fact the holistic framework set out in his *Logical Investigations* (1900–01). And in the Prolegomena of the *Investigations* Husserl explicitly outlined a vision of "pure logic": a semantic conception of metalogic or metamathematics even before those terms took shape in Tarski's expressly "semantic" conception of "metalogic" and therewith of truth. The paramount structure in Husserl's semantic system of "pure logic" is the structure of <act-content-object>, the defining structure of intentionality, ideally expressible in language. That structure remains essential throughout Husserl's subsequent writing. Accordingly, rather than treating Husserl's "transcendental turn" (around 1907) as leaving behind the "logical" results of the *Logical Investigations* in favor of the "transcendental" phenomenology of *Ideas* I (1913), we should see Husserl's "transcendental" perspective as an extension of his "logical" perspective. (This metaphilosophical view of Husserl's system of philosophy is a guiding theme in my reconstruction of Husserl's system in Smith 2013.)

And then we can see in a new light the revolutionary significance of Husserl's methodology of epoché set forth in *Ideas* I. For the ancient skeptics, "epoché" meant withholding judgment. For Husserl, the practice of epoché meant we are to "bracket" the question of the actual existence of our surrounding world in order to turn our focus from *things in the world* to our *consciousness of* such things. In the practice of phenomenology, we reflect on the essence of consciousness, especially the way our acts of consciousness are intentionally directed (via their meaning-contents) as if toward things in the world around us. As we enter into *phenomenological reflection* on experience, then, we move from cognition to *meta-cognition*, from everyday consciousness-of-the-world to meta-consciousness of everyday consciousness.

That shift in focus is exactly parallel to a shift in logic from, for example, the sentence "snow is white" (asserting that in fact snow is white) to the metalinguistic sentence " 'snow is white' is true", and specifically to a formulation of truth-conditions for the sentence "snow is white":

"'Snow is white' is true if and only if snow is white".

In this metalinguistic sentence, our concern is the form of truth-conditions à la Tarski for our everyday sentence. Notice that the bi-conditional "if and only if" specifies the conditions that *would* make the sentence true *if and only if* those conditions obtain in the actual world. So in stating the truth-conditions for the sentence "snow is white" we have in effect "bracketed" the question of the actual truth of the sentence we are talking about. We are not therein asserting of the world that in actuality snow is white, though we still understand what that condition would consist in.

Similarly, in phenomenological reflection on, say, my experience of thinking "snow is white", by the practice of epoché I move from my concern with snow in thinking "snow is white" to a focus on the *meaning-content* in my thinking, which is the proposition <snow is white>, not on the actual state of affairs in the world [snow is white]. Yet I understand the intentional relation between the proposition and the state of affairs. In this way the methodology of epoché is based on the "semantic" conception of intentionality as the structure of act-content-object.

For Husserl as for Tarski, the meta-theoretical perspective opens into interesting complexities of phenomenological and logical structure. For instance, Husserl took the "determinable X" content in a perceptual experience to track the ostensible object through various possible scenarios, whereby the experience is successfully "of" that object just in case the object is appropriately "determined" or propertied in those scenarios. Similarly, at the level of language, Tarski took the variable "x" in (say) "some object x is white" to be assigned various possible objects, whereby the quantified sentence is true if and only if at least one such assignment to "x" actually "satisfies" the formula "x is white". Our immediate aim here, in any case, is simply to emphasize the significance of the shift in perspective to a higher "meta" level. (Husserl's notion of the "determinable X" in a noema is studied in Smith 2013 and Beyer 2013, as well as prior works including Smith and McIntyre 1982.)

One way of reading Husserl's phenomenology places Husserl's theory of intentionality primarily in the context of post-Kantian German idealism. This approach focuses, naturally enough, on "phenomena": phenomenology is the study of phenomena. But in what sense? Kant's doctrine of phenomena and noumena is interpreted in different ways, but the status of things in themselves is problematic on most interpretations. Husserl himself rejected the notion of a *Ding an sich* beyond the reach of intentional experience. But Husserl's own take on "phenomena" has in turn been interpreted in different ways. In particular, Husserl's notion of "noemata" can be seen as refining or simply replacing the prior notion of "phenomena", that is, insofar as Husserl falls within a Kantian tradition.

A very different way of reading Husserl's phenomenology places Husserl's theory of intentionality squarely in the context of emerging logical theory. From Bolzano to Lotze to Frege, the notion of ideal logical meanings took shape in contrast to any Kantian notion of "phenomena" as contents of consciousness. Remember that Husserl's intellectual milieu included Georg Cantor, David Hilbert, Herman Weyl, and Rudolf Carnap – Husserl worked explicitly with these foundational thinkers in modern mathematical logic. Then, in the 1930s, Kurt Gödel and Alfred Tarski changed mathematical logic with their ground-breaking mathematical results. Tarski referenced Husserl explicitly, we noted, as he formulated his technical "definition" of truth for formalized languages. Gödel later saw in Husserl's phenomenology a philosophical framework for a broadly Platonistic vision of logic. (On Husserl, Gödel, and varieties of Platonism in mathematics and phenomenology, see Tiezzen 2005 and 2011.)

Accordingly, the "semantic" conception of intentionality, hence of phenomenology, comes into a sharp focus as we come to appreciate the results of Tarski's subsequent "semantic" conception of truth and thus of metalogic and metamathematics. In Tarski's truth definition, we separate the metalanguage from the object language, but we keep the object language in view (on the right of the formula) as we say, " 'snow is white' is true if and only if snow is white". Similarly, in Husserl's phenomenology, by epoché we turn from (say) snow itself to our experience in seeing snow, but we keep the world of snow in view as we say, in phenomenological reflection, "my *seeing* snow is directed as if toward *snow*". In the methodology of epoché, then, we move back and forth between world and consciousness. With the structure of intentionality in mind, we know where we are: focused on snow in the Alps, or focused on our *experience* in seeing Alpine snow.

To the heart of Tarski's view of truth we now turn.

§5 Tarski's Conception of Semantics in his Semantic Conception of Truth

Opening the present essay, we outlined Tarski's semantic theory of truth. Now I should like to reflect on Tarski's theory considered as a formalization of a theory of intentionality expressed in language. "Semantics" can thus be seen as a theory of relations of "reference" not only between language and world, but also between consciousness and world.

In "The Semantic Conception of Truth and the Foundations of Semantics" (2001/1944), Tarski characterized *semantics* in a way that reflects a basic de facto conception of intentionality. In Tarski's words:

> *Semantics* is a discipline which, speaking loosely, *deals with certain relations between expressions of a language and the objects* (or "states of affairs") *"referred to"* by those expressions. ...
> While the words *"designates," "satisfies,"* and *"defines"* express relations (between certain expressions and the objects "referred to" by these expressions), the word *"true"* is of a different logical nature: it expresses a property (or denotes a class) of certain expressions, viz., of sentences. ... And, moreover, it turns out that the simplest and the most natural way of obtaining an exact definition of truth is one which involves the use of other semantic notions, e.g., the notion of satisfaction. It is for these reasons that we count the concept of truth which is discussed here among the concepts of semantics, and the problem of defining truth proves to be closely related to the more general problem of setting up the foundations of theoretical semantics. (Tarski 2001/1944, p. 336.)

As is clear from the course of Tarski's presentation, the theory of truth belongs to metalogic, and thus to metamathematics inasmuch as a mathematical theory is ideally a deductive theory formulated in the language of modern logic. Thus Tarski speaks of "the deductive system of logic—or of any discipline based upon logic, e.g., of semantics" (p. 350).

Tarski's characterization of semantics, in the passage above, can be seen as a mathematical-logical image – with duly increased precision – of a phenomenological theory of intentionality. If we replace "expression" with "experience", we can offer a paraphrase as follows:

> *Semantics* is a discipline which, speaking loosely, *deals with certain relations between experiences in a stream-of-consciousness and the objects* (or "states of affairs") *"referred to"* by those experiences. ...
> Thus, we count the concept of truth, or veridicality of experience, among the concepts of semantics, and the problem of truth proves to be closely related to the more general problem of setting up the foundations of theoretical semantics in phenomenology.

The *relations* between experiences and objects (or "states of affairs") "referred to" by those experiences are *intentional relations*, relations of *intentionality*. Each experience has a particular formal structure in what we may call the "logic" of consciousness. As expressions take their places in the logical structure of a given language, so experiences take their places in the phenomenological structure of a given stream of consciousness (with its intersubjective dimension in full force, like that of a language). Thus, on Husserl's analysis of time-consciousness, a presently occurring experience takes its place in a structure of *Ur*-experiences joined with retentions of past experiences and protentions of anticipated future experiences. Then, moving beyond this temporal "syntax", we can say that *truth* consists in the *veridical fit* between an experience (with noematic meaning) and its *object* if such exists. Hence, the problem of truth is central to the foundations of intentionality theory – or theoretical "semantics" in phenomenology.

When Tarski spoke of the "foundations" of semantics, as above (in Tarski 1944), he wrote in the context of *metalogic* or *metamathematics* – a discipline that was emerging around him in the 1930s. In a textbook titled *Introduction to Logic and to the Methodology of Deductive Sciences* (Tarski 1965/1941/1936), Tarski presented logic as the theory of "the deductive sciences", viz., mathematical sciences such as arithmetic, geometry, etc. The 1936 Polish edition of this text was titled *Introduction to Mathematical Logic and to the Methodology of Mathematics* (translating the title into English). Now, Husserl had conceived "pure logic" as "the theory of theories" – in the Prolegomena of the *Logical Investigations* (1900–01). By the time Tarski was writing, logic itself had become a mathematical deductive science – with theorems about decidability, completeness, and incompleteness in axiomatic theories. Indeed, it was in that period that Tarski presented his formal theory of truth in the "*Wahrheitsbegriff*" (Tarski 1983/1936/1933) – where, we noted earlier, Tarski alluded to Husserl's conception of categories in the Prolegomena.

And so we find Tarski writing in this textbook on logic as the methodology of deductive sciences, in effect, the mathematical theory of mathematical theories:

> The methodology of the deductive sciences became a general theory of deductive sciences in an analogous sense as arithmetic is the theory of numbers and geometry is the theory of geometrical configurations.

— whence:

> Methodology [of the deductive sciences] has become like those sciences which constitute its own subject matter – it has assumed the form of a deductive discipline. ... [I]ndeed, "methodology" means merely "the science of method". Consequently this expression is now often

replaced by others – for instance, by a (not altogether happy) term "theory of proof", or by a (much better) term "metalogic and metamathematics", which means about the same as "the science of logic and mathematics". Still another term is used, "syntax and semantics of deductive sciences", which stresses the analogy between the methodology of deductive sciences and the grammar of everyday language. (Tarski 1965: first passage above, p. 138; second passage, p. 140.)

In a footnote to the latter passage, Tarski adds:

> Methodology of the deductive sciences in its widened meaning is a young discipline. Its intensive development began only after 1920 – simultaneously (and, it seems, independently) in two different centers: Göttingen ... and Warsaw ...

Tarski there cites Hilbert and Bernays in Göttingen and Lesniewski and Lukasiewicz in Warsaw, and nods to "the contemporary American philosopher and logician (of German origin) R. Carnap", citing appreciatively Carnap's *Logische Syntax der Sprache* (Vienna, 1934; translated as *The Logical Syntax of Language* in Carnap 2002/1934).

§6 Semantics in Context with Husserl, Carnap, and Tarski

Husserl worked with Hilbert during Husserl's years in Göttingen, 1901–1916. In *Ideas* I (1913) Husserl developed his new "methodology" for phenomenology called "bracketing" or "phenomenological epoché" (§32); emphasizing "methodological considerations for phenomenology" (§63), he cited "phenomenology's relating back [*Rückbeziehung*] to itself" (§65). Accordingly, the *meta-phenomenological* structure in Husserl's methodology for phenomenology parallels the *meta-logical* structure in the emerging methodology for logic: in Hilbert et al., and subsequently in Carnap and Tarski.

But notice that Tarski spoke of "syntax *and* semantics" (as quoted above), whereas Carnap focused initially on "logical syntax" alone. Indeed, Carnap closed *The Logical Syntax of Language* (Carnap 2002/1934) with a declaration, "The Logic of Science is Syntax" (§86). For Carnap, we are most properly restricted – in a logically proper philosophy, as it were – to the "formal mode" of speech (syntax), where semantics is in effect collapsed into syntax. In fact, he warns of "The Dangers of the Material Mode of Speech" (§80) – as if we could refer to things in the world apart from the expressions we use. Is this anti-"semantic" perspective not a logical version of the method of "bracketing" any actual reference to objects in the world beyond our linguistic presentations of such objects?

Recall that Carnap studied with Husserl in 1924 in Freiburg, and in his *Aufbau* (1928) Carnap spoke of "methodological solipsism" in relation to Husserl's methodology of "bracketing" questions of the existence of the surrounding world. Under Tarski's influence, however, Carnap soon embraced semantics, albeit in his own terms. In the 1930s, as we noted earlier, Tarski pressed the case for "semantics" in the emerging discipline of mathematical logic, and Carnap adapted Tarski's theory of truth while retaining an empiricist suspicion of "metaphysics". (We noted Carnap's autobiographical report in Carnap 1963, p. 60 ff, and the biography of Tarski, Feferman and Feferman 2004.)

Reading Tarski's own words above, in this historical context, we should see that Tarski's methodology for logic, the methodology he called "metalogic" or "metamathematics", properly parallels Husserl's methodology for phenomenology. In this light we might speak of "transcendental" phenomenology as "meta-phenomenology". For in the *practice* of phenomenology we must analyze the structure of the experience of *phenomenological reflection* along with the structure of everyday experiences of perception and thought about the surrounding world. We can face the world itself in everyday experience, but we can reflect on consciousness itself in a *different level* of experience as we "bracket" the existence of the world beyond consciousness. Similarly, with Tarski's theory of truth we can knowingly move back and forth between reference to objects in the world and semantic reflection on expressions that ostensibly refer to objects in the world: between a sentence in the object-language and its quotation in the meta-language.

Accordingly, a Tarskian "semantic" perspective on Husserlian phenomenology helps us to put *intentionality* in a clear light. Not only are we *conscious of* things in the world around us, as we see and touch and think about objects like a ball or a hammer or a bicycle or an automobile. In the practice of phenomenology we are also *conscious of* our familiar *experiences* of seeing and touching and thinking about these objects in the world. These *intentional relations* between our experiences and their objects belong to the subject matter of *intentional semantics* in phenomenology, we might say.

In light of the historical links among Husserl, Carnap, and Tarski, it is interesting to consider how Carnap tended to link semantics with syntax: by staying within the purview of a "bracketed" semantics – a kind of reductive "transcendental idealism" for semantics. In his *Introduction to Semantics* (1942), Carnap explicitly addressed the status of "semantics" with an eye to principled philosophical views. Carnap wrote:

> While many philosophers today urge the construction of a system of semantics, others, especially among my fellow empiricists, are rather skeptical. They seem to think that prag-

matics – as a theory of the use of language – is unobjectionable, along with syntax as a purely formal analysis; but semantics arouses their suspicions. They are afraid that a discussion of propositions – as distinguished from sentences expressing them – and of truth – as distinguished from confirmation by observations – will open the back door to speculative metaphysics, which was put out at the front door. ...

... But the use of this method [i.e., the semantical method] for the construction of a theory of truth by Tarski and its use in the present book for the construction of a theory of logical deduction and a theory of interpretations of formal systems seems to justify the expectation that semantics will not only be of accidental help to pure logic but will supply the very basis for it. In addition, I believe, semantics will be of great importance for the so-called theory of knowledge and the methodology of mathematics and of empirical science. (Carnap 1942, pp. vii-viii.)

In this meta-theoretical passage we hear Carnap's logical echoes of a style of neo-Kantian "theory of knowledge and the methodology of mathematics and of empirical science". That perspective has been drawn in illuminating studies of Carnap's "logical empiricism" (see Friedman 1999.)

I have dwelt on these quotations above, as a conversation between Tarski and Carnap, because we see these two celebrated logicians wrestling in mathematical logic with a key issue in Husserl's phenomenology, an issue they would have been familiar with in their times and places. Where does "transcendental phenomenology" require – in Kantian terms – a stance of "empirical realism" (as in our object language) and where instead a stance of "transcendental idealism" (as in our meta-language)? Do we leave objects in the world behind as we ascend to contents of our consciousness?

Husserl characterized the *noema* of an act of consciousness in two quite different ways: (i) as the act's *sense*, or *Sinn*, and (ii) as the act's *object-as-intended*. In terms shared by Husserl and Kant, "phenomena" are objects *as they appear*, as they are given or "intended" in consciousness. In logical terms shared by Husserl and Frege, *Sinne* are timeless *meanings* in virtue of which acts are directed toward objects in consciousness. As metalogic wrestles with meaning and truth, so phenomenology wrestles with meaning and veridical intentionality. The *semantic* conception of truth and of intentionality leads to a sharp demarcation of the roles of act, content, and object in the structure of intentionality. We may have our phenomena and our worldly objects too, if we clearly distinguish objects in the world from contents presenting such objects: if we keep track of where we speak or think of each as we move between object language and metalanguage. (My take on this cluster of issues weaves through several chapters in Smith 2013.)

§7 From Tarskian Semantics to Hintikka's Possible Worlds Semantics for Intentional Modalities

The story we have been unfolding finds in Tarski's theory of truth a formal model of aspects of Husserl's theory of intentionality. We might well say that Tarski's mathematical model theory itself affords a metamathematical model of aspects of Husserl's theory of intentionality. Well, if only Husserl's theory, at least a part of it, could itself be "mathematized" to Tarski's "satisfaction" and in line with Husserl's *Crisis* intervention (differentiating a mathematical model from what it models).

A crucial part of Tarski's conception of metalogic is his conception of *model theory*, which is central to his conception of theoretical semantics and to his formal theory of truth. In model theory, an axiomatic theory (such as geometry) can be "modeled" by an *interpretation* that correlates a formal *model* with sentences in the theory: where a *model* is defined as a set-theoretic structure, an ordered tuple, consisting of a set of objects, called the *domain*, and a set of relations among objects in the domain, where an n-place *relation* is treated as a set of ordered n-tuples of objects in the domain. Then a sentence in the theory is *true in a given model* just in case it is "satisfied" by appropriate objects in appropriate relations in the model. (The technical construction of the truth-definition features the satisfaction of open sentences with variables, as detailed in the *Wahrheitsbegriff*, Tarski 1983/1936/1933, and cited in the more informal essay, Tarski 2001/1944. Tarski 1965/1941/1936 includes an introduction to model theory: see pp. 120 ff.)

In the 1940s and 1950s, formal semantics was extended to systems of modal logic, and since the 1960s *models* have been treated as formal analogues of possible situations or "possible worlds", with metaphysics resurgent. Truth-conditions are formulated for *modal* sentences accordingly:

"Necessarily p" is true if and only if "p" is true in all possible worlds.

"Possibly p" is true if and only if "p" is true in some possible world.

Jaakko Hintikka, one of the founders of possible worlds semantics, proposed to treat the language of "propositional attitudes" in the form of modal logic. Thus, truth-conditions for propositional (intentional) attitudes would take the form:

"A believes that p" is true if and only if "p" is true in all doxastically possible worlds for the believer A.

> "A perceives that p" is true if and only if "p" is true in all perceptually possible worlds for the perceiver A.

In Hintikka's model for intentionality, an act of consciousness is, as it were, *directed* toward objects bearing properties and relations *in various possible worlds*, "small worlds" or situations, that are *compatible with* the content of the intentional state ascribed. Where Leibniz conceived of metaphysically possible worlds, Hintikka conceived of limited "worlds" delimited by a subject's beliefs or perceptions, depending on the intentional "modality" at stake. (See Hintikka 1962, 1969, 1975.)

In our book *Husserl and Intentionality* (Smith and McIntyre 1982), Ronald McIntyre and I developed a reconstruction of Husserl's theory of intentionality that drew on both Frege's semantics of *Sinn*-and-*Bedeutung* and Hintikka's possible worlds semantics for intentional experiences in the form of propositional attitudes. On our construction, an intentional experience is directed via its noematic Sinn toward objects in a potential "horizon" of possibilities left "open" or "motivated" by the Sinn in the content of the experience. Husserl's theory of *horizon*, we proposed, can be elaborated in a possible-worlds framework along Hintikkian lines. (See Smith and McIntyre 1982, Chapters V–VIII.)

Of special interest to phenomenology is Hintikka's semantics for perception sentences. Consider a striking case of perception as described by Husserl. Suppose I am visiting a wax museum. I see a woman on a staircase waving toward me. We may describe my visual experience by saying (in the third person):

> "Smith sees that the woman on the stair is waving".

On Hintikka's possible-worlds semantics, this sentence has truth-conditions we may formulate as follows:

> "Smith sees that the woman on the stair is waving" is true (in the actual world) if and only if: in every perceptually possible world W compatible with what Smith sees, the woman on the stair is waving.

Following Husserl's example, I soon notice that "the woman on the stair" is a wax figure. So as it happens the propositional content of my perception is not satisfied in the actual world – there is no woman on the stair, but only a wax figure. Yet the content of my perception is satisfied in each world *compatible with what I see*. As Husserl would say, the situation that "she" is a wax figure is not a "motivated" possibility for my original visual experience, and the content of my original experience "explodes" as I realize my mistake.

As semantic theory has evolved in logic, then, from Tarski to Hintikka, we can see in these formal constructions reflections of phenomenological structures in our language describing intentional experience.

§8 Intentionality, Truth, and Paradox

Within his theory of truth Tarski sought to block the ancient *liar paradox* by distinguishing object language and metalanguage. The liar paradox can take shape in several forms of sentence including:

"I am now lying",

"this sentence is not true",

or an adaptation from Tarski's variant:

(L) "L is not true",

where "L" is a name of the sentence so quoted. This sentence, L, is self-contradictory. For its truth-conditions, in Tarskian style, are:

(TL)   "L is not true" is true if and only if L is not true.

That is to say:

L is true if and only if L is not true.

On pain of contradiction, then, L can be neither true nor false.

On Tarski's diagnosis, the problem is that the liar sentence (in one form or another) applies the predicate "is true" *within the same language* as that of the sentences to which the predicate is applied. If we place sentences ascribing truth in a separate *metalanguage*, then we block truth-ascriptions like the "liar" sentence from the assumed base object language. (See the discussion in Tarski 2001/1944, sections 7–9. Compare Sainsbury 2009, Chapter 6, and note the discussion of indexicality in sections 6.7 and 6.8.)

Husserl did not address the liar paradox. But we may formulate a parallel paradox in "inner speech". Consider an act of consciousness wherein:

(N)   I think "this very thought is not true".

The *truth-conditions* for my thought – for my act of so thinking, with noematic content <this very thought is not true> – are as follows:

(TN)   My thinking "this very thought is not true" is true

if and only if this very thought is not true.

Well, now, this very thought – my act N of so thinking – just is:

my thinking "this very thought is not true".

So, by TN: the thought N is true if and only if the thought N is not true.

Thus, we land in contradiction. Here we face an *inner liar* paradox.

I take "thinking" here to carry assertoric or "positing" force in thinking that something is actually the case. Husserl spoke of "judgment" (*Urteil*) in this sense, but the flavor of the English term "judging" is rather too loaded with active deliberation, so I prefer the simpler "thinking" for present purposes.

As observed above, Husserlian epoché can be seen as paralleling semantic ascent into a Tarskian metalanguage. As we "bracket" factual claims about the surrounding world, claims in our everyday *object language* (about "objects" in the world), we move into a *metalanguage* of "pure" phenomenology. Suppose:

I think "snow is white".

Then in phenomenological reflection I may proceed to make claims about the *content* of my experience of thinking "snow is white", say, as I think in reflection:

I think "the content of my thinking 'snow is white'

is propositional in form".

For present purposes we treat my act of so thinking as an "inner speech act". (We'll not worry here about what it is to think in a language, merging language and thought.)

Now suppose I ascribe *truth* to my thought about snow, as I think thus:

I think "my thinking 'snow is white' is true".

In this higher-order experience I think that my prior thought is *true*, i.e., that my experience of thinking "snow is white" is *intentionally related* to *the actual condition* that snow is white. In that case I mix object language – in my thinking-about-*snow* – with metalanguage – in my thinking-about-*my-thinking-about-snow*. When we ascribe *truth* to a thought, then, we break back through the "brackets" and ascribe to the "pure" act-of-thinking a successful intentional relation to an existing *condition in the world*. The semantic theory of intentionality recognizes truth as a successful intentional relation of this sort. No problem so far in thinking about truth.

But now our inner Tarski steps forth. If I think "this very thought is not true", then my thought is self-contradictory: it is true if and only if it is not true.

Here we face a problematic form of intentionality: *in the same thought* I reflect on my "pure" act-of-thinking and I deny the *truth* of my act of so thinking, i.e. its veridical intentional relation to some ostensible condition in the actual world. What could that condition be – the thought's condition of truth being its untruth? In metaphenomenological analysis we should see that the *phenomenology* of this form of thinking is uniquely paradoxical. Its *content* <this very thought is not true> renders the *act* self-negating, self-defeating. Indeed, as I attempt to think "this very thought is not true", I cannot even understand *what I have thought* in so thinking.

What has gone wrong in this proposed form of thinking? With an eye to the practice of epoché, we may find a diagnosis. For, in the *very same act of consciousness* as I think "this very thought is not true":

(i) I place the world, and any question of truth, in brackets as I think about my "pure" act of thinking,

and

(ii) I break back through the brackets as I deny the truth of my so thinking.

Interestingly, the "logical" problem is both *semantic*, featuring a logically corrupt noematic *Sinn*, and *pragmatic*, featuring an act of thinking that cannot be executed consistently or coherently owing to its own noematic content. The logical problem lies not in thinking about truth per se, but in attempting to think – in phenomenological reflection – about the untruth of that very act of thinking.

Phenomenology does not live by epoché alone. Epoché is a technique for helping us to focus on consciousness itself, even on our own activities of consciousness. As we learn to distinguish the contents from the objects of our own acts of consciousness, we come to frame the principles of the theory of intentionality – articulating, along broadly Husserlian lines, the structure of a successful intentional relation between act and object via content. We then see *truth* as a successful intentional relation between a thought and what it "intends" in the world. The problem with the inner liar thought is that it pretends to step inside the act of thinking "this very thought is not true" – bracketing the role of that act in the surrounding world – while also stepping outside that act in asserting the untruth of that very act of thinking, that is, asserting the failure of the "intended" state of affairs in the act. But I cannot both pull back from the world and simultaneously stand in the world.

While the intentionality of consciousness is brought to the fore in the practice of epoché, we do not remain stranded in "pure" consciousness. As we distinguish act, content, and object, in the semantic conception of intentionality, we zig-zag back and forth between world and consciousness in the structure <act, noematic content, object>. ... By the way, in the *Crisis* (1935–38) Husserl himself spoke of a "zig-zag" (*Zickzack*) in "a sort of circle" in this movement between life-world and consciousness in the methodology of phenomenology. (See Husserl 1970/1935 – 38, § 9 l, p. 58.)

Bibliography

Betti, Arianna, "Kazimierz Twardowski", The Stanford Encyclopedia of Philosophy (Summer 2011 Edition), Edward N. Zalta (ed.), URL = <http://plato.stanford.edu/archives/sum2011/entries/twardowski/>.

Beyer, Christian. 2013. "Noema and Reference". In Michael Frauchiger, editor, *Reference, Rationality, and Phenomenology: Themes from Føllesdal*. Frankfurt and Paris: Ontos Verlag. pp. 73 – 88.

Carnap, Rudolf. 2003/1928. *The Logical Structure of the World and Pseudoproblems in Philosophy*. Translated by Rolf A. George. Chicago and La Salle, Illinois: Open Court. German original, *Der Logische Aufbau der Welt*, 1928, published by Felix Meiner Verlag.

Carnap, Rudolf. 2002/1934. *The Logical Syntax of Language*. Translated by Amethe Smeaton. Chicago and LaSalle, Illinois: Open Court. German original, 1934. English translation originally published, 1937.

Carnap, Rudolf. 1942. *Introduction to Semantics*. Cambridge, Massachusetts: Harvard University Press.

Carnap, Rudolf. 1963. "Intellectual Autobiography". In Paul Arthur Schipp, editor, *The Philosophy of Rudolf Carnap*. LaSalle, Illinois: Open Court, 1963. pp. 3 – 84.

Coffa, J. Alberto. 1991. *The Semantic Tradition from Kant to Carnap: To the Vienna Station*. Cambridge and New York: Cambridge University Press.

Davidson, Donald. 1984/1967. "Truth and Meaning". In Donald Davidson, Inquiries into Truth and Interpretation. Oxford and New York: Oxford at the Clarendon Press. pp. 17 – 36. Originally published in 1967.

Dreyfus, Hubert L. 1982. Editor (with Harrison Hall). *Husserl, Intentionality, and Cognitive Science*. Cambridge, Massachusetts: MIT Press.

Feferman, Anita Burdman, and Feferman, Solomon. 2004. *Alfred Tarski: Life and Logic*. Cambridge and New York: Cambridge University Press.

Friedman, Michael. 1999. *Reconsidering Logical Positivism*. Cambridge and New York: Cambridge University Press.

Hill, Claire Ortiz, and Rosado Haddock, Guillermo E. 2000. *Husserl or Frege?: Meaning, Objectivity, and Mathematics*. Chicago and LaSalle, Illinois: Open Court.

Hintikka, Jaakko. 1962. *Knowledge and Belief: An Introduction to the Logic of the Two Notions*. Ithaca, New York: Cornell University Press.

Hintikka, Jaakko. 1969. *Models for Modalities: Selected Essays*. Dordrecht and Boston: D. Reidel Publishing Company, now Springer.

Hintikka, Jaakko. 1975. *The Intentions of Intentionality and Other New Models for Modalities*. Dordrecht and Boston: D. Reidel Publishing Company, now Springer.

Husserl, Edmund. 2001/1900 – 01. *Logical Investigations*, Volumes One and Two. Translated by J. N. Findlay. Edited and Revised by Dermot Moran. London and New York: Routledge,

2001. German original, first edition, 1900–01; second edition, 1913, 1920. English translation, first edition, 1970. 1900/2001.

Husserl, Edmund. 1965/1911. "Philosophy as Rigorous Science". In *Edmund Husserl: Phenomenology and the Crisis of Philosophy*, including the essays "Philosophy as Rigorous Science" and "Philosophy and the Crisis of European Man", translated with an introduction by Quentin Lauer. New York: Harper & Row, 1965. "Philosophy as Rigorous Science", translated from the German original, "Philosophie als strenge Wissenschaft" (written in 1911), *Logos*, I (1910–11), pp. 289–341.

Husserl, Edmund. 2014/1913. *Ideas* I, i.e. *Ideas for a Pure Phenomenology and Phenomenological Philosophy. First Book: General Introduction to Pure Phenomenology*. Translated by Daniel O. Dahlstrom. Indianapolis/Cambridge: Hackett Publishing Company. German original, 1913. Called *Ideas* I.

Husserl, Edmund. 1969/1929. *Formal and Transcendental Logic*. Translated by Dorion Cairns. The Hague: Martinus Nijhoff. (Now: New York: Springer.) 1969. German original 1929.

Husserl, Edmund. 1960/1929. "Phenomenology", translated by C. V. Solomon, reprinted from the article, "Phenomenology", by Edmund Husserl, in the 14th edition of the *Encyclopaedia Britannica* (1929).

Husserl, Edmund. 1970/1935–38. *The Crisis of European Sciences and Transcendental Phenomenology: An Introduction to Phenomenological Philosophy*. Translated by David Carr. Evanston: Northwestern University Press, 1970. Original German manuscripts written, 1935–1938. German edition first published 1954. 1935–38/1970.

Lynch, Michael P., editor. 2001. *The Nature of Truth: Classic and Contemporary Perspectives*. Cambridge, Massachusetts: MIT Press.

Parsons, Charles. 2012. *From Kant to Husserl: Selected Essays*. Cambridge, Massachusetts: Harvard University Press.

Sainsbury, R. M. 2009. *Paradoxes*. Cambridge and New York: Cambridge University Press. Third edition, slightly revised from prior editions, the first edition published in 1987.

Smith, David Woodruff. 1975. "Meinongian Objects". *Grazer Philosophische Studien*, Vol. 1 (1975), pp. 43–71.

Smith, David Woodruff. 1989. *The Circle of Acquaintance: Perception, Consciousness, and Empathy*. Dordrecht and Boston: Kluwer Academic Publishers, now Springer.

Smith, David Woodruff. 2002. "Mathematical Form in the World". *Philosophia Mathematica* (3) Vol. 10 (2002) 102–129.

Smith, David Woodruff. 2002a. "Intentionality and Picturing: Early Husserl vis-à-vis Early Wittgenstein". In Terry Horgan, John Tienson, and Matjaz Potrc, editors, *Origins: The Common Sources of the Analytic and Phenomenological Traditions* (proceedings of the Spindel Conference 2001; *The Southern Journal of Philosophy*, Volume XL, Supplement 2002; published by the Department of Philosophy, The University of Memphis), pp. 153–180.

Smith, David Woodruff. 2005. "Truth and Experience: Tarski vis-à-vis Husserl". In M. E. Reicher and J. C. Marek, editors, *Experience and Analysis. Erfahrung und Analyse. The Proceedings of the 27th International Wittgenstein Symposium*. Vienna: öbv Et hpt, Verlagsgesellschaft mbH & Co. KG, Vienna, 2005), pp. 270–284. [Publisher: öbv Et hpt = Österreicher Bundesverlag Schulbuch / Hölder Pichler Tempsky.]

Smith, David Woodruff. 2013. *Husserl*. London and New York: Routledge. Second edition, revised and expanded from the first edition published by Routledge in 2007.

Smith, David Woodruff. 2016. "Truth and Epoché: The Semantic Conception of Truth in Phenomenology". In Bell, Jeffrey A.; Cutrofello, Andrew; and Livingston, Paul. Editors. *Beyond the Analytic-Continental Divide: Pluralist Philosophy in the Twenty-First Century*. London and New York: Routledge.

Smith, David Woodruff, and McIntyre, Ronald. 1982. *Husserl and Intentionality: A Study of Mind, Meaning, and Language*. Dordrecht and Boston: D. Reidel Publishing Company, now Springer.

Tarski, Alfred. 1983/1936/1933. "The Concept of Truth in Formalized Languages". In Alfred Tarski, *Logic, Semantics, Meta-Mathematics: Papers from 1923 to 1938*. Translated by J. H. Woodger. Oxford: Oxford at the Clarendon Press, 1956, reprinted 1983, pp. 152–278. Translated from the German edition of 1936, following the original Polish edition of 1933 from the 1931 presentation. New edition, Indianapolis: Hacket, 1983. Often referred to as "the *Wahrheitsbegriff*", from the title of the 1936 German version.

Tarski, Alfred. 1965/1941/1936. *Introduction to Logic and to the Methodology of Deductive Sciences*. New York: Oxford University Press, New York. First published in 1941. Translated into English by Olaf Helmer from the German edition of 1937. Based with some revision on the original Polish edition published in 1936, translated into German in 1937 as *Einführung in die mathematische Logik und in die Methodologie der Mathematik* (*Introduction to Mathematical Logic and to the Methodology of Mathematics*).

Tarski, Alfred. 2001/1944. "The Semantic Conception of Truth and the Foundations of Semantics". In Michael P. Lynch, editor, *The Nature of Truth: Classic and Contemporary Perspectives*. Cambridge, Massachusetts: MIT Press, 2001, pp. 331–363. Reprinted from the original edition in *Philosophy and Phenomenological Research*, 4 (1944).

Thomasson, Amie. 2015. *Ontology Made Easy*. Oxford and New York: Oxford University.

Tieszen, Richard. 2005. *Phenomenology, Logic, and the Philosophy of Mathematics*. Cambridge and New York: Cambridge University Press.

Tieszen, Richard. 2011. *After Gödel: Platonism and Rationalism in Mathematics and Logic*. Oxford and New York: Oxford University Press.

Twardowski, Kasimir. 1977/1894. *On the Content and Object of Presentations* [*Vorstellungen*]. Translated by R. [Reinhardt] Grossmann. The Hague: Martinus Nijhoff. German original 1894.

Verena Mayer
Der *Logische Aufbau* als Plagiat
Oder: Eine Einführung in Husserls System der Konstitution

Abstract: When Carnap published his famous book *Der logische Aufbau der Welt* in 1928 he was a member of the Vienna Circle and seemingly had nothing to do with the phenomenology of Edmund Husserl. However, as diaries and letters prove, he was Husserl's student for several years and even wanted him to supervise his „Habilitationsschrift". In this paper the biographical background of the *Aufbau* is reconstructed in some detail. Hereafter close similarities between the *Aufbau* and writings of Husserl are detected. There are many striking parallels between the *Aufbau* and Husserl's genetic phenomenology, especially as presented in *Ideen II*. They concern basic ideas and notions, as well as the constitutional steps and the transitional definitions from bottom to top. The many correlations between the *Aufbau* and Husserl's phenomenology even suggest the suspicion of plagiarism.

1	**Die Frage nach der Urheberschaft**	**176**
2	**Der biographische Hintergrund**	**179**
2.1	Die Jahre 1920–1923(1)	179
2.2	Die Jahre 1923(2)-26	186
3	**Die offenen Bezugnahmen auf Husserl und die Phänomenologie**	**195**
3.1	Die Bedeutung der „Phänomenologie"	195
3.2	Das Konstitutionssystem als eine „Mathesis der Erlebnisse"	196
3.3	Die Epoché, die eigenpsychische Basis und der Erlebnisstrom	199
4	**Der *Aufbau* und das Stufenmodell der *Ideen II***	**201**
4.1	Die naturalistische Einstellung	204
4.2	Der Begriff der Konstitution	206
4.3	Das Konstitutionssystem	208
4.4	Das materielle Ding und das unwirkliche Ding	210
4.5	Sinnendinge, Sehdinge und Empfindungen	211
4.6	Mein Leib	215
4.7	Das physikalische Ding	217
4.8	Das Eigenpsychische und das reale seelische Subjekt	218
4.9	Animalia und die biologischen Gegenstände	221
4.10	Einfühlung und Ausdrucksbeziehung	222
4.11	Der Mensch und die intersubjektive Welt	225
4.12	Die geistige Welt	227
4.13	Werte	229
4.14	Zusammenfassung	231
5	**Andere Anleihen bei Husserl**	**231**
5.1	Rationale Nachkonstruktion	232

5.2 Die Ähnlichkeitserinnerung —— 234
6   Die Methoden der Maskierung —— 236
6.1 Übersetzung und definitorische Umdeutung —— 237
6.2 Der Umgang mit Literaturangaben —— 238
6.3 Der vorgebliche Stellenwert des Konstitutionssystems —— 239
6.4 Biographische Angaben —— 240
6.5 Scheinbare und implizite Husserlkritik —— 241
7   Einwände —— 248
7.1 Weshalb das Plagiat nicht entdeckt wurde —— 248
7.2 Carnap als ethische Persönlichkeit —— 249
7.3 Carnap als Neukantianer? —— 250
8   Fazit —— 254
    Literatur —— 256

1 Die Frage nach der Urheberschaft

Ein Plagiat ist nach allgemeiner Auffassung eine bewusste Aneignung fremden Geistesguts unter Anmaßung der eigenen Urheberschaft und stellt in vielen Fällen juristisch eine Verletzung des Urheberrechts dar. Obwohl die Kriterien für die Bewertung eines Textes als Plagiat und gleichzeitig die Kriterien für die korrekte Verwendung fremder Gedanken in eigenen Werken sich in den letzten Jahrzehnten in mancher Hinsicht verändert haben, wird doch das Plagiieren schon lange verurteilt. Viel zitiert wird heute die Definition von Paul Englisch aus dem Jahr 1933, in der es, zeitnah zum *Aufbau*, heißt:

> Plagiat ist [...] die aus freier Entschließung eines Autors oder Künstlers betätigte Entnahme eines nicht unbeträchtlichen Gedankeninhalts eines anderen für sein Werk in der Absicht, solche Zwangsanleihe nach ihrer Herkunft durch entsprechende Umgestaltung zu verwischen und den Anschein eigenen Schaffens damit beim Leser oder Beschauer zu erwecken. (Englisch 1933, S.81f.)

Der heute im Vordergrund stehende Fall des wörtlichen Abschreibens steht hier also gar nicht erst zur Debatte. Vielmehr geht es um eine undeklarierte Übernahme von Ideen.

Um zu zeigen, dass ein bestimmtes Werk ein Plagiat *im Sinne von Englisch* ist (der juristische Nachweis sei hier ausgeklammert), muss also gezeigt werden, dass nicht unbeträchtliche Gedankeninhalte aus dem Werk eines anderen Autors stammen, ohne dass diese Urheberschaft angezeigt wurde. Drei Punkte sind dabei erwähnenswert: Zum einen würde man im Sinne Englischs eine Schrift auch dann als Plagiat bezeichnen, wenn das ungenannte Quellenwerk zum Zeitpunkt der Veröffentlichung des Plagiats noch nicht publiziert war. Dies würde wohl sogar einen besonders perfiden Fall des Ideendiebstahls darstellen. Ein zweiter Punkt betrifft den Inhalt: Man würde auch dann ein Werk als Plagiat bezeichnen, wenn die Darstellung den Inhalt des Originals nicht exakt so wiedergibt, wie es vom Autor intendiert war. Ein Plagiator beabsichtigt nicht eine werkgetreue Exegese, sondern bedient sich der Ideen des Anderen zu eigenen Zwecken, wobei diese Ideen in der Regel wohl mehr oder weniger modifiziert werden dürften. Wir würden den Vorwurf des Plagiats nicht mit dem Hinweis zurückweisen können, dass die entwendeten Stellen ja im Original nicht genau so gemeint waren wie im Plagiat. Drittens würden wir ein Werk auch dann als Plagiat bezeichnen, wenn Schlüsselbegriffe der Quelle umbenannt oder umdefiniert, aber inhaltlich im selben Sinne verwendet wurden. Die Umbenennung zählt dann zur Verschleierung des Ideendiebstahls. Man könnte einwenden, dass die beiden letzten Kriterien den Begriff des Plagiats unanwendbar machen, da im Einzelfall schwer nachweisbar sein dürfte, ob ein Teil eines Werkes originale Leistung des Autors oder verfälschte und umbenannte Übernahme von Gedanken eines Anderen ist. In einem solchen Fall jedoch würde eine große Menge von Ähnlichkeiten zusammen mit anderen Hinweisen aus dem Umfeld und der Motivation des Autors den Plagiatsverdacht wesentlich erhärten. Alle diese Punkte betreffen, wie sich noch zeigen soll, das hier diskutierte Werk, und zwar bezüglich einer ganzen Anzahl von Übernahmen.

Im Vorwort zur ersten Auflage seines Buchs *Der logische Aufbau der Welt* von 1928 scheint Carnap die Frage der Urheberschaft unmittelbar anzusprechen. Dort heißt es:

> Was ist die Absicht eines wissenschaftlichen Buchs? Es stellt Gedanken dar und will den Leser von ihrer Gültigkeit überzeugen. Darüber hinaus aber will der Leser auch wissen: woher kommen diese Gedanken und wohin führen sie? (*Aufbau*, XVII)

Diese zweite Frage möchte Carnap in seinem Vorwort kurz andeutungsweise beantworten. Carnap nennt keine Namen. Er verweist auf die „neue Logik", welche zur Begriffsklärung eingesetzt werden solle, auf die Idee, mit ihrer Hilfe die Erkenntnisse auf wenige „Wurzelbegriffe" zurückzuführen, und auf eine gewisse wissenschaftliche Grundeinstellung. In diesem Zusammenhang schreibt er:

> Die Grundeinstellung und die Gedankengänge dieses Buchs sind nicht Eigentum des Verfassers allein, sondern gehören einer bestimmten wissenschaftlichen Atmosphäre an, die ein Einzelner weder erzeugt hat, noch umfassen kann. (LA XVIII)

Generationen von Lesern haben dies wohl als Ausdruck von wissenschaftlicher Bescheidenheit verstanden, wobei jene Atmosphäre, aus der die Gedanken des *Logischen Aufbau* entsprungen sein sollen, selbstverständlich als die des Wiener Kreises und ihres Logischen Empirismus gedeutet wurde. Dass es sich hier um das implizite Geständnis eines Plagiators handeln könne, erscheint geradezu abwegig. In wohltuendem Unterschied zu den akademischen Gepflogenheiten seiner Zeit führt Carnap nämlich in seinem Literaturverzeichnis eine beträchtliche Anzahl von Autoren auf, die darüber hinaus (und zur Verwirrung der Interpreten) keineswegs alle oder auch nur in der Mehrzahl dem Umfeld des Wiener Kreises zuzurechnen sind, darunter Cassirer, Rickert und Husserl. Auch zu den einzelnen Kapiteln gibt es oft mehr oder weniger ausführliche Literaturverweise. Von Husserl nennt Carnap zwei Werke: die *Logischen Untersuchungen* und den ersten Band der *Ideen zu reinen Phänomenologie und phänomenologischen Philosophie* (im Folgenden abgekürzt als *Ideen I*[1]). Der Vorwurf des Plagiats betrifft Carnaps *Aufbau* zum einen in Bezug auf diese beiden Werke. Es lässt sich zeigen[2], dass Carnap eine ganze Reihe von Begriffen und Ideen aus beiden Schriften entnimmt, ohne ihre Herkunft zu kennzeichnen. Wesentlich jedoch ist auch eine Schrift Husserls, die zur „heißen Phase" der Entstehung des *Aufbau*, nämlich im Wesentlichen im Jahr 1925, nicht in publizierter Form vorlag. Es geht hier um den zweiten Band der *Ideen zu einer reinen Phänomenologie*, der den Titel *Phänomenologische Untersuchungen zur Konstitution* trägt (im Folgenden abgekürzt als *Ideen II*).[3] Der Vorwurf lautet, dass Carnap wesentliche Teile und Grundgedanken des *Aufbau* durch „Zwangsanleihen" aus diesem Manuskript erstellt und diese Herkunft im Folgenden bewusst maskiert hat. Die Verschleierung betrifft sowohl Maßnahmen in der publizierten Version des *Aufbau*, als auch die Darstellung von der Entstehung des Werkes, die Carnap später in seiner Autobiographie zeichnet. Im Folgenden wird der Frage des Plagiats vor allem in Bezug auf diesen zweiten Band der *Ideen* nachgegangen.

Ich gebe zunächst einen Überblick über die biographische Sachlage (2), stelle unter (3) die offenen und unter (4) und (5) die verborgenen Bezüge auf Husserl dar, behandle anschließend unter (6) die Methoden, mit deren Hilfe Carnap seine Zwangsanleihen maskiert und diskutiere unter (7) einige Einwände gegen die Plagiatsthese.[4]

---

1 HUA III/1.
2 und ist bereits von Rosado-Haddock 2008 gezeigt worden.
3 Husserliana Band IV. Die Edition der Husserliana wird im Folgenden wie üblich als Hua zitiert.
4 Die folgende Untersuchung wäre nicht möglich gewesen ohne die freundliche Unterstützung durch verschiedene Personen und Institutionen. Ich danke insbesondere Thomas Vongehr und dem Husserl Archiv Leuven, Brigitte Parakenings vom Philosophischen Archiv der Universität Konstanz sowie Margret Heitmann vom Jonas Cohn Archiv des Steinheim Instituts Essen; ebenso danke ich den Herausgebern der Urtexte der *Ideen II*, Dirk Fonfara und Dieter Lohmar, die mir das Manuskript zur Verfügung gestellt haben, sowie Christian Damböck für seinen unermüdlichen Einsatz für die Transkription und Herausgabe des Carnap-Nachlasses. Ganz besonders aber danke

2 Der biographische Hintergrund

Carnap hat seine Beziehung zu Husserl und dem phänomenologischen Kreis in Freiburg Zeit seines Lebens verschwiegen. Lange hielt sich deshalb das Gerücht, es habe keinerlei Kontakt zwischen Carnap und Husserl und auch kein Interesse Carnaps an der Phänomenologie bestanden – wohl ein Grund, weshalb die vorhandenen phänomenologischen Bezugnahmen im *Aufbau* von den Interpreten nie verfolgt wurden.[5] Da das Manuskript der *Ideen II* zur Zeit der Abfassung des *Aufbau* nicht veröffentlicht war, muss also zunächst gezeigt werden, dass und wie Carnap darauf Zugriff gehabt haben könnte. Allgemeiner ist zu klären, womit sich Carnap in dieser Zeit philosophisch beschäftigt hat und welche Themen im Vordergrund standen.

Im Folgenden geht es um die Jahre 1920–1926, in denen Carnap in Buchenbach bei Freiburg lebte. Im ersten Teil werden die Jahre 1920–1923 dargestellt, soweit sie durch Briefe, Tagebücher oder andere Schriften dokumentiert sind. Im zweiten Teil befassen wir uns mit den Jahren 1924–1926, der Zeit der konkreten Arbeit an der Habilitationsschrift, aus welcher der *Aufbau* hervorging. Diese Darstellung geht auf den Inhalt der Texte, die Carnap zwischen 1920 und 1926 verfasst hat – abgesehen vom *Aufbau* selbst – nur oberflächlich und nur insoweit ein, als Bezüge zum *Aufbau* erkennbar sind. Eine Interpretation ist hier nicht beabsichtigt. Die Frage, inwieweit diese Texte außerdem auch neukantianische oder andere Bezugnahmen enthalten, bleibt hier unberücksichtigt.[6]

2.1 Die Jahre 1920–1923(1)

2.1.1 Das philosophische Forschungsprogramm

Im Jahr 1919 siedelte Carnap mit seiner Frau und den beiden Töchtern von Jena nach Buchenbach bei Freiburg über, wo seine Schwiegereltern lebten. Carnap hatte zuerst erwogen, Lehrer zu werden und in Jena auch das Oberlehrerexamen

---

ich Guillermo Rosado Haddock für seine kenntnisreiche Unterstützung und die Bereitschaft, dieses weit über alles übliche Maß angewachsene Manuskript zu publizieren.

5 In der Ausgabe der *Scheinprobleme der Philosophie* aus dem Jahr 1966 schreibt etwa der Herausgeber Günther Patzig, Carnap habe wohl keinen Kontakt zu Husserl aufgenommen, als er in den Jahren 1919–1926 in Buchenbach lebte. Carnap hat dem nicht öffentlich widersprochen. In seinem Exemplar des Buchs findet sich allerdings die Randbemerkung: „Doch!". (Vgl. Carus 2007, 129)

6 Vgl. jedoch unten 7.3.

abgelegt, arbeitete jedoch nun an seiner Dissertation bei dem Jenaer Neukantianer Bruno Bauch. Über die Zeit in Buchenbach schreibt Carnap in seiner intellektuellen Autobiographie kurz:

> After the war, I lived for a while in Jena, and then in Buchenbach near Freiburg/i.B. In this period, I first passed my examinations, and then I began my own research in philosophy, first in relative isolation, but later in contact with Reichenbach and others who worked in a similar direction. (Carnap 1963, 10)[7]

In der auf das Zitat folgenden Darstellung ist von einem Studium bei Husserl oder irgendeinem Bezug zum phänomenologischen Kreis in Freiburg an keiner Stelle die Rede. Auch in den im Carnap-Archiv in Pittsburgh überlieferten Dokumenten finden sich nur wenige Informationen über die Jahre 1919 bis 1924, die den philosophischen Werdegang Carnaps betreffen. Erhalten sind neben einem Rundbrief an den Serakreis – einem freistudentischen Zirkel, dem Carnap in Jena angehört hatte – einige frühe Notizen zum *Aufbau*, einige Aufsätze und Aufsatzentwürfe sowie Briefe und Notizen Carnaps in Tagebüchern. Aus diesen ergibt sich das folgende Bild.

In dem erwähnten Rundbrief an den Serakreis[8], in dem er seine Freunde über seinen Umzug informiert, schreibt Carnap, er habe die Lehrerpläne aufgegeben und wolle sich nun der „reinen Wissenschaft", insbesondere der „Philosophie der exakten Wissenschaften" widmen. Diese habe in den letzten zwei Jahrzehnten sehr an Bedeutung gewonnen, da die exakten Wissenschaften, d. h. diejenigen, die nach mathematischer Methode vorgehen (Mathematik, Physik, Logik), im 19. Jahrhundert einen großen Aufschwung genommen hätten, ohne dabei viel Zeit

---

7 Die Beziehung zwischen Reichenbach und Carnap war anfangs wohl keineswegs ungetrübt. Eine Tagung in Erlangen 1923 wurde von beiden organisiert, ohne dass sie sich persönlich gekannt hätten. (Reichenbach 1923/24, Brief an Schlick vom 3.2.1923) Reichenbach schreibt am 13.6.1923 an Schlick: „Carnap ist ein Mensch, bei dem man immer wieder auf große Kritiklosigkeit gefasst sein muss, gegen fremde und leider auch gegen eigene Arbeiten". Dies war offenbar schon bei der Erlanger Tagung deutlich geworden. Er dürfe deshalb, schreibt Reichenbach, auch keinesfalls in das Herausgebergremium der geplanten „Zeitschrift für exakte Philosophie" aufgenommen werden, wegen der Reichenbach damals intensiv mit Schlick korrespondierte. Vorausgegangen war eine Kritik Schlicks an Carnaps in den Kantstudien erschienenem Aufsatz „Über die Aufgabe der Physik und die Anwendung des Grundsatzes der Einfachstheit", Kantstudien 28 (1923), 90–107. Die Kritik hinderte allerdings weder Schlick daran, Carnap später als Habilitanden zu akzeptieren, noch Reichenbach, sieben Jahre später mit Carnap die Zeitschrift *Erkenntnis* zu gründen. – Als Herausgeber der neuen Zeitschrift, über die Reichenbach mit Schlick korrespondierte, standen überraschenderweise zunächst auch Jaspers und Heidegger zur Diskussion.

8 Rundbrief an den Serakreis vom 7.11.1920 in Carnap 1908–1920, 081–47–01.

auf die kritische Nachprüfung ihrer Fundamente und Methoden zu verwenden. In der militanten Sprache seiner Kriegserfahrung schreibt Carnap, im „Bewegungskrieg" der Wissenschaften sei dabei der Kontakt zwischen „Front und Stab" verloren gegangen, so dass die Philosophie (der Stab) keine Meldungen mehr von den neuesten wissenschaftlichen Entdeckungen mehr erhalte. Inzwischen sei die Sache so fortgeschritten, dass „seit längerem schon in der Geometrie, später auch in der Arithm. und Analysis, und jetzt auch in der Physik [...] die Meldungen von vorn gar nicht mehr zur Stabskarte passen".[9] Die axiomatischen Wissenschaften arbeiteten mit Begriffen, von denen sie nicht genau wüssten, was sie bedeuten, während die traditionellen Methoden der Philosophie ihnen bei der Begriffsklärung nicht helfen könnten. Carnap positioniert nun seine wissenschaftlichen Absichten im Feld zwischen Philosophie und exakten Wissenschaften recht genau, daher sei die Stelle hier ausführlicher zitiert:

> Und so ist man denn jetzt schon seit einiger Zeit dabei, und an manchen Stellen schon mit sehr erfreulichem Erfolg, eine Gesamtkarte zu entwerfen, die sowohl den Genauigkeitsansprüchen der Topographen und Generalstäbler genügt, als auch alle eroberten Punkte aufzuweisen imstande ist, d.h. ein System der Wissenschaft (und vorerst der mathemat. Wissenschaftsgebiete) aufzubauen, das logisch einwandfreie Grundlagen und methodische Begriffsbildung aufweist und dabei imstande ist, alle Einsichten der Fachgebiete zu umfassen und möglichst einfach und einheitlich darzustellen. In der Richtung auf dieses (natürlich im Unendlichen liegende) Ideal ist nun in der letzten Zeit von den verschiedenen Seiten aus eifrig gearbeitet worden; ich nenne einige allgemeiner bekannte Namen: von Philosophen Natorp, Husserl, Cassirer, Nelson; von Math. Russell, Couturat, Frege, Hilbert, Klein; von Phys. Mach, Poincaré, Dühring, Ostwald, Klein. Nun sind aber bei dieser Zusammenarbeit doch leider Missverständnisse und teils wirkliche, teils scheinbare Meinungsverschiedenheiten zwischen den beiden Gruppen sehr häufig; durch die lange Trennungszeit sind eben auf beiden Seiten Terminologie (und auch die Begriffe selbst) sehr verschieden entwickelt. Deshalb kann sich hier als Helfer besonders nützlich machen, wer sowohl für Philosophie, als auch für die mathem. Wissenschaften Neigung und Verständnis hat.[10]

Es dürfte dies die erste und letzte Stelle sein, an der Carnap die Bedeutung Husserls für sein Denken wenigstens gegenüber einem Freundeskreis kundtut. Bemerkenswert an der zitierten Stelle ist auch, dass er Russell und Frege nicht als Mitglieder des philosophischen „Stabs" erwähnt, sondern der wissenschaftlichen „Front" zuordnet. Für die Strategie und die Grundlagen schienen sie ihm also damals nicht zuständig zu sein.

---

9 Ebd., Blatt 2.
10 Ebd., Blatt 3.

Carnaps Interesse lag demnach in der philosophischen Fundierung der exakten Wissenschaften in einer Weise, die den Wissenschaften einen „topologischen Ort" zuweist und gleichzeitig eine gemeinsame „Sprache" für alle Gebiete verwendet. Den philosophischen Grundlagen kommt in diesem Projekt eine richtungsweisende Funktion zu. Deutlich ist zudem, dass das Programm für Carnap mehr oder weniger einen „Zeitgeist" kennzeichnet, der von Philosophen unterschiedlicher Richtungen verfolgt wird.

2.1.2 Die Vorläuferschriften des *Logischen Aufbau:* Vom Chaos zur Wirklichkeit

Die Dissertation „Der Raum" war für Carnap sicherlich ein Teil der Durchführung des im Sera-Brief skizzierten Programms. Wie Sarkar 2003 und Rosado-Haddock 2008 gezeigt haben, ist hier der Bezug zu Husserls Phänomenologie an vielen Stellen nachweisbar. Auch die Schriften bis zum Jahr 1924, die im Nachlass oder in publizierter Form vorliegen, befassen sich mit dem philosophischen Fundierungsprogramm in verschiedener Hinsicht. Zum einen betreffen sie die Axiomatisierung oder die formalsprachliche Darstellung von mathematischen oder physikalischen Teilgebieten oder Begriffen. Carnap publizierte zudem in den Jahren 1923 und 1924 zwei Aufsätze: „Über die Aufgabe der Physik und die Anwendung des Grundsatzes der Einfachstheit"[11] und „Dreidimensionalität des Raumes und Kausalität: eine Untersuchung über den logischen Zusammenhang zweier Fiktionen"[12]. Der zweite dieser beiden Aufsätze zeigt eine gewisse Affinität zum *Aufbau* insofern, als es auch hier um ein Teilproblem der Wirklichkeitskonstruktion geht, nämlich die Frage, wie wir von der Zweidimensionalität der Sinnesempfindungen zur Mehrdimensionalität des (erlebten oder physikalischen) Raumes gelangen. Dennoch handelt sich es hier zwar um Überlegungen, die sich im weitesten Sinne mit der Frage der Konstitution der Welt aus Sinnesqualitäten befassen, sie gehen aber von einem konventionalistischen Standpunkt aus. Nach der Darstellung seines philosophischen Werdegangs in der Autobiographie rechnete Carnap selbst sie daher nicht zu den Vorarbeiten des *Aufbau*. (Carnap 1963, 16)

Im Nachlass findet sich von den vorbereitenden Arbeiten nur wenig. Neben Skizzen zur Methode der Quasizerlegung liegt hier ein Ordner mit Notizen und Entwürfen unter dem Titel „Vom Chaos zur Wirklichkeit" vor (Carnap 1921–1926), der ein 14-seitiges Manuskript mit demselben Titel und der Datierung 1922 enthält,

---

[11] Kantstudien Bd. 28, 1923, 90–107.
[12] Annalen der Philosophie und philosophischen Kritik Bd. 4, 1924, 105–130.

sowie einige wenige Seiten über die „Analyse von Erlebnissen" und die „Analyse des Weltbildes" (1921), die man ebenfalls zu den Vorüberlegungen rechnen kann. Die übrigen Texte betreffen bereits die Jahre 1924 und später: ein Plan oder ein Inhaltsverzeichnis mit dem Titel „Entwurf einer Konstitutionstheorie der Gegenstandsarten" vom Dezember 1924, den Carnap Schlick als Skizze seines Habilitationsprojekts vorgelegt, sowie eine thematische Liste für einen Vortrag, den Carnap 1925 in Wien über dieses Projekt gehalten hat.

Da Carnap das Manuskript mit dem Titel „Vom Chaos zur Wirklichkeit" selbst als den „Kern der Konstitutionstheorie des ‚Logischen Aufbau'" gekennzeichnet hat[13], sei dessen Inhalt hier kurz skizziert. Carnap beginnt mit der Feststellung, dass wir die Welt als geordnet erleben, aber gewisse kleinere und größere Unstimmigkeiten in ihr feststellen, die den Wunsch nach einer Umordnung motivieren. Wir betrachten deshalb die Welt fiktiv als aus einem Chaos entstanden, um sie von Grund auf neu aufzubauen, und zwar mit dem Ziel „zu einem einheitlichen System der Wirklichkeit zu gelangen".[14] Das fiktiv-ursprüngliche Chaos wird dadurch hergestellt, dass aus der Wirklichkeit alles gestrichen wird, „was schon fertige Ordnung und Einzelbestimmbarkeit" bedeutet. (*Chaos*, 1) Dazu gehören der Unterschied zwischen Psychischem und Physischem, Räumlichkeit und Zeitlichkeit, Sinnesklassen und -qualitäten, Begriffe sowie überhaupt die meisten Elemente. „Es gibt da nur Gegenwart". (Ebd., 2) Um vom Chaos zu einer Ordnung gelangen zu können, müssen allerdings im Chaos bereits gewisse minimale Grundunterscheidungen oder Grundrelationen gegeben sein. Carnap unterscheidet erstens den „lebendigen" vom „toten" Teil von Erlebnissen, nämlich Sinnesempfindungen von Vorstellungen. Innerhalb des toten Teils werden dann „fertige" Bestandteile (Erinnerungen) und „neutrale" Bestandteile (Vorstellungen) unterschieden.

---

[13] Handschriftliche Notiz auf Manuskript RC081–05–01 aus Carnap 1921–1926. Das Manuskript wird im Folgenden als *Chaos* zitiert.

[14] Chaos, 1; Auf welche Unstimmigkeiten" und „Risse" Carnap hier anspielt, ist unklar. Mormann 2006 vermutet, dass Carnap sich auf Rickerts *System der Philosophie I* (Tübingen 1921) stützt. Carus 2007 sieht den Ursprung in Vaihingers *Die Philosophie des Als-Ob* (1911). Für letzteren ist der Begriff der Fiktion wesentlich, den auch Carnap verwendet. Rickert wie Vaihinger sprechen von einem ursprünglichen „Chaos" der Empfindungen. (Vaihinger 1922, 332, 446; Rickert 1921, 8) Vaihinger etwa schreibt: „Aus dem Chaos der Empfindungen tritt die geschiedene Anschauung hervor, in jenem Chaos ist noch keine Vorstellung von einem besonderen Dinge, denn die große, unklare Nebelmasse der Empfindungen kommt erst allmählich in eine rotierende Bewegung und es ballen sich die einzelnen zusammengehörigen Stücke erst allmählich zu Wahrnehmungsdingen, zu Anschauungen des Einzelnen zusammen." (Vaihinger 1922, 332) Wesentlich konkreter wird Vaihinger nicht.

Die fertigen Bestandteile können in Mannigfaltigkeiten auseinander gelegt werden derart, dass (verkürzt gesagt) Erinnerungsketten entstehen, deren Teile in einer asymmetrisch-transitiven Beziehung zueinander stehen. Mit Hilfe dieser „Bausteine" der so definierbaren „Z-Reihe" wird der Aufbau der Wirklichkeit durchgeführt. Die Bausteine, vergleichbar den „Elementarerlebnissen" im *Aufbau*, stehen nun noch in anderen Relationen zueinander: zum einen in der Relation der „Hauptgleichheit" (G), wenn sie „in der Qualität des Aufmerksamkeitszentrums übereinstimmen" (ebd., 3), also etwa farbgleich sind; des Weiteren in der Relation der Hauptähnlichkeit (A), wenn zwei Qualitäten verwandt sind. Mit Hilfe von G und A werden Qualitätsklassen und im Folgenden Sinnesklassen definiert. Weitere Unterscheidungsmöglichkeiten werden durch die „Nebengleichheit" (G2) eingeführt, welche „Außenglieder" einer Qualitätsklasse erzeugt, die nicht im Blickpunkt der Aufmerksamkeit stehen. Mit Hilfe einiger weiterer Umformungen und Definitionen werden dann Phänomene wie eine „langsame Gesichtsveränderung" beschrieben, etwa der Übergang eines Farbtons in einen anderen.

Zwei „Tendenzen" führen zum Aufbau der „Wirklichkeit": die Tendenz zur Erhaltung der Zustandsgleichheit und die Tendenz zur Erhaltung der Ablaufgleichheit, welche die Fiktionen von Substanz, Kausalität und Zukunft erzeugen. Durch sie werden Lücken im Wahrnehmungsfeld sukzessive gefüllt. Gewisse nunmehr konstruierte Sehdinge werden durch eine Klasse von Tastempfindungen als „mein Leib" ausgezeichnet. Die Tastklasse gehört zu einer umfassenderen Sinnesklasse („Druckklasse") aus Muskel- und kinästhetischen Empfindungen; über diese wird auch eine „Gefühlsklasse" definiert. Nach der Definition weiterer Sinnesklassen können andere Leiber als ähnlich bestimmt und ihnen analoge Sinnesklassen zugewiesen werden. Die Leiber stehen in Kausalbeziehungen und in Zeichenbeziehungen zu ihrer Umgebung. Carnap versucht die Zeichenbeziehung ebenfalls durch formale Kennzeichen zu bestimmen, indem er etwa „Dinglaute" und „Beziehungslaute" durch gewisse Gleichzeitigkeitserlebnisse definiert. (Ebd. 10 f) Durch das Zeichenverständnis werden dann der „Erlebnisbereich" und anschließend der „Wirklichkeitsbereich" des anderen Leibes L darstellbar. Nun wird eine gewisse Übereinstimmung zwischen diesem Bereich (4. Stufe) des L und dem Bereich 2. Stufe des L, den Sinneswahrnehmungen, beobachtet, der auf eine ursprüngliche Ordnung schon im „Chaos" deutet. Dadurch können weitere Lücken in den einzelnen Stufen beseitigt werden.

In einem eigenen Kapitel werden nun Vorschläge für die Konstruktion des Seelischen entwickelt. Und zwar soll dies nicht nur das „Erlebnismäßige" (das Bewusstsein) enthalten, sondern auch einen Teil, der „einen gesetzmäßigen Ablauf" zeigt, womit Carnap das Unbewusste meint. (Ebd., 12) Im Unterschied zum „Wirklichen" ist der Bereich des Seelischen nicht durchgängig gesetzmäßig bestimmt, die Empfindungen „gehorchen keiner Gesetzmäßigkeit dieses Bereichs; sie springen unvermittelt und unerklärt in diesem Bereiche auf". (Ebd., 12f) Sie sind vielmehr die Folge von Reizen aus der „Wirklichkeit", so dass die Wirklichkeit dem Seelischen methodisch vorhergeht. Die Konstruktion des Unbewussten durch bloße „Umordnung" von Bausteinen bezeichnet Carnap hier als ungelöstes Problem.

Es folgt der Bereich des Physikalischen, der allein formal, als vierdimensionales Beziehungsgefüge, definiert wird. Er unterscheidet sich vom Bereich des Wirklichen durch das Fehlen von Qualitäten und zeigt eine strenge Kausalität. Weitere Stufen entwickelt das Chaos-Manuskript nicht.

Während dieses Manuskript zunächst in der Rede vom fiktiven Chaos (das dann doch keines ist) und den „toten" und „lebendigen" Erlebnisteilen vom späteren *Aufbau* abweicht, ist die Stufenfolge doch schon recht ähnlich und auch einzelne Elemente wie „mein Leib" oder die Qualitätsklassen entsprechen sich. Schon in diesem Manuskript sind gleichzeitig die Parallelen zu Husserls Phänomenologie, vor allem in den *Ideen I*, deutlich. Wenn Carnap eine „Nebengleichheit" definiert, die Elemente betrifft, die nicht im Zentrum der Aufmerksamkeit stehen, aber dennoch wahrgenommen werden, dann könnte er dafür auf die Einführung des Horizontbegriffes in §27 der *Ideen I* verweisen, wo Husserl schreibt:

> Das aktuell Wahrgenommene, das mehr oder minder klar Mitgegenwärtige und Mitbestimmte (oder mindestens einigermaßen bestimmte) ist teils durchsetzt, teils umgeben von einem **dunkel bewussten Horizont unbestimmter Wirklichkeit**. Ich kann Strahlen des aufhellenden Blickes der Aufmerksamkeit in ihn hineinsenden, mit wechselndem Erfolge, [...] eine Kette von solchen Erinnerungen schließt sich zusammen, der Kreis der Bestimmtheit erweitert sich immer mehr. (*Ideen I*, 57)[15]

Auch die anderen Subjekte und ihre Umwelten, die jeweils auf diese selbst bezogen sind, und die Tatsache, dass wir uns darüber verständigen und so eine intersubjektive Welt gewinnen, sind Thema in den *Ideen I*. Die hier nur ange-

---

[15] Wenn hier und im Folgenden Auszüge aus dem *Aufbau* mit Textstellen aus Husserls Schriften kontrastiert werden, dann ergibt sich dadurch eine Schwierigkeit, die nicht leicht zu beheben ist. Husserl hat während der Entwicklung seines Denkens eine eigene Terminologie entwickelt, deren Ausdrücke zumeist präzise Bedeutungen innerhalb des Gesamtsystems der Phänomenologie haben, und deren Erklärung deshalb voraussetzungsreich ist, hier z. B. der Begriff des Horizonts. Eine jeweils ausführliche Erläuterung würde den Rahmen dieses Aufsatzes sprengen. Ich verweise den Leser auf das Husserl-Lexikon von Gander 2010 sowie auf das Husserl Dictionary von Moran/Cohen 2012.

deuteten Parallelen zwischen Husserls und Carnaps Konstitutionssystem werden im Folgenden ausführlich und in den Einzelheiten expliziert.

2.2 Die Jahre 1923(2)–26

2.2.1 Habilitationspläne bei Husserl

Mormann (2000) vermutet, dass Carnap mit der Absicht nach Buchenbach umzog, bei Husserl zu studieren. In den privaten Notizen finden sich zu den Gründen des Umzugs keine Informationen. Eingeschriebener Student war Carnap zu keiner Zeit, das bedeutet jedoch nicht, dass er nicht bis zum Jahr 1923 Husserl-Vorlesungen besucht haben könnte.[16] Ab dem Jahr 1923 jedenfalls ist der Kontakt zu Husserl in den Tagebüchern belegt. Offenbar suchte Carnap im Oktober 1923 intensiv nach einer Möglichkeit zur Habilitation und dachte dabei an Jena oder Kiel. Sein Doktorvater Bruno Bauch rät ihm von Jena ab – er hatte offenbar kein Interesse daran, Carnap „nach Hause zu holen".[17] Der Kieler Logiker Heinrich Scholz sagt ebenfalls ab und schlägt ihm vor, bei Husserl zu habilitieren.[18] Carnap folgt diesem Rat offenbar. Am 13.11. notiert er den Besuch von Husserls „Kolleg", der Vorlesung „Erste Philosophie", die ihm „nicht sehr gefallen" hat.[19] Dennoch bittet er Husserl am 17.11. schriftlich um die Erlaubnis, an seinem Oberseminar „Phänomenologische Übungen für Fortgeschrittene" teilnehmen zu dürfen, die Husserl am 21.11. zwischen Tür und Angel und offenbar nicht sonderlich gesprächsfreudig gewährt.[20] Im Husserl-Archiv in Leuven befindet sich ein Exemplar von Carnaps Dissertation *Der Raum* mit undatierter handschriftlicher Widmung: „Herrn Geh.-

---

[16] Vgl. zum Folgenden Carnap 2015. Carnaps Tagebücher enthalten überwiegend Notizen zu privaten Ereignissen (Einkäufen, Spaziergängen, Befindlichkeiten, Besuche von Freunden etc.), die vielleicht als Gedächtnisstütze dienen sollten. Daneben sind auch gelegentlich wichtige berufliche Vorkommnisse vermerkt, dies jedoch keineswegs zuverlässig. So findet sich z. B. kaum ein Hinweis auf die Arbeit an und keiner auf die Abgabe der Habilitationsschrift. Die Tagebücher sind also nicht Dokumente, aus denen sich auf das Sein oder Nichtsein nicht vermerkter Ereignisse schließen ließe.
[17] Vgl. Awodney et al. 2004. Über Bauch heißt es im Tagebuch: „Er rät zu Kiel zu, winkt von Jena ab; erstens weil sehr viel besser an preußischen Universitäten Aussicht, zweitens weil hier schon viele Dozenten". Carnap 2015, Eintrag vom 2.1.1923, 548.
[18] „Ich berichte ihm, dass Familie in Wiesneck bleiben würde; er rät mir dringend von dieser Trennung ab; ich soll bei Husserl versuchen." Carnap 2015, Eintrag vom 25.10.1923, 546.
[19] Ebd., 552.
[20] Ebd., 553.

R. Prof. Edmund Husserl in dankbarer Verehrung überreicht v.V." [21], das Carnap vielleicht bei dieser Gelegenheit übergeben hat. Am 25.11 notiert Carnap ein Erlebnis, das er als vielversprechend empfunden haben muss:

> Zu Merten <später unterstrichen>: Mit ihm ½ 4 zu Husserl, das ganze Seminar. Zum Tee dort. Dort auch Professor Tschichmanoff und der russische Professor Stepun. Beim Teetisch setzt Husserl mich sich gegenüber, spricht über die beneidenswerte Lage in Buchenbach, dann über Habilitation im allgemeinen, er sei 14 Jahre Privatdozent gewesen, habe immer nur gelesen, was er selbst dachte, darum oft längere Pausen mit Vorlesungen gemacht.[22]

In der Folge wird der Besuch des Husserl-Seminars immer wieder einmal vermerkt. Am 19.12. hält Carnap dort ein Referat, am 29.12 besucht er Husserl und notiert: „Er sieht sich in Galileis Rolle als Begründer der wissenschaftlichen Philosophie."[23] Am 23.1.1924 referiert Carnap bei Husserl über Quasizerlegung.[24] Auch der Besuch eines Husserl-Kollegs, also vermutlich der Vorlesung „Erste Philosophie", ist wieder vermerkt. Carnap nimmt an Husserls Oberseminar auch noch in den folgenden drei Semestern, also im Sommersemester 1924, im Wintersemester 1924/25 und im Sommersemester 1925 teil.[25]

Am 4.10.1924 schreibt Carnap: „Mit Roh ins Ibental. Über meine Habilitation Kiel, Wien".[26] Wohl kurz zuvor hatte Carnap bei Husserl um eine Habilitation nachgefragt. Ein Jahr später, am 26.9.1925 berichtet er in einem Brief an den Freiburger Neukantianer Jonas Cohn:

---

21 Für diese Auskunft sowie für weitere wertvolle Hinweise danke ich Thomas Vongehr.
22 Carnap 2015, Eintrag vom 25.10.1923, 554.
23 Ebd., 561.
24 Ebd., 613.
25 Schuhmann 1977, 281. Dies wird durch einen Brief von Landgrebe an Schuhmann vom 6.8.1976 bestätigt. Es handelte sich um Husserls Übungen für Fortgeschrittene, die im Anschluss an Vorlesungen stattfanden und die folgenden Titel trugen: Sommersemester 1924: „Phänomenologische Übungen für Fortgeschrittene", Wintersemester 1924/25: „Phänomenologische Übungen für Fortgeschrittene über Berkeleys Abhandlung über die Prinzipien der menschlichen Erkenntnis", Sommersemester 1925: „Übungen in der Analyse und Deskription rein geistiger Akte und Gebilde (im Anschluss an die Vorlesungen über phänomenologische Psychologie)". (Diese Auskunft verdanke ich Thomas Vongehr.) Es ist sinnvoll, anzunehmen, dass Carnap nicht nur die Übungen zur Vorlesung, sondern auch die Vorlesungen selbst besucht hat. – Benoist 2001 glaubt, dass Carnap nur ein einziges Semester bei Husserl studiert habe, und zwar als er bereits bei der Endredaktion des *Aufbau* gewesen sei (192). Dies trifft also nicht zu. Vielmehr war Carnap über vier Semester und während der gesamten konkreten Arbeit an seiner „Konstitutionstheorie" Husserls Student.
26 Carnap 2015, Eintrag vom 25.10.1923, 651.

> Vor einem Jahr habe ich Herrn Prof. Husserl einmal darum [um die Habilitation, V.M.] gefragt, worauf er antwortete, daß er mir einstweilen keine Hoffnung machen dürfe, da einer seiner Schüler die Habilitation vorhabe und dann vorläufig die wünschenswerte Zahl der Dozenten voll sei.[27]

Carnap ist jedoch offenbar nicht endgültig entmutigt, wie seine fortgesetzte Teilnahme an den Seminaren Husserls zeigt. In dem Brief an Cohn macht er einen erneuten Vorstoß: Er habe gehört, dass die Zahl der Privatdozenten nun um zwei verringert sei und frage, ob dadurch vielleicht „eine Habilitation in den Bereich der Möglichkeit gerückt ist". Er fügt hinzu, dass er sich nach der Absage durch Husserl „nicht gern [...] noch einmal mit einer Frage an ihn wenden möchte"[28] Die Frage ist aber wohl dennoch über den Umweg Cohns an Husserl gerichtet, da Cohn Mitdirektor Husserls am Freiburger psychologischen Institut war und als Extraordinarius keine Habilitation betreuen konnte.

Carnap betont in diesem Brief seine Habilitationswürdigkeit: Er habe von einer ungenannten anderen Universität (Kiel?) ungefragt die Aufforderung zur Habilitation erhalten. Wieder eine andere habe ihm Hoffnung gemacht, falls er noch im Verlauf des Winters 1925 eine Habilitationsschrift einreiche. Moritz Schlick nämlich hatte Carnap auf Anregung von Reichenbach diesen Vorschlag in einem Brief vom 9. August 1924 unterbreitet.[29] Schon am 16. August 1924 war es zu einer Besprechung zwischen Carnap und Schlick gekommen.[30] Aus dem Briefwechsel geht hervor, dass Carnap daraufhin tatsächlich mit dieser Arbeit, dem späteren *Aufbau*, begann. Die Möglichkeit einer Habilitation bei Husserl oder wenigstens in Freiburg war aber noch im September 1925 seine erklärte Präferenz. Im Brief an Cohn (vgl. Anm. 25) schreibt er:

---

[27] Carnap Brief an Jonas Cohn vom 26.9.1925, abgedruckt in diesem Band. Original im Jonas-Cohn-Archiv, Steinheim-Institut Essen. Zur Stellung Cohns am Freiburger psychologischen Institut vgl. auch Fahrenberg 2006 und Heitmann 2001.
[28] Carnap 2015, Eintrag vom 25.10.1923, 651.
[29] Brief Schlicks vom 9. August 1924, Carnap 1922–1927a, 029–32–50. Vgl. Auch Carnap an Reichenbach, am 10.3.1925: „Im Jan. war ich ein paar Wochen in Wien. Es scheint mit den Aussichten auf Habilitation günstig zu stehen. Ich bin jetzt mit der Hab.-Schrift beschäftigt („Prolegomena zu einer Konstitutionstheorie der Wirklichkeit', die Ausführung einiger Gedanken aus meinem Wiener Vortrage). Ich will mich bemühen, bald fertig zu werden, um zu Beginn des S.-S. das Hab.-Gesuch einreichen zu können. Die Hab. wird wohl erst zu Beginn des W.-S- möglich sein, so dass ich in diesem Jahr nicht mehr lesen werde, vielleicht auch nicht vor Ostern 1926." (Carnap 1905–1970, Box 102d, Folder 64, 11) Für diesen Hinweis danke ich Thomas Vongehr.
[30] Im von Carnap angefertigten Protokoll heißt es: „Zunächst müsste ich noch eine längere philosophische Textarbeit schreiben." Carnap 1922–1927a, RC-029–32–51.

> Dort [in Wien V.M.] glaube ich auch, günstige Wirkungsbedingungen finden zu können. Trotzdem würde ich Freiburg vorziehen, wenn sich hier die Möglichkeit ergäbe.

Cohns Antwort ist nicht erhalten, sie kann jedoch nicht ermutigend gewesen sein, da Carnap im November 1925 seine Habilitationsschrift, vermutlich unter dem Titel „Konstitutionstheorie", in Wien einreicht.

2.2.2 Die Entstehung des *Logischen Aufbau*

Obwohl Carnap noch im September 1925 einen zweiten Anlauf zu einer Habilitation in Freiburg unternimmt, betrachtet Schlick die Sache schon ein Jahr vorher als abgemacht: Er drängt darauf, dass Carnap in der zweiten Hälfte des Wintersemesters nach Wien kommen solle, „um Fühlung zu nehmen" und seine Arbeiten in einem Seminar Schlicks vorzustellen. Der Besuch findet tatsächlich im Januar 1925 statt. Gleichzeitig bittet Schlick Carnap um eine Monographie über symbolische Logik für die von Schlick und Frank herausgegebene Reihe „Bausteine zu einer exakten Weltauffassung".[31] Carnap antwortet, dass er ein solches Buch in wenigen Monaten fertig stellen könne, aber nun nicht dazukommen werde, da die Arbeit an der Habilitationsschrift Vorrang habe.

> Die Habilitationsschrift wird noch mehr Zeit in Anspruch nehmen, als ich glaubte. Ich möchte *das Problem der Kategorien oder Konstitutionsprinzipien der verschiedenen Realitätssphären bearbeiten*, das mir jetzt am meisten am Herzen liegt, aber es sind noch eine Reihe Steine aus dem Weg zu schaffen, über die ich immer noch nicht hinwegkomme. (Hervorh. V.M.)[32]

Am 18. Dezember 1924 schickt Carnap an Schlick den vorläufigen Plan der Habilitationsschrift, der im Nachlass unter dem Titel „Entwurf einer Konstitutionstheorie der Erkenntnisgegenstände" erhalten ist. Er bemerkt dazu:

> Fertig geschrieben ist noch nichts davon. In einer ganz vorläufigen Form niedergeschrieben sind auch nur Teile, nämlich bis jetzt: I,1–3,5; II, III, IV A–D1. Das Thema der Arbeit steht seit längerer Zeit im Zentrum meines Interesses. Sie geht zurück auf einen (unveröffentlichten) Aufsatz ‚Vom Chaos zur Wirklichkeit', den ich im Sommer 1922 geschrieben habe. Mein Hauptreferat in Erlangen 1923 war auf denselben Gegenstand gerichtet. Doch ist das Problem immer noch nicht genügend ausgereift.[33]

---

[31] Der Text erscheint 1929 unter dem Titel „Abriß der Logistik" in der nun *Schriften zur wissenschaftlichen Weltauffassung* genannten Reihe bei Springer.
[32] Brief Carnaps an Schlick vom 11.11.1924, in Carnap 1922–1927a, 029-32-48.
[33] Brief Carnaps an Schlick vom 19.12.1924, Ebd., 029-32-46.

Die „in einer ganz vorläufigen Form" niedergeschriebenen Kapitel lassen sich den im Nachlass erhaltenen Texten nur zu einem geringen Teil zuordnen. Gegenüber dem *Chaos*-Text lässt Carnap im Entwurf die Idee des fiktiven Chaos, die Motivation einer Korrektur von Unstimmigkeiten sowie die Unterscheidung zwischen Sinnesempfindungen und Vorstellungen fallen und erweitert die Konstitutionsstufen um die geistige Welt. Es gibt nun fünf statt vier Grundrelationen, während die Elemente der Basis unbestimmt bleiben. Formale Merkmale wie die Quasianalyse und die Qualitätsklassen, Relationen wie Ähnlichkeit und Teilgleichheit sowie die Idee einer formalen Darstellung der Wirklichkeitsgenese mit Hilfe der Relationslogik bleiben erhalten.

Am 31. Mai 1925 schreibt Carnap ein weiteres Mal, dass die Arbeit noch Zeit zur Ausarbeitung brauche und stellt die Fertigstellung zum Sommersemester in Aussicht. Schlick antwortet im Juni, Carnap könne auch noch im Oktober einreichen, drängt aber nun zunehmend auf baldige Abgabe. Am 23. September 1925, also kurz vor seinem Brief an Cohn, schreibt Carnap, ein Viertel der Arbeit läge nun in Maschinenschrift vor. Am 13. November heißt es, dass die Arbeit 560 Seiten haben werde und Weihnachten oder im Januar abgegeben werden könne. Schlick will die Sache beschleunigen und schlägt vor, dass Carnap einen Teil sofort als Habilitationsschrift einreicht (18. November). Carnap geht schließlich, vermutlich nach einem negativen Bescheid durch Cohn, darauf ein. Er fragt nun im Dezember:

> Würden Sie mir raten, bei der späteren Einsendung von Bd. II (oder vielleicht jetzt schon) nur S. 1–346 des Manuskripts als Habilitationsschrift zu bezeichnen, also die Untersuchung der Formprobleme ohne den Entwurf des Konstitutionssystems? Es kommt mir jetzt vor, als würde ich mit dem ganzen MS die Kommissionsmitglieder in allzuhohem Grade belasten.[34]

Nach Zustimmung Schlicks reicht Carnap die Arbeit in den folgenden Tagen ein und wird im Herbst 1926 erfolgreich habilitiert.

Carnaps Habilitationsschrift bestand also schließlich nur aus einem Teil des umfangreichen Manuskripts von 560 Seiten, das er zwischen Dezember 1924 und November 1925 erstellt hatte. Dieser Teil behandelte „Formprobleme" und schlägt sich im publizierten *Aufbau* als Abschnitt III nieder, während das Konstitutionssystem als solches nicht als Habilitationsschrift vorgelegt wurde. Obwohl Schlick selbst, um das Verfahren zu beschleunigen, die Einreichung eines Teiltextes vorgeschlagen hatte, erscheint Carnaps Begründung merkwürdig. In Abschnitt III des *Aufbau* geht es um Quasigegenstände, Sphärenverwandtschaft, Klassen, Relationen, die extensionale Methode und ähnliche Themen aus der Philosophie der Logik. Die gesamte Arbeit am Text im Jahr 1925 war dagegen „den Kategorien und

---

34 Brief Carnaps an Schlick vom 2. Dezember 1925, Carnap 1922–1927a, 029–32–33.

Konstitutionsprinzipien", mithin dem inhaltlichen Teil des Systems gewidmet, wurde nun aber letztlich nicht für die Habilitation verwendet. Die Kommission bestand aus Heinrich Gomperz, Karl Bühler und Robert Reininger[35] – Professoren, die wohl mehr von einer Darstellung der Formprobleme als von dem Konstitutionssystem „belastet" gewesen wären. In Bezug auf diese Gutachter wäre es sinnvoller gewesen, die „Formprobleme" zu streichen und stattdessen das inhaltliche Konstitutionssystem vorzulegen. Worauf beziehen sich also Carnaps Bedenken?

Schlick jedenfalls zeigt sich von Carnaps Habilitationsschrift restlos begeistert. Er schreibt:

> dass die Lektüre Ihres Buches mir wirklich ganz außerordentliche Freude bereitet hat. Ich bin überzeugt, dass Ihrem Werk in mancher Beziehung eine schlechthin grundlegende Bedeutung zukommt, und gratuliere Ihnen von ganzem Herzen zu dieser Leistung. Dieses Urteil würde ich auch dann fällen, wenn ich sachlich nicht so weitgehend mit Ihnen übereinstimmte. In Wirklichkeit ist diese Übereinstimmung aber sehr groß, noch viel größer, als man aus der 2. Aufl. meiner Erkenntnislehre würde schließen können [...] Einige Gedankenübereinstimmungen waren mir besonders erfreulich, *so das über die Metaphysik Gesagte* [Hervorh. V.M.].[36]

Dieser letzte Satz wirft ein besonderes Licht auf die Beziehung zwischen Schlick, Carnap und Husserl und soll daher an dieser Stelle vorgreifend kommentiert werden.

Exkurs: Schlick und die intuitive Metaphysik

Im *Aufbau* §182 grenzt Carnap die Konstitutionstheorie von der „intuitiven Metaphysik" ab.[37] Die intuitive Metaphysik sei eine philosophische Methode, die im Sinne Bergsons ohne Symbole, also „unsprachlich", vorgehe, und zwar im Unterschied zum rational-rekonstruktiven („sprachlichen") Verfahren der Konstitutionstheorie.[38] Damit spielt Carnap offensichtlich auf eine These Schlicks an. In

---

[35] oder einer Auswahl aus diesen Personen, vgl. Brief Schlicks an Carnap vom 13. Juni 1925, Carnap 1922–1927a, 029-32-42.
[36] Brief Schlicks an Carnap vom 7.3.1926, Carnap 1922–1927a, 029-32-27.
[37] Vgl. dazu unten 6.5.2. Da die Habilitationsschrift nicht erhalten ist, muss hier die publizierte Fassung des *Aufbau* zugrunde gelegt werden. Dass sich die Argumente decken, kann hier nur unterstellt werden. Es gibt jedoch keine Hinweise darauf, dass Carnap wesentliche Änderungen vorgenommen hat.
[38] Carnap qualifiziert diese Aussage aber sogleich dahingehend, dass man von Metaphysik auch in anderem Sinne sprechen könne, etwa im Sinne einer „Grundwissenschaft". Tut man dies, dann

der *Allgemeinen Erkenntnislehre* sowie in dem Aufsatz „Gibt es intuitive Erkenntnis" (Schlick 1913) kritisiert Schlick das Konzept einer nicht-sprachlich vorgehenden, und daher für die Erkenntnis irrelevanten Intuition. Einen solchen Intuitionsbegriff schreibt Schlick Bergson zu, richtet seine Kritik aber zugleich gegen Husserl, dessen Position er mit derjenigen Bergsons identifiziert.[39]

Husserl weist Schlicks Darstellung der Phänomenologie in seinem Vorwort zur zweiten Auflage des zweiten Teils der *Logischen Untersuchungen* aus dem Jahr 1920 zurück. Er schreibt dort in Bezug auf einen Satz, den Schlick dann in der zweiten Auflage gestrichen hat[40], ungewöhnlich scharf:

> Wie bequem es sich manche Autoren mit wegwerfenden Kritiken machen, mit welcher Gewissenhaftigkeit sie lesen, welchen Unsinn sie mir und der Phänomenologie zuzumuten die Kühnheit haben, das zeigt die „Allgemeine Erkenntnislehre" von Moritz Schlick […]. Die völlige Unmöglichkeit, dass ich je eine tolle Behauptung, wie sie mir von Schlick […] zugeschrieben ist, ausgesprochen haben könnte, und ebenso die Unwahrheit seiner sonstigen Darstellung des Sinnes der Phänomenologie muß jeder, dem diese vertraut ist, im ersten Blick erkennen. […] Ich muß noch ausdrücklich bemerken, dass es sich bei M. Schlick nicht bloß um irrelevante Entgleisungen handelt, sondern um sinnverkehrende Unterschiebungen, auf die seine ganze Kritik aufgebaut ist. (HUA XIX/2, 535 f.)

Schlicks Kritik an der Phänomenologie bleibt trotz der Streichung des Satzes in der Auflage von 1925 im Wesentlichen dieselbe.[41] Wenn Carnap also in der Habilitationsschrift wie im §182 des *Aufbau* die „intuitive Metaphysik" unter Verweis auf Schlick aus der Konstitutionstheorie ausschloss, konnte Schlick dies als kaum verhüllte Kritik an Husserl verstehen. Dies könnte ein Grund für die enthusiastische Rede von „sehr großen Übereinstimmungen" seiner eigenen Philosophie mit dem *Aufbau* gewesen sein.[42]

---

ließe sich wohl auch die Konstitutionstheorie als Metaphysik bezeichnen. Eine weitere Bedeutung erhält der Begriff der Metaphysik im Abschnitt VD. (*Aufbau*, 245 ff) Vgl. dazu im Folgenden 6.5.2.
39 Der Angriff gilt vor allem der eidetischen Intuition und Wesensschau (Schlick 1979, 103, 113); vgl. auch die Darstellung von Ideation und Evidenz. (Ebd. 162 ff)
40 „Es wird die Existenz einer besonderen Anschauung behauptet, die kein psychischer realer Akt sein soll; und vermag jemand ein solches nicht in den Bereich der Psychologie fallendes Erlebnis nicht aufzufinden, so wird ihm bedeutet, er habe die Lehre eben nicht verstanden, er sei noch nicht zu der richtigen Erfahrungs- und Denkeinstellung vorgedrungen, das erfordere nämlich ‚eigene und mühselige Studien'". (Schlick 2009, 387)
41 Vgl. die Anm. 38 zum zweiten Teil in Schlick 1997, 447. Diese zweite Auflage lag zur Zeit des Beginns von Carnaps konkreter Arbeit am *Aufbau* nicht vor, wird aber im Literaturverzeichnis der Ausgabe von 1928 angeführt. Zu Husserls Begriff der Wesensschau vgl. Mayer 2011.
42 Schlicks Opposition gegen Husserl, der seinerseits auf Schlick nie wieder Bezug nimmt, ist noch Jahre später ungebrochen. So fragt er Wittgenstein einmal in Bezug auf Husserl: „Was kann man einem Philosophen erwidern, der meint, dass die Aussagen der Phänomenologie syntheti-

Die Auseinandersetzung zwischen Schlick und Husserl demonstriert hinreichend, dass Carnap keinesfalls mit einer von Husserl inspirierten Arbeit bei Schlick hätte habilitieren können. Nebenbei wirft sie auch ein Licht darauf, weshalb Carnap, der in seiner Dissertation noch von der Wesensschau Gebrauch macht, im *Aufbau* auf deren Einführung verzichtet. Vor allem aber zeigt sich hierin die prekäre Situation, in der Carnap seine Habilitationsschrift verfasste: wie der Brief an Cohn beweist, hielt er sich während der Arbeit am Text fast bis zuletzt die Möglichkeit offen, damit bei Husserl oder wenigstens in Freiburg mit Unterstützung Husserls zu habilitieren; und während der gesamten Zeit, als er an der Qualifikationsarbeit für Schlick schrieb, der Husserl scharf kritisierte, besuchte er Husserls Veranstaltungen – nach der öffentlich ausgetragenen Kontroverse eine Konstellation, die in der akademischen Lebenswelt nicht oft vorkommen dürfte.
Exkurs Ende

Als Zwischenbilanz sei festgehalten, dass Carnap die Habilitationsschrift, aus welcher der *Aufbau* hervorging, wohl erst ab Ende 1924 und im Jahr 1925 unter großem zeitlichem Druck verfasst hat, wobei die Durchführung der Gedankengänge, die er in seinem Chaosmanuskript skizziert hatte, seinem eigenen Bekunden nach erst in dieser Zeit entstand. Diese Durchführung betrifft nun vor allem die Einzelheiten der Konstitution, d. h. die Frage, wie auf der Basis von „Erlebnissen" Gegenstände wie mein Leib oder andere Personen dargestellt werden können, und zwar in aufeinanderfolgenden Konstitutionsstufen. Diese Übergänge bilden wohl die „Steine", die Carnap, wie er es in seinem Brief an Schlick vom 11.11.1924 ausdrückt, aus dem Weg schaffen musste.

Während der Zeit der konkreten Arbeit am Manuskript nahm Carnap mindestens an Husserls Übungen, wohl aber auch an den Vorlesungen, denen sie zugeordnet waren, teil. Seit dem Sommersemester 1923 war Ludwig Landgrebe Student und seit dem Herbst 1923 Privatassistent Husserls.[43] In den Jahren 1924 und 1925 wurde er mit der Typoskriptfassung und Umarbeitung des Stein-Manuskripts der *Ideen II* nach Husserls Notizen betraut.[44] Landgrebe suchte in den folgenden Jahren wie viele andere Postdoktoranden jener Zeit eine Möglichkeit zur Habilitation. Im Jahr 1932 eröffnete sich die Aussicht, bei Oskar Kraus in Prag zu

---

sche Urteile a priori sind?" (Wittgenstein 1984, 67) Vgl. auch Schlicks Bemerkungen über die Phänomenologie in seiner Vorlesung aus dem Wintersemester 1933/34, Schlick 1986, 98 ff. – Nach Husserls Auffassung wären insbesondere die Aussagen der Konstitutionstheorie synthetisch apriori.
43 Vgl. Schuhmann 1977, 269 und 273.
44 Vgl. dazu die Einleitung der Herausgeberin Marly Biemel in *Ideen II* (XVIII) und den textkritischen Anhang (398 f.).

habilitieren. Landgrebe hatte allerdings Bedenken, weil Kraus ein Brentanoschüler war und sich in Brentanoausgaben kritisch gegen Husserl geäußert hatte. In diesem Zusammenhang schreibt er an Husserl:

> Aber jetzt ist ja auch noch Carnap dort, der trotz ganz anderer Einstellung die Phänomenologie doch schätzt und sich von seiner Freiburger Zeit wohl noch an mich erinnern wird. Ich habe damals viel mit ihm diskutiert.[45]

Landgrebe war auch Teilnehmer an einem Seminar über Erkenntnistheorie, das Carnap privat organisiert hatte.[46] Carnap hat also nicht nur während der gesamten Zeit seiner Arbeit am *Aufbau* bei Husserl studiert. Während dieser Zeit, als er an einer Habilitationsschrift schrieb, die sowohl für Schlick, als auch für Husserl annehmbar sein sollte, befand er sich in nächster Nähe des Typoskripts der *Ideen II*, in welchem – wie sich nun zeigen soll – die Fragen, die ihn am meisten beschäftigten, beantwortet wurden. Die Diskussionen mit Landgrebe müssen in die beiden Jahre 1924 und 1925 fallen, da Landgrebe erst kurz zuvor Husserls Student geworden war und Carnap nicht lange danach nach Wien übersiedelte.

Wie bereits bemerkt unterschlägt Carnap später den biographischen Kontakt zu Husserl und Landgrebe ebenso wie seine damalige Wertschätzung der und die inhaltlichen Parallelen zur Phänomenologie. Dem Fachpublikum konnte allerdings spätestens seit 1957 durch einen Aufsatz von Bar-Hillel bekannt sein, dass Carnap einige Zeit bei Husserl studiert hatte und Husserlsche Ideen aufgreift. (Bar Hillel 1957, 362)[47] In der Autobiographie beschreibt Carnap dennoch das System des *Aufbau* als eine Realisierung von Russells Ideen in *Our Knowledge of the External World*. Seiner eigenen Darstellung nach war der *Aufbau* in seinen formalen Teilen von Frege und in seinen Inhaltlichen außer von Russell auch u. a. von Mach sowie der Gestalttheorie motiviert. Das Konstitutionssystem im engeren Sinne, d. h. die einzelnen Schritte und Stufen der „rationalen Rekonstruktion" unserer Gegenstandserkenntnis, stellt er jedoch durchweg als eigene Erfindung dar.

---

45 Brief an Husserl vom 2.11.1932, in Husserl 1994 Bd. IV, 298. Auf diese Stelle verweist Rosado-Haddock 2008. Dass Landgrebe von Carnaps „Freiburger Zeit" spricht, deutet auf eine ausführlichere Präsenz Carnaps.
46 Carnap 2015, Dokument 37: 01–1924 bis 12–1924, Eintrag vom 17.1.1924, 612.
47 Bar Hillel weist darauf hin, dass Carnaps Unterscheidung von Formations- und Transformationsregeln in der *Logischen Syntax der Sprache* schon in den *Logischen Untersuchungen* zu finden ist. (366 ff) Man kann Bar-Hillels Aufsatz als einen frühen leisen Hinweis auf eine plagiatorische Tendenz Carnaps lesen. – In diesem Zusammenhang ist eine Tagebuchnotiz Carnaps zu einem Treffen mit Landgrebe am 19.6.1933 interessant: „Wir sprechen über Phänomenologie; ich erkläre ihm, warum ich die Phänomenfragen für syntaktische Fragen halte." Carnap 2015, 52: 01–1933 bis 01–1934, 1099.

3 Die offenen Bezugnahmen auf Husserl und die Phänomenologie

In den letzten Jahren hat sich zunehmend die Auffassung durchgesetzt, dass der *Aufbau* wesentlich vom Neukantianismus inspiriert sei.[48] Demgegenüber wird hier die These vertreten, dass der *Aufbau* in großen Teilen der Phänomenologie Husserls entnommen ist. Dabei geht es vor allem um das inhaltliche Konstitutionssystem, also die Art und Weise, wie die Welt aus Elementarerlebnissen „aufgebaut" wird. Die These lautet, dass Carnap dieses System von Husserl übernommen, die Quelle dann aber systematisch verleugnet hat. Da es um einen Plagiatsvorwurf geht, soll hier zunächst darauf hingewiesen werden, dass Carnap im *Aufbau* nicht alle Bezüge zu Husserl und zur Phänomenologie unterdrückt hat. Es finden sich fünf explizite Referenzen auf Husserl, vier Verweise auf die Phänomenologie allgemein und zwei Verweise auf die phänomenologische Enthaltung, die sich teilweise überschneiden. Wir betrachten diese Bezugnahmen im Folgenden etwas genauer.

3.1 Die Bedeutung der „Phänomenologie"

Der *Aufbau* skizziert eine logisch-genetische Entwicklung der Welt aus Elementarerlebnissen in Konstitutionsstufen, die von Sinnesdaten bis zu Werten reichen. Carnap gibt dabei jeweils Kriterien an, mittels derer die jeweilige Stufe aus den vorangegangenen zu „definieren" ist. Die meisten dieser Konstitutionsstufen sind dabei nicht im Detail nach ihrer Konstitutionsstruktur bestimmt. Vielmehr verweist Carnap insbesondere auf den höheren Stufen auf diejenigen Wissenschaften, die sich mit diesen Details zu befassen hätten. An verschiedenen Stellen wird diese Aufgabe „der Phänomenologie" zugeschrieben, wobei Carnap gelegentlich die Phänomenologie als „Realwissenschaft" anspricht.
1. „Im Einzelnen wird die Beschaffenheit der Erlebnisse der verschiedenen Wertarten von der Wertphänomenologie untersucht." (*Aufbau*, 204)
2. „[...] eine Phänomenologie der Geisteswissenschaften müsste dann für den einzelnen primären geistigen Gegenstand feststellen, auf Grund welcher psychischen Gegenstände als seiner Manifestationen und in welcher Art er zu konstituieren ist." (Ebd., 201)

---

[48] Vgl. u. a. *Friedman/Creath* 2007, Richardson 1998 und Awodney et al. 2004. Ich gehe auf die neukantianische Interpretation im Kapitel 7.3 kurz ein.

3. „Der Inhalt [des dargestellten Konstitutionssystems] ist von den inhaltlichen Ergebnissen der Realwissenschaften, und zwar für die unteren Stufen insbesondere der Phänomenologie der Wahrnehmungen und der Psychologie abhängig." (Ebd., 148)
4. „Im Unterschied zu den Empfindungen, die zum Gegenstandsbereich der Psychologie gehören, gehören die Qualitäten zum Bereich der Phänomenologie oder der Gegenstandstheorie." (Ebd., 130)

Wenn manche Interpreten den *Aufbau* deshalb als „neukantianisch" qualifizieren, weil er die Konstitutionsschritte von den Wissenschaften definieren lasse, dann muss ihnen an dieser Stelle entgegengehalten werden, dass als definierende Wissenschaft häufig die Phänomenologie fungieren soll. In einem pauschalen Sinne wird dadurch der Phänomenologie sogar beträchtliche Bedeutung für die Konstitutionstheorie zugeschrieben. Diese Bedeutung wird allerdings entwertet dadurch, dass die Phänomenologie gemeinsam mit der Psychologie als „Realwissenschaft" apostrophiert wird, also, im Sinne des Serabriefs, nicht der „Generalstabskarte" angehört.[49] Durch diesen Kunstgriff gelingt es Carnap zudem, das von der Phänomenologie wesentlich inspirierte Konstitutionssystem als „empiristisch" erscheinen zu lassen.[50] Namentlich genannt wird in diesem Zusammenhang kein Phänomenologe; der Verweis bleibt unbestimmt.

3.2 Das Konstitutionssystem als eine „Mathesis der Erlebnisse"

Neben den allgemeinen Hinweisen auf die Phänomenologie wird Husserl im *Aufbau* auch gelegentlich direkt als Quelle von Aspekten des Konstitutionssystems genannt. Schon im §3 erwähnt Carnap Husserl (unter vielen anderen) im Zusammenhang mit der grundliegenden Idee der Konstitution. Er schreibt bezüglich dieser Idee, nachdem er Mach, Avenarius, Ziehen, Driesch und Dubislav als Vorläufer genannt hat:

> Berührungspunkte liegen ferner vor mit dem von Husserl als ‚mathesis der Erlebnisse' angedeuteten Ziel. (*Aufbau*, 4)

---

[49] Die Identifikation von Phänomenologie und Psychologie entspricht dem damaligen Verschleif der Begriffe und findet sich u. a. bei Driesch 1913, passim.

[50] Vgl. etwa den Verweis auf die Empirie in §103. Gleichzeitig kann Carnap damit das kantische synthetische Apriori zurückweisen: die definitorischen Übergänge zwischen den Konstitutionsstufen sind nun einer „Realwissenschaft" geschuldet (*Aufbau* §106, 148).

Roy 2004 hat versucht zu zeigen, dass der erwähnte Bezug von einer oberflächlichen Lesart der *Ideen I* herrühre und dem *Aufbau* daher keine echte Verwandtschaft zum phänomenologischen Programm zuzuschreiben sei. Dem sei hier ausdrücklich widersprochen.[51] Es ist schon biographisch unplausibel, dass Carnap, der während mehrerer Semester Husserls „Übungen für Fortgeschrittene" besuchte, ein oberflächlicher Rezipient der *Ideen I* war. Carnap zeigte sich vielmehr schon in der Dissertation als ein scharfsinniger und vorurteilsfreier, wenn auch durchaus selektiver und eklektischer Leser Husserls, der nicht nur die *Logischen Untersuchungen* und die *Ideen I* sehr gut kennt. Dies wird im Folgenden noch ausführlicher zu zeigen sein.

Husserls Idee einer Mathesis der Erlebnisse steht im Zusammenhang der in den §§71–75 der *Ideen I* diskutierten Frage, ob und inwiefern die Phänomenologie als eine deskriptive *Wissenschaft* auftreten könne, da sie doch von subjektiven Erlebnissen, d.h. von einer fluktuierenden Sphäre von Individualitäten (einem Erlebnisstrom), ihren Ausgang nimmt. Husserls erste Antwort lautet, dass es ihr um die Beschreibung nicht der Individualitäten, sondern der Wesen („Typen") geht, worauf sich die Frage stellt, ob die Phänomenologie etwa mit den Methoden der exakten „eidetischen" Wissenschaften, d.h. der Arithmetik und Geometrie, durchführbar sei. Dies ist in der Tat die entscheidende Frage auch für den *Aufbau*, ganz unabhängig vom Bezug zu Husserl. Husserl entwickelt sie in den angeführten Paragraphen mit aller wünschenswerten Klarheit und spitzt sie auf folgende Frage zu: Kann die Phänomenologie in der Weise der mathematischen Wissenschaften vorgehen, nämlich so

> dass eine e n d l i c h e A n z a h l, gegebenenfalls aus dem Wesen des Gebietes zu schöpfender Begriffe und Sätze die Gesamtheit aller möglichen Gestaltungen des Gebietes in der Weise rein analytischer Notwendigkeit vollständig und eindeutig bestimmt, so dass also in ihm prinzipiell nichts mehr offen bleibt. (*Ideen I* §72, 152)

Ohne auf die Einzelheiten einzugehen, sei hier festgehalten, dass Husserl diese Frage selbstverständlich verneint: Die Phänomenologie ist keine formale, sondern eine materiale Wesenswissenschaft, und sie geht nicht axiomatisch, sondern

---

51 Roys Darstellung ist in mehreren Hinsichten zurückzuweisen. Es geht Carnap nicht, wie Roy behauptet, um eine Reduktion wissenschaftlicher Begriffe auf das Gegebene, und Carnap setzt die formale Logik nicht schlechthin voraus, sondern verweist in §107 auf ihre Konstitution durch Russell/Whitehead. Sachlich unzutreffend ist jedoch vor allem Roys Identifikation einer „Mathesis der Erlebnisse" mit einer „formalen Wesenswissenschaft". Allerdings ist Roy zuzustimmen, wenn er schreibt, „Husserlian phenomenology can provide the theory of the epistemic order required by the sort of epistemic constructional system sought for in the 1928 book." (Roy 2004, 44)

deskriptiv vor; sie beschreibt den Zusammenhang der reinen Erlebnistypen. Während nun die untersten „fließenden Konkreta" weiter nicht begrifflich fixierbar sind, können die Wesen höherer Stufe, d. h. die Arten und Gattungen, streng begrifflich gefasst werden.

> So beschreiben wir und bestimmen damit in s t r e n g e n Begriffen das gattungsmäßige Wesen von Wahrnehmung überhaupt oder von untergeordneten Arten, wie Wahrnehmung von physischer Dinglichkeit, von animalischen Wesen u. dgl. (Ebd. §75, 157)

Und da dies die Aufgabe der Phänomenologie ist, so drängt sich die Frage auf

> ob es nicht im eidetischen Gebiet der reduzierten Phänomene (sei es im Ganzen, sei es in irgendeinem Teilgebiete) n e b e n dem beschreibenden auch ein idealisierendes Verfahren geben könne, das den anschaulichen Gegebenheiten reine und strenge Ideale substituiert, die dann gar als Grundmittel für eine Mathesis der Erlebnisse – als Gegenstück der beschreibenden Phänomenologie – dienen könnten. (Ebd., 158)

Diese Frage lässt Husserl ausdrücklich offen. Eine solche Mathesis der Erlebnisse hätte sicher keinen axiomatischen Charakter wie eine reine Wesenswissenschaft – sie würde den Bewusstseinsstrom nicht in eine „definite Mannigfaltigkeit", d. h. eine endliche Menge, verwandeln, aus der alle möglichen Konkretionen mit Notwendigkeit vollständig bestimmt werden könnten – sondern hätte vielmehr den Charakter einer reinen Strukturbeschreibung der Erlebnistypen, würde mithin das erfüllen, was der *Aufbau* eben generell leisten will.

Es erscheint plausibel, anzunehmen, dass Carnap glaubte, mit der Relationslogik ein Instrument zur Verfügung zu haben, das eine solche Mathesis ermöglicht. Hier fände sich also ein Beispiel für eine von Husserl entworfene Generalsstabskarte, zu welcher die (an der logischen Front entdeckten) formalen Mittel so exakt passen, dass damit womöglich auch bisher unentdeckte wissenschaftliche Zusammenhänge aufgedeckt werden könnten. Dies, die formale Durchführung einer Mathesis der Erlebnisse, scheint ein Projekt, mit dem sich Carnap bei Husserl hätte habilitieren können. Einschränkend ist allerdings zu bemerken, dass Husserl eine mengentheoretische Rekonstruktion von Universalien schon in den §§ 4 und 5 der zweiten Logischen Untersuchung zurückgewiesen hatte, und zwar wegen des Problems der koextensionalen Eigenschaften, das sehr viel später Nelson Goodman gegen den *Aufbau* ins Feld führen wird. (Goodman 1966) So bleibt unentschieden, ob Husserl das Carnapsche Habilitationsprojekt nicht auch aus inhaltlichen Gründen abgelehnt hat.

3.3 Die Epoché, die eigenpsychische Basis und der Erlebnisstrom

Im §64 des *Aufbau* finden sich zwei offene Verweise auf Husserl: einmal wird die phänomenologische Enthaltung Epoché als methodischer Ausgangspunkt der Konstitution aufgeführt (ebd., 86), zum zweiten wird Husserl unter vielen anderen Protagonisten als Verfechter einer „eigenpsychischen Basis" erwähnt. In Bezug auf die Epoché schreibt Carnap:

> Zu Beginn des Systems sind die Erlebnisse einfach so hinzunehmen, wie sie sich geben; die in ihnen vorkommenden Realsetzungen und Nichtrealsetzungen werden nicht mitgemacht, sondern ‚eingeklammert'; es wird also die phänomenologische ‚Enthaltung' (ἐποχή) *im Sinne Husserls* ausgeübt. (*Ideen I* §§31,32; Hervorh. V.M.)

Hatte Carnap im *Chaos*-Text noch mit einem erkenntnistheoretischen „Kahlschlag" begonnen, der jede vorgegebene Ordnung, alle Bestimmungen sowie die meisten Erlebnisse wegstrich, übt er hier eine phänomenologisch korrekte Enthaltung, indem er lediglich die mit den Urteilen verbundenen Existenzannahmen „außer Vollzug setzt". Die Bedeutung dieses Schritts wird in der Rezeption des *Aufbau* systematisch unterschätzt. Die Epoché ist nicht ein gängiges philosophisches Verfahren, von dem Carnap hier unter anderem Gebrauch macht; vielmehr kennzeichnet sie die Phänomenologie Husserls nach den *Logischen Untersuchungen* und dient, wie es in den *Ideen I* heißt, der „Entdeckung einer neuen wissenschaftlichen Domäne" (*Ideen I*, 65), der Domäne des reinen Bewusstseins. Ausdrücklich grenzt Husserl im von Carnap angeführten §32 der *Ideen I* die Epoché von der positivistischen Forderung nach Metaphysikfreiheit ab:

> Man wird die hier fragliche ἐποχή nicht verwechseln mit derjenigen, die der Positivismus fordert, und gegen die er freilich selbst, wie wir uns überzeugen mussten, verstößt. Es handelt sich jetzt nicht um Ausschaltung aller, die reine Sachlichkeit der Forschung trübenden Vorurteile, nicht um die Konstitution einer ‚theoriefreien', ‚metaphysikfreien' Wissenschaft durch Rückgang aller Begründung auf die unmittelbaren Vorfindlichkeiten, und auch nicht um Mittel, dergleichen Ziele, über deren Wert ja keine Frage ist, zu erreichen. Was wir fordern liegt in einer ganz anderen Linie. (Ebd., 65)

Husserl fordert nun, dass ein auf Epoché beruhendes System keine Sätze der positiven Wissenschaften voraussetzen darf, während Carnap auf der anderen Seite für die Ableitung der Konstitutionsregeln wissenschaftliche Erkenntnisse einsetzen will. (*Aufbau* §106) Steht dies nicht in Widerspruch zu Carnaps Ankündigung, er wolle Epoché „im Sinne Husserls" üben? Im §179 kommt Carnap auf das Problem direkt zu sprechen – antwortet also auf einen möglichen Einwand

Husserls – und gesteht zu, dass praktisch gesehen die wissenschaftlichen Aussagen für das Konstitutionssystem vorausgesetzt sind. Systematisch oder „logisch" gesehen wird aber ein Satz erst dann zu einem wissenschaftlichen, wenn der Gegenstand, über den er spricht „von den Grundgegenständen her konstituiert ist" (*Aufbau*, 253), im Sinne Husserls also von der durch die Epoché gewonnenen Sphäre des reinen Bewusstseins. Es ist dieser systematisch-logische Sinn, der das Aufbauprogramm bestimmt.

Noch in einem weiteren wesentlichen Punkt übernimmt Carnap im §64 und danach Husserls *Ideen I*, allerdings diesmal ohne sich ausdrücklich dazu zu bekennen. In Husserls *Ideen I* folgt auf die Einführung und Darstellung der Epoché in den §§27–32 unmittelbar ein Kapitel über „Bewusstsein und natürliche Wirklichkeit" (§§33–46), in dem Husserl das Feld der reinen Phänomene, das durch die Epoché freigelegt wird, beschreibt. Der Zusammenhang kann nicht eng genug gedacht werden: Hat man Epoché geübt, also Existenzvoraussetzungen „eingeklammert", so erscheint die Welt als Strom von Erlebnissen, in dem sich verschiedenartige Erlebnistypen („cogitationes") unterscheiden lassen, aus denen sich die Gegenstände als intentionale Objekte konstituieren (oder in welchem sie sich als solche darstellen). „Erlebnis" und „Erlebnisstrom" sind Grundbegriffe der *Ideen I*. Erlebnisse können intentional und nichtintentional (Empfindungsdaten) sein sowie reflektiert und unreflektiert („im Modus aktueller Zuwendung", „im Modus der Inaktualität"; Ebd. 72) auftreten. Die Frage nach dem Wesen des Bewusstseins betrifft nach Husserl

> da wir hier Bewusstsein in jedem noch so weiten, sich schließlich mit dem Begriff des Erlebnisses deckenden Sinn verstehen können, die Eigenwesenheit des Erlebnisstromes und aller seiner Komponenten (ebd., 80).

Carnap, nachdem er im §64 die Epoché offen von Husserl übernommen hat, übernimmt diesen Begriff des Bewusstseins, wenn er im nächsten Absatz schreibt:

> [D]as Grundgebiet liegt nur im Bewusstsein (im weiteren Sinne): zu ihm gehören alle Erlebnisse, ob gleichzeitig oder nachträglich auf sie reflektiert wird oder nicht. Wir sprechen deshalb lieber vom ‚Erlebnisstrom'. (*Aufbau*, 86)

Diese terminologische und sachliche Entscheidung, die dem engen Zusammenhang von Epoché und Bewusstsein bei Husserl genau entspricht, wird nun aber nur mehr beiläufig und unter vielen anderen Husserl zugeschrieben. Carnap erwähnt vielmehr als Hauptvertreter einer eigenpsychischen Basis mit methodischem Anspruch („methodischer Solipsismus") Driesch und fährt fort:

> Es seien hier noch einige Vertreter dieser Auffassung genannt, die aber zum Teil die solipsistische Methode nur zu Beginn anwenden und später einen Sprung in das Fremdpsychische hinüber machen. (*Aufbau*, 86)

In dem folgenden mehr als einseitigen Literaturverweis nennt Carnap (in dieser Reihenfolge) v. Schubert-Soldern, Gomperz, Ziehen, Husserl, Dingler, Reiniger, Jacoby und Volkelt und verweist bei Husserl auf S. 316 der *Ideen I*. Die Seitenangabe ist irreführend, da an der angegeben Stelle der *Ideen I* nur marginal vom Bewusstsein die Rede ist, während das Thema im zweiten und dritten Kapitel ausführlich behandelt wird.[52] Auch kann Carnap kaum behaupten, dass Husserl im Gegensatz zu ihm „einen Sprung in das Fremdpsychische" mache, da er Husserls Konstitutionsschritten genau folgt. Carnaps Vorgehen in §64 ist symptomatisch für den ganzen *Aufbau*: Das im Text enthaltene Habilitationsprojekt für Husserl wird im veröffentlichten Text des *Aufbau* in einer Vielzahl zumeist irrelevanter oder irreführender Verweise und Umdeutungen unsichtbar gemacht.

4 Der *Aufbau* und das Stufenmodell der *Ideen II*

Wir wenden uns nun dem zweiten Band der *Ideen* zu. Husserl arbeitete seit 1912 an diesem Band, der bis 1928 immer wieder umgearbeitet und erweitert wurde und vermutlich in die *Cartesianischen Meditationen* einging. Das umfassende Thema der *Ideen II* ist das Problem der systematischen Konstitution aller möglichen Gegenstandsbereiche, wobei die Frage ihrer „Rückführbarkeit" aufeinander oder umgekehrt: ihrer genetischen Analyse im Hintergrund steht. Von den verschiedenen Manuskripten hatte Edith Stein seit 1916 handschriftliche Abschriften angefertigt, die sie 1918 zum Teil selbstständig zu einem größeren Manuskript zusammenstellte. Dieses war dann Grundlage einer Schreibmaschinenabschrift, die in den Jahren 1924–25 von Landgrebe angefertigt wurde, also in jener Zeit, in der Carnap an seiner Habilitationsschrift arbeitete. Dieser Text wurde erst 1952 als Band IV der Husserliana publiziert.[53]

---

52 Das zweite Kapitel mit den Paragraphen 3–46 trägt den Titel „Bewusstsein und natürliche Wirklichkeit, das dritte mit den Paragraphen 47–55 „Die Region des reinen Bewusstseins".
53 Die *Ideen II* stellen den Interpreten vor die Schwierigkeit, dass die Textzusammenstellung nicht von Husserl, sondern von Stein stammt, und Husserl daher nicht im selben Sinne als „Autor" angesprochen werden kann, wie er etwa Autor der *Logischen Untersuchungen* oder der *Ideen I* ist. Dennoch stammen alle in Hua IV veröffentlichten Texte tatsächlich von Husserl. Auch versucht die Steinsche Anordnung die phänomenologische Genese mehr oder weniger in der sinngemäßen Reihenfolge darzustellen. Husserl war mit der Zusammenstellung nicht zufrieden. In einem voraussichtlich 2016 erscheinenden neuen Band der Husserliana (im Folgenden abgekürzt mit

Wie nahe verwandt Carnaps Idee des Konstitutionssystems überhaupt mit derjenigen Husserls ist, zeigt sich schon in den *Ideen I* an verschiedenen Stellen, so etwa im § 151, wo Husserl schreibt:

> Diese Untersuchungen sind wesentlich bestimmt durch die verschiedenen Stufen und Schichten der Dingkonstitution im Rahmen des originär erfahrenden Bewusstseins. Jede Stufe und jede Schicht in der Stufe ist dadurch charakterisiert, dass sie eine eigene Einheit konstituiert, die ihrerseits notwendiges Mittelglied ist für die volle Konstitution des Dinges. (*Ideen I*, 352)

Dieses Konstitutionssystem, dessen Aufbau in den *Ideen I* nur angedeutet ist, wird also in den verschiedenen Manuskripten, aus denen die *Ideen II* eine Synopse bilden, detailliert ausgeführt.

Die *Ideen II* sind selbst für den Kenner von Husserls Hauptwerken kein leicht verständlicher Text. Es handelt sich eben nicht um eine vom Verfasser für die Publikation fertig gestellte Monographie, sondern wenigstens zum Teil um von Stein und Landgrebe sinngemäß angeordnete Manuskripte. Obwohl dem Inhalt nach klar gegliedert in drei Abschnitte „Die Konstitution der materiellen Natur", „Die Konstitution der animalischen Natur" und „Die Konstitution der geistigen Welt", tauchen daher doch immer wieder Gedanken und Themen aus dem zweiten und dritten auch im ersten Abschnitt auf und fließen in die Überlegungen zur Konstitution der materiellen Natur ein. Der Text mäandert in diesem Sinne und ist in seinem letzten Impetus nicht leicht zu durchschauen. Dennoch ist auch für den flüchtigen Leser ohne weiteres klar, dass es sich um ein Konstitutionssystem handelt, das untere und höhere Konstitutionsstufen beschreibt, und das insofern exakt in die Problematik passt, die Carnap in seiner Habilitationsschrift bearbeiten wollte. Insbesondere hatte Carnap im Brief an Schlick im November 1924 angekündigt, dass er im Folgenden „das Problem der Kategorien oder Konstitutionsprinzipien der verschiedenen Realitätssphären bearbeiten" wolle, das ihm nun am meisten am Herzen liege.[54] Dafür sind die *Ideen II* unmittelbar einschlägig.

Urtexte) werden daher die Originalmanuskripte der *Ideen II* mit entsprechenden Ergänzungstexten versammelt. – Obwohl Carnap sicher keinen Zugriff auf die Originalmanuskripte hatte, werden auch die *Urtexte* im Folgenden gelegentlich herangezogen. Für die Forschung an der genetischen Phänomenologie werden sie in Zukunft maßgeblich sein.

54 Brief Carnaps an Schlick vom 11.11.1924, in Carnap 1922–1927. Bemerkt sei an dieser Stelle, dass der Begriff der Realitätssphäre aus den *Ideen I* stammt und dort von Husserl im Zusammenhang mit der Durchführung eines Konstitutionssystems verwendet wird: „Zu beachten ist aber, dass unser Ziel hier nicht darin lag, eine ausführende Theorie solcher transzendentaler Konstitution zu geben und damit eine neue ‚Erkenntnistheorie' hinsichtlich der Realitätssphären zu entwerfen, sondern nur allgemeine Gedanken zur Einsicht zu bringen, die für die Gewinnung

Es ist, wie bereits dargestellt, unklar, inwiefern Carnap Zugang zu den von Stein und Landgrebe zusammengestellten Abschriften hatte. Ob Landgrebe Carnap Einblick in das Manuskript gewährte oder Einzelheiten mündlich weitergab, oder ob einzelne Konstitutionsschritte in Husserls Seminaren zur Sprache kamen, wird wohl nicht mehr zu rekonstruieren sein. Bei der großen Anzahl an detailgetreuen Parallelen, die zu keinem anderen philosophischen System nachweisbar sind, sollte die Frage des Zugangs jedoch sekundär sein. Mindestens die Paragraphen 1–11 der Ideen II waren jedenfalls unter Husserls Studenten bekannt. Sie sind der Vorlesung „Natur und Geist" aus dem Jahr 1913 entnommen und existierten als Abschriften u. a. von Edith Stein.[55]

Bei einem Vergleich der Konstitutionssysteme des *Aufbau* und der *Ideen II* darf man nicht eine lineare Übereinstimmung *in der Darstellung* erwarten. Während Carnap die Konstitutionsstufen von unten (Elementarerlebnisse) nach oben (geistige Welt und Werte) abarbeitet, beginnen die *Ideen II* bei den materiellen Gegenständen, die zunächst mit den Werten kontrastiert werden. Der Text geht von diesen zurück zu den Empfindungen und von dort zu den höheren Stufen wie den anderen Personen und geistigen Gegenständen. Dies ist kein systematischer Unterschied, sondern lediglich einer im methodischen Vorgehen: Die *Ideen II* folgen zunächst der Nachfrage des Wissenschaftlers nach der konstitutiven Herkunft seiner Gegenstände, während Carnap die Antworten schon als gegeben voraussetzt.

Auch in der groben Gliederung weicht der *Aufbau* von den *Ideen II* etwas ab: Carnap unterteilt die Konstitutionsstufen in „eigenpsychische Gegenstände", „physische Gegenstände" und „fremdpsychische und geistige Gegenstände" (wobei die Werte als eigener Bereich zu ergänzen wären), während in den *Ideen II* die „eigenpsychischen Gegenstände" nicht eigens ausgezeichnet, sondern bei der Konstitution der materiellen und der seelischen Realität mitbehandelt und die Sphären des Seelischen und des Geistigen deutlicher getrennt werden. Auch dies sind keine systematischen Unterschiede, da die Konstitutionsstufen mit ihren definitorischen Übergängen im Wesentlichen dieselben sind. Terminologisch gibt es sowohl Übereinstimmungen („mein Leib"), als auch Carnapsche Synonyme („das Fremdpsychische" und das „Eigenpsychische" bei Carnap; „das Fremdseelische" und „das Idiopsychische" bei Husserl). Husserls Darstellung in den *Ideen II* ebenso wie in den *Urtexten* ist darüber hinaus wesentlich detaillierter und geht in die phänomenologischen Zusammenhänge im Einzelnen ein, während der

---

der Idee des transzendental reinen Bewusstseins hilfreich sein können." (*Ideen I*, 121) Die Ausführung fand dann in den *Ideen II* statt.
55 Für diese Auskunft danke ich Dirk Fonfara.

Aufbau geradezu als knappe Zusammenfassung der Ergebnisse Husserls gelesen werden kann, die sich Einzelheiten weitgehend erspart. Insgesamt kann man die Unterschiede zu Husserl in Terminologie und Organisation des *Aufbau* zu den Maskierungen der Herkunft rechnen; eine inhaltliche Differenz ergibt sich daraus nur in wenigen Fällen, auf die im Folgenden jeweils hingewiesen wird. Wir widmen uns nun einigen der auffallendsten Parallelen.

4.1 Die naturalistische Einstellung

Von Interesse sind die *Ideen II* für den *Aufbau* nicht nur, weil sie Konstitutionsprinzipien für die Realitätssphären der materiellen, seelischen und geistigen Realität formulieren, sondern vor allem insofern, als sie dies im ersten und zweiten Abschnitt unter der „naturalistischen Einstellung", d. h. der Einstellung des Naturwissenschaftlers tun. Genauer: in den ersten beiden Abschnitten geht es nicht um die Konstitution von Teilen unserer alltäglich vorfindlichen oder schlechthin vorhandenen Realität, sondern um die Konstitution der Gegenstände der Wissenschaften, d. h. um „Naturobjekte". Das Interesse Husserls entspricht hier ganz den ersten Paragraphen des *Aufbau*, in denen Carnap deutlich macht, dass es ihm um ein Konstitutionssystem der Begriffe der *Wissenschaften* zu tun sei, wobei er Begriff und Gegenstand als austauschbar behandelt. (*Aufbau* §5)[56]

Husserls Zugriff auf dieses Thema sei hier zunächst grob umrissen. Husserl beobachtet, dass wir es in der natürlichen Einstellung, in der wir im Alltag mit Dingen und Personen umgehen, nicht mit „Naturobjekten" im Sinne der Naturwissenschaften zu tun haben, sondern mit vielfach „wertgetränkten" Gegenständen. Ein Ding als Naturobjekt zu betrachten heißt dagegen geradezu, es als wertneutral ins Auge zu fassen. So mag der Naturwissenschaftler, der den blauen Himmel in der „naturalistischen Einstellung" betrachtet, diesen zwar nebenbei auch noch bewundern, aber sein wissenschaftliches Interesse abstrahiert von dieser Wertung, er als Wissenschaftler „lebt" nicht darin. Nun sind nach Husserl alle unsere Bewusstseinsakte an der Basis „doxischer" Natur, das heißt auch unsere Gefühls- und wertenden Akte sind in einem basalen Urteilsakt, einer „Urdoxa" fundiert. Die naturalistische Einstellung ist dann dadurch charakterisiert, dass sie in der Hauptsache thetisch, doxisch, urteilend vorgeht und die

---

[56] Carnaps Identifikation von Begriff und Gegenstand über die Quasigegenstände, sowie Husserls Begriff des Begriffs und des kategorialen Gegenstandes würden ein weiteres interessantes Feld von Vergleichsmöglichkeiten abgeben, das wir hier aus Raumgründen aussparen.

mitverknüpften Wertungen „einklammert".[57] Die Sphäre der Natur, wie sie von den Naturwissenschaften untersucht wird, ist das Korrelat dieser theoretischen Einstellung. Die Beschränkung auf diese Sphäre hat zur Folge, dass in der naturalistischen Einstellung genau genommen keine anderen Personen zur Verfügung stehen; diese begegnen dem Naturwissenschaftler als materielle Körper und müssen erst auf höheren Stufen konstituiert werden. Daher beginnt die Untersuchung methodisch in einer „solipsistischen Sphäre" und mit einer Art Epoché

> [W]ir lassen uns nur durch das doxisch objektivierende Bewusstsein und nicht durch das wertende ‚Gegenstände konstituieren'. Die uns so erfahrbare Sachsphäre soll uns jetzt die naturwissenschaftliche bestimmen. Wir halten uns also von jetzt an rein in der naturwissenschaftlichen Einstellung und sind uns dabei klar, dass wir damit eine Art Ausschaltung, e i n e A r t ἐποχή, vollziehen. (*Ideen II*, 27)

Als Carnap im §64 die Husserlsche Epoché als methodischen Ausgangspunkt einführt, beruft er sich explizit auf den ersten Band der *Ideen*. Tatsächlich ist es eher die naturalistische Epoché des zweiten Bandes, die sein Vorgehen bestimmt. Denn anders als Husserl in den *Ideen I* geht es ihm nicht darum, das Feld des reinen Bewusstseins als solches offen zu legen und in seinen Konstitutionsleistungen zu erfassen (von denen dann die Welt der naturwissenschaftlich bestimmten Natur einen spezifischen Ausschnitt bildet), sondern zu zeigen, wie sich die wissenschaftlichen Aussagen in Elementarerlebnisse eines solipsistischen Subjekts übersetzen lassen. Carnap braucht daher nicht alle wissenschaftlichen Existenzannahmen einklammern, sondern nur Epoché in Bezug auf Wertgegenstände zu üben. Dies würde die Inkonsistenz, die aus der Einführung der Epoché und der Forderung nach Wissenschaftlichkeit entsteht, entschärfen.

Zusammenfassend sei festgehalten, dass das Interesse Carnaps – die „Reduktion" naturwissenschaftlicher Aussagen auf Erlebnisse – dem Interesse Husserls in der ersten Hälfte der *Ideen II* genau entspricht. Beide fragen: wie viel lässt sich von der Welt der Naturwissenschaften von einem *solus ipse* ausgehend konstituieren?

---

[57] „[D]ie thematische Einstellung der naturalen Erfahrung und Erfahrungsforschung des Naturwissenschaftlers ist die doxisch-theoretische. Ihr gegenüber gibt es andere Einstellungen, nämlich die wertende (die im weitesten Sinne schön und gut wertende) und die praktische Einstellung." (Ideen II, 2) „Im gewöhnlichen Leben haben wir es gar nicht mit Naturobjekten zu tun. Was wir Dinge nennen, das sind Gemälde, Statuen, Gärten, Häuser, Tische, Kleider, Werkzeuge usw. All das sind Wertobjekte verschiedener Art, Gebrauchsobjekte, praktische Objekte. Es sind keine naturwissenschaftlichen Objekte." (Ebd., 27)

4.2 Der Begriff der Konstitution

Der Begriff der Konstitution ist wohl die erste augenfällige Übereinstimmung zwischen den *Ideen II* und dem *Aufbau*. Carnap wollte ursprünglich der aus der Habilitationsschrift hervorgegangenen Monographie den Titel „Konstitutionstheorie" geben, ließ sich aber von Schlick davon abbringen. Dennoch taucht nun der Begriff der Konstitution bereits im ersten Kapitel auf, welches als Ziel der Arbeit „ein Konstitutionssystem der Begriffe" bestimmt. (*Aufbau*, 1) Der Titel von Husserls *Ideen II* wiederum lautet „Phänomenologische Untersuchungen zur Konstitution". Bedenkt man, dass die Phänomenologie nach Carnaps eigenem Bekunden wesentliche Teile seines Systems konkret ausgestalten sollte, so wäre ein Text mit diesem Titel für ihn unbedingt einschlägig gewesen und kaum verständlich wäre es, wenn er ihn nicht berücksichtigt hätte.

Husserl hat den Begriff der Konstitution nie explizit definiert, sondern nur verwendet, weshalb er Gegenstand umfangreicher Kontroversen geworden ist.[58] Dennoch ist der Grundgedanke intuitiv nachvollziehbar. Dass sich ein Gegenstand im Bewusstsein konstituiert, heißt grob gesprochen, dass er sich auf der Basis der „Deckung" von verschiedenen intentionalen Erlebnissen (z. B. Wahrnehmungen) herauskristallisiert. So kann man sich etwa in Zeitlupe vorstellen, wie aus verschiedenen Erlebnissen, die eine unterschiedlich rot gefärbte Scheibe zum Gegenstand haben, schließlich die Wahrnehmung eines Apfels hervorgeht. Das Deckungserlebnis lässt sich nicht auf die Zusammensetzung von bloßen Sinnesdaten reduzieren (ist also intentional zu verstehen), und auch die einzelnen sich deckenden Erlebnisse können ihrerseits als Ergebnis fundamentalerer Deckungen verstanden werden. Umgekehrt konstituiert sich über die Wahrnehmung verschiedener Äpfel zu verschiedenen Zeiten und in verschiedenen Zuständen der Gegenstand Apfel, daraus z. B. Obst, Baumfrucht, Nahrungsmittel oder ganz allgemein Gegenstand. So entsteht eine Ontologie (Husserl: „regionale Ontologie") von Gegenstandsarten und Gegenstandssphären, deren Elemente sich durch einen stufenförmigen Aufbau auf der Basis immer fundamentalerer Gegenstände bestimmen lassen.

Während die „Verallgemeinerung" von Äpfeln zum Begriff Apfel oder Obst relativ unproblematisch erscheint, gibt es kritische Übergänge, etwa von der zweidimensionalen zur dreidimensionalen Wahrnehmung, von materiellen zu belebten Körpern, von Tieren zu Menschen, von wertneutralen zu werthaltigen

---

58 Ströker 1984, Kern 1964, Lohmar 2009. Zu den Literaturverweisen sei an dieser Stelle angemerkt, dass hier keine Vollständigkeit angestrebt, sondern jeweils nur eine knappe Auswahl genannt wird. Es geht um den Plagiatsnachweis, nicht um die Aufklärung der exegetischen Zusammenhänge im Einzelnen. Diese müssen zukünftiger Forschung vorbehalten bleiben.

Gegenständen und schließlich von dem subjektiven Ausgangspunkt in den Erlebnissen zu einer objektiven Welt. Will man wirklich solche Gegenstände und Gegenstandssphären als Ergebnis der Deckung fundamentaler Erlebnisse auffassen, so muss man zeigen, wie aus den Erlebnissen niedrigerer Stufe diejenigen höherer Stufe hervorgehen, ohne dass man den höheren Gegenstand selbst ad hoc einführt. Genau dies ist „das Problem der Kategorien oder Konstitutionsprinzipien der verschiedenen Realitätssphären", das Carnap im Brief an Schlick vom 11.11. 1924 als seine Hauptschwierigkeit bezeichnet hatte.[59]

Carnaps Begriff der Konstitution scheint jedoch zunächst zumindest verbal ein ganz anderer als derjenige Husserls. Carnap nämlich definiert den Begriff nicht über die Deckung von Erlebnissen, sondern über die Umformung von Aussagen. So heißt es im §2 des *Aufbau*:

> Ein Gegenstand (oder Begriff) heißt auf einen oder mehrere andere Gegenstände ‚zurückführbar', wenn alle Aussagen über ihn sich umformen lassen in Aussagen über andere Gegenstände. (*Aufbau*, 1)

„Zurückführen" ist nun ein Synonym für „konstituieren", und es gilt,

> 'a aus b, c konstituieren' soll bedeuten: eine allgemeine Regel aufstellen, die angibt, in welcher Weise man in jedem einzelnen Falle eine Aussage über a umformen muss, um eine Aussage über b, c zu erhalten. (*Aufbau*, 2)

Jedoch bedeutet dieses Umformen nicht, dass nun Begriff oder Gegenstand a auf die Begriffe oder Gegenstände b und c „reduziert" würde. Dies macht Carnap deutlich, wenn er „summative Verbindung" von „logischem Komplex" unterscheidet. So ist etwa der Gegenstand Staat aus psychischen Vorgängen zu konstituieren, „das bedeutet aber nicht etwa, dass er eine Summe psychischer Vorgänge sei". (*Aufbau*, 5) Der logische Komplex ist nicht ein Konglomerat aus seinen Elementen, sondern ein eigenständiger Gegenstand. Daher „konstruiert" der Aufbau auch nicht etwa neue Gegenstände, sondern stellt einen erlebten („fundierten") genetischen Zusammenhang dar. Darin ist er dem Konstitutionssystem Husserls ganz analog.[60]

---

59 Vgl. oben 2.2.
60 Aus diesem Grund ist auch die Übersetzung von „Konstitution" durch „construction" in der englischen Ausgabe des *Aufbau* irreführend. (Der Titel von §1 etwa lautet im Deutschen: „Das Ziel: Konstitutionssystem der Begriffe", im Englischen: „A constructional sytem of concepts". (*Aufbau*, 1; Carnap 1967, 5) Diese Übersetzung wirkt bis heute zurück auf die Interpretation. So schreiben Moran und Cohen 2012 unter dem Stichwort „construction (Aufbau)", dass Husserl zwischen Konstitution und Aufbau unterschieden habe und Carnap einen Aufbau, nicht eine Konstitution

Auch das Ziel der Carnapschen Konstitution deckt sich mit demjenigen Husserls. Beiden geht es darum, ein Konstitutionssystem der Erkenntnisgegenstände aufzustellen. Darunter versteht Carnap

> eine stufenweise Ordnung der Gegenstände derart, dass die Gegenstände einer jeden Stufe aus denen der niederen Stufen konstituiert werden. (Ebd.)

Das „Problem der Konstitutionsprinzipien" besteht dabei darin, die Regeln zu finden, durch welche die Übergänge zwischen den einzelnen Stufen bewältigt werden.[61] Betrachten wir nun, wie Husserl und Carnap diese Übergänge bestimmen.

4.3 Das Konstitutionssystem

In den ersten beiden Abschnitten der *Ideen II* geht es um die systematische Konstitution der Naturobjekte als Korrelate der theoretischen Einstellung. Folgt man dem konstitutiven Gedankengang der *Ideen II*, so fragt Husserl zunächst, wie sich uns materielle Gegenstände darstellen. (§§13,15) Sie tun dies als sinnlich „erfüllte Raumgestalten" (Schemata), die im Wechsel der Erscheinungen, also im zeitlichen Ablauf, als „dieselben" erscheinen, und die sich gegenüber bloßen Phantomen (Träumen, Halluzinationen etc.) dadurch als materiell auszeichnen, dass sie in systematischen, wiederholbaren, kausalen Beziehungen stehen. Will

---

beschreibe: „Rudolf Carnap, who attended Husserl's Seminars in the 1920s, refers, in his *Logical structure of the world*, to the ‚logical construction' or ‚structure' of the world. [For Husserl] constituton includes the idea of reference to an intending consciousness, whereas construction suggests the a priori arrangement of elements and parts of conscious experience." (Moran/Cohen 2012, 72) Dabei berücksichtigen sie jedoch nicht, dass Carnap im Deutschen das Wort Konstitution verwendet und dass der ursprüngliche Titel des Werks gerade „Konstitutionstheorie" lauten sollte. Zu Carnaps Begriff der Intentionalität vgl. unten 6.5.1.

61 In den §§103 und 104 führt Carnap einige allgemeine Konstitutionsregeln und -prinzipien an, die allerdings formalen Charakter haben. Er behauptet hier, dass auf ihnen der Übergang von einer Konstitutionsstufe zur nächsten beruhe, weshalb sie „apriori" seien, dass sie aber dennoch durch „Abstraktion" aus der Erfahrung gewonnen wurden. Carnap analysiert, mit anderen Worten, die inhaltlich gegebenen Übergänge (nach der Art der nun im Folgenden betrachteten) auf ihre formalen relationslogischen Kennzeichen hin. Die inhaltlichen Übergänge selbst muss er dabei schon zur Verfügung haben, also wissen, wie z.B. „mein Leib" sich aus der Klasse der Wahrnehmungsdinge auszeichnet. Diese Übergänge stellen das eigentliche Problem dar. Wenn Carnap nicht konkret zeigen kann, auf welche Weise sich eine höhere Stufe wie etwa das Fremdseelische aus niedrigeren Stufen heraus „definieren" lässt, dann macht das Konstitutionssystem keinen Sinn. Dies im Einzelnen zeigen zu können, ist aber gerade Carnaps im §64 formulierter Anspruch.

ich wissen, ob die Erscheinung vor mir ein physikalischer Gegenstand ist, werde ich also etwa versuchen, diesen systematisch physikalischen Einwirkungen (Stoß, Druck etc.) auszusetzen.

Nachdem die konstitutive Differenz der Kausalität im Sinne von funktionaler Abhängigkeit gewonnen ist, geht Husserl als nächstes der Frage nach, wie sich die erfüllten Raumgestalten, die Wahrnehmungsdinge, konstituieren, und kommt von diesen auf die wesentliche Rolle, die „mein Leib" bei der Konstitution spielt. (§18a) Die Wahrnehmungsdinge sind immer in Bezug auf diesen Leib als „Zentrum" bestimmt. In der naturalistischen Einstellung ist also als nächstes dieser Leib als *solus ipse* zu betrachten, eine Aufgabe, die bereits in die Konstitution der seelischen Realität fällt und dort ein ganzes Kapitel bestimmt. (§§35–42) Zuvor allerdings macht Husserl noch klar, dass das physikalische Ding, also der eigentliche Gegenstand der Physik, nicht mit dem materiellen Körper, wie er bisher konstituiert wurde, identisch ist, da der letztere wesentlich die für den physikalischen Gegenstand irrelevante Abhängigkeit vom Leib impliziert. Das physikalische Ding stellt sich vielmehr als ein rein mathematisch bestimmter Gegenstand dar. (§18d) In später folgenden Kapiteln (§§43–47) fragt Husserl, wie wir bestimmte materielle Dinge als animalische Wesen auszeichnen – dies geschieht durch die Einfühlung – wonach er sich der Konstitution der geistigen Welt zuwendet. Ein wesentlicher Punkt dabei, der in Carnaps *Aufbau* nicht reflektiert wird, ist der Wechsel der Einstellung: wie oben bemerkt geschieht die Konstitution der materiellen und der seelischen Realität in der naturalistischen Einstellung. Da aber in die Konstitution der geistigen Welt Werte wesentlich involviert sind, muss die naturalistische Einstellung schließlich aufgegeben werden. Daraus folgt, dass keine echte genetische Kontinuität von den untersten Stufen zur Welt der geistigen Gegenstände reicht. Die geistigen Gegenstände „bekunden" sich zwar in der physischen und seelischen Realität, sind aber nicht auf diese rückführbar – ein Standpunkt, den Carnap, wie wir noch sehen werden, übernimmt, allerdings ohne ihn weiter zu begründen.[62]

Mit diesem ungefähren Fahrplan vor Augen lässt sich nun die Übereinstimmung zwischen den *Ideen II* und dem *Aufbau* recht genau nachvollziehen. Sie liegt zunächst in den einzelnen Konstitutionsschritten, also der Frage, wie sich denn aus der „eigenpsychischen Basis", d.h. dem leiblich lokalisierten Zentrum des *solus ipse*, die Welt der Natur- und schließlich auch der Geisteswissenschaften etabliert. Genau für diese Konstitutionsschritte, die getreu mit denen der *Ideen II* übereinstimmen, hat Carnap im §64 des *Aufbau* und in der Autobiographie Ur-

---

[62] Eine Zusammenfassung des Konstitutionssystems findet sich auch in Beilage XIII zum zweiten Urtext. (*Urtexte*, 313 ff)

heberschaft beansprucht. Dieser Anspruch wird im Folgenden zurückgewiesen. Wir gehen dazu dem Stufensystem in der Reihenfolge der *Ideen II* schrittweise nach.

4.4 Das materielle Ding und das unwirkliche Ding

a) Husserl

Husserl begreift das materielle Ding in Überstimmung mit der Tradition als *res extensa*, das bedeutet für ihn: als (mit sinnlichen Qualitäten) erfüllten Raumkörper. Im Unterschied zur Tradition stellt er jedoch im Zuge phänomenologischer Differenzbetrachtung (d. h. „Wesenserschauung") fest, dass diese Bestimmung nur ein notwendiges, aber kein hinreichendes Kriterium dafür ist, dass ein Ding als materielles Ding erscheint (Ideen II, 37). Eine in einem Stereoskop gesehene rote, raue Pyramide ist ein erfüllter Raumkörper ohne Materialität, ein „sinnliches Schema" oder Sinnending. Husserl stellt fest, dass wir, solange wir das Ding außerhalb seiner kausalen Zusammenhänge betrachten, und zwar auch dann, wenn wir es als Abfolge von Schemata ansehen,

> keine Möglichkeit finden, ausweisend zu entscheiden, ob das erfahrene materielle Ding wirklich sei, oder ob wir einer bloßen Täuschung unterliegen und das Erfahrene ein bloßes Phantom sei. (Ebd., 40)

Diesen Unterschied können wir nicht am Schema selbst feststellen, sondern nur, indem wir die Abhängigkeit des Dinges von „Umständen" berücksichtigen. Eine reale Pyramide sieht bei wechselnder Beleuchtung immer wieder systematisch anders aus, eine Phantompyramide dagegen nicht. (Ebd., 41) Den funktionalen gesetzlichen Zusammenhang von Umständen und Veränderung nennt Husserl Kausalität. Das Schema erweist sich als wirklich, sofern es in kausale Zusammenhänge eingeordnet ist. (Ebd., 43)

b) Carnap

Carnap verhandelt den hier angesprochenen Punkt unter dem Thema der wirklichen und unwirklichen Gegenstände im *Aufbau* in §170. An Stelle der Rede von erfüllten Raumkörpern benutzt er die Sprache der Physik. Ein erfüllter Raumkörper stellt sich bei ihm wie folgt dar:

> [Die physischen Dinge] heißen ‚wirklich', wenn sie konstituiert sind als Klassen physikalischer Punkte, die auf zusammenhängenden Weltlinienbündeln liegen und in das vierdimensionale Gesamtsystem der physikalischen Raum-Zeit-Welt eingeordnet sind. Dinge hingegen, die für sich genommen eine gleiche oder ähnliche Beschaffenheit haben wie die wirklichen physischen Dinge, die also insbesondere auch vierdimensionale Ordnungen von Weltpunkten mit physikalischer Zuschreibung sind, die aber nicht Teilgebiete des einen, umfassenden, vierdimensionalen Systems der physikalischen Welt bilden, heißen wegen der gleichen Beschaffenheit zwar auch ‚physisch', aber wegen der Nichtzugehörigkeit zu dem Gesamtsystem ‚unwirkliche' physische Dinge. (*Aufbau*, 237)

Als Beispiel führt Carnap ein „Sehding" an (eine Reihe von visuellen Wahrnehmungen), für das noch nicht feststeht, ob es „in das System der Wahrnehmungswelt eingebaut" werden kann, ohne damit in Widerspruch zu treten. Um zu sehen, was es heißt, dass ein Ding in die Wahrnehmungswelt eingebaut werden kann, muss man zum §165 („Das Wesen der Kausalität") zurückgehen. Dort schreibt Carnap, dass die Wahrnehmungswelt nach Kausalgesetzen geregelt ist, die in funktionalen Abhängigkeitsbeziehungen zwischen Wahrnehmungsdingen der folgenden Art bestehen:

> wenn den Weltpunkten eines (vierdimensionalen) Gebietes Qualitäten in der und der Weise zugeschrieben sind, so sind den Weltpunkten eines anderen Gebietes, das zu jenem ein Lageverhältnis von der und der Art hat, Qualitäten in der und der Art zugeschrieben oder zuzuschreiben. [...] Innerhalb der Wissenschaft bedeutet also Kausalität nur funktionale Abhängigkeit bestimmter Art. (Ebd., 229)

Mit anderen Worten: das Ding im Sinne eines erfüllten raumzeitlichen Schemas ist auch für Carnap nur wirklich, insofern es in Kausalzusammenhänge eingeordnet werden kann. Für Husserl wie für Carnap gibt es unwirkliche Sehdinge – eine interessante frühe Vorwegnahme der Idee einer virtuellen Realität. Carnaps Kausalitätsbegriff entspricht im Wesentlichen demjenigen Husserls.

4.5 Sinnendinge, Sehdinge und Empfindungen

a) Husserl

Als Husserl die naturalistische Einstellung deskriptiv auszeichnet, argumentiert er, dass theoretische Akte vortheoretisch konstituierte Gegenstände voraussetzen, und gelangt im § 8 zu der These, dass die „Sinnengegenstände als konstitutive

Urgegenstände" aufzufassen seien (*Ideen II*, 17). Eine Teilklasse der Sinnengegenstände sind die „Sehdinge".[63]

Was aber ist ein Sinnengegenstand? Generell handelt es sich um Gegenstände, die sich durch einzelne Wahrnehmungssinne präsentieren. Da es hier um vortheoretisch konstituierte Gegenstände geht, ist an ihrer Konstitution keine kategoriale Synthesis, kein Urteil, beteiligt. Vielmehr sind sie das Ergebnis einer ästhetischen Synthese, die sich „unwillkürlich" vollzieht. Dabei ordnen sich offenbar „Merkmale", etwa Farben, in charakteristischer Weise zueinander, wobei die Elemente nicht selbst Synthesen sein können. Sie müssen auf andere Weise konstituiert werden. Husserl schreibt:

> Der gegenständliche Sinn eines reinen Sinnengegenstandes (reine Sache) ist eine Synthesis von E l e m e n t e n , die nicht wieder durch aesthetische Synthesis gewonnen sind: das sind die letzten sinnlichen Merkmale. (*Ideen II*, 19)

Es ist überraschend, dass Husserl hier von Elementen und Merkmalen spricht, da er nach Auffassung der meisten Interpreten die Rede von vorgängigen Empfindungsinhalten, die im Bewusstseinsakt „aufgefasst" werden, nach den *Logischen Untersuchungen* aufgegeben hat. (Lohmar 2009) Jedoch behauptet er hier klar, dass wir von einfachen Sinnengegenständen noch zurückgeführt werden

> auf die in der primitivsten Weise konstituierten Empfindungsdaten, die sich als Einheiten konstituieren im ursprünglichen Zeitbewusstsein. (*Ideen II*, 24)

Diese Daten also werden so „aufgefasst", dass sie als Merkmale von Sinnesdingen einen Raumkörper „erfüllen".[64] Jedem Sinn entspricht eine eigene Weise der Erfüllung: es ist etwas anderes, wie Farbe einen Raumkörper „überdeckt" oder Wärme ihn „durchstrahlt". Sinnendinge sind dabei nicht statische „Momentaufnahmen" eines Gegenstandes, sondern durch eine Mannigfaltigkeit in der Zeit wechselnder *Aspekte* als dieselben erlebt. Die Aspekte sind die vom Leib, etwa den Augenbewegungen abhängigen Teilansichten der Gegenstände. Sinnengegenstände ergänzen sich zu vollständigen Wahrnehmungsgegenständen – der gese-

---

[63] Husserl verwendet den Begriff des Sehdinges häufig in *Urtexte*, 160, 165, 176, 264, 372. Carnap definiert das Sehding in *Aufbau* §94 und konstituiert es in §128, weitere Verweise gibt es in §124, §129, §133 und §170.
[64] Dies ist eine metaphorische Redeweise, da es keinen „leeren" Raumkörper gibt; vgl. *Ideen II*, 31.

hene Körper kann auch getastet werden – aber auch einzelne Sinne können zusammenhängende Raum-Zeit-Welten konstituieren.[65]

b) Carnap

Carnap beginnt die Konstitution nicht mit Sinnendingen überhaupt, sondern mit der Teilklasse der visuellen Gegenstände, also der Sehdinge. Die Konstitution der Sehdinge gestaltet sich im *Aufbau* detailliert und aufwändig, da sie denjenigen Teil des Konstitutionssystems darstellt, der formal ausgearbeitet ist. Hier finden sich wohl auch die ältesten Teile des *Aufbau*, die schon vor 1924 vorlagen. Wenn für Husserl ein Sinnending darin besteht, dass zeitlich wechselnde Empfindungsdaten so aufgefasst werden, dass sie in (je nach Wahrnehmungssinn) spezifischer Weise einen Raumkörper erfüllen, dann besteht für Carnap ein Sehding darin, dass in zeitlicher Folge in Nachbarschaft befindliche Farbempfindungen benachbarten „Weltpunkten" zugeschrieben werden. (*Aufbau* §§126, 127) Auch für Carnap geschieht diese Zuschreibung offenbar nicht „synthetisch", also nicht durch ein Urteil, sondern unwillkürlich, also synästhetisch. Carnaps weitergehende These lautet, dass sich der Gesichtssinn formal vor anderen Sinnen durch die Dimensionszahl 5 auszeichnet, so dass keine qualitativen Beschreibungen notwendig sind (was der strukturalistischen Ausgangsthese zugutekommt), eine These, die dann noch durch allerlei Ergänzungen bezüglich Ausblickspunkten, Lichtgeschwindigkeit und Sehwinkel präzisiert wird. Hierfür gibt es bei Husserl keine direkten Entsprechungen. [66] Die einfachen Empfindungsdaten konstituiert Carnap aus unzerlegbaren Elementarerlebnissen durch einen Prozess der Quasianalyse; sie sind also nicht, wie im Sensualismus, unmittelbar „gegeben". Aber auch für Husserl sind die Empfindungsdaten in der Zeit konstituiert, werden also nicht etwa durch bloße Zerstückung der Erlebnisse gewonnen. Auffällig sind noch zwei andere Parallelen, die wir im Folgenden etwas genauer betrachten werden: die „Zuschreibung" von nicht wahrgenommenen Eigenschaften und die Normalität der Wahrnehmungsbedingungen.

---

[65] In den *Urtexten* findet sich eine Vielzahl von Beschreibungen dessen, wie sich auf der untersten Stufe Sinnendinge konstituieren, zentral etwa im §17 des 3. Urtextes. Auch in den Paragraphen 8 und 9 der *Ideen II* wird darauf eingegangen.
[66] Vgl. jedoch unten 4.5.1.

4.5.1 „Unsichtiges" und Weltlinien

Husserl betont, dass uns ein Sinnending nicht nur in „synthetisch geeinigten Teilmeinungen" vor Augen steht, sondern selbst schon verschiedene „Schichten" aufweist. In diesem Zusammenhang spricht er auch von einem „auffassenden Strahl", der durch gewisse Aspekte der Dingerscheinung hindurchgeht und z. B. die Wahrnehmungsumstände, darunter den räumlichen Horizont oder die kinästhetischen Empfindungen des auffassenden Subjekts, mit erfasst. Wesentlich ist dabei, dass die Dingerscheinung in spezifischer Weise auch Merkmale enthält die unbestimmt bleiben oder gar nicht gesehen werden. In den *Urtexten* nennt er dies auch das „Unsichtige". (*Urtexte*, B, §2, 513 f) Das Sinnending besteht also keineswegs bloß aus den aktuell aufgefassten Empfindungsdaten oder Aspekten. Er schreibt:

> [W]ährend wir das Ding unter dem Gesichtspunkt des einen Merkmals betrachten, steht es zugleich da als mit anderen Merkmalen ausgestattet; zum Teil sind es bestimmte, schon im Wahrnehmungsfeld unerfasst liegende [...]. Teils sind sie unbestimmte. In diesem Fall werden Horizont, und ev. bestimmt gerichtete Meinungsstrahlen reaktiviert, die in Form nicht-aktivierter ‚Verworrenheiten' zum Auffassungssinn beitrugen. (*Ideen II*, 20 f)

Analog lässt Carnap zu, dass Farben auch nichtgesehenen Weltpunkten zugeschrieben werden, wobei die Zuschreibung auf bestimmten systematischen „Vermutungen" beruht, etwa derjenigen, dass ein einmal gesehener Punkt der Außenwelt „auch vorher und nachher da ist. Seine Orte bilden eine stetige Weltlinie." (*Aufbau* §126, 9) Auch Carnap spricht vom Aspekt eines Gegenstandes:

> Die Klasse derjenigen Gesichtsempfindungen eines Elementarerlebnisses, die den gesehenen Punkten eines bestimmten Dinges entsprechen, heißt ‚Aspekt' des Dinges in dem Erlebnis. (Ebd., 170)

Die technisch verklausulierten Beschreibungen in *Aufbau* §126 kann man als Übersetzung eines wesentlichen Gedankens Husserls verstehen: Wir sehen zwar in der visuellen Wahrnehmung faktisch nur „Aspekte" von Gegenständen, etwa Vorderseiten, nehmen aber regelmäßig dreidimensionale Körper mit nichtgesehenen Eigenschaften wahr. Sinnendinge sind insofern aus einem „kontinuierlich[en] System von Aspekten bzw. Seitenerscheinungen" (*Urtexte*, Urtext 2, B §2) mit Hilfe von „Meinungsstrahlen" oder Zusatzannahmen konstituiert. Dadurch würde etwa sowohl für Husserl, als auch für Carnap zum im Stereoskop gesehenen „Phantom" einer roten Pyramide auch die nicht gesehene Rückseite zählen. Zwischen Carnaps und Husserls Sehdingen besteht demnach weitgehende Übereinstimmung.

4.5.2 Normale Wahrnehmungsbedingungen

Eine weitere erwähnenswerte Parallele in diesem Zusammenhang findet sich in einer Nebenbemerkung Carnaps zur Zuschreibung der Farbpunkte. Die Erfüllung der Konstitutionsbedingungen kann, so schreibt er hier, verhindert werden durch „Halluzinationen, Störungen des Auges und des Zwischenmediums, Deformationen und Zerreißungen der Körper und dergl." (*Aufbau*, 166) Husserl widmet diesem Thema in den *Ideen II* einige Aufmerksamkeit, wenn er im §18b und c die Abhängigkeit der Wahrnehmung von normalen Wahrnehmungsbedingungen untersucht, darunter die Beleuchtung, aber auch das Sehen durch ein „drittes Medium" (die rosa Brille), eine „anormale Veränderung eines Organs", die Einnahme von bestimmten Substanzen oder psychische Zustände. Auch in den *Urtexten* spielt die Durchbrechung der Normalität der Wahrnehmungsbedingungen durch solche Eingriffe eine wesentliche konstitutive Rolle. Wahrnehmungen stehen in „orthoästhetischen Wahrnehmungssystemen" (*Urtexte*, B Nr. 6, 480 ff), sie haben gewissermaßen eine Normalform. Wird das Wahrnehmungssystem gestört, so setzt Reflexion über die Abhängigkeit des Gegenstandes von Umständen ein, womit die Konstitution des Sinnendinges als kausal determiniert beginnt. Systematisch abhängig sind nun Sinneswahrnehmungen von Veränderungen des eigenen Leibes, etwa Bewegungen, so dass auf der nächsten Stufe die Konstitution von „mein Leib" erfolgt.

Auch hinter Carnaps Erwähnung der möglichen Wahrnehmungsdeformationen steht die Idee einer optimalen Normalität, die sich durch die in §126 des *Aufbau* geschilderten Bedingungen ausdrückt. Mit ihnen expliziert Carnap, was ein orthoästhetisches Sehsystem im Sinne Husserl ist. Es folgt daher bei Carnap wie bei Husserl auf die Konstitution der Sinnendinge die Konstitution des eigenen Leibes. Diese Stufenfolge ist eine der auffallendsten Parallelen zwischen dem *Aufbau* und den *Ideen II*.

4.6 Mein Leib

a) Husserl

Obwohl die Konstitution des materiellen Dinges zunächst „selbstvergessen" vor sich geht, kann die Rolle des Leibes dabei also nicht dauerhaft übergangen werden. Die Schemate sind mit Qualitäten erfüllt, die aus der Wahrnehmung stammen, die vom Leib als Wahrnehmungsorgan „getätigt" wird: der Leib also

„ist bei aller Wahrnehmung immer notwendig dabei". (*Ideen II*, 56)

Es gibt nun nach Husserl nicht nur die üblichen visuellen, taktilen etc. Empfindungsqualitäten, sondern eine zweite Reihe von Empfindungen, die mit den ersteren systematisch verknüpft sind. Eine visuelle Wahrnehmung ist z. B. mit einer bestimmten Augenstellung, des Weiteren auch mit einer Körperhaltung systematisch so verbunden, dass sich der visuelle Eindruck in Abhängigkeit von Augenstellung und Körperhaltung ändert. Diese leiblichen Faktoren werden selbst empfunden und verbinden sich mit den Sinneseindrücken erst zu den vollständigen Wahrnehmungen.

> Bei aller Konstitution von Raumdinglichkeit sind zweierlei Empfindungen mit durchaus verschiedenen konstituierenden Funktionen beteiligt und notwendig beteiligt, wenn Vorstellungen von Räumlichem möglich sein sollen. – Fürs erste die Empfindungen, die durch die Auffassungen, die ihnen zuteilwerden, entsprechende Merkmale des Dinges als solche abschattend konstituieren. [...] Fürs zweite die ‚Empfindungen', welche solche Auffassungen nicht erfahren, andererseits aber bei allen derartigen Auffassungen anderer Empfindungen notwendig beteiligt sind, sofern sie dieselben in gewisser Weise motivieren. (Ebd., 57)

Während Husserl im §18 diese beiden grundsätzlichen leiblichen Empfindungsfunktionen nur einführt, geht es ihm im §36 um die Konstitution des Leibes selbst. Und zwar kennzeichnet er den Leib zunächst als einen gesehenen Raumkörper (Sehding), der im Gegensatz zu anderen Raumkörpern nur „innerhalb gewisser Grenzen" sichtbar ist:

> So gibt es Teile des Körpers, die zwar tastend wahrgenommen, aber nicht gesehen werden können. (Ebd., 144)

Neben dieser Besonderheit zeichnet sich mein Leib auch dadurch aus, dass er, wenn ich mit einer Hand die andere berühre, nicht nur in der berührenden Hand, sondern auch in der berührten Empfindungen hat und dass ich diese Empfindungen zudem durch visuelle Wahrnehmung einem Ort im Raum zuordnen kann.

> Die ‚Berührungs'-empfindungen gehören zu jeder erscheinenden objektiven Raumstelle der berührten Hand, wenn sie eben an dieser Stelle berührt wird. (Ebd., 145)

In dieser Möglichkeit der Doppelempfindung unterscheidet sich das taktile Gebiet vom visuellen, bei dem dergleichen nicht vorkommt und durch das allein sich daher kein Leib manifestieren könnte. „Der Leib kann sich als solcher nur konstituieren in der Taktualität." (*Ebd.*, 150) Diese Aspekte, die den wesentlichen Teil von Husserls Analysen der Leiblichkeit ausmachen, sind für den Vergleich mit Carnap ausreichend.

b) Carnap

Auch Carnap konstituiert den Leib als ein Sehding, das sich von anderen Sehdingen durch gewisse Kennzeichen abhebt. Wir geben die Merkmale in „realistischer Sprache" wieder:

> 1. Mein Leib ist immer in der Nähe meiner Augen.
> 2. [...] Bei meinem Leib [...] ist auch die überhaupt sichtbare Fläche eine offene, da einige Teile seiner Oberfläche, z. B. Auge und Rücken, nicht sichtbar sind.
> 3. Den Stellen der Oberfläche meines Leibes entsprechen die Qualitäten (oder Lokalzeichen) des Drucksinnes derart, dass eine Druckempfindung von bestimmter Art erlebt wird, wenn die entsprechende Hautstelle durch einen anderen Körper oder durch einen anderen Teil meines Leibes berührt wird.
> 4. Die Qualitäten der kinästhetischen Empfindungen entsprechen bestimmten Arten von Bewegungen meines Leibes. (*Aufbau*, 171)

Die Übereinstimmungen müssen nicht weiter kommentiert werden: Die konstitutionelle Definition des Leibes ist mit derjenigen Husserls nahezu identisch.

4.7 Das physikalische Ding

Der Gegenstand der Physik – das Paradigma des naturwissenschaftlichen Objekts – ist dadurch gekennzeichnet, dass er von aller Relativität auf Wahrnehmungsumstände oder Subjekte frei ist. Diese Unabhängigkeit konstituiert sich für Husserl darin, dass das wahrgenommene Ding aller sinnlichen Qualitäten entkleidet wird und nur noch mit seinen „primären", das heißt den mathematisch-geometrischen Eigenschaften charakterisiert wird.

> [D]as Ding an sich selbst besteht aus kontinuierlich oder diskret erfülltem Raum in Bewegungszuständlichkeiten [...] Das Raumerfüllende untersteht gewissen Gruppen von Differentialgleichungen, entspricht gewissen physikalischen Grundgesetzen. Aber sinnliche Qualitäten gibt es da nicht. Und das sagt: es gibt da überhaupt keine Qualitäten. (*Ideen II*, 84)

Carnap ist derselben Auffassung:

> Von der Wahrnehmungswelt, die durch Zuschreibung von Sinnesqualitäten konstituiert wird, ist die physikalische Welt zu unterscheiden, bei der den Punkten des vierdimensionalen Zahlenraumes bloße Zahlen, die ‚physikalischen Zustandsgrößen' zugeschrieben werden. (*Aufbau*, 180)

In seiner näheren Charakterisierung der physikalischen Gegenstände spricht Husserl zwar von der intersubjektiven Identität solcher Dinge, es wird aber doch deutlich, dass diese nichts zur physikalischen Bestimmungen (etwa im Sinne gemeinsamer Qualitäten) beiträgt. Die physikalische Welt lässt sich naturalistisch schon auf der Stufe des *solus ipse* konstituieren, wenn dieser sich einen hinreichenden Begriff vom Unterschied der gleichbleibenden mathematischen von den wechselnden qualitativen Bestimmungen gebildet hat. Dies ist wohl auch der Grund, weshalb Carnap, der die physikalische Welt an derselben Stelle einführt, von Intersubjektivität hier schweigt. In seinen Literaturangaben verweist Carnap auf sich selbst und Schlick, der gezeigt habe „dass die physikalische Welt v ö l l i g f r e i v o n S i n n e s q u a l i t ä t e n ist". (*Aufbau*, 182) Husserl wird nicht erwähnt.

4.8 Das Eigenpsychische und das reale seelische Subjekt[67]

a) Husserl

Den zweiten Abschnitt der *Ideen II* über die Konstitution der seelischen Realität leitet Husserl mit einer ganzen Reihe von Differenzierungen zwischen verschiedenen Begriffen der Seele ein, die bei Carnap nicht ausdrücklich unterschieden werden. Im Folgenden werden wesentliche Aspekte schrittweise herausgehoben, um den Vergleich mit Carnap zu erleichtern.

(i) Zunächst wird das Feld des Seelischen überhaupt durch den Erlebnisstrom gebildet, dessen zeitlich geordnete Erlebnisse und Erlebnistypen durch Introspektion unmittelbar zugänglich sind. Innerhalb dieser Realität lassen sich insbesondere das reine Ich und das reale seelische Subjekt unterscheiden.

(ii) Das reine Ich versteht Husserl als den Ich-Pol intentionaler Akte. Vom reinen Ich gehen Aufmerksamkeitsstrahlen aus[68], die ihr Objekt im Verlauf der Zu-

---

[67] Husserl schließt mit der Konstitution des physikalischen Dinges den ersten Abschnitt über die Konstitution der materiellen Realität ab und geht zum Thema des zweiten Abschnitts über, zur Konstitution der seelischen Realität. Carnap dagegen behandelt das „Eigenpsychische" vor der physikalischen Realität und zwar mit einer gewissen Notwendigkeit, da ja das Konstitutionssystem auf der „eigenpsychischen Basis" beruht. Hierin könnte man eine Abweichung in der Stufenfolge zu sehen, die aber nicht relevant ist. Wie oben betont, handelt es sich bei der unterschiedlichen Reihenfolge nur um Unterschiede in der Darstellung, nicht im Konstitutionssystem selbst.

[68] Die Rede von „Strahlen", die vom Ich ausgehen, durchzieht den ganzen Abschnitt. Husserl reflektiert auf die Metaphorik z. B. in §25, wo es heißt. „Die Frage ist, ob diese Bilder eine ursprüngliche Bedeutung haben und eine ursprüngliche Analogie ausdrücken. D. h. liegt im Auf-

wendung immer besser erfassen. (*Ideen II*, 106)
Dies bedeutet auch, dass das reine Ich nicht „da" ist, wenn keine intentionalen Akte vollzogen werden, also etwa im Schlaf. Es tritt dann, wie Husserl sagt, ab oder wird inaktuell. Es gibt in diesem Sinne unbewusste Ichakte:

> Das reine Ich kann nie verschwinden, es ist immerfort in seinen Akten, aber je nachdem: sind sie oder werden sie aktuelle Akte, dann tritt das Ich sozusagen in ihnen auf [...] oder es ist sozusagen verborgenes Ich, es wirft nicht einen aktuellen Blick auf etwas." [Es gibt also] „eine Ichstruktur, die es eben gestattet und fordert zu sagen, das Ich im Stadium des spezifischen ‚Unbewusstseins', der Verborgenheit, sei nicht ein Nichts, [...] sondern ein Moment der Struktur. (Ebd., 100)

(iii) Ein anderer Aspekt des organisierten Erlebnisstroms ist das „reale seelische Subjekt" (Ebd., §§30 ff), das im Wesentlichen die passiven Wahrnehmungs- und Empfindungsfunktionen umfasst, die vom Leib abhängen, nicht aber (oder jedenfalls nur mittelbar) die spontanen Denk- und Willensfunktionen, die Husserl dem Geistigen und der Person zurechnet. Die Seele ist also „als eine mit der Leibesrealität verbundene oder in ihr verflochtene Realität konstituiert" (ebd., 93), oder, wie es an anderer Stelle heißt, „in eigentümlich inniger Weise mit dem Leibe eins" (ebd., 121). Die Seele in diesem Sinne erscheint als „Substrat" von seelischen Eigenschaften parallel zum physischen Körper, der als „Substrat" (oder Träger) seiner physischen Eigenschaften auftritt. Wie sich die physische Eigenschaft eines Dinges, z. B. seine Wasserlöslichkeit, in verschiedenen *Zuständen* zeigt, so offenbaren die Erlebnisse des Subjekts die seelischen Eigenschaften. Hat das Subjekt also ein Wahrnehmungserlebnis, so ist es im Zustand des Wahrnehmens, in dem sich die Wahrnehmungsfähigkeit ausdrückt oder, wie Husserl sagt, „bekundet". Ähnlich bekundet sich in den verschiedenen Seherlebnissen die Eigenschaft der Sehschärfe:

> [Z]wischen materiellen Eigenschaften, die sich im wechselnden physischen Verhalten des Dinges bekunden, und seelischen Eigenschaften, die sich in entsprechenden Erlebnissen als seelischen Verhaltensweisen bekunden, [besteht] volle Analogie. (Ebd., 121)

b) Carnap

Die entsprechenden Stellen im *Aufbau* betreffen im Wesentlichen „das Eigenpsychische".

---

merken, vom Räumlichen abgesehen, dem das Bild entstammt, etwas Richtungsartiges, das von einem Punkt ausgeht?" (*Ideen II*, 106)

(i) Zunächst rechnet Carnap zum Eigenpsychischen die konstitutiv geordneten Elementarerlebnisse und nennt diesen Bereich auch „mein Bewusstsein". (*Aufbau*, 174) Dem Ausdruck „Bewusstsein" zieht er allerdings im §64 den Begriff des Erlebnistroms vor. Das Eigenpsychische (Bewusstsein, Erlebnisstrom) wird unmittelbar (introspektiv) erkannt. (Ebd., 79)

(ii) Das Eigenpsychische wird dann ergänzt durch „das Unbewusste", für dessen Existenz Carnap ganz entschieden eintritt. Und zwar argumentiert er hier mit einer Analogie zwischen dem Seelischen und Wahrnehmungen, wobei er auf die Konstitution der nichtgesehenen Farbpunkte zurückgreift. Explizit fasst Carnap dabei nun das Bewusstsein (im Unterschied zu (i)) als einen „Ausblickspunkt" (Husserls Ich-Pol). Das Bewusstsein „blickt" auf eine Zeitkoordinate, auf der auch „nicht erlebte" Qualitätsklassen liegen, also solche, auf die sich kein „Aufmerksamkeitsstrahl" richtet, und die in diesem Sinne „unbewusst" sind. Das Ich in diesem Sinne als „Ausblickspunkt" entspricht in etwa dem „reinen Ich" Husserls.

(iii) Zwischen physischem Ding und Seele besteht die folgende Analogie: „Entsprechend den ‚Zuständen' des ‚physischen Dinges' pflegt auch hier das, was einem einzelnen Zeitpunkt als Eigenpsychisches zugeordnet ist [...] als ‚Zustand' eines beharrenden Trägers, gewissermaßen eines physischen Dinges, aufgefasst zu werden." (*Aufbau*, 176) Das Eigenpsychische in diesem letzteren Sinne entspricht dem „realen seelischen Subjekt" im Sinne Husserls. Carnap betrachtet dieses Subjekt wie Husserl analog zum physischen Ding als ein Substrat von Eigenschaften, die sich in Zuständen manifestieren.

Während die Identifikation des Eigenpsychischen mit den bewussten Erlebnissen wenig spektakulär erscheint, ist die Rede vom Ich als Ausblickspunkt und die Einbeziehung des Unbewussten ungewöhnlich. Die Analogie des Bewusstseins mit der Wahrnehmung und gleichzeitig die Auffassung des seelischen Ich als Träger von Zuständen dürften in dieser Weise wohl nur in Husserls *Ideen II* zu finden sein. Carnap erwähnt Husserl an dieser Stelle nicht. Im §65 jedoch grenzt er sich von Husserl (unter vielen anderen) durch die These ab, dass das Gegebene „subjektlos" sei. Dies ist richtig in dem Sinne eines realen seelischen Subjekts (iii), das erst durch das Gegebene konstituiert wird. Die Rede von „Ausblickspunkten" in §132 zeigt aber, dass das Gegebene nicht subjektlos im Sinne des reinen Ich (ii) ist: Der Ausblickspunkt entspricht dem Ich-Pol im Sinne Husserls.

4.9 Animalia und die biologischen Gegenstände

Nach der Unterscheidung der verschiedenen Formen der Seele folgt in den *Ideen II* eine Reflexion über die Realität des Seelischen. Da nämlich zuvor die Wirklichkeit des materiellen Objekts durch seine Abhängigkeit von Umständen charakterisiert worden war, und da auch das Seelische (im Sinne der Wahrnehmungs- und Empfindungsfunktionen) von Umständen abhängt, folgt, dass auch ihm eine Art von Realität zugesprochen werden muss. Allerdings wird dies zweifach qualifiziert: Zum einen handelt es sich um eine andere Art der Realität, insofern sie durch die „physio-psychische" und nicht durch die „physio-physische" Beziehung konstituiert wird. Zum zweiten ist das Seelische so sehr „mit dem Leibe eins", dass nicht die Seele als Substrat, sondern die leibseelische Einheit als besondere Form der Realität erscheint.

> Die Einheit der Seele ist r e a l e Einheit dadurch, dass sie a l s E i n h e i t d e s s e e l i s c h e n L e b e n s v e r k n ü p f t i s t m i t d e m L e i b als Einheit des leiblichen Seinsstroms, der seinerseits Glied der Natur ist. [...] was wir der materiellen Natur als zweite Art von Realitäten entgegenzustellen haben, ist nicht die ‚Seele', sondern die k o n k r e t e E i n h e i t von Leib und Seele, das menschliche (bzw. animalische) Subjekt. (*Ideen II*, 139)

Da Husserl die Wahrnehmungs- und Empfindungsfunktionen von Leibern als Konstituens der „realen seelischen Subjekte" auffasst, sind für ihn alle Leib-Wesen auch seelische Subjekte. Schon in den *Ideen I* spricht Husserl von „tierischen Ichsubjekten" (§35, §73) und scheut sich nicht, Tieren sogar Personalität zuzuschreiben.

In diesem Punkt nun will ihm Carnap ersichtlich nicht folgen. Obwohl er in der Stufenfolge weiterhin nach dem Husserlschen System vorgeht und nun also zu den biologischen Gegenständen gelangt, will er deren Konstitution allein auf Grund von physischen Kennzeichen vornehmen und nicht auf Grund ihrer seelischen Empfindungsfähigkeit. Die biologischen Gegenstände werden deshalb auf der Basis von physischen Kennzeichen wie Fortpflanzung und Ernährung konstituiert. Dabei behandelt Carnap nun auch gleich die „vom Menschen verfertigten Gegenstände" mit; kurz: das gesamte Gebiet der „physischen Gegenstände", und das sind alle Gegenstände überhaupt, wird nun auf Grund der materiellen Eigenschaften ausdifferenziert.

Man beachte jedoch, dass selbstverständlich auch für Husserl die biologischen und kulturellen Gegenstände materielle Gegenstände sind, die mit ihren physischen Eigenschaften konstituiert werden. Die Frage für Husserl ist jedoch, ob sie sich *als Gegenstandsarten* allein durch ihre physischen Eigenschaften ausweisen. Diese Frage verneint Husserl. Während also für Carnap die biologischen Gegenstände rein physisch konstituierbar und daher mit den physikalischen

Gegenständen sozusagen erledigt sind (man fragt sich, weshalb sie dann überhaupt eine eigene Konstitutionsstufe erhalten), sind sie nach Husserl durch ihre Sensibilität charakterisiert. Da man diese aber den materiellen Körpern nicht ohne weiteres ansieht, bedarf es für ihre Konstitution eines besonderen Verfahrens. Dieses Verfahren wendet auch Carnap im nächsten Schritt an, allerdings nur, um den Menschen innerhalb der Klasse der physischen (bzw. biologischen) Gegenstände gesondert zu spezifizieren.

4.10 Einfühlung und Ausdrucksbeziehung

a) Husserl

Unter dem Titel „Einfühlung" finden sich in den *Ideen II* zwei Verfahren, die dazu dienen, zum einen die animalischen Wesen, insbesondere den Menschen, zum anderen Personen zu konstituieren.[69] Carnap verwendet im Aufbau nur das erste Verfahren, weshalb wir uns hier auf dieses beschränken. Husserl geht es zunächst um die Animalia. Kurz zusammengefasst erfahren wir andere Lebewesen auf Grund ihres Ausdrucksverhaltens als Analoga zu uns selbst und insofern als „beseelt", darunter die anderen Menschen als Wesen, die uns in dieser Hinsicht besonders ähnlich sind. Die Konstitution des Menschen nimmt im System eine wichtige Position ein, denn

> [m]it der Mensch-Apperzeption ist eo ipso auch gegeben die Möglichkeit der Wechselbeziehungen, der Kommunikation zwischen Mensch und Mensch. Sodann auch die Identität der Natur für alle Menschen und Tiere. Gegeben sind ferner die einfacheren und komplexeren sozialen Verbindungen, Freundschaften, Ehen, Vereine. (*Ideen II*, 162)

Mit anderen Worten: die folgenden höheren Gegenstandsarten sind alle nur auf der Basis der Konstitution des Menschen möglich.

Die Konstitution der seelischen Realität des Anderen geschieht durch den Leib, denn die Anderen sind uns nur als Leibkörper gegeben (präsentiert). Husserl beobachtet aber, dass ihre „Innerlichkeit" immer schon mitgegeben (appräsentiert) ist. So sehen wir nicht etwa ein Lächeln, dem wir Freude nachträglich zuschreiben, sondern die Freude ist mit dem Lächeln so „direkt" gegeben, dass wir ohne weiteres sagen, wir *sehen*, dass sich jemand freut. Da wir selbst Empfin-

---

[69] Menschen als animalische Wesen sind also von Menschen als Personen noch zu unterscheiden. Zu Husserls beiden Begriffen der Einfühlung vgl. Mayer 2013; zum Vergleich von Husserls und Carnaps Positionen Rosado-Haddock 2008.

dungen und Wahrnehmungen am Leib lokalisiert erfahren, appräsentieren sich solche Wahrnehmungen und Empfindungen mit der Wahrnehmung des fremden Leibkörpers an denselben Körperstellen. Indem ich also den anderen als Leib wahrnehme, „übertrage" ich ihm auch analoge Erlebnisse, so dass seine leiblichen Erscheinungsformen zu „Anzeichen" mit einer eigenen „Grammatik" werden:

> So bildet sich allmählich ein System von Anzeichen aus, und es ist schließlich wirklich eine Analogie zwischen diesem Zeichensystem des ‚Ausdrucks' seelischer Vorkommnisse, und zwar der passiven und aktiven, und dem Zeichensystem der Sprache für den Ausdruck von Gedanken. (Ebd., 166)

Eine kritische Frage der gesamten Debatte über Empathie lautet, ob ich in der Einfühlung nur mich selbst erfahre (also dem Anderen meine eigenen Erlebnisse zuschreibe), oder ob ich auf irgendeine Weise wirklich in die Erlebnisse des Anderen „hineinreiche". Diese Frage beantwortet Husserl mit einem „sowohl – als auch": Was ich erlebe, wenn ich jemandes Schmerzen wahrnehme, ist nicht eigener Schmerz, sondern ein Analogon des Schmerzes des Anderen; diese Analogierfahrung ist aber dennoch eigenes Erlebnis.

b) Carnap

Auch Carnap verwendet gelegentlich (etwa in *Aufbau* §21) den Begriff der Einfühlung, allerdings bezeichnet er damit ein intuitives Vorgehen, das durch wissenschaftliche Kennzeichen ersetzt werden müsse. (*Aufbau* §49) In seiner Konstitution des Fremdpsychischen jedoch verwendet er dann ein Verfahren, das Husserls Einfühlung entspricht. Carnap stellt zunächst fest, dass die Konstitution des anderen Menschen für das Konstitutionssystem von besonderer Bedeutung ist, denn „[a]n sie werden die Konstitutionen des Fremdpsychischen und damit die aller höheren Gegenstände anknüpfen". (*Aufbau*, 183) Die Konstitution findet statt über die „Ausdrucksbeziehung" (§138)[70], worunter Carnap Gesten, Mienenspiel etc. versteht. Die Anderen sind uns nur als Leib gegeben, denn:

---

[70] Rosado-Haddock 2008 hat gezeigt, dass Carnap in §19, 138 und 141, als er die Ausdrucksbeziehung und die Zeichengebung diskutiert, stillschweigend Husserls Bedeutungstheorie aus der ersten Logischen Untersuchung übernimmt.

> bei der Konstitution des Fremdpsychischen kann es sich nur um eine Zuschreibung an den Leib des Anderen handeln, nicht etwa an seine Seele, die ja nicht anders als auf Grund erst dieser Zuschreibung konstituiert werden kann. (*Aufbau*, 186)

> Es gibt kein Fremdpsychisches ohne Leib. (Ebd., 140)

Die Zuordnung geschieht wie bei Husserl auf Grund des Ausdrucksverhaltens des anderen Leibes. Etwas verklausulierter ist die weitere Charakterisierung der Einfühlung als Analogieerfahrung. Carnap schreibt:

> [D]ie zugeschriebenen psychischen Vorgänge sind eigenpsychische [...], nämlich weil anderes Psychische als das Eigenpsychische noch nicht konstituiert ist (ebd.),

jedoch sind es nicht einfach eigene Erlebnisse, etwa des Schmerzes, sondern es handelt sich um eine „Umordnung meiner Erlebnisse und ihrer Bestandteile" und es gilt:

> was mir nicht seiner Art nach von mir aus bekannt ist, auf das kann ich auch nicht bei dem anderen Menschen aus den Ausdrucksvorgängen, die ich beobachte, schließen (ebd.).[71]

Eine „Umordnung" der Erlebnisse „in derselben Art" ist für Carnap regelmäßig gleichbedeutend mit einer „Konstitution nach Analogie", so etwa auch bei der Konstitution des Unbewussten (*Aufbau*, 176), der Konstitution nicht gesehener Farbpunkte (§126) und in der Vervollständigung der Wahrnehmungswelt (§133). Wie Husserl also begreift Carnap die Konstitution anderer Menschen über die Zuordnung der eigenen analogen Erfahrungen an den fremden Leib auf Grund von Ausdrucksverhalten, also über die Einfühlung.

In seinen Literaturangaben nennt Carnap die üblichen Protagonisten (Kauffmann, Driesch, Dingler). Russell wird angeführt mit der allgemeinen Bemerkung, dass erschlossene Entitäten durch logische Konstrukte zu ersetzen seien, und dies obwohl Carnap gleichzeitig zugibt, dass Russell gar nichts zur Konstitution von Fremdpsychischem geschrieben hat – ein Beispiel für die Willkür, mit der im *Aufbau* Literaturhinweise verteilt werden. Husserl bleibt nach wie vor ungenannt.

---

[71] Carnap meint hier nicht wirklich einen Schluss, denn in der folgenden Literaturangabe kritisiert er andere Autoren dafür, dass sie das Fremdpsychische erschließen anstatt es zu konstituieren. (*Aufbau, 187*)

4.11 Der Mensch und die intersubjektive Welt

a) Husserl

Schon im oben unter 4.6 angeführten ersten Zitat wird deutlich, dass für Husserl die Einfühlung Voraussetzung für die Konstitution der intersubjektiven Welt und letztlich der Natur ist. Dieser Gedanke wird im §47 unter dem Titel „Einfühlung und Naturkonstitution" weiter ausgeführt. Hier fasst Husserl den Konstitutionsprozess noch einmal kurz zusammen:

> [E]s konstituiert sich zu unterst in der früher beschriebenen Weise die anschauliche materielle Welt und korrelativ dazu das erfahrende Subjekt, das Leib und Seele hat, aber noch nicht reale Einheit ‚Mensch', noch nicht Naturobjekt ist. Es konstituieren sich dann die fremden Subjekte, die als Analoga des eigenen und zugleich als Naturobjekte apperzipiert werden, es konstituiert sich die Natur als intersubjektiv gemeinsame und objektiv (exakt) bestimmbare und das eigene Subjekt als Glied dieser ‚objektiven Natur'. (*Ideen II*, 170 f)

Vom solipsistischen Standpunkt aus erfahre ich mich nicht als einen Leib, „in dem" seelische Erlebnisse statthaben. Erst wenn ich die anderen als materielle Körper mit einem „Innenleben" durch Einfühlung konstituiert habe, gewinne ich einen echten Begriff des Menschen als beseeltem Leib und erfahre mich dann auch selbst als ein Menschen-Ich in diesem Sinne, gelange also über den solipsistischen Standpunkt hinaus. Durch Einordnung des Anderen in die Raum-Zeit-Welt etabliert sich nun eine merkwürdige Doppelnatur: einerseits gibt es eine Unzahl subjektiver Welten, die aus Gegenständen bestehen, die nur *relativ* zu den wahrnehmenden Subjekten existieren.

> Setze ich, der Erfahrungsforscher, ein Ding als objektiv wirklich, so setze ich damit für jedes gesetzte Subjekt auch seiende Erscheinungseinheiten, d.i. Geltungseinheiten, die Indices sind für Regeln von Erlebnissen des Wahrnehmens und möglichen Wahrnehmens, intentional bezogen auf diese ‚Erscheinungen'. (Ebd., 170)

Andererseits lassen sich nun intersubjektive Gemeinsamkeiten ebenso etablieren wie die von allen als identisch akzeptierte mathematisch-quantitativ beschreibbare objektive Welt. Diese Welt ist so gestaltet, dass es möglich ist

> das intersubjektiv Gesetzte so zu bestimmen, dass der Bestimmungsgehalt unabhängig wird von den einzelnen Subjekten, bzw. dass er ausschließlich aus Bestimmungen besteht, die jedes Subjekt aus seinen Gegebenheiten der Erscheinungen durch das methodische Verfahren der Naturwissenschaft herausgewinnen kann. (Ebd., 171)

Der intersubjektive Gegenstand ist ein exakt bestimmbarer „Index" für subjektive Erscheinungsreihen.

b) Carnap

Carnap widmet der intersubjektiven Welt vergleichsweise viel Raum. (§§141–149) Sie ist ja der ursprünglich ausgewiesene Zielpunkt des Konstitutionssystems, insofern als dieses die Gegenstände der Wissenschaften etablieren soll. Die wissenschaftlichen Objekte müssen aber intersubjektiv verfügbar sein. Carnap baut hier Aspekte aus, die bei Husserl selbstverständlich mitgedacht und angedeutet, aber nicht eigens ausgeführt sind. So betont er (i) besonders ausführlich, dass die Welten des konstituierenden Subjekts S und des konstituierten M sich grundsätzlich dadurch unterscheiden, dass die des M *innerhalb* der Welt von S konstituiert wird, während diese Relativität für die Welt des M natürlich nicht gilt. Er charakterisiert (ii) zunächst das Verfahren der Zuordnung von zwei Subjekten, um dieses dann in §148 auf alle Subjekte auszudehnen. Schließlich führt er (iii) nach der Konstitution des Fremdpsychischen in §§141, 142, 144 ausführlich die „Zeichengebung" ein, d.h. die sprachliche Kommunikation, mit deren Hilfe die Gegenstände anderer Menschen beschrieben werden und wodurch die bis dato konstituierte Welt ergänzt werden kann. Auf dieser Basis der Angaben des Anderen wird dann dessen subjektive Welt expliziert – wobei Carnap betont, dass es sich bei dieser Beschreibung letztlich nur um eigenpsychische Elementarerlebnisse handelt – es werden also subjektive Konstitutionssysteme mit Gegenständen relativ zu einem Subjekt S aufgestellt. Die Gegenstände dieser Konstitutionssysteme können dann nach §146 einander zugeordnet werden. Denn einmal wird es gewisse Gemeinsamkeiten geben etwa in dem Sinn, dass die raumzeitlichen Gegenstände in allen Konstitutionssystemen vorkommen; zum anderen lassen sich die physikalischen Welten der verschiedenen subjektiven Systeme einander zuordnen:

> [Z]wischen der physikalischen Welt in S und der in S_M besteht eine eineindeutige Zuordnung derart, daß zwischen den physikalischen Weltpunkten von S_M dieselben raum-zeitlichen und qualitativen (d.h. auf Grund der Zuschreibung geltenden) Beziehungen gelten wie zwischen den zugeordneten Weltpunkten von S. (*Aufbau*, 195)

Auf Grund der Konstitution des Fremdpsychischen über die Ausdrucksbeziehung bzw. Einfühlung können auch psychische Gegenstände intersubjektiv zugeordnet werden. Ich kann also sagen, der andere sehe „dieselbe" Farbe wie ich.

Auch in diesem Punkt ist die inhaltliche Übereinstimmung mit Husserl deutlich: die wesentliche These des §47 der *Ideen II* besteht eben darin, dass die intersubjektive Welt aus einer Zuordnung und mathematischen Verallgemeinerung der subjektiv-relativen Welten besteht. Die Idee der „Doppelnatur" der intersubjektiven Welt – einerseits eine Menge aus subjektiven Konstitutionen, andererseits eine objektive Welt der Gemeinsamkeiten – ist auch für Carnaps Darstellung grundlegend. Für Carnap wie für Husserl ist die intersubjektive Welt Gegenstand der Wissenschaft. Deren Aufgabe besteht in der Umformung von nicht-intersubjektiven in intersubjektive Aussagen. So schreibt Carnap ganz analog zu Husserl:

> Die Umformung gehört zur Aufgabe der Wissenschaft; das Bestreben der Wissenschaft geht dahin, zu einem Bestande von nur intersubjektiven Aussagen zu gelangen. (*Aufbau*, 200; vgl. dazu das letzte Zitat von (a))

Relevante Literaturangaben zu diesem Teil gibt es im *Aufbau* nicht.

4.12 Die geistige Welt

Sowohl für Carnap als auch für Husserl ist mit der Konstitution der intersubjektiven Welt oder Welt der Natur eigentlich ein methodischer Schlusspunkt erreicht, allerdings aus unterschiedlichen Gründen. Carnaps Ziel, die Gegenstände der Wissenschaften zu konstituieren, ist nun mindestens für die Naturwissenschaften erreicht. Husserl verfolgt aber mit dem Konstitutionssystem ein ganz anderes Bestreben. Die Genese der Natur im Rahmen der naturalistischen Einstellung soll nämlich zeigen, dass diese Einstellung nicht hinreichend ist, um alle lebensweltlichen Dinge zu konstituieren, insbesondere nicht die geistigen Gegenstände und die anderen Menschen als Personen. Das liegt im Wesentlichen daran, dass der Naturalismus von vornherein die Werte und ihre zugehörigen Konstitutionsmechanismen ausgeschaltet hatte. Gerade darin bestand ja die naturalistische Epoché. Es gibt aber noch einen tieferen Grund: der Naturwissenschaftler kann zwar Menschen als Subjekte setzen und beschreiben; er kann aber nicht die Subjektivität seiner eigenen Konstitution, das „absolute Subjekt", innerhalb dessen all diese Konstitutionsschritte stattfinden, in den Blick bekommen.

> Die Analyse der Natur und Naturbetrachtung zeigt also, dass sie ergänzungsbedürftig ist, dass sie in sich Voraussetzungen birgt und somit über sich hinausweist auf ein anderes Gebiet des Seins und der Forschung: das ist das Feld der Subjektivität, die nicht mehr Natur ist. (*Ideen II*, 172)

Diese reine Subjektivität verfolgt Husserl im dritten Abschnitt der *Ideen II*. In unserem Rahmen muss auf die Konstitution der geistigen Welt nicht näher eingegangen werden. Es sei nur angedeutet, dass sie den Übergang von der naturalistischen in eine personalistische Einstellung verlangt, die nicht nur Kausalitätsbeziehungen, sondern vor allem Motivationsbeziehungen betrachtet. Da dieser Übergang nicht seinerseits aus der Welt der Natur entspringt, obwohl das Seelische seinen „Untergrund" bildet, ergeben sich daraus für Husserl starke Argumente für die Unabhängigkeit des Bewusstseins vom Sein. Für unser Thema ist wichtig, dass die geistigen und kulturellen Gegenstände auf der Basis der motivationalen, interpersonalen Beziehungen konstituiert sind und deshalb in besonderer Weise einen eigenen „ontologischen Status" aufweisen. Zwar sind es wenigstens zum Teil physische Gegenstände, ihr Wesen erschöpft sich aber in keiner Weise in ihrer physischen und auch nicht in ihrer „psychischen" Beschaffenheit, sondern wird durch einen „Sinn" bestimmt, dessen „Ausdruck" sie sind. In der im Sommersemester 1925 gehaltenen Vorlesung *Phänomenologische Psychologie*, zu der Carnap mindestens die Übung besucht hat, spricht Husserl in diesem Kontext auch von der „Verkörperung" des Sinns geistiger Gegenstände.[72]

Den besonderen ontologischen Status der geistigen Objekte setzt Carnap ohne weiteren Kommentar als gegeben voraus. So sagt er in §23:

> Die geistigen Gegenstände sind [...] n i c h t a u s P s y c h i s c h e n (und etwa physischen) z u s a m m e n g e s e t z t. Es handelt sich um völlig disparate Gegenstandsarten. (*Aufbau*, 30)

Carnap geht so weit, die Existenz geistiger Gegenstände unabhängig von ihrer Manifestation oder Dokumentation (s. u.) zu behaupten:

> Ein geistiger Gegenstand, der während einer gewissen Zeit existiert, braucht nicht zu allen Zeitpunkten dieser Zeitstrecke aktuell zu sein, d.i. in Erscheinung zu treten. (Ebd., 31)

Anders als Husserl gibt Carnap aber keine „Einstellung" an, als deren „Korrelat" die Klasse von Gegenständen auftreten würde. Dieses Thema, und also auch der Übergang von der naturalistischen in die personalistische Einstellung, wird im *Aufbau* ausgespart; der für einen logischen Empiristen ziemlich überraschende Realismus gegenüber den geistigen Gegenständen, für den sich Carnap auch auf Frege hätte berufen können, bleibt unmotiviert.

Die geistigen Gegenstände stehen nach Carnap zur intersubjektiven Welt in der Beziehung der Manifestation oder Dokumentation:

---

72 Vgl. dazu insbesondere §18: „Die Gestalten, in denen das Geistige in der Erfahrungswelt auftritt" (Hua IX, 110 ff.)

> Die psychischen Vorgänge, in denen [der geistige Gegenstand] jeweils in Erscheinung tritt oder ‚manifest' wird, nennen wir seine (psychischen) Manifestationen. […] Als Dokumentationen eines geistigen Gegenstandes bezeichnen wir dauernde physische Gebilde, in denen das geistige Leben gewissermaßen erstarrt ist, Produkte, dingliche Zeugen und Dokumente des Geistigen. (Ebd.)

Über diese Beziehungen der Manifestation und Dokumentation lassen sich die geistigen auf psychische Gegenstände zurückführen und letztlich als Klassen von Elementarerlebnissen konstituieren. Somit kann man Carnaps Position bezüglich der geistigen Gegenstände trotz des Fehlens der personalistischen Einstellung als „husserlianisch" bezeichnen: die wesentlichen Charakteristika, d. h. ontologische Unabhängigkeit bei gleichzeitiger Fundierung im Psychischen sowie die Verkörperung in Verhaltensweisen oder physischen Dingen, sind dieselben.

4.13 Werte

Die Konstitution der Werte, die in *Aufbau* §152 verhandelt wird, betrachtet Carnap, wie die Beschreibung der geistigen Gegenstände, als eine Aufgabe der (namentlich nicht spezifizierten) Phänomenologie.[73] Husserl hatte zu dieser Zeit nichts zum Thema Werte veröffentlicht, weshalb der zeitgenössische Leser hier vermutlich an Scheler dachte, der allerdings im Literaturverzeichnis des *Aufbau* nur marginal vorkommt. In Vorlesungen[74] und kursorisch auch in den *Ideen II* hat Husserl jedoch eine Wertphänomenologie dargestellt, die erst in jüngster Zeit größere Beachtung findet. (Vongehr 2011) Kennzeichnend für diese Wertphänomenologie ist, dass Werte über eine bestimmte Form von Wahrnehmungen konstituiert werden, die Husserl „Wertnehmungen" nennt, und dass in diese Wertnehmungen Gefühle wesentlich involviert sind. So schreibt Husserl in den *Ideen* II in Bezug auf die ästhetische Betrachtung eines Kunstobjekts:

> Die ursprüngliche Wertkonstitution vollzieht sich im Gemüt als jene vortheoretische (in einem weiten Wortsinne) genießende Hingabe des fühlenden Ichsubjektes, für die ich den Ausdruck Wertnehmung schon vor Jahrzehnten in Vorlesungen verwendet habe. Der Ausdruck bezeichnet also ein der Gefühlssphäre zugehöriges Analogon der Wahrnehmung, die in der doxischen Sphäre das ursprüngliche (selbsterfassende) Dabeisein des Ich bei dem Gegenstande selbst bedeutet. (*Ideen II*, 9)

---

73 Vgl. oben, 3.1.
74 Vgl. die Vorlesungen über Ethik und Wertlehre 1908–1914 (Hua XXXVIII), und die Vorlesungen zur Einleitung in die Ethik aus den Jahren 1920 und 1924. (Hua XXXVII) Die letzte Vorlesung könnte Carnap gehört haben.

Carnaps Darstellung im §152 liest sich wie ein Resümee dieser Theorie. Carnap schreibt:

> Die Konstitution der Werte aus gewissen Erlebnissen, den ‚Werterlebnissen', zeigt in mehrfacher Hinsicht eine Analogie zur Konstitution der physischen Dinge aus ‚Wahrnehmungserlebnissen' (genauer: aus den Sinnesqualitäten). [...] So kommen etwa (unter manchen anderen) für die Konstitution der ethischen Werte Gewissenserlebnisse, Erlebnisse der Pflicht oder der Verantwortung und dergl. in Betracht; für die ästhetischen Werte Erlebnisse des (ästhetischen) Gefallens oder anderer Haltungen bei Kunstbetrachtung und Erlebnisse der Kunstschöpfung usw. (*Aufbau*, 204)

Für einen radikalen Antimetaphysiker bemerkenswert ist der damit involvierte Werterealismus, zu dem Carnap sich ganz ausdrücklich bekennt:

> Der Wert ist nicht selbst erlebnishaft oder psychisch, sondern besteht unabhängig vom Erlebtwerden und wird in dem Erlebnis (genauer: in dem Wertgefühl, dessen intentionales Objekt er bildet[75]) nur erkannt; ebenso, wie das physische Ding nicht psychisch ist, sondern unabhängig von der Wahrnehmung besteht und in der Wahrnehmung, deren intentionales Objekt er ist, nur erkannt wird. (Ebd.)

In den *Ideen II* hatte Husserl entsprechend ausgeführt:

> Die Schönheit schaue ich am Gegenstand an, freilich nicht wie seine Farbe oder Gestalt in schlichter sinnlicher Wahrnehmung; aber am Gegenstande selbst finde ich das Schöne. Das Schön sagt nichts weniger als ein Reflexionsprädikat, wie etwa, wenn ich sage, er sei ein mir gefallender. (*Ideen II*, 14)[76]

Quellenliteratur in Bezug auf die Konstitutionsstufe der Werte nennt Carnap nicht.[77]

---

75 Das könnte wörtlich von Husserl stammen.
76 Vgl. zur Objektivität der Werte und zur Kritik an der hedonistischen Verwechslung von Werten und Wert vor allem Husserls Ausführungen in den Vorlesungen *Einleitung in die Ethik* 1920 und 1924, §§15 ff. Dort heißt es auch: „Das Fühlen ist subjektiv, der Wert objektiv." (68 f.)
77 Mormann 2007 hat zu zeigen versucht, dass Carnaps Konstitution der Werte dem Südwestdeutschen Neukantianismus Rickerts geschuldet ist. Die Assimilation von Werturteilen an Wahrnehmungen, die sich bei den Neukantianern auch aus systematischen Gründen nicht findet, spricht jedoch sehr viel mehr für eine Adaption der phänomenologischen Werttheorie. Mormann ist zudem zu widersprechen in der Behauptung, die Werte seien im *Aufbau* geistige Gegenstände. (Mormann 2007, 180) Das Gebiet der Werte ist vielmehr ein selbstständiger Bereich, der „an einer früheren Stelle des Konstitutionssystems wieder an[knüpft]." (*Aufbau* §152, 203), eben bei den sinnlichen Wahrnehmungen. Der von Carnap und Husserl vertretene Werterealismus hat deshalb einen ganz anderen Charakter als der neukantianische.

4.14 Zusammenfassung

Es sei zuletzt noch einmal festgehalten, dass Carnaps „Beispiel" eines Konstitutionssystems Schritt für Schritt demjenigen Konstitutionssystem entspricht, das im damals noch unveröffentlichten Entwurf des zweiten Bandes der *Ideen* dargestellt wird. Die Parallele gilt dabei nicht nur in dem Sinne, als Carnap die einzelnen Stufen Husserls übernimmt, vielmehr lehnt sich Carnap auch in den Übergangskriterien („Regeln") von einer Stufe zur anderen an die Ausführungen Husserls an. Wie eingangs bemerkt kommt es dabei nicht darauf an, ob Carnap den Husserlschen Intentionen exakt gerecht wird und ihren tiefsten Sinn wiedergibt. Sein Ziel und Zweck war es, die Idee des Konstitutionssystems konkret an den einzelnen „Seinssphären" durchzuführen. Aus den dargestellten Parallelen ergeben sich starke Argumente dafür, dass Carnap die *Ideen II* für die Beschreibung der Konstitutionsschritte verwendet hat. Zu keinem der anderen von Carnap zitierten Werke besteht auch nur annähernd (wenn überhaupt) eine derart vollständige Parallele. Obwohl sich gelegentlich Übereinstimmungen, z. B. zu Kauffmann 1893 und Driesch 1912 finden, und obwohl die Philosophie um die Jahrhundertwende die Frage des Zusammenhangs von subjektiven Empfindungen und objektiver Welt vielfach und auf unterschiedliche Weise thematisiert hat: die genetische Entwicklung eines Konstitutionssystems in einzelnen phänomenologischen Details unter der Einstellung der Epochè war Hauptthema der Phänomenologie Husserls nach den *Logischen Untersuchungen*. Carnap hat Husserls Veranstaltungen während der Abfassung seiner Habilitationsschrift besucht, mit Husserls Assistenten Ludwig Landgrebe diskutiert, Wertschätzung der Phänomenologie bekundet und Husserl im Serabrief als philosophischen „General" bezeichnet. Der *Aufbau* führt aus, was Carnap im Serabrief angekündigt hatte: er übersetzt die Generalstabskarte Husserls in eine formale Sprache, die vom Naturwissenschaftler verstanden wird, so dass der Zusammenhang zwischen Philosophie und Naturwissenschaft wieder hergestellt werden kann. Hätte Carnap seine Quelle benannt, wäre dagegen auch weiter nichts einzuwenden.

5 Andere Anleihen bei Husserl

Mit den Parallelen im Stufenmodell und den Definitionen der einzelnen Gegenstandstypen sind die Anleihen, die Carnap bei Husserl nimmt, keineswegs schon erschöpft. Rosado-Haddock 2008 hat darauf aufmerksam gemacht, dass Carnap Husserls Bedeutungstheorie aus der ersten Logischen Untersuchung übernimmt und den Begriff der Fundierung aus der Dritten Logischen Untersuchung. Erwähnt wurde bereits die Horizontintentionalität, die im *Aufbau* mit den „Weltlinienbündeln" und der Konstitution des Nichtgegebenen durch Analogie eine wichtige Rolle spielt. Ergänzen ließe sich die Liste z. B. durch die Gegenstandssphären – man vergleiche Husserls regionale Ontologie aus den *Ideen I* – oder die Quasigegenstände, die Husserls kategorialen Gegenständen in der sechsten Logischen Untersuchung ähnlich sind. Nebenbei bemerkt entstammen Wortschöpfungen mit der Vorsilbe „Quasi", für die der *Aufbau* berühmt ist, Husserls Terminologie, etwa wenn in der sechsten Logischen Untersuchung von einer Quasi-Erfüllung gesprochen wird (HUA XIX/2, 656), in den *Ideen I* von einer „Quasi-Region Gegenstand überhaupt" die Rede ist (*Ideen II*, 126) oder es in den *Ideen II* heißt, das Seelische habe „eine Quasi-Natur und eine Quasi-Kausalität". (Ebd., 138)[78] Im Folgenden seien noch zwei weitere Fälle genannt, in denen sich Carnap ohne Hinweis für den Leser an Husserl anlehnt.

5.1 Rationale Nachkonstruktion

Unter den Begriffen, die vom Aufbau in die „analytische" Philosophie geradezu als ihr differenzierendes Merkmal eingegangen sind, ist einer der wichtigsten derjenige der rationalen Re- oder Nachkonstruktion. Die anglo-amerikanische Mythologie, die von Carnap (nicht zuletzt im Vorwort) entscheidend mitgeprägt wurde, besagt, dass Husserl-und-Heidegger in Personalunion Vertreter einer „intuitiven Metaphysik" gewesen seien, die Gegenstände durch einen „instantanen geistigen Blick" zu erkennen beanspruche (*Aufbau* §§181 f), während die im *Aufbau* verfolgte Methode intuitive Erkenntnisprozesse durch Einordnung in ein Konstitutionssystem und die Angabe einer konstitutionalen Definition rational nachkonstruiere. Liest man den §100 des *Aufbau* vor dem Hintergrund der Husserlschen Phänomenologie, so handelt es sich bei der rationalen Rekonstruktion jedoch um nichts anderes als Husserls Vorgehen, wie er es an vielen Stellen in den *Ideen I* und *II* beschreibt. Zunächst zu den Voraussetzungen. Carnap schreibt:

> Das Gegebene liegt im Bewusstsein niemals als bloßes, unbearbeitetes Material vor, sondern immer schon in mehr oder weniger verwickelten Bindungen und Gestaltungen. [...] BEISPIEL: Beim Anschauen eines Hauses wird dieses unmittelbar und intuitiv als körperlicher Gegenstand wahrgenommen, seine nicht wahrgenommene Rückseite wird mitgedacht, seine Fortexistenz beim Wegblicken wird gedacht, es wird das bestimmte, erkannte Haus in ihm

---

[78] In den *Urtexten* ist die Rede von Phantasien als „quasierfahrenen Raumgestalten" (126), von einer Quasi-Zukunft und einem Quasi-Modus (445). Die Liste ließe sich beliebig verlängern.

wiedererkannt usw., meist ohne dass dabei Schlussketten in ausdrücklichem Denken vollzogen würden. (*Aufbau*, 138) [79]

Dass wir raum-zeitliche Gegenstände als Ganze wahrnehmen, obwohl uns nur ihre Vorderseiten gegeben sind, dass wir also Rückseiten und alle möglichen anderen „Sinnbestandteile" immer schon mitdenken, ohne sie uns erschließen zu müssen, gehört jedoch zum Grundbestand der Logik unserer Phänomene, wie sie *Husserl* darstellt. In den *Ideen I* schreibt er etwa in §44:

> Ein Ding kann prinzipiell nur ‚einseitig' gegeben sein. [...] Ein Ding ist notwendig in bloßen ‚Erscheinungsweisen' gegeben, notwendig ist dabei ein Kern von ‚wirklich Dargestelltem' auffassungsmäßig umgeben von einem Horizont uneigentlicher ‚Mitgegebenheit' und mehr oder minder vager Unbestimmtheit. (*Ideen I*, 91)[80]

Die Phänomenologie analysiert die Dingwahrnehmung nach den verschiedenen Komponenten des wirklich Gegebenen (Erscheinenden) und des in der Wahrnehmung jeweils mit Gemeinten durch systematische „eidetische Variation", um schließlich den präzisen Sinn des Dinges zu erfassen und ihm, wie Husserl in den *Ideen II* sagt, „in strenger Analyse und Deskription Ausdruck zu geben".[81] Den Sinn des Dinges erfassen heißt zu unterscheiden, in welchen Gegebenheiten das Ding „fundiert" ist (von welchen es ontologisch abhängig ist) und welche Ergebnis der spezifischen Auffassung oder Apperzeption sind. Dadurch erweist sich das Ding dann als Glied einer „Gattung regionaler Gegenständlichkeiten", es zeigt, wiederum mit Carnap zu sprechen, seine Konstitutionsstruktur.

Carnap beschreibt die Aufgabe durchaus analog: Die rationale Nachkonstruktion betrifft die intuitiven Wahrnehmungserlebnisse. Der Botaniker, der eine Pflanze intuitiv als physisches Ding von der und der Art erkennt,

> muß sich bei der Nachkonstruktion der Erkennung der Pflanze fragen: was war in der erlebten Wiedererkennung das eigentlich Gesehene und was war daran die apperzeptive Verarbeitung? (*Aufbau*, 139)

---

[79] Eine solche Darstellung der Hauswahrnehmung ist regelmäßig Teil von Einführungen in Husserls Phänomenologie; so etwa schon bei Ingarden 1967 (1992), 111 f.
[80] Vgl. *Ideen II*, 34 ff.
[81] Der ganze Satz lautet: „Es gilt [...], in der Wesensintuition das Wesen von Erfahrenem überhaupt und als solchem zu erwägen, so wie es in einem beliebigen, sei es wirklich oder imaginativ vollzogenen Erfahren (in einem Sich-in-ein-mögliches-Erfahren-Hineinfingieren) sich expliziert, um dann in der Entfaltung der in solchem Erfahren wesensmäßig liegenden Intentionen den Sinn des Erfahrenen als solchen – der betreffenden Gattung regionaler Gegenständlichkeiten – schauend zu erfassen und ihm in strenger Analyse und Deskription Ausdruck zu geben." (*Ideen II*, 91)

Während Husserl nun die „Konstitutionsformel" durch Wesensschauung gewinnt, nämlich durch eine systematisch induzierte Wahrnehmung von Differenzreihen, schreibt Carnap, der Botaniker könne die beiden Komponenten „nur durch Abstraktion" trennen, und ebenso

> muss die Konstitutionstheorie in der rationalen Nachkonstruktion, nicht für den einzelnen Fall, sondern für den gesamten Bewusstseinsverlauf, durch eine Abstraktion die Trennung zwischen dem reinen Gegebenen und der Verarbeitung machen. (Ebd.)

Liegt hier also der wesentliche Unterschied und die besondere Leistung, die Carnap dem Husserlschen Konstitutionssystem hinzufügt? Die wesentliche Frage lautet, was Carnap unter Abstraktion versteht. Seine technische Verwendung des Begriffs in Wortverbindungen wie „Abstraktionsprinzip" und „Abstraktionsklasse" setzt die inhaltliche Bedeutung bereits voraus, die in §67 beiläufig eingeführt wird. Dort heißt es nämlich, die Bestandteile von Elementarerlebnissen, etwa eine Gehörwahrnehmung, seien aus den Elementarerlebnissen „durch Inbeziehungsetzung und Vergleichung, also durch Abstraktion" gewonnen, also nicht unmittelbar gegeben. (*Aufbau*, 92) Mit anderen Worten: eine Abstraktion ist hier nicht etwa ein begriffsanalytisches Verfahren, sondern entsteht aus dem unmittelbaren Vergleichen von als Totalitäten zugrunde gelegten sinnlichen Erlebnissen. Der ganze Prozess des „Aufbaus" entwickelt sich in diesem Sinne als eine immer weiter fortschreitende Abstraktion und der Begriff der Abstraktion selbst erweist sich als synonym zu dem Begriff der Konstitution. Eine Kluft zwischen Carnaps rationaler („abstrahierender") Nachkonstruktion und Husserls Wesensschau lässt sich hier nicht mehr erkennen.

5.2 Die Ähnlichkeitserinnerung

Das formale Konstitutionssystem Carnaps wird auf der Basis einer einzigen Grundrelation entwickelt, der Ähnlichkeitserinnerung. Diese Relation besagt:

> ‚x ER y' oder ‚zwischen x und y besteht die Ähnlichkeitserinnerung' besagt also: ‚x und y sind Elementarerlebnisse, die durch Vergleich einer Erinnerungsvorstellung von x mit y als teilähnlich erkannt sind'. (*Aufbau*, 110)

Carnap betont, dass diese Relation „erkenntnismäßig grundlegend" ist. Er präzisiert:

> Unter Erinnerung ist hier nicht nur die Reproduktion eines schon entschwundenen Erlebnisses gemeint, sondern auch die Retention eines kurz vorher gewesenen, noch nicht entschwundenen, sondern nachklingenden Erlebnisses, z. B. einer Wahrnehmung. (Ebd.)

Der Begriff der Retention, den Carnap hier einführt, ist von Husserl im Rahmen der Phänomenologie des Zeitbewusstseins geprägt worden.[82] Carnap kennt ihn mindestens aus den *Ideen I*. So heißt es dort in §77, dass Erlebnisse „innerhalb der Retention (der ‚primären' Erinnerung) als soeben gewesene ‚noch bewußt' sind" (Hua III, 163), und in §78, dass „jedes Erlebnis seine Parallelen in verschiedenen Formen der Reproduktion [hat], die wie ideelle ‚operative' Umformungen des ursprünglichen Erlebnisses angesehen werden können", darunter die Wiedererinnerung. (Hua III, 167)

Aus der Ähnlichkeitserinnerung wird im *Aufbau* die Teilähnlichkeit abgeleitet, aus der wiederum die Ähnlichkeitskreise konstituiert werden. Ähnlichkeitskreise sind insofern eigentlich Reihen von Erinnerungen mit einem gemeinsamen Bestand. Sie repräsentieren das „konstitutionale Wesen" des entsprechenden Gegenstandes. Husserl sagt im § 78 des ersten Bandes der *Ideen* zu diesem Thema:

> Natürlich denken wir uns alle parallelisierten Erlebnisse als solche eines gemeinsamen Wesensbestandes: die parallelen sollen also dieselben intentionalen Gegenständlichkeiten bewusst haben, und bewusst in identischen Gegebenheitsweisen aus dem Umkreise aller derjenigen, die in anderen Hinsichten möglicher Variation statthaben können. (Hua III, 167)

In den *Ideen II* spricht Husserl auch vom „Inhalt" der Erinnerungen, der als eine Einheit gesetzt wird:

> In wiederholten Erinnerungen kommt diese Einheit zur Deckung: sie steht als Objektives da. (*Ideen II*, 115)

Diese Funktion der Erinnerung könnte man als gegenstandsstiftend bezeichnen, wenn man beachtet, dass dabei eine „Urstiftung", nämlich eine originäre Wahrnehmung, vorausgesetzt ist – ein Punkt, den Carnap systematisch übergeht. Husserl jedenfalls stellt fest, dass die Erinnerung „in Akten jeder Gattung, bei Erlebnissen jederlei Qualifizierung" eine Rolle zu spielen scheint „und überall in gleicher Weise". (Ebd., 117) Mit anderen Worten: die Ähnlichkeitserinnerung, denn um diese handelt es sich, ist auch in Husserls Konstitutionssystem eine Grundrelation.

Zusammenfassend sei noch einmal betont, dass Carnap bis in die formalen Grundbegriffe hinein eine Vielzahl von Begriffen und Ideen aus dem Werk Hus-

---

[82] Vgl. dazu den Band X der Husserliana.

serls entnimmt. Berücksichtigt wurden hier bewusst nur die beiden von Carnap selbst angegebenen Texte, das Manuskript der *Ideen II*, zu dem Carnap höchstwahrscheinlich Zugang hatte, sowie die Urtexte dieses Manuskripts. Nicht systematisch einbezogen sind die Vorlesungen und andere Veranstaltungen Husserls, die Carnap in den Jahren 1920–1925 besucht haben könnte, und die ebenfalls Quelle seiner Informationen gewesen sein könnten.

6 Die Methoden der Maskierung

Wie gelingt es Carnap, seine zahlreichen inhaltlichen und terminologischen Anleihen bei Husserl so zu verbergen, dass bis heute trotz der seit langem vorliegenden Hinweise kaum ein Interpret sie erkennt? In einer entlarvend ehrlichen Passage aus seiner Autobiographie der frühen Jahre schildert Carnap, wie er in seinen philosophischen Gesprächen mit Freunden verschiedene „Sprachen" benutzte, um sich an die Denkweisen seines Gegenüber anzupassen. So sprach er einmal in „realistischer" oder „materialistischer" Sprache, ein anderes Mal verwendete er idealistisches Vokabular, oder er redete wie ein Nominalist oder im Gegenteil wie Frege in der Terminologie abstrakter Entitäten. Carnap fährt fort:

> I was surprised to find that this variety in my way of speaking appeared to some objectionable and even inconsistent. I had acquired insights valuable for my own thinking from philosophers and scientists of a great variety of philosophical creeds. When asked which philosophical positions I myself held, I was unable to answer. (Schilpp 1963, 17)

Diese Anekdote gibt in mehr als einer Hinsicht Aufschluss über Carnaps Methoden auch noch im Aufbau. Zum einen fiel ihm die „Übersetzung" von Aussagen in andere Terminologien leicht, zum zweiten vertrat er keine dezidierte eigene Position und konnte daher auch die eines anderen Denkers ohne weiteres übernehmen, zum dritten wusste er, wie man sich der Denkweise einer anderen Person (hier vor allem Schlicks) anpasst. Als anstößig empfand er dieses Verfahren offenbar nicht. So bildet die Übersetzung in verschiedene „Sprachen" einen wichtigen und sogar einen explizit als Vorteil ausgewiesenen Bestandteil des *Aufbau*. Da Carnap die formale Sprache für grundlegend erklärt (§95) und die anderen Sprachen zu „erleichternden Hilfssprachen" degradiert, liegt von vornherein der Verdacht fern, dass es sich gerade andersherum verhalten könnte und die formale Sprache im Gegenteil eine Formalisierung schon anderweitig vorliegender Gedanken darstellt. Durch die Übersetzung in vier Sprachen – die realistische Sprache, die Sprache der fiktiven Konstruktion, die formale Sprache und deren wortsprachlichen Ausdruck – werden die Anleihen bei Husserl zudem schrittweise maskiert, so dass etwa in den Relationen „Er" oder „Aq" (§§108, 114) kein Hinweis mehr auf Husserls reproduktive Wiedererinnerung zu finden ist. Dieses offene Vorgehen des *Aufbau* bildet aber nur die Spitze des Eisbergs, wie sich an der vorangegangenen Darstellung bereits gezeigt hat. Carnaps weitere Maskierungsmethoden betreffen in grober Unterteilung (1) Übersetzung und definitorische Umdeutung im *Aufbau* selbst und danach, (2) den Umgang mit Literaturangaben, (3) Verlautbarungen über den Stellenwert des Konstitutionssystems, (4) biographische Angaben, (5) scheinbare oder implizite Husserlkritik. Ich gebe im Folgenden für jedes dieser Verfahren Beispiele, die allerdings keineswegs erschöpfend sind.

6.1 Übersetzung und definitorische Umdeutung

Es wurde hier schon mehrfach darauf hingewiesen, dass Carnap Husserlsche Begriffe durch eigene Begriffe ersetzt, die er dann aber in Husserls Sinn verwendet. Ein augenfälliges Beispiel ist die „Ausdrucksbeziehung", die im *Aufbau* Husserls „Einfühlung" ersetzt. Sucht man im Index nach „Einfühlung", wird man dagegen an das Stichwort „Intuition" verwiesen, das bei Husserl mit Einfühlung wiederum nichts zu tun hat. Ein zweites Beispiel ist der Begriff des Eigenpsychischen, der Husserls Begriff des Idiopsychischen übersetzt. (*Urtexte*, u. a. 18, 21, 34)

Eine andere Vorgehensweise, die man die Politik der scheinbaren Umdeutung nennen könnte, verfolgt Carnap mit dem Wort „Konstitution". Der Verdacht, es könne sich um Husserls Konstitutionsbegriff handeln, wird schon mit den ersten Sätzen des *Aufbau* ausgeräumt. Carnap schreibt hier, durch das Konstitutionssystem sollten *Begriffe* „aus gewissen Grundbegriffen stufenweise abgeleitet, ‚konstituiert' werden, so dass sich ein Stammbaum der Begriffe ergibt, in dem jeder Begriff seinen bestimmten Platz findet". (*Aufbau*, 1) Der Begriff „Begriff" hat in Husserls damals veröffentlichten Schriften keinen wesentlichen Stellenwert[83] und die Rede von Konstitution steht bei Husserl selten im Zusammenhang mit einer begrifflichen Ableitung. Carnap erklärt jedoch im §5 Begriffe und Gegenstände für austauschbar, so dass er im §6 dann die Rede von Begriffen fallen lassen kann. Tatsächlich geht es ihm um ein Konstitutionssystem der Erkenntnisgegenstände aus Erlebnissen in Husserls Sinn.

Ein drittes Beispiel, das den Umgang mit der Phänomenologie im Allgemeinen betrifft, ist die Tatsache, dass Carnap die Basis rückblickend für „phänomena-

---

[83] Anders in den Manuskripten der *Urtexte* und im dritten Band der *Ideen*. Auf dieses Detail soll hier nicht eingegangen werden.

listisch" anstatt für „phänomenologisch" erklärt, und damit vermutlich die in der anglo-amerikanischen Philosophie übliche Verschleifung der Begriffe „phenomenalism" und „phenomenology" einleitet.[84] Wenn man unter Phänomenalismus wie im Deutschen üblich eine erkenntnistheoretische Position versteht, welche die Welt auf der Basis von Sinnesdaten konstruieren möchte, ist die Auszeichnung des *Aufbau* als phänomenalistisch unzutreffend, da Sinnesdaten erst auf einer höheren Stufe konstituiert werden und die Totalität der Elementarerlebnisse eine berühmte Grundthese des *Aufbau* darstellt. Dennoch schreibt Carnap in seiner Autobiographie entgegen besserem Wissen: „The system of concepts was constructed on a phenomenalistic basis". (Schilpp 1963, 18)

Ein viertes Beispiel betrifft schließlich die englische Übersetzung des *Aufbau*, an der Carnap sicher nicht unbeteiligt war. Hier ist der verdächtige Ausdruck „Konstitution" fast ganz eliminiert und durch „construction" ersetzt worden. Diese Ersetzung ist sachlich ebenfalls falsch: das Konstitutionssystem konstruiert nicht neue Gegenstände, sondern analysiert gegebene Gegenstände nach ihrer logisch-genetischen Entwicklung. Nicht umsonst soll die Relation FUND, die formale Entsprechung zu Husserls Begriff der Fundierung der Gegenstände ineinander, „erlebbare" Beziehungen ausdrücken, also nicht etwa beliebige mögliche Gegenstände „erschaffen". Der englischsprachige Leser des *Aufbau* hat auf Grund der Übersetzung von Konstitution durch „construction" und der Auszeichnung der Basis als „phenomenalistic" kaum noch eine Chance, die Verwandtschaft zu Husserls *Phänomenologischen Untersuchungen zur Konstitution* (1990 erschienen als *Studies in the Phenomenology of Constitution*) zu erkennen.

6.2 Der Umgang mit Literaturangaben

In der vorangegangenen Darstellung wurde mehrfach darauf hingewiesen, dass Carnap seine Anleihen bei Husserl in der überwiegenden Zahl der Fälle nicht kennzeichnet, sondern als eigene Ideen verkauft. In solchen Fällen gibt es zumeist keine Literaturverweise. Gelegentlich führt Carnap jedoch für Husserlsche Gedanken andere Literatur an, so wenn er in §129 darauf verweist, dass auch Kauffmann, Ziehen und Driesch sich mit der Konstitution des Leibes beschäftigt haben. Wer diese Angaben ernsthaft versucht, zu verifizieren, wird bald entmutigt. Zwar lassen sich in den genannten Texten gelegentlich Stellen finden, die Ähn-

---

[84] Der Bedeutungswandel des Wortes „phenomenology", das im Englischen heute den Bereich des irgendwie Fühlbaren bezeichnet, macht die These der phänomenologischen Herkunft des *Aufbau* für den englischsprachigen Leser noch unplausibler.

lichkeiten zu den entsprechenden Konstitutionsstufen im *Aufbau* aufweisen (manchmal gibt es aber auch keine erkennbaren Parallelen), keines der genannten Werke passt jedoch in einem größeren Argumentationszusammenhang zum Konstitutionssystem des *Aufbau*. Irreführende Literaturangaben sind zahlreich dann, wenn Carnap einen expliziten Verweis auf Husserl entwerten möchte, etwa in §64, wo Husserl unter einer Vielzahl anderer Autoren erscheint. Carnap gibt hier wie bemerkt sogar Seitenzahlen der *Ideen I* an; dort ist aber nichts von dem Thema des Eigenpsychischen zu finden, um das es im §64 geht.[85] Wer also hier nachschlägt, wird ebenso wenig wie bei den anderen Autoren auf charakteristische inhaltliche Bezüge stoßen.

Eine andere Methode verfolgt Carnap, wenn er über den Text zahlreiche Hinweise auf Russell verstreut, die dennoch keine echte Verwandtschaft zu Russell etablieren[86], sondern gelegentlich sogar irrelevant oder nicht nachvollziehbar sind. Die Verweise auf Russell haben mehrere erwünschte Effekte: zum einen legen sie eine falsche Spur in Bezug auf die Herkunft von Carnaps Ideen – eine Spur, die er in der Autobiographie massiv bekräftigt –; zum zweiten positionieren sie den *Aufbau* innerhalb der empiristischen Tradition und stärken damit Carnaps Position gegenüber Schlick; zum dritten könnte Carnap damit auch einfach um das Wohlgefallen Russells, mit dem er von Buchenbach aus Kontakt aufgenommen hatte, geworben haben.

Generell erweckt der *Aufbau* durch die Vielzahl der Literaturverweise den Eindruck, Carnap gehe besonders akribisch mit der Offenlegung seiner Quellen um, ein Eindruck, der, wie sich gezeigt hat, in eklatanter Weise täuscht.

6.3 Der vorgebliche Stellenwert des Konstitutionssystems

Der *Aufbau* ist berühmt geworden dafür, dass er ein Konstitutionssystem auf eigenpsychischer Basis entwickelt. Ohne dieses System hätte das Buch kaum einen sinnvollen Gehalt: die Behauptung einer möglichen Entwicklung der Welt aus Grundgegenständen bliebe rein theoretisch; der gesamte formale Apparat wäre überflüssig, wesentliche technische Bestandteile wie die Quasianalyse würden keinen Sinn erfüllen. Tatsächlich zeigen auch die wenigen erhaltenen Skizzen und Entwürfe, dass Carnap von Anfang an über eine Entwicklung auf der eigenpsy-

---

[85] Allerdings fasst Husserl gerade auf den beiden genannten Seiten (316, 317) sein Konstitutionsprogramm zusammen; die Stelle ist also für den *Aufbau* durchaus einschlägig. Ob es sich hier um ein Versehen Carnaps handelt oder vielleicht sogar um einen versteckten Hinweis an den Leser, ist schwer einzuschätzen.
[86] Dies hat z. B. Michael Friedman 1997 gezeigt; vgl. auch Richardson 1998.

chischen Grundlage nachgedacht hat; diese erscheint an keiner Stelle als eine bloße Anwendung der Idee eines schon konzipierten Konstitutionssystems. Dennoch betont Carnap im *Aufbau* und danach immer wieder, dass es sich bei den vorgestellten Entwicklungsschritten um ein bloßes Beispiel handle, dass man die Konstitution auch auf einer anderen Basis (z. B. einer physikalischen) vornehmen könne, und dass nur die „erkenntnismäßige Ordnung", die durch das vorliegende System am besten wiedergegeben werde, ihn zu diesem Vorgehen motiviert habe. (§§62,63) Diese Äußerungen sind wohl ebenfalls als Mittel zur Maskierung der Quellen zu werten, vielleicht auch als Ausdruck davon, dass Carnap sich von der Last des Plagiats befreien wollte. Dass Carnap später kein anderes System entwickelt hat, weist ebenfalls darauf hin, dass die Rede vom Beispielcharakter leer ist. Vielmehr hat Carnap im *Aufbau* getan, was er im Sera-Brief von 1920 angedeutet hatte: den Generalstabsplan eines Konstitutionssystems, den Husserl formuliert hatte, mit Hilfe der neuen Methoden der Logik, insbesondere derjenigen Freges und Russells, auszubuchstabieren.

6.4 Biographische Angaben

Der erste Verdacht, dass es sich beim *Aufbau* um ein bewusstes Plagiat handelt, entsteht durch Carnaps systematisches Verschweigen der faktischen Beziehungen zu Husserl. In einer intellektuellen Autobiographie, die von zukünftigen Forschern und Interpreten für bare Münze genommen wird und deren Interpretationen bestimmt, kommt dies Verschweigen einer absichtlichen Irreführung der Scientific Community gleich. Es ist zu fragen, welches Motiv, außer Opportunismus und anschließender Angst vor Entdeckung, diesem Verhalten zu Grunde lag. Zur Zeit der Abfassung der Habilitationsschrift war Husserl der wohl berühmteste Philosoph Deutschlands und besaß internationales Renommee, eine Vielzahl von Schülern und Forschern aus den verschiedensten Ländern und wissenschaftlichen Disziplinen besuchte ihn, seine Publikationen, insbesondere die *Prolegomena* und die *Logischen Untersuchungen*, waren einflussreich und hatten schulbildend gewirkt, er besaß eine Ausbildung als Mathematiker und war u. a. mit Hilbert befreundet, und er stand gewiss nicht in dem Ruf, den ihm die Nachcarnapsche Ära analytischer Philosophen zuschrieb, ein irrationaler Metaphysiker zu sein. Im Gegenteil schreibt er in seinem Nachwort zu den *Ideen I* aus dem Jahr 1930, dass ihm von Seiten der „Lebensphilosophie, mit ihrer neuen Anthropologie, ihrer Philosophie der ‚Existenz'" Intellektualismus und Rationalismus vorgeworfen würden. (Husserl 1930, 549) Ernst Cassirer schreibt an Husserl 1925, er halte

Husserl „nach Natorps Tode, für de[n] Vertreter der wissenschaftlichen Philosophie in Deutschland".[87]

Carnap hätte also, sofern er nichts zu verbergen gehabt hätte, die Beziehung wenigstens dann offen legen können, als seine Karriere gesichert war. Stattdessen hat er jedoch mit seiner Heidegger-Attacke im „Manifest" des Wiener Kreises „Überwindung der Metaphysik durch logische Analyse der Sprache" (1931/32) die Kontroverse, die er im Vorwort zum *Aufbau* bereits eröffnet hatte, verschärft. Da es gleichzeitig Heidegger gelang, Husserl zu seinem Vorläufer zu erklären, war durch diesen Angriff auch Husserl für die „rational rekonstruktive Philosophie" zur *persona non grata* geworden. Carnap hat damit nicht nur eine irreführende Interpretation des *Aufbau* initiiert, sondern wesentlich zur Ausbildung des „Schismas" zwischen angloamerikanischer und kontinentaler Philosophie beigetragen.

6.5 Scheinbare und implizite Husserlkritik

Carnap bezieht sich, wie gezeigt wurde, an einigen Stellen im *Aufbau* explizit auf Husserl, an vielen anderen Stellen dagegen macht er implizit von seinen Ideen Gebrauch. Ähnliches gilt auch für kritische Einwände gegen Husserl, die Carnap gelegentlich explizit vorbringt, zumeist aber indirekt suggeriert. Für die Habilitation bei Schlick war wohl wesentlich, dass sich Carnap wenigstens an einigen Stellen von Husserl absetzte. Im Folgenden gehe ich auf zwei Kritikpunkte ein, die für den *Aufbau* einschlägig sind: die Zurückweisung des Begriffs der Intentionalität sowie die Kritik an der „intuitiven Metaphysik".

6.5.1 Intentionalität

Das Thema Intentionalität ist für den *Aufbau* offenbar nicht unwesentlich, da dieser ja seine Gegenstände im Rahmen eines „methodischen Solipsismus" konstituiert. Versteht man unter Intentionalität nun den Objektbezug von Akten oder Aussagen, dann fragt sich, wie ein solcher möglich sein sollte, wenn nicht die Objekte selbst Akte oder Aussagen sind? Diese Frage stellt Carnap nicht explizit, sie lässt sich aber doch aus seinen Bemerkungen im § 164 rekonstruieren.

Der *locus classicus* für Husserls Auffassung von Intentionalität ist die 5. Logische Untersuchung. Husserl kritisiert hier zunächst Brentanos Intentionalitätsbegriff, nach welchem sich intentionale Akte wie Wahrnehmen oder Wün-

---

[87] Cassirer an Husserl, Brief vom 10.IV.1925, Husserl 1994,6.

schen auf einen „immanenten Gegenstand" beziehen. Damit verbindet sich jedoch auch eine Kritik an einer „relationalen" Auffassung überhaupt, der zufolge Intentionalität in einer Beziehung zwischen einer mentalen Repräsentation und einem extramentalen Gegenstand bestünde. Der Objektbezug intentionaler Akte ist vielmehr ein Merkmal (Moment) des intentionalen Erlebnisses selbst:

> Es sind nicht [...] zwei Sachen erlebnismäßig präsent, es ist nicht der Gegenstand erlebt und daneben das intentionale Erlebnis, das sich auf ihn richtet; es sind auch nicht zwei Sachen wie Teil und umfassendes Ganzes, sondern nur eines ist präsent, das intentionale Erlebnis, dessen wesentlicher deskriptiver Charakter eben die bezügliche Intention ist. (Hua XIX/1, 386)[88]

Daher ist es auch für die Intentionalität eines Aktes unwesentlich, ob der intendierte Gegenstand ein realer, ein fiktiver oder ein widersinniger ist:

> *Jupiter* stelle ich nicht anders vor als *Bismarck*, den *Babylonischen Turm* nicht anders als den *Kölner Dom*, ein *regelmäßiges Tausendeck* nicht anders als einen regelmäßigen Tausendflächner. (Ebd., 387)

Carnap behandelt den Begriff der Intentionalität ausschließlich im §164. Im ersten Absatz schildert er Husserls Auffassung in der fünften Logischen Untersuchung, jedoch ohne Husserl beim Namen zu nennen. Dass Carnap die fünfte Logische Untersuchung vor Augen hat, ergibt sich daraus, dass er als Beispiel ebenfalls den Kölner Dom anführt:

> Die intentionale Beziehung besteht zwischen einem inhalthabenden psychischen Vorgang und seinem Inhalt, z. B. zwischen meiner augenblicklichen Vorstellung des Kölner Doms und diesem Gebäude als dem Inhalt oder ‚Gemeinten' dieser Vorstellung. (*Aufbau*, 226)[89]

Er fügt (wie Husserl) hinzu, dass es für die intentionale Beschaffenheit z. B. der Wahrnehmung sekundär sei, ob der sich darstellende Gegenstand geträumt oder real ist. Carnap behauptet nun, dass nach der „üblichen Auffassung" solche intentionalen Erlebnisse „aus sich heraus" auf das in ihnen gemeinte Objekt weisen. Er konzediert dieser Auffassung, dass Objekt und Erlebnis nicht identisch seien, wendet aber kritisch gegen sie ein, dass die intentionale Beziehung „nicht eine Beziehung ganz eigener Art" sei. Denn

---

88 Zum Begriff der Intentionalität Erhard 2014, Mayer 2009, 4.6 und Mayer/Erhard 2008.
89 Carnap zitiert die *Logischen Untersuchungen* auch in den Literaturverweisen zu diesem Paragraphen nicht, sondern bezieht sich nur auf die *Ideen I*.

vom Standpunkt der Konstitutionstheorie ist ja der gemeinte Baum eine gewisse, schon recht komplizierte Ordnung von Erlebnissen, von denen wir sagen, dass der Baum ihr intentionales Objekt sei. (Ebd., 227)

Mohanty 1972 bemerkt dazu:

Carnap's constructionism looks surprisingly alike Husserl's later theory of intentionality as constitutive, or of the intended object as being constituted in the noetic acts (Mohanty 1972, 74).[90]

Tatsächlich beschreibt Husserl in den *Ideen I* die intentionale Beziehung als eine Beziehung der Konstitution von intentionalen Objekten, den Noemata, durch komplexe noetische Akte. So schreibt er:

In Wesensnotwendigkeit gehört zu einem ‚allseitigen', kontinuierlich einheitlich sich in sich selbst bestätigenden Erfahrungsbewusstsein vom selben Ding ein vielfältiges System von kontinuierlichen Erscheinungs- und Abschattungsmannigfaltigkeiten [...]. (*Ideen I*, 85)

Auch Husserl vertritt also den „Standpunkt der Konstitutionstheorie". In seinem Literaturverweis behauptet Carnap nun:

Die traditionelle Theorie der Intentionalität stammt von Brentano und ist von Husserl [Phänomenol., 64 ff) weitergeführt worden. (Aufbau, 228)

Obwohl also tatsächlich Husserl Brentano kritisiert und Carnaps mit Husserls Intentionalitätsbegriff übereinstimmt, erweckt Carnap den Anschein, als ob er eine von Husserl verschiedene Theorie der Intentionalität vertrete, so dass er Husserls Auffassung „vom Standpunkt der Konstitutionstheorie" aus zurückweisen könne. Der Verweis auf §64 ff der *Ideen I* ist dabei irreführend, denn dort wird der Begriff der Intentionalität nur als Merkmal des Bewusstseins behandelt. Erst in den §§87 ff der *Ideen I* werden die Begriffe von Noesis und Noema eingeführt, auf deren Basis sich dann Intentionalität als Konstitution darstellt.[91]

Carnap behauptet nun an dieser Stelle nicht nur wider besseres Wissen, dass Husserls Intentionalitätsbegriff relational und nicht-konstitutiv sei. Er fügt hinzu, dass die intentionale Beziehung nicht eine irreduzible Beziehung „ganz eigener Art", sondern bloß ein Spezialfall der Relation zwischen einem Ordnungsgefüge und einem Gegenstand innerhalb dieses Gefüges sei, so wie etwa eine Pflanze

---

[90] Den Hinweis auf Mohanty verdanke ich Christopher Erhard.
[91] Dies ist ein zweiter Fall, in welchem Carnap den Verweis auf Husserl durch Angabe falscher Seitenzahlen missverständlich macht; vgl. oben 3.3.

auch auf das System der Pflanzen „verweise". Wie sinnvoll diese Parallele ist, sei hier dahingestellt[92]; sie dient Carnap an dieser Stelle jedenfalls mehreren Zwecken: zum einen den *Aufbau* scheinbar kritisch von Husserl abzurücken, zum zweiten die Rolle der Intentionalität für den *Aufbau* zu minimieren, und zum dritten Russell als angebliche Quelle der Inspiration ins Feld zu führen. Mit Russell, so behauptet Carnap in der Literaturanmerkung, stimme seine Auffassung nämlich wesentlich überein.

Es fällt schwer in Russells *The Analysis of Mind* Ähnlichkeit zu Carnaps Auffassung zu entdecken. Russell bezieht sich dort auf Brentano und Meinong, deren Theorie er unter anderem wie folgt als *relational* beschreibt:

> Speaking in popular and unphilosophical terms, we may say that the content of a thought is supposed to be something in your head when you think the thought, while the object is usually something in the outer world. It is held that knowledge of the outer world is constituted by the relation to the object, while the fact that knowledge is different from what it knows is due to the fact that knowledge comes by way of contents. (Russell 1921, 19)

Russell weist die Brentano-Meinong-Position zurück, weil sie erstens von Akten rede (Russell kann keinen Unterschied zwischen Akt und Inhalt erkennen), und zweitens, weil es keine einfache Beziehung zwischen Inhalt und Objekt gebe, vielmehr werde diese Beziehung hauptsächlich durch „beliefs" etabliert, die in inferentiellen und kausalen Beziehungen zum Objekt stehen:

> the relation of a mental occurrence to its 'object' is regarded as merely indirect and causal. [...] The mental content is, of course, always particular, and the question as to what it 'means' (in case it means anything) is one which cannot be settled by merely examining the intrinsic character of the mental content, but only by knowing its causal connections in the case of the person concerned. (Ebd., 227)

Diese Antwort passt nicht zu Carnaps These, wonach Intentionalität eine spezifische Form von Hinweisstruktur sei. Die Hinweisstruktur zwischen Erlebnis und Erlebnisordnung oder von Pflanze und botanischem System, von der Carnap spricht, wird von ihm weder inferentiell noch kausal begründet. Die Referenz auf Russell ist daher in mehrfacher Weise irreführend: Weder bezieht sich Russells Rekonstruktion der „üblichen Theorie der Intentionalität" auf Husserl, noch lässt sie sich auf diesen sinnvoll anwenden noch entspricht Russells Antwort auf die „übliche" Theorie derjenigen Carnaps. Wenn Carnap also in den Literaturverweisen schreibt, seine Auffassung stimme „im Wesentlichen überein mit der von

---

[92] Man könnte etwa bezweifeln, dass sich der Begriff des Verweises definieren ließe, ohne von dem der Intentionalität Gebrauch zu machen.

Russell" (*Aufbau*, 228), und den Eindruck erweckt, er kritisiere gemeinsam mit Russell Husserl, so sind beide Behauptungen schlicht nicht nachvollziehbar – es sei denn als Manöver, mit dem die faktische Übereinstimmung mit Husserl unkenntlich gemacht werden sollte.

6.5.2 Die intuitive Metaphysik und Carnaps Antimetaphysik

Für Schlick war Carnaps Kritik an der „intuitiven Metaphysik" besonders bedeutungsvoll; zumindest wird man wohl seine enthusiastische Reaktion auf den *Aufbau* auf diesen Punkt beziehen müssen.[93] Carnaps Kritik hat gleichzeitig zur anglo-amerikanischen Mythologiebildung entscheidend beigetragen. Die Kritik, die in den §§181/182 ausgeführt wird, richtet sich vor allem gegen die Rede von „Anschauung" oder „Intuition" in der Erkenntnistheorie, womit Carnap ein irrationales, nicht sprachlich rekonstruierbares Verfahren der Begründung meint. So stellt er – offenbar auf Husserls Wesensschau anspielend – in §181 die Frage nach der Möglichkeit außerbegrifflicher Erkenntnis „etwa im Glauben, z. B. auf Grund religiöser Offenbarung, in mystischer Versenkung oder sonstiger Schau (Intuition)". (*Aufbau*, 256) Carnap folgt Schlicks Erkenntnislehre, wenn er darlegt, dass Intuition, auch wenn darin etwas erfasst werde, keine Erkenntnis ergebe, da „Erkenntnis erst dann vorliegen [kann], wenn bezeichnet, formuliert wird, wenn in Worten oder anderen Zeichen eine Aussage gegeben wird". (Ebd.) Im §182 kennzeichnet Carnap dann die Metaphysik als „das Ergebnis eines nicht rationalen, sondern rein intuitiven Prozesses". (Ebd., 258) Im Folgenden sei zunächst Husserls Begriff der Anschauung oder Intuition erläutert, um anschließend Carnaps Position gegenüber der Metaphysik in Augenschein zu nehmen.

Für Husserl hat der Begriff der Anschauung oder Intuition einen klaren Sinn: er bezeichnet Akte, in denen ein Gegenstand unmittelbar präsent oder gegeben ist, und zwar im Unterschied zu Akten, in denen der Gegenstand nur repräsentiert oder appräsentiert ist. Husserls These, von der er sich allerdings nicht abbringen lässt, lautet, dass uns wesentliche Ähnlichkeiten und Differenzen wie die zwischen Farbe und Ton unmittelbar, und zwar auch in der Vorstellung oder Phantasie, gegeben sind, dass wir sie also in diesem Sinne „anschauen" oder „intuitiv erfassen". Wesenserschauung beruht auf Ähnlichkeits- und Differenzwahrnehmung in Bezug auf Gegebenheiten irgendeiner Art.

Auch Carnaps Quasianalyse setzt im Grunde genau diese Fähigkeit voraus. Wie sonst sollte ein solipsistisches Subjekt, das noch nicht über Begriffe verfügt,

---

[93] Vgl. oben 2.2.

sich diese auf der Basis von Ähnlichkeiten zwischen Elementarerlebnissen bilden?[94] Die Frage, wie denn „erkenntnistheoretisch" die Quasianalyse funktioniert, wird jedoch im *Aufbau* an keiner Stelle thematisiert. Carnap macht seine Interpretation der Metaphysik dann im Vorwort zum *Aufbau* endgültig manifest, wenn er fordert, die ganze Metaphysik sei aus der Philosophie zu verbannen, weil sie sich in ihren Begründungen nicht auf rationale Methoden, sondern auf Irrationales berufe.

> [D]ie Begründung hat vor dem Forum des Verstandes zu geschehen; da dürfen wir uns nicht auf eine erlebte Intuition oder auf Bedürfnisse des Gemüts berufen. (*Aufbau*, XX)

Spätestens nach dem neopositivistischen Manifest von 1931/32 mit seinem expliziten Angriff auf Heidegger, dürfte eine große Zahl an Lesern diese Worte auch auf Husserl bezogen haben. Antimetaphysisch in diesem Sinne ist Carnap also insofern, als er mit Schlick Intuition für irrational und nichtsprachliche Erkenntnis für unmöglich erklärt.

Der Begriff der Metaphysik, wie er heute von anglo-amerikanischen Philosophen verwendet wird, hat nichts mit Carnaps Begriff der „intuitiven Metaphysik" zu tun, sondern meint im Allgemeinen Fragen, die „das Sein als solches" angehen.[95] Auch Carnap verwendet den Begriff manchmal in diesem Sinne, etwa wenn er sich in Abschnitt VD unter dem Titel „Das metaphysische Wirklichkeitsproblem" von den Positionen des Realismus, Idealismus und Phänomenalismus absetzt. Da man nicht sinnvoll annehmen kann, dass nach Carnap alle diese Positionen „Intuition" voraussetzen, ist Carnaps Begriff der Metaphysik zumindest zweideutig: er meint zum einen eine Position, die den Anspruch erhebt, durch nicht sprachlich fassbare Anschauung Erkenntnis zu erlangen, zum zweiten eine Position, die Aussagen über das Sein als solches macht. Antimetaphysisch ist Carnap in dem zweiten Sinn nur insofern, als er sich gegenüber den genannten philosophischen Standpunkten für „neutral" erklärt: Soweit die drei Positionen erkenntnistheoretische Thesen aufstellen, steht die „Konstitutionstheorie" mit

---

[94] Burg 1933 weist bereits darauf hin, dass „Gleichheit und Ähnlichkeit bei der Quasianalyse schon vorausgesetzt werden als Ordnungsbegriffe wie auch als material Erlebtes. Es sollen rein formale Relationen sein, aber sie können in Wirklichkeit erst ausgesagt werden, nachdem man nicht nur einen Begriff von dem hat, was im allgemeinen Gleichheit Ähnlichkeit bedeuten, sondern, nachdem auf Grund einer vorangegangenen Untersuchung gesagt werden kann, diese Dinge seien gleich oder ähnlich." (38)

[95] In diesem heutigen Sinne versteht offenbar auch Friedman 2007 Carnaps Begriff der Metaphysik. Den §182, in dem Carnap die Frage, was Metaphysik ist, beantworten will, erwähnt Friedman nicht.

ihnen nicht im Widerspruch, sie stellt vielmehr „das ihnen gemeinsame neutrale Fundament dar". (*Aufbau*, 250)

Man kann bestreiten, dass Husserls Phänomenologie im ersten Sinne als intuitive Metaphysik bezeichnet werden kann, und zwar auch nach Carnaps eigenen Kriterien. Carnap schreibt in §182, dass die Tatsache der Verbalisierung angeblicher mystischer Erkenntnis diese nicht schon rational werden lasse – so dass man sich vergeblich darauf berufen würde, dass Husserl die Ergebnisse seiner Wesensschau auf etwa 80000 Manuskriptseiten schriftlich fixiert hat. Vielmehr, fährt Carnap fort, könnten Worte nur dann als Zeichen von Begriffen angesehen werden, wenn sie definierbar seien und das bedeute, dass sie „in ein erkenntnismäßiges Konstitutionssystem entweder eingeordnet sind oder eingeordnet werden können." (*Aufbau*, 259) Husserl bestand nun allerdings darauf, dass Wesensschau nicht in einer „Begriffsanalyse" bestehen kann, sondern dadurch geschieht, dass man sich die konstitutive Struktur der Gegenstände anschaulich gegenwärtig macht. So wird die Konstitutionsstruktur von „mein Leib" durch Wesensschau erkannt, nämlich durch in freier Phantasie erzeugte anschauliche Deckungserlebnisse („eidetische Variation"). Das Ziel ist aber gerade, was Carnap fordert, nämlich die Einordnung des Gegenstandes in ein Konstitutionssystem. Da Carnap sehr genau wusste, dass die Wesensschau die Konstitutionsstruktur des Gegenstandes offenlegt, zeigt sich in den §§181 und 182 des *Aufbau* eine kuriose Doppelstruktur. Einerseits erweckt Carnap an die Adresse von Schlick den Anschein, als ob er sich Schlicks Husserlkritik anschließe; andererseits rettet er Husserl vor Schlick, indem er ein „Irrationalitätskriterium" formuliert, das ausgerechnet auf Husserl nicht zutrifft.

Im zweiten Sinne von Metaphysik, d.h. als Untersuchung von Seinsfragen, kann man nicht nur bestreiten, dass Husserl Metaphysiker ist, sondern muss wohl abermals überraschende Ähnlichkeit zwischen Carnaps und Husserls Standpunkt konstatieren. So schreibt Husserl in den *Logischen Untersuchungen* einmal:

> Erlebnis ist das Die-Welt-Meinen, die Welt selbst ist der intendierte Gegenstand. Für diese Unterscheidung ist es, wie ich noch ausdrücklich betonen will, gleichgültig, wie man sich zu den Fragen stellt, was das objektive Sein, das wahre, wirkliche An-sich-sein der Welt oder eines beliebigen sonstigen Gegenstandes ausmacht, und wie man das objektive Sein als ‚Einheit' zum subjektiven Gedacht-sein mit seiner ‚Mannigfaltigkeit' bestimmt; desgleichen, in welchem Sinne metaphysisch immanentes und transzendentes Sein gegenübergestellt werden dürfe usw. Es handelt sich hier vielmehr um eine Unterscheidung, die vor aller Metaphysik und an der Pforte der Erkenntnistheorie steht, also auch keine Fragen als beantwortet voraussetzt, die eben die Erkenntnistheorie allererst beantworten soll. (HUA XIX/1, 401)

Carnaps vor allem durch sein „Scheinprobleme in der Philosophie" bekannt gewordener, gegenüber metaphysischen Fragen neutraler Standpunkt hat demnach ebenfalls sein Gegenstück in Husserls Phänomenologie.

7 Einwände

Carnaps *Aufbau* ist eines der einflussreichsten und meist diskutierten Werke der Philosophie des 20. Jahrhunderts und gilt im Allgemeinen als Carnaps Hauptwerk. (Mormann 2000) Die Beziehungen des *Aufbau* zu verschiedenen philosophischen Richtungen oder einzelnen Philosophen, die wesentlichen Thesen, der philosophische Charakter des Buchs und viele seiner einzelnen Aspekte sind Gegenstand einer Unzahl wissenschaftlicher Untersuchungen geworden. Die These, die in diesem Aufsatz verfochten wird, wonach sich im *Aufbau* nicht etwa nur „Einflüsse" Husserls auf Carnap zeigen, und auch nicht nur etwa „oberflächliche Ähnlichkeiten" (Richardson 2010), sondern dass es sich um ein systematisches Plagiat handelt, erscheint schon allein wegen der Resonanz, die das Buch fand, unwahrscheinlich. Hätten nicht trotz der verschiedenen Maskierungen Carnaps „Zwangsanleihen" in den mehr als 80 Jahren, die seit seiner Publikation vergangen sind, entdeckt werden müssen? Hätte nicht wenigstens Husserl Einspruch erheben müssen? Wie steht es mit der in den letzten Jahren vor allem von Michael Friedman massiv vorgetragenen neukantianischen Interpretation des *Aufbau*? Kann man einem so engagierten Philosophen wie Carnap, der sich an der Bürgerrechtsbewegung beteiligte und sich aktiv gegen den Vietnamkrieg einsetzte, ernsthaft ein derartig unethisches Verhalten unterstellen? Im Folgenden wird einigen dieser Einwände nachgegangen.

7.1 Weshalb das Plagiat nicht entdeckt wurde

Das Manuskript der *Ideen II* war beim Erscheinen des *Aufbau* unveröffentlicht und nur einem engen Kreis von Schülern Husserls näher bekannt, darunter Landgrebe und Stein. Deren philosophische Interessen waren jedoch nicht so gelagert, dass man annehmen kann, dass sie den *Aufbau* sorgfältig, wenn überhaupt gelesen haben. Eine sorgfältige Lektüre ist aber notwendig, um durch die vielfältigen Maskierungen hindurch die Verwandtschaft zu den *Ideen II* zu erkennen. Im Umfeld des Wiener Kreises war Felix Kaufmann mit Husserls Phänomenologie vertraut und mit Husserl persönlich bekannt. Er kannte aber wohl nicht das Manuskript der *Ideen II* und damit die genetische Phänomenologie, so dass er Carnaps formale Rekonstruktion nicht auf Husserl zurückbeziehen konnte. So bleibt wohl nur Husserl selbst, der sowohl die formale Kompetenz besaß, als auch der beste Kenner seines eigenen Werkes war.

Husserl war mit dem Phänomen, dass seine Ideen von anderen undeklariert verwendet wurden, vertraut. So verweist er in einer Anmerkung der *Ideen I* bezüglich der Formalisierbarkeit von Axiomensystemen auf die *Prolegomena* und schreibt: „Einzelnes aus diesem Gedankenkreis ist in die Literatur gedrungen, ohne dass die Ursprungsquelle genannt worden wäre. (*Ideen I*, 153) Mehr als solche kursorischen Äußerungen findet sich zu dem Thema in den veröffentlichten Schriften nicht.[96] Ein deutlicherer Einspruch hätte auch dem Geist widersprochen, in dem er die Phänomenologie verstanden wissen wollte: als ein offenes Forschungsprogramm, das durch Generationen von Phänomenologen präzisiert und weiterentwickelt werden sollte. Gegen Carnaps vielfach verklausulierte Anleihen an einem unveröffentlichten Werk wäre ohnehin schwer Einspruch zu erheben gewesen. So ließ Husserl wohl die Sache auf sich beruhen.

7.2 Carnap als ethische Persönlichkeit

Dass die Schwierigkeiten einer Qualifikationsschrift auch einen Menschen überfordern können, der sich als ethisch verantwortlich versteht, insbesondere wenn so beträchtlicher Druck ausgeübt wird wie damals durch Schlick, ist inzwischen hinlänglich bekannt. Carnaps freimütiges Geständnis in der Autobiographie, dass er nichts dabei fand, je nach Gegenüber verschiedene „Sprachen" zu verwenden, wie sie eben von den zahlreichen Philosophen „gesprochen" wurden, die er gelesen hatte, deutet auf eine Gewissenslücke in diesem Punkt. Auch der Vorwurf der „Kritiklosigkeit", der ihm von Reichenbach gemacht wurde, weist in diese Richtung. Im Übrigen ist es nicht das erste Mal, dass der Vorwurf des Plagiats gegen Carnap erhoben wird. Auch Wittgenstein beschuldigte Carnap des Diebstahls an Ideen, die er in den Gesprächen mit dem Wiener Kreis geäußert hatte. (Stadler 1992) Ob Wittgensteins Vorwurf zutrifft, kann hier dahingestellt bleiben. Ausgeschlossen ist es jedenfalls nicht, dass Carnap die so erfolgreiche Methode

---

96 Vgl. jedoch den Plagiatsprozess gegen Theodor Lessing, der in Husserls Göttinger Zeit fiel; dazu Schuhmann 1977, 115 und Baron 1983. Auf diesen Fall hat mich Thomas Vongehr hingewiesen. Die Ähnlichkeiten zwischen den Vorfällen sind nicht von der Hand zu weisen: Bei Lessing ging es wie bei Carnap um eine Habilitationsschrift und Lessing hatte ebenso wie Carnap ohne Immatrikulation bei Husserl studiert. Womöglich haben die Erfahrungen mit dem Fall Lessing dazu beigetragen, dass der nun wesentlich ältere Husserl das Plagiat Carnaps mit Stillschweigen überging.

des unkenntlich Machens fremder Ideen durch Übersetzung in eine formale Redeweise auch in anderen Zusammenhängen verwendet hat.

7.3 Carnap als Neukantianer?

Seit Michael Friedman 1987 gezeigt hat, dass der *Aufbau* nicht mit den Merkmalen einer empiristischen Erkenntnistheorie übereinstimmt, hat sich eine einflussreiche neukantianische Interpretationsrichtung entwickelt. Diese beruft sich u. a. auf zwei Kennzeichen: Erstens, dass Carnap die Objektivität wissenschaftlicher Erkenntnis in den Vordergrund stellt, und zweitens, dass er die wissenschaftlichen Aussagen wenigstens potentiell als reine Strukturaussagen darzustellen versucht. Bestärkt fühlt sich diese Interpretation dadurch, dass Carnap bei dem Neokantianer Bruno Bauch promoviert hatte. Man könnte hinzufügen, dass Carnap im eingangs zitierten Sera-Brief neben Husserl zwar nicht Bauch und Rickert, aber doch Natorp und Cassirer als philosophische „Generäle" bezeichnet.

Auf die neukantianische Interpretation kann hier nicht im Einzelnen eingegangen werden.[97] Es sei aber doch im Folgenden kurz auf einige Aspekte hingewiesen, die eine neukantianische Deutung des *Aufbau* unplausibel erscheinen lassen.[98] Dabei muss zunächst festgehalten werden, dass die neukantianische Interpretation eine phänomenologische Deutung keineswegs ausschließt, und zwar deshalb nicht, weil Husserls Phänomenologie und der Neukantianismus, insbesondere derjenige Natorps, in vieler Hinsicht übereinstimmen. Iso Kern findet in seiner klassischen Monographie zum Thema (Kern 1964) kaum Divergenzen und Husserl wird sogar noch in Moran und Cohens *Husserl Dictionary* als „broadly neokantian" dargestellt. (Moran/Cohen 2012, 70 f) Die Frage, ob der *Aufbau* mehr neukantianisch oder mehr phänomenologisch „beeinflusst" ist, muss sich also daran entscheiden, welche Position Carnap in Bezug auf die wesentlichen verbleibenden Differenzen zwischen beiden Systemen bezieht. Es genügt deshalb nicht, weitläufige Ähnlichkeiten zum Neukantianismus aufzuzeigen; vielmehr muss, vor allem angesichts der vielen Übereinstimmungen zwischen

---

[97] Das Ziel dieser Untersuchung ist es nicht, zu zeigen, dass Carnap in Wirklichkeit Phänomenologe im Sinne Husserls war oder die Auffassung Husserls für wahrer gehalten habe als den Neukantianismus oder eine andere Position, sondern dass er sich der Ideen Husserl bedient hat, um eine Habilitationsschrift zu erstellen – eine These, die zunächst unabhängig von seinen eigenen Überzeugungen zu betrachten ist.
[98] Legt man die Position zugrunde, die Carnap im Sera-Brief formuliert, dann mag es allerdings müßig scheinen, ihn vor seiner Habilitation auf eine philosophische Richtung verpflichten zu wollen.

Carnaps und Husserls Konstitutionssystem, auf die Verwandtschaftsbeziehungen zwischen Phänomenologie und Neukantianismus im Einzelnen eingegangen werden. Husserl und Natorp standen in engem Kontakt; beide thematisieren die Frage ihrer Übereinstimmung und Nichtübereinstimmung an verschiedenen Stellen, so etwa Natorp in seiner Rezension der *Ideen I*. [99] Für eine Klärung der philosophischen Herkunft des *Aufbau* gäbe es also hinreichende Textgrundlagen. Die folgenden Bemerkungen verstehen sich lediglich als erste Hinweise.

(1) Carnap hat neukantianische Auffassungen[100] selbst an mehreren Stellen mit gutem Grund kritisch bewertet oder zurückgewiesen. So macht er in §64 (*Aufbau*, 87) darauf aufmerksam, dass die Neukantianer Natorp und Rickert eine erkenntnistheoretische Begründung auf „eigenpsychischer Basis" ablehnen. Ein Konstitutionssystem auf einer solchen Grundlage kann Carnap selbst daher wohl kaum als neukantianisch verstanden haben. Dieser Aspekt betrifft insbesondere die Rolle der Subjektivität im Konstitutionssystem, eine Frage, in der Natorp 1912 sich gegenüber seinen früheren Auffassungen neu orientiert. (Sieg 1994, 413 ff)[101] Das Problem der Bedeutung des in Husserls Sinne „transzendentalen" Subjekts steht auch im Hintergrund der folgenden Einwände.

---

99 Natorp schreibt in seiner Rezension: „Eine Auseinandersetzung mit Husserls Standpunkt der ‚Phänomenologie' ist für jeden in den Grundfragen der Philosophie vorwärtsstrebenden eine Notwendigkeit; sie ist es doppelt für den, der sich in einer Reihe von fundamentalen Voraussetzungen von Anfang an mit ihm auf einer Linie findet." (Natorp 1914 [1917–18], 224) In dieser lesenswerten ausführlichen Besprechung geht Natorp sehr genau auf die Gemeinsamkeiten und Unterschiede zwischen Husserls Phänomenologie und seiner eigenen Variante des Neukantianismus ein, darunter findet sich auch Kritik an der Epoché und den regionalen Ontologien ebenso wie – entgegen seinen früheren Auffassungen – Zustimmung zur Bestimmung der Noemata durch die noetischen „Charaktere".
100 Der Neukantianismus ist keine einheitliche philosophische Schule und die Zugehörigkeiten sind auch zur Zeit der Entstehung des *Aufbau* unklar und strittig. (Sieg 1989; Köhnke 1886; Häusser 1989, 155 Anm.10) Als prototypische Vertreter gelten die Marburger (Cohen, Natorp) und die Südwestdeutsche (Rickert) Schule. Carnap führt im Literaturverzeichnis neben seinen Doktorvater Bauch Cassirer, Natorp und Rickert auf. Auf diese sei die Bezeichnung „Neukantianer" hier bezogen.
101 Einen anderen Unterschied zwischen dem Neukantianismus (in diesem Falle Rickerts) und der Phänomenologie Husserls arbeitet Kreis 1930 heraus: demnach ist es der für Husserl wesentliche Begriff der Anschauung oder des unmittelbar Gegebenen, der die Differenz zum Neukantianismus markiert. Der Neukantianismus besteht darauf, dass „Gegebenes" immer schon in Urteilen geformt ist. Wenn Carnap in §67 schreibt, das Gegebene seien „die Erlebnisse selbst in ihrer Totalität und geschlossenen Einheit" und in §68 die Elementarerlebnisse als „unzerlegbare Einheiten" beschreibt (*Aufbau*, 92 f), dann positioniert er sich deutlich gegen die neukantianische Erkenntnistheorie.

(2) Ein wichtiger Divergenzpunkt zwischen Neukantianismus und Phänomenologie findet sich in der Frage der Bestimmtheit des Erkenntnisgegenstandes. Für den Neukantianer Natorp, zumindest vor seiner „subjektivistischen Wende" 1912, ist Objekt der Erkenntnis das unbestimmte und vage X, das in einer unendlichen wissenschaftlichen Objektivierung immer genauer präzisiert wird. Nicht die Subjektivität, sondern die Wissenschaft liefert uns daher Erkenntnisgegenstände. (Natorp 1888, 1892, 1910) Husserl widerspricht dieser Auffassung schon in der fünften Logischen Untersuchung. Die Erkenntnisgegenstände sind immer schon durch Bewusstseinsakte vorstrukturiert, deren Korrelate sie sind:

> Der Inhalt ist für mich in anderer Weise da, je nachdem ich ihn nur impliziert, ohne Sonderabhebung in einem Ganzen, oder abgehoben, wieder ob ich ihn nur nebenbei bemerke oder ihn bevorzugend im Auge, es besonders auf ihn abgesehen habe. (Hua XIX/1, 394f)

In den *Ideen I* entspricht dem die komplexe Korrelation zwischen Noesis und Noema[102]; in den *Ideen II* wird dies dann dahingehend expliziert, dass die Gegenstandstypen durch den genetischen Konstitutionszusammenhang strukturiert werden. Carnap verfolgt eine ganz ähnliche Argumentationslinie wie Husserl, wenn er in § 179 *gegen* Natorp schreibt:

> Nach Auffassung der Marburger Schule (vgl. Natorp [Grundlagen] 18 ff.) ist der Gegenstand das ewige X, seine Bestimmung ist eine unvollendbare Aufgabe. Demgegenüber ist darauf hinzuweisen, dass zur Konstitution des Gegenstandes, also zu seiner eindeutigen Kennzeichnung innerhalb der Gegenstände überhaupt, *endlich viele Bestimmungen genügen.* (Hervorhebung V.M.) Ist eine solche Kennzeichnung aufgestellt, so ist der Gegenstand kein X mehr, sondern etwas eindeutig Bestimmtes, dessen vollständige Beschreibung dann freilich noch eine unvollendbare Aufgabe bleibt. (*Aufbau*, 253)[103]

Die „endlich vielen Bestimmungen" sind diejenigen Kriterien, durch die ein Gegenstand im Konstitutionssystem definiert ist, etwa mein Leib durch das „bei jeder Wahrnehmung dabei sein" oder die Gleichzeitigkeit von Seh- und Fühlerlebnissen im Falle der Selbstberührung. Hier bezieht also Carnap in einer zentralen Frage

---

102 Vgl. dort die §§87 ff.
103 Richardson 1998, der den Neukantianismus Natorps als eine der wesentlichen Inspirationsquellen des *Aufbau* darstellt, zitiert die Auffassung Natorps, wonach die Bestimmung des Gegenstandes eine „unendliche Aufgabe" sei (ebd., 132); dass Carnap Natorp in eben diesem Punkt zurückweist, erwähnt er jedoch nicht. Friedman dagegen bemerkt die Abweichung vom Marburger Neukantianismus in 2007, 140, Fn.13. Die Kontroverse zwischen Natorp und Husserl über diesen Punkt kennt auch er offenbar nicht.

explizit Stellung gegen den Neukantianismus und positioniert sich gleichzeitig implizit auf der Seite Husserls.

(3) Auch in einer spezifischeren Hinsicht lässt sich gegen die neukantianische Interpretation argumentieren. Im zuletzt zitierten Abschnitt aus den *Logischen Untersuchungen* betont Husserl, dass eine eindeutige Beziehung zwischen dem *Akttypus* und seinem intentionalen Gegenstand bestehe: der wahrgenommene Gegenstand ist ein anderer als der erinnerte oder phantasierte.[104] Natorp leugnet dagegen, zumindest vor seiner Rezension der *Ideen I* 1914, dass Bewusstseinsakte etwas zum Wesen des Gegenstandes beitragen. Vielmehr sind die Unterschiede zwischen solchen Akten durch die Unterschiede zwischen den Gegenständen bestimmt. So schreibt Natorp: „In dem Grundphänomen der Bewusstheit liegt ganz und gar keine Mannigfaltigkeit und Besonderung; sie ist schlechterdings einfach und an Belehrung arm". (Natorp 1888, 19)[105] Welche Position in Bezug auf diese Frage nimmt Carnap ein? Mindestens in Bezug auf die Werte besteht für Carnap eine Korrelation zwischen Wertwahrnehmung und Wert, die den Gegenstand, den Wert, inhaltlich vorstrukturiert. (*Aufbau*, 203 f.) In diesem Zusammenhang erwähnt Carnap dann auch eine Analogie zum Verhältnis zwischen Wahrgenommenem und physischem Gegenstand. Die Konstitutionstheorie nämlich

> übersetzt die genannte Aussage über das Verhältnis von Wert und Wertgefühl in die konstitutionale Sprache in einer bestimmten Weise, die analog ist zu der Weise, in der sie die Aussage über das Verhältnis zwischen physischem Ding und Wahrnehmung übersetzt, nämlich durch Heraushebung der rein logischen Beziehung des Bestimmtseins des Einen durch die Beschaffenheit des Anderen. (*Aufbau*, 204)

(4) Die Einstellung der Epochè ist für Husserls Phänomenologie vor allem nach den *Logischen Untersuchungen* grundlegend.[106] Carnap setzt diese Einstellung ebenfalls an den Anfang der inhaltlichen Entwicklung seines Konstitutionssystems.[107] Natorp dagegen lehnt die Epochè als erkenntnistheoretisches Werkzeug ab. Für ihn stellt sie eine Objektivierung des Subjektiven dar, die sachlich und theoretisch nicht gerechtfertigt werden kann. In diesem Punkt konstatiert Natorp eine wesentliche Differenz zu Husserl (Natorp 1912, 281; 1914).

---

104 XIX/1, 397 ff; vgl. zur Auseinandersetzung Natorp-Husserl insbesondere Kern 1964, 321 ff.
105 Husserl argumentiert gegen Natorp in XIX/1, 400. Natorp hat seine Position in diesem Punkt später derjenigen Husserls angenähert.
106 Vgl. oben 3.3.
107 Vgl. oben 3.3.

(5) In einem Brief an Natorp aus dem Jahr 1900 schreibt Husserl: „Bei der Lektüre Ihrer ‚Einleitung in die Psychologie' hatte ich so oft das Bedürfnis nach einer Erkenntniskritik aus Ihrer Feder, aber – ganz auf Kleingeld, in E i n z e l d u r c h f ü h r u n g ."[108] Natorp hat jedoch im Folgenden ebenso wenig wie andere Neukantianer eine solche Detailanalyse, wie sie Husserl und Carnap beispielsweise bei der Konstitution des Sehdinges vornehmen, vorgelegt. Die neukantianische Philosophie bleibt im Wesentlichen programmatisch; eine analytische Beschreibung der Erkenntnisprozesse liegt auch aus systematischen Gründen nicht in ihrem Interesse.

Dieses Merkmal findet sich übrigens ebenso in der neukantianischen *Aufbau*-Interpretation. Auch diese widmet dem Konstitutionssystem in seinen Einzelheiten keine Aufmerksamkeit, sondern übernimmt den von Carnap initiierten Mythos, es handle sich um Übernahmen aus der Gestaltpsychologie.

(6) Schließlich sollte für eine Einordnung des *Aufbau* in eine philosophische Schule auch von Bedeutung sein, wie die Mitglieder dieser Schule selbst auf das Werk reagiert haben. Hier wäre etwa die Kritik von Jonas Cohn 1936 am *Aufbau* zu nennen. Cohn rechnete sich nicht nur dem Neukantianismus zu, er hat sich, wie der Briefwechsel mit Husserl bezeugt, zudem mit der Phänomenologie und der Frage ihrer Differenz zum Neukantianismus intensiv auseinandergesetzt.[109]

Insgesamt ergibt sich: Die neukantianische Carnap-Deutung kennt weder Husserl noch die vielfältigen inhaltlichen Beziehungen und Auseinandersetzungen zwischen Husserls Phänomenologie und neukantianischen Auffassungen. Sie hält daher für neukantianisch, was tatsächlich phänomenologisch begründet ist. Diese Verwechslung würde ihr nur dann erkennbar werden, wenn sie sich auf das Studium der Phänomenologie einließe. Erst auf dieser Grundlage könnten die echten Bezugnahmen auf die eine oder andere Richtung offen gelegt und vorurteilsfrei diskutiert werden.

8 Fazit

Der *Aufbau* weist nach der hier vorgelegten Analyse mehrere Schichten auf. Im eigentlichen und vielleicht auch ursprünglich beabsichtigten Sinne stellt er eine Übersetzung des genetischen Konstitutionsprogramms Husserls in eine formale

---

[108] Brief an Natorp vom 8. VII. 1900, Husserl 1994, Bd. V, 74.
[109] Vgl. den Brief Cohns an Husserl vom 31. 3. 1911 in Husserl 1994, Bd. V, 17 ff.

Sprache dar. Darüber legt Carnap eine Schicht der irreführenden Verweise und falschen Spuren, die er im Nachhinein weiterführt und bestärkt. Auf einer dritten Ebene finden sich schließlich Hinweise, dass Carnap womöglich die phänomenologische Herkunft des *Aufbau* nicht ganz unsichtbar machen wollte. Dafür spricht, dass er dem Werk auch in der veröffentlichten Fassung den Titel „Konstitutionstheorie" geben wollte, dass die Phänomenologie an entscheidenden Stellen zur ausführenden „Wissenschaft" erklärt wird, und vor allem, dass er im §182 seinen eigenen impliziten Verweis auf Husserl konterkariert, indem er die Einfügung eines Begriffs in ein Konstitutionssystem als das Merkmal eines „wissenschaftlichen" Konzepts bezeichnet – wohl wissend, dass er damit Husserls Projekt einer „Philosophie als strenge Wissenschaft" beschreibt. Diese Hinweise sind jedoch für den uneingeweihten Leser so kryptisch, dass sie den hier erhobenen Plagiats-Vorwurf nicht aus der Welt schaffen können.

Nach der eingangs zitierten Definition eines Plagiats aus dem Jahr 1933, wonach ein solches in einer Übernahme „nicht unbeträchtlichen Gedankeninhalts eines anderen" besteht, „in der Absicht, solche Zwangsanleihe nach ihrer Herkunft durch entsprechende Umgestaltung zu verwischen und den Anschein eigenen Schaffens damit beim Leser oder Beschauer zu erwecken", muss man den *Aufbau* wohl als Plagiat bewerten. Die Fülle der inhaltlichen, strukturellen und terminologischen Ähnlichkeiten, die Interessenlage Carnaps zur Zeit der Abfassung, der mögliche Zugang zur Quelle, das absichtliche Verschweigen der biographischen Kontakte zu Husserl und seinem Kreis in Freiburg sowie die vielfältigen anderen hier aufgelisteten Hinweise, lassen kaum eine nachsichtigere Interpretation zu. Wenn Michael Friedman schreibt, „[t]he Aufbau [...] explains a new philosophical discipline Carnap calls constitutional theory and presents a particular constitutional system against the background of this general theory" (Friedman 2007, 132), dann muss dagegen gehalten werden, dass System wie Theorie weder neu noch originell sind. Die Beschreibung des *Aufbau*-Programms, die Friedman seinem Aufsatz 2007 voranstellt, kann man auch als eine knappe Darstellung von Husserls genetischer Phänomenologie lesen. Man muss dabei allenfalls den Bezug zu Russells Typentheorie durch den Verweis auf Husserls Begriff der Fundierung aus der dritten Logischen Untersuchung ersetzen.

Für viele anglo-amerikanische Philosophen ist die Phänomenologie Husserls, insbesondere dessen genetische Konstitutionstheorie, zu der das System der *Ideen II* gehört, nach wie vor *terra incognita*. Husserls Terminologie ist schwierig und ungewohnt, gelegentlich pathetisch, es ist nicht leicht, den greifbaren Sinn dahinter zu verstehen oder die geforderte Einstellung der Epochè einzunehmen, Reizwörter wie „Wesensschau" tun ein Übriges. Dies sind wohl einige der Gründe, weshalb den schon seit 1992 vorliegenden Hinweisen auf die auffallenden Parallelen zu den *Ideen II* nicht nachgegangen wurde.

Carnap jedoch verstand Husserl sehr gut; die Widmung in Husserls Exemplar der Dissertation, die Auskunft Landgrebes, und nicht zuletzt die ausgreifenden Anleihen im *Aufbau* deuten auf Wertschätzung, die dann allerdings der Karriere weichen musste. Die hier vorgelegte ausführliche Aufzählung der Ähnlichkeiten zwischen dem *Aufbau* und Husserls Phänomenologie, vor allem der *Ideen II*, sollte deshalb auch nicht nur dazu dienen, den *Aufbau* als aus dem Wunsch nach einer Habilitation entstandenes Plagiat zu entlarven. Es soll dadurch auch gezeigt werden, wie viel Potential Husserls Werk für die Interpretation des *Aufbau* und darüber hinaus für die dort behandelten Fragen überhaupt enthält. Nicht nur in den Einzelheiten der Konstitution ist Husserl weitaus detaillierter und näher an den „Sachen selbst" als Carnap, dem es nur um eine grobe Skizze geht. So erfährt man über die Konstitution der Sinnendinge – z. B. der Töne – weit mehr in den *Ideen II* als im Aufbau, der sich auf eine Charakterisierung der visuellen Gegenstände beschränkt. Bei Husserl finden sich zudem grundsätzliche Überlegungen, die nicht nur die Möglichkeit der Konstitution der Welt auf der Basis von Erlebnissen betreffen, sondern die Begriffe der Konstitution, der Subjektivität, der Natur, der Wissenschaftlichkeit und andere weitaus tiefgehender reflektieren, als dies Carnap in seinem scheinbar alles integrierenden Übersetzungsmanual auch nur annähernd zu leisten vermag. Die Verdienste Carnaps für den Versuch einer formalen Durchführung des Programms sind von diesen Einwänden nicht betroffen; für seine inhaltliche Begründung jedoch sollte man in Zukunft auf das Original zurückgreifen.

Literatur

Awodney, Steve/Klein, Carsten (2004): *Carnap Brought Home. The Jena Connection*, Chicago and LaSalle: Open Court.

Bar-Hillel, Yehoshua (1957): „Husserl's Conception of a purely Logical Grammar", *Philosophy and Phenomenological Research* Vol. 17, 362–369.

Baron, Lawrence (1983): „Discipleship and Dissent: Theodor Lessing and Edmund Husserl", *Proceedings of the American Philosophical Society* Vol. 127, 32–44.

Benoist, Jocelyn (2001): „L'Aufbau comme phénoménologie", in: S. Laugie (ed.), *Carnap et la Construction du monde*, Paris: Librare Philosophique J. Vrin.

Burg, Josef (1933): *Konstitution und Gegenstand im logischen Neopositivismus Rudolf Carnaps*. Inaugural-Dissertation, Leipzig: Albert Teicher.

Rudolf Carnap Papers (1905–1970): Briefwechsel mit Reichenbach, Box 102d, Folder 64, *Rudolf Carnap Papers*, ASP.1974.01, Special Collections Department, University of Pittsburgh.

Carnap, Rudolf (1908–1920): Alte Aufzeichnungen und Tagebuch, Box 81d, Folder 47, *Rudolf Carnap Papers*, 1905–1970, ASP.1974.01, Special Collections Department, University of Pittsburgh.

Carnap, Rudolf (1921–1926): „Vom Chaos zur Wirklichkeit" (mit Notizen zum Konstitutions-System), Box 81a, Folder 5, *Rudolf Carnap Papers, 1905–1970*, ASP.1974.01, Special Collections Department, University of Pittsburgh.

Carnap, Rudolf (1922–1927a): Briefwechsel mit Schlick 1922–1927, Box 29, Folder 32, *Rudolf Carnap Papers*, 1905–1970, ASP.1974.01, Special Collections Department, University of Pittsburgh..

Carnap, Rudolf (1922–1927b): Tagebuch, Jan. 1925 – Jan. 1926, Box 25, Folder 72, *Rudolf Carnap Papers*, 1905–1970, ASP.1974.01, Special Collections Department, University of Pittsburgh.

Carnap, Rudolf (1928a): *Der Logische Aufbau der Welt*, Berlin-Schlachtensee : Weltkreis. [*Aufbau*]

Carnap, Rudolf (1928b): *Scheinprobleme in der Philosophie. Das Fremdpsychische und der Realismusstreit.* Berlin-Schlachtensee : Weltkreis.

Carnap, Rudolf (1925): *Brief an Jonas Cohn vom 14. März 1925*, Original im Jonas Cohn-Archiv, Salomon Ludwig Steinheim Institut für deutsch-jüdische Geschichte, Essen.

Carnap, Rudolf (1963): „Intellectual Autobiography", in Schilpp, P.-A. (ed.), *The Philosophy of Rudolf Carnap*, LaSalle: Open Court, 3–83.

Carnap, Rudolf (1967): *The Logical Structure of the World; and : Pseudoproblems in Philosophy.* Translated by Ralph A. George, Berkeley: University of California Press.

Carnap, Rudolf (2015): *Tagebücher 1908–1935*. Transkribiert von Brigitta Arden und Brigitte Parakenings, Fassung vom 30.9.2015, http://homepage.univie.ac.at/christian.damboeck/carnap_diaries_2015–2018/diaries_1908–1935_transcriptions_2015.pdf (abgerufen am 16.10.2015).

Carus, André W. (2007): *Carnap and Twentieth Century Thought*, Cambridge: Cambridge University Press.

Cohn, Jonas (1936): „Kritische Bemerkungen zur neupositivistischen Erkenntnislehre, namentlich zu der Carnaps (Methodenmonismus und Problemabweisung)", *Philosophische Hefte*, Hrsg.: Maximilian Beck. Verlag: Maximilian Beck, Prag – Dejvice 1936, 5. Jg., Heft 1/2, S. 51–74.

Driesch, Hans (1913): *Die Logik als Aufgabe. Eine Studie über die Beziehung zwischen Phänomenologie und Logik. Zugleich eine Einführung in die Ordnungslehre*, Tübingen: Mohr.

Driesch, Hans (1923): *Ordnungslehre. Ein System des nichtmetaphysischen Teils der Philosophie.* Jena: Diederichs.

Englisch, Paul (1933): *Meister des Plagiats oder Die Kunst der Abschriftstellerei*, Berlin-Karlshorst: Hannibal.

Erhard, Christopher (2014): *Denken über Nichts. Intentionalität und das Problem der Nichtexistenz bei Husserl.* Berlin: De Gruyter.

Fahrenberg, J. (2006): „Vom psychophysischen Labor zum Psychologischen Institut". In: E. Wirbelauer (Hrsg.), *Die Freiburger Philosophische Fakultät 1920–1960*, Freiburger Beiträge zur Wissenschafts- und Universitätsgeschichte. Freiburg: Karl Alber, 468–476.

Friedman, Michael (1987): „Carnap's Aufbau Reconsidered", *Nous* 21, 521–545.

Friedman, Michael (1997): „Erkenntnistheorie in Carnaps Aufbau", in: *Bausteine wissenschaftlicher Weltauffassung*, Lecture Series, Hg. Friedrich Stadler, Wien: Springer, 101–124.

Friedman, Michael (2007): „The *Aufbau* and the Rejection of Metaphysics", in Friedman/Creath 2007, 129–152.
Friedman, Michael/Creath, R. (Hgg.) (2007): *The Cambridge Companion to Carnap*, Cambridge: Cambridge University Press.
Gander, Hans-Helmuth (2010): *Husserl-Lexikon*. Darmstadt: Wissenschaftliche Buchgesellschaft.
Goodman, Nelson (1963): „The Significance of Der logische Aufbau der Welt", in: Schilpp 1963, 545–558.
Häusser, Hans-Dietrich (1989): *Transzendentale Reflexion und Erkenntnisgegenstand. Zur transzendentalphilosophischen Erkenntnisbegründung unter besonderer Berücksichtigung objektivistischer Transformationen des Kritizismus; ein Beitrag zur systematischen und historischen Genese des Neukantianismus*, Bonn, Bouvier.
Heitmann, Margret (2001): „'Jedes Gefühl der Zugehörigkeit fehlt'. Jonas Cohn (1869–1947) – Einblicke in ein deutsch-jüdisches Gelehrtenleben", *Kalonymos, Beiträge zur deutsch-jüdischen Geschichte aus dem Salomon Ludwig Steinheim Institut* 4(4), 1–4.
Husserl, Edmund (1930): „Nachwort zu meinen Ideen zu einer reinen Phänomenologie und phänomenologischen Philosophie", *Jahrbuch für Philosophie und phänomenologische Forschung* Bd. 11, 549–570.
Husserl, Edmund (1952): *Ideen zu einer reinen Phänomenologie und phänomenologischen Philosophie. Zweites Buch: Phänomenologische Untersuchungen zur Konstitution*, hrsg. von Marly Biemel, Den Haag: Martinus Nijhoff = Husserliana Bd. IV. [*Ideen II*]
Husserl, Edmund (1968): *Phänomenologische Psychologie. Vorlesungen Sommersemester 1925*, hrsg. von Walter Biemel, Den Haag: Martinus Nijhoff = Husserliana Bd. IX.
Husserl, Edmund (1976) *Ideen zu einer reinen Phänomenologie und phänomenologischen Philosophie. Erstes Buch: Allgemeine Einführung in die reine Phänomenologie*, 1. Halbband: Text der 1.–3. Auflage, [*Ideen I*] 2. Halbband: Ergänzende Texte (1912–1929). Neu hrsg. von Karl Schuhmann, Den Haag: Martinus Nijhoff = Husserliana Bd. III/1 und 2.
Husserl, Edmund (1984): *Logische Untersuchungen. Zweiter Band. Untersuchungen zur Phänomenologie und Theorie der Erkenntnis*, hrsg. von Ursula Panzer, Den Haag: Martinus Nijhoff = Husserliana Bd. XIX/1 und 2.
Husserl, Edmund (1994): *Briefwechsel*. Hrsg. von Elisabeth Schuhmann in Verbindung mit Karl Schuhmann, Den Haag: Kluwer Academic Publishers = Husserliana Dokumente 3, in zehn Bänden.
Husserl, Edmund (2016): *Ideen zu einer reinen Phänomenologie und phänomenologischen Philosophie. Zweites Buch: Phänomenologische Untersuchungen zur Konstitution und Wissenschaftstheorie. Die drei Urtexte mit ergänzenden Texten sowie einem Nachwort (1908–1930)*, hrsg. von Dirk Fonfara, Dordrecht: Brill-Nijhoff = Husserliana Band IV-2/V-2. [*Urtexte*]
Husserl, Edmund (1969): *Zur Phänomenologie des inneren Zeitbewusstseins (1893–1917)*, hrsg. von Rudolf Boehm. Den Haag: Martinus Nijhoff = Husserliana Bd. X.
Ingarden, Roman (1992): *Einführung in die Phänomenologie Edmund Husserls: Osloer Vorlesungen 1967*, hrsg. von Gregor Haeflinger, in: Gesammelte Werke, Hgg. Rolf Fieguth und Guido Küng, Tübingen: Niemeyer, Bd. IV.
Kauffmann, Max (1893): *Immanente Philosophie*. Leipzig: Wilhelm Engelmann.
Kern, Iso (1964): *Husserl und Kant. Eine Untersuchung über Husserls Verhältnis zu Kant und zum Neukantianismus*, Den Haag: Martinus Nijhoff.

Köhnke, Klaus Christian (1986): *Entstehung und Aufstieg des Neukantianismus*, Frankfurt a. M.: Suhrkamp.
Kreis, Friedrich (1930): *Phänomenologie und Kritizismus*, Tübingen: Mohr.
Lohmar, Dieter (2009): „Die Entwicklung des Husserlschen Konstitutionsmodells von Auffassung und Inhalt", *Studia Universitatis Babes-Bolyai, Philosophia*, LIV, 2, 3–19.
Mayer, Verena (2009): *Edmund Husserl*, München: Beck.
Mayer, Verena (1992): „Die Konstruktion der Erfahrungswelt – Carnap und Husserl", *Erkenntnis* 35, 1991, S. 287–304.
Mayer, Verena (2011): „Husserl und die Kognitionswissenschaften", in: Verena Mayer, Christopher Erhard, Marisa Scherini (Hgg.), *Die Aktualität Husserls*, Freiburg: Alber 2011, 114.
Mayer, Verena (2011): „Regeln, Spielräume und das offene Undsoweiter. Die Wesensschau in *Erfahrung und Urteil*", in: *Die Aktualität Husserls*. Hgg. Verena Mayer, Christopher Erhard, Maria Scherini, Alber, Freiburg 2011, 145–171.
Mayer, Verena/Erhard, Christopher (2008): „Die Bedeutung objektivierender Akte", in: Verena Mayer (Hrsg.), *Edmund Husserl: Logische Untersuchungen*, (= Klassiker Auslegen Bd. 35), Berlin: Akademieverlag, 159–188.
Mohanty, Jitendranath (1972): The Concept of Intentionality, St. Louis: Warren H. Green.
Moran, Dermot/Cohen, Joseph (2012): *Husserl Dictionary*, London, New York: Continuum International.
Mormann, Thomas (2007): „Werte bei Carnap", *Zeitschrift für philosophische Forschung*, Vol. 60/2, 169–189.
Mormann, Thomas (2000): *Rudolf Carnap*. München: Beck.
Natorp, Paul (1888): *Einleitung in die Psychologie nach kritischer Methode*, Freiburg im Br.: Mohr.
Natorp, Paul (1892): „Über objektive und subjektive Begründung der Erkenntnis", *Philosophische Monatshefte* 23, Berlin.
Natorp, Paul (1910): *Die logischen Grundlagen der exakten Wissenschaften*, Leipzig, Berlin: B.G. Teubner.
Natorp, Paul (1914): „Husserls Ideen zu einer reinen Phänomenologie", in: *Die Geistwissenschaften* 1, 426 f. Wieder abgedruckt in: *Logos. Internationale Zeitschrift für Philosophie und Kultur* VII (1917–18), 224–246.
Reichenbach, Hans (1923/24): „Scientific Philosophy and Modern Physics: Hans Reichenbach and Moritz Schlick, Correspondence 1923/24".
http://echo.mpiwg-berlin.mpg.de/content/space/space/reichenbach1923–24 (abgerufen am 20.4.2015).
Richardson, Alan (1998): *Carnap's construction of the world*, Cambridge: Cambridge University Press.
Richardson, Alan (2010): „On Husserl's influence on Carnap: Guillermo E. Rosado Haddock: The young Carnap's unknown master: Husserl's influence on Der Raum and Der logische Aufbau der Welt", Book Review, *Metascience* Vol. 19 (2010), 297–299.
Rickert, Heinrich (1910): „Vom Begriff der Philosophie", *Logos. Internationale Zeitschrift für Philosophie der Kultur*, Tübingen: Mohr.
Rickert, Heinrich (1921): *System der Philosophie, Erster Teil: Allgemeine Grundlegung der Philosophie*, Tübingen: Mohr.

Rosado-Haddock, Guillermo (2008): *The Young Carnap's Unknown Master. Husserl's Influence on Der Raum and Der Logische Aufbau der Welt*. Aldershot: Ashgate.
Rosado-Haddock, Guillermo (2012): „On the Interpretation of the Young Carnap's Philosophy", in ders., *Against the Current*, Ontos Verlag, Frankfurt am Main 2012, 261–284.
Roy, Jean-Michel (2004): „Carnap's Husserlian Reading of the Aufbau", in: *Carnap Brought Home: The View from Jena*, Steve Awodey, Carsten Klein (eds.), Illinois: Open Court, S. 41–62.
Russell, Bertrand (1921): *The Analysis of Mind*, London: Allen & Unwin.
Ryckman, Thomas (2007): „Carnap and Husserl", in Michael Friedman, Richard Creath (eds.), *The Cambridge Companion to Carnap*, Cambridge: Cambridge UP, 81–105.
Sarkar, Sahotra (2003): „Husserl's Role in Carnap's *Der Raum*", in: Thomas Bonk (ed.), *Language, Truth and Logic. Contributions to the Philosophy of Rudolf Carnap*, Dordrecht, Boston, London: Kluwer Academic Publishers, 179–190.
Schilpp, Paul Arthur (Hg.) (1963): *The Philosophy of Rudolf Carnap*, La Salle, Illinois: Open Court.
Schlick, Moritz (1913): „Gibt es intuitive Erkenntnis?", *Vierteljahrsschrift für wissenschaftliche Philosophie*, Bd. 37, Leipzig.
Schlick, Moritz (1986): *Die Probleme der Philosophie in ihrem Zusammenhang. Vorlesung aus dem Wintersemester 1933/34*, hrsg. von Henk Mulder, Anne J. Knox und Rainer Hegselman, Frankfurt a.M.: Suhrkamp.
Schlick, Moritz (2009): *Allgemeine Erkenntnislehre*, hrsg. von Hans Jürgen Wendel und Finn Ole Engler, Wien, New York: Springer.
Schuhmann, Karl (1977): *Husserl-Chronik: Denk- und Lebensweg Edmund Husserls*, Den Haag: Martinus Nijhoff.
Sieg, Ulrich (1994): *Aufstieg und Niedergang des Marburger Neukantianismus*, Würzburg: Königshausen & Neumann.
Sokolowski, Robert (1970): *The Formation of Husserl's Concept of Constitution*, Den Haag: Martinus Nijhoff.
Stadler, Friedrich (1992): „Wittgenstein und der Wiener Kreis – zwischen Rezeption und Plagiat", in: Muhr, Peter/Feyerabend, Paul/Wegeler, Cornelia (Hgg.), *Philosophie – Psychoanalyse – Emigration, Festschrift für Kurt Rudolf Fischer zum 70. Geburtstag*, Wien: WUV Universitätsverlag, 398–414.
Ströker, Elisabeth (1984): „Intentionalität und Konstitution", *Dialectica* 38, 191–208.
Vaihinger, Hans (1922): *Die Philosophie des Als Ob. System der theoretischen, praktischen und religiösen Fiktionen der Menschheit auf Grund eines idealistischen Positivismus*, Leipzig: Felix Meiner.
Vongehr, Thomas (2011): „Husserls Studien über Gemüt und Wille", in: *Die Aktualität Husserls*, hrsg. von Verena Mayer, Christopher Erhard und Marisa Scherini, Freiburg: Alber, 335–360.
Wittgenstein, Ludwig (1984): *Wittgenstein und der Wiener Kreis. Gespräche, aufgezeichnet von Friedrich Waismann*, Frankfurt: Suhrkamp.

Guillermo E. Rosado Haddock
The Old Husserl and the Young Carnap

Abstract: Carnap, whose dissertation, *Der Raum*, had the imprint of Husserl's phenomenology, was also decisively influenced by Husserl in *Aufbau*, and to a lesser degree in *Logische Syntax*. Nonetheless, he tried to mask that influence, what resulted in incoherent and even incompatible explanations in his *Autobiography* of the influences on his 1922 and 1928 books. In this paper it is shown that not only the empiricist-positivist interpretation of *Aufbau* is unsustainable, but also that the Kantian or Neo-Kantian rendering is untenable, whereas Husserl's masked influence emerges as the strongest.

§1 Introduction

The relation between Edmund Husserl and Rudolf Carnap is without doubt one of the less known and most problematic in the history of philosophy. However, if we take into account only what Carnap says in his 1963 sort of 'Intellectual Autobiography'[1] there never existed any relation between the two philosophers at all. Husserl is mentioned only twice, on pp. 20 and 40, of the 'Intellectual Autobiography', and in both cases Husserl is related to other philosophers, namely, to Felix Kaufmann and to some unnamed American philosophers. When Carnap refers to his dissertation, *Der Raum*[2], on pp. 11–12 he mentions that, with regard to intuitive space, Kant and the neo-Kantians, especially Natorp and Cassirer exerted a decisive influence. And when he refers to influences in *Der logische Aufbau der Welt*[3], he mentions Frege and Russell (p. 12), the Gestalt psychology of Wertheimer and Köhler (pp. 16–17), Ernst Mach, Richard Avenarius, Richard von Schubert-Soldern and Wilhelm Schuppe (p. 18), once more Mach and Russell (p. 50) and, finally, Mach, Russell and Wittgenstein (p. 57).

All translations in this paper were done by the present author.

[1] In Paul A. Schilpp (ed.), *The Philosophy of Rudolf Carnap*, Open Court, La Salle et al., pp. 3–84
[2] *Der Raum* 1922, reprint, Topos Verlag, Vaduz 1991.
[3] *Der logische Aufbau der Welt* 1928, second edition, F. Meiner, Hamburg 1961.

It were Adolf Grünbaum and Robert Cohen in their respective commentaries[4] on aspects of Carnap's philosophy that refer to Husserl's influence on Carnap's early writings, namely, Grünbaum on p. 666 on *Der Raum* and Cohen on p. 146 on *Der logische Aufbau der Welt*. Grünbaum's comment forces Carnap to reply (p. 957)[5] that in his conception of intuitive space in *Der Raum* he had followed Kant and Husserl. With respect to Cohen's remark nothing similar occurs.

Moreover, on pp. 50 and 57 Carnap tries to make us believe that in *Aufbau* – as we will call *Der logische Aufbau der Welt* from now on- the basis of the system consisted of Ernst Mach's sense data. This clearly contrasts with his remarks two years earlier on page XII of the Preface to the second edition of *Aufbau*, in which he said that the basic elements of his constitutional system were the 'Elementarerlebnisse' but that if he were to write that book in 1961 he would take Ernst Mach's sense data as the basis. Hence, he had acknowledged two years before the publication of his 'Intellectual Autobiography' that he had not taken Mach's sense data as the basis of the system. In fact, in the same 'Intellectual Autobiography' he had written on pp. 16–17 that, following the Gestalt psychologists – presumably Köhler and Wertheimer –, he used the instantaneous whole experiences (Elementarerlebnisse) as the basis of his *Aufbau*. At first sight, such a remark concerning the basis of his *Aufbau* system seems more nearer to the truth than those referring to Mach, Avenarius *et alia* or to Russell. However, the fact of the matter is that the writings of Köhler and Wertheimer included in the references of *Aufbau* are from 1922 and 1925, respectively, whereas Husserl's *Ideen I*, in which "Erlebnisse" and "Erlebnisstrom" are central grounding notions, was published in 1913 and, as will be shown below, already when he wrote *Der Raum* Carnap was very well acquainted with that central work of Husserl's phenomenology. By the way, one can wonder how a paper published by Wertheimer in 1925 could have influenced Carnap in choosing the basis of his system, since at that time he had already written a substantial part of the book. Hence, it should by now be perfectly clear that, with regard to Husserl, Carnap's *Intellectual Autobiography* turned to be a glaring case of intellectual dishonesty. It will be shown below that such signs of dishonesty began much earlier.

---

[4] Adolf Grünbaum, 'Carnap's Views on the Foundations of Geometry', and Robert S. Cohen, 'Dialectical Materialism and Carnap's Logical Empiricism', in Paul A. Schilpp (ed.), *The Philosophy of Rudolf Carnap*, pp. 599–684 and 99–158, respectively.
[5] 'Replies and Systematic Expositions', in Paul A. Schilpp (ed.), *The Philosophy of Rudolf Carnap*, pp. 859–1013.

§2 The Truth about *Der Raum*

An examination of Carnap's dissertation easily refutes Carnap's commentaries on it in his 'Intellectual Autobiography'. First of all, Cassirer and Natorp are barely mentioned, though included in the references. Moreover, when mentioned, as happens on p. 81 in the notes at the end of the small book, it is not precisely in a favourable way. On that page, Carnap refers to Natorp and Cassirer, as well as to Russell and others, as examples of philosophers that erroneously considered the notions of Euclidean space and of homogeneous space as extensionally equivalent.

With respect to Husserl's influence, it is true that Grünbaum's remarks referred to above 'refreshed Carnap's memory' and made him 'acknowledge' that his conception of intuitive space in *Der Raum* was influenced by 'Kant and Husserl'. In fact, so much has been already accepted by some of the best known Carnapian scholars, among them Michael Friedman[6] in his 'Carnap and Weyl on the Foundations of Geometry and Relativity Theory'. However, things are not exactly as Carnap put it in his answer to Grünbaum. Husserl's influence on Carnap's *Der Raum* is by far greater than that of Kant.[7] In fact, the influence of Hans Driesch seems to be stronger than that of Kant, from whose specific views on space Carnap clearly disassociates. Thus, a more exact phrasing of the situation would have been that 'with respect to intuitive space Carnap was strongly influenced by Husserl, in a lesser degree by Driesch and in an even lesser one by Kant'. Let us now quote some of the passages of *Der Raum*, in which Carnap refers to Husserl or explicitly uses Husserl's terminology.

> By intuitive space, on the other hand, is understood the structure of relations between "spatial" figures in the usual sense...whose particularity we apprehend by means of perception or mere representation. One is still not concerned there with spatial facts present in empirical reality, but only with the "essence" of those figures, which can be recognized in any representative of the species. [*Der Raum*, pp. 5–6][8]

---

6 See the above mentioned paper in U. Majer and H. J. Schmidt (eds.), *Reflections on Spacetime*, Kluwer, Dordrecht et al. 1995.
7 Besides Cohen's brief remark already referred to, for a detailed discussion of Husserl's influence on *Der Raum* see Sahotra Sarkar's paper 'Husserl's Role in Carnap's *Der Raum*', in Thomas Bonk (ed.), *Language, Truth and Logic*, Kluwer, Dordrecht 2003, pp. 179–190, and especially the present author's by far more detailed treatment in his book *The Young Carnap's Unknown Master*, Ashgate, Aldershot 2008.
8 "Unter Anschauungsraum dagegen wird das Gefüge der Beziehungen zwischen den im üblichen Sinne "räumlichen" Gebilden verstanden, also den Linien-, Flächen- und Raumstücken, deren bestimmte Eigenheit wir bei Gelegenheit sinnlicher Wahrnehmung oder auch bloßer Vor-

Anyone familiar with Husserl's philosophy, especially with Husserl's 1913 *Ideen zu einer reinen Phänomenologie und einer phänomenologischen Philosophie I*[9] – from now on *Ideen I* – will recognize that Carnap is assuming Husserl's conception of the contemplation of essences. But there is much more, and the following two passages should leave little doubt that they were written by someone who at that moment considered himself a disciple of Husserl in philosophical matters.

> Since here one is concerned, as Husserl has shown, not with facts in the sense of empirical reality, but with the essence ("Eidos") of certain given objectualities [Gegebenheiten], which being as they are, can be apprehended by means of [their] being given [Gegebensein] only once. [*Der Raum*, p. 22][10]
>
> Since we refer here not to the isolated fact..., but to the non-temporal species, its "essence", it can be important to distinguish this mode of experience from intuition in the strict sense, which refers to the fact itself, by means of the designation "contemplation of essences [Wesenserschauung]" (Husserl), where there could seem to be [some] confusion. But, in general, it can be the case that the expression intuition also includes the contemplation of essences, since in this wide sense is also used by Kant. [*Der Raum*, pp. 22–23][11]

The reference to Kant at the end of the last passage, after a clear acknowledgment of the author of *Der Raum* of his allegiance to Husserl's phenomenology, is certainly unnecessary, regardless of whether Kant's notion of intuition could be rendered in some sense as a forerunner of the contemplation of essences. In any case it seems like a wart on the corpus of the passage. The reason for this unnecessary addition is certainly an attempt to please and appease his dissertation's director, the neo-Kantian Bruno Bauch. A little bit of history should make things clearer.

---

stellung erfassen. Dabei handelt es sich aber noch nicht um die der Erfahrungswirklichkeit vorliegenden räumlichen Tatsachen, sondern nur um das "Wesen" jener Gebilde selbst, das an irgendwelchen Artvertretern erkannt werden kann."

9 *Ideen zu einer reinen Phänomenologie und phänomenologischen Philosophie I* 1913, Hua III M. Nijhoff, Den Haag, 1950, revised edition 1976.

10 Denn es handelt sich hier, wie Husserl gezeigt hat, gar nicht um Tatsachen im Sinne der Erfahrungswirklichkeit, sondern um das Wesen ("Eidos") gewisser Gegebenheiten, das in seinem besonderen Sosein schon durch einmaliges Gegebensein erfaßt werden kann."

11 "Weil wir hierbei nicht auf die einzelhafte Tatsache eingestellt sind...sondern nur um seine zeitlose Art, sein "Wesen", kann es von Wichtigkeit sein, diese Erfahrungsweise von der Anschauung im engeren Sinne, die auf die Tatsache selbst geht, durch die Benennung "Wesenserschauung" (Husserl) zu unterscheiden, wo Verwechslung möglich erscheint. Im Allgemeinen mag aber der Ausdruck Anschauung auch die Wesenserschauung mit umfassen, da er in diesem Sinne auch schon von Kant her gebräulich ist."

In 1911 Husserl was by far the first candidate to occupy a vacancy as full professor of philosophy at the University of Jena, the university where Frege was associate professor of mathematics. Because of still unclear reasons, at the last moment the faculty decided to give the chair to Bruno Bauch instead of Husserl. Uwe Dathe has tried to explain this decision in a very superficial way by referring to Husserl's presumed tendency to acknowledge only one sort of dialogue, namely monologues in which Husserl spoke and the other person heard.[12] More plausible explanations are that Frege intervened with Rudolf Eucken to block Husserl's appointment and that Husserl's Jewish origin played a decisive role in the faculty's decision. Those two explanations can very well be complementary. The fact of the matter is that Bruno Bauch, a neo-Kantian and an incomparably inferior philosopher was appointed to the vacant chair of philosophy, and precisely the same year of 1911 in which Carnap entered the university. By the way, all that occurred a decade after the publication of Husserl's *Logische Untersuchungen*, one of the really great books in the history of philosophy.

It seems pertinent here to quote two additional passages from *Der Raum*, which should leave no doubt about Husserl being the primary philosophical influence in *Der Raum* and of the cautious rejection of specific Kantian theses, while agreeing with Kant "in principle".

> Here [in intuitive space] we have distinguished between the principles in the strict sense and the requirements. Those build the result of a determined sort of "contemplation of essences" [Wesenserschauung] (in Husserl's sense) and as such, like all knowledge from this source, do not need of the accumulation of empirical facts, [and] as such are not to be referred to as empirical knowledge, but also are not independent of every experience, since they are obtained from any representative of the kind of objects concerned. Requirements, on the other hand, are not knowledge but stipulations that have to be made in order to obtain a total structure "space" from such knowledge, which in virtue of their own nature [ihrem Wesen nach] seem limited to an incomplete region. Topological space presents [darstellt] what is common to all [those possibilities] and on this ground ought to be seen as the form of the spatial apprehensible in the contemplation of essences. Intuitive metric spaces, on the contrary, also depend on the choice of the stipulations, and as such lack the property of unlimited validity, which possess [both] intuitive topological space and all knowledge originating in this source. [*Der Raum*, pp. 62–63][13]

---

12 Uwe Dathe, 'Eine Ergänzung zur Biographie Edmund Husserls', in Werner Stelzner (ed.), *Philosophie und Logik*, Walter de Gruyter, Berlin 1993, pp. 160–166.
13 "Hier haben wir unterschieden zwischen den Grundsätzen im engeren Sinne und den Forderungen. Jene bilden den Befund einer bestimmten Art der "Wesenserschauung" (im Husserlschen Sinne) und sind daher wie alle Erkenntnisse dieser Quelle nicht auf Häufung von Erfahrungstatsachen angewiesen, daher nicht als Erfahrungserkenntnisse zu bezeichnen, aber auch nicht unabhängig von jeder Erfahrung, insofern als sie an irgendwelchen Vertretern der betref-

The principles of intuitive space are equally *a* priori. According to the well-known distinction of Kant between "to originate [Entspringen] in experience" and "to begin [Anheben] with experience", this does not mean apprehensible without experience, but "independent of the quantity of experience" (Driesch) and on this ground does not contradict that for the contemplation of essences is required what is given in experience, be it immediately [given] in perception or mediately in representation. In these principles of intuitive space we have before us the synthetic a priori propositions asserted by Kant. But the same is not valid of the theorems derived from them, except to the point in which they concern only topological space, since those [theorems] that refer us to metric spaces are dependent not only on the principles, but also on the requirements, on whose base the complete structure of intuitive space is obtained, thus, on determinations that are not a priori knowledge, since they are not knowledge, but stipulations. Kant's assertion is, thus, indeed correct, but is not valid for the whole domain of those propositions to which he referred. [*Der Raum*, pp. 63–64][14]

The references to Kant in the last passage should not make us believe that Carnap was endorsing any fundamental specific concrete thesis. What Carnap says in the two passages amounts to the following: there is a sort of synthetic *a priori* knowledge in the topological level of intuitive space, and this knowledge is obtained by means of Husserl's method of the contemplation of essences. On the

---

flichen Art von Gegenständen gewonnen werden. Die Forderungen dagegen sind nicht Erkenntnisse, sondern Festsetzungen, die getroffen werden, um ein geschlossenes Gesamtgefüge "Raum" aus jenen Erkenntnissen zu gewinnen, die ihrem Wesen nach auf ein nicht vollständiges Gebiet beschränkt erscheinen. Für diese Erweiterungen zum vollständigen Gefüge zeigten sich verschiedene Möglichkeiten. Der topologische Raum stellt das ihnen allen gemeinsame dar und ist deshalb als Form in der Wesenserschauung des Räumlichen faßbar anzusehen. Die metrischen Anschauungsräume dagegen sind noch von der Wahl jener Festsetzungen abhängig; daher fehlt ihnen die dem topologischen Anschauungsraum wie allen dieser Quelle entstammenden Erkenntnisse zukommende Eigenschaft der unbedingten Gültigkeit."

14 "Die Grundsätze des Anschauungsraumes sind gleichfalls *a priori*. Nach der bekannten Unterscheidung Kants zwischen dem "der Erfahrung Entspringen" und dem "Anheben mit der Erfahrung" bedeutet dies ja nicht: ohne Erfahrung erfaßbar, sondern "unabhängig von der Menge der Erfahrung" (Driesch) und steht deshalb nicht im Widerspruch dazu, daß zu der Wesenserschauung des Gegebenseins von Erfahrung entweder unmittelbar in der Wahrnehmung oder mittelbar in der Vorstellung, erforderlich ist. In diesen Grundsätzen des Anschauungsraumes haben wir die von Kant behaupteten synthetischen Sätze *a priori* vor uns. Dasselbe gilt aber nicht für die aus ihnen abgeleiteten Lehrsätze, sondern nur, soweit sie den topologischen Raum betreffen; denn diejenigen, die sich auf einen der metrischen Räume beziehen, sind nicht nur von den Grundsätzen, sondern auch von den Forderungen abhängig, auf Grund deren das vollständige Gefüge des Anschauungsraumes sich ergibt, also von Bestimmungen, die nicht Erkenntnisse *a priori* sind, weil überhaupt nicht Erkenntnisse, sondern Festsetzungen. Kants Behauptung ist also zwar richtig, aber nicht für den ganzen Bereich derjenigen Sätze gültig, auf die er selbst sie bezog."

other hand, Kant's specific metric theses about the synthetic *a priori* character of the three-dimensionality and Euclidicity of space are false.

Furthermore, on pp. 64–65, where Carnap makes a very interesting classification of our geometrical knowledge of the different sorts of spaces, and in which he uses the abbreviation 'W' for 'contemplation of essences', 'S' for 'freely chosen stipulation' and 'T' for 'factual knowledge', while referring to Husserl, he mentions that 'W' is present in all cases, though with respect to formal topological space –be it three- or n-dimensional-, the application is of a formal nature, since those formal spaces belong to what Husserl had called since the last chapter of the Prolegomena 'formal ontology'. In fact, Carnap seems to be echoing Husserl's distinction, already present in the Sixth Logical Investigation and especially underscored in *Ideen I* between formal essences and the more familiar for phenomenologists material essences.

Finally, it seems pertinent to mention that in Appendix II of Carnap's first book there are many – always positive – references to Husserl, including one on p. 85 in which Carnap correctly observes that the distinction between formal, intuitive and physical space, which is central to the book, is just a special case of Husserl's distinction between formal ontology, regional ontology and factual science. If there still were some doubt, that remark on p. 85 is a clear acknowledgement of Carnap that what he has done in *Der Raum* is a clarification of the relation between formal, intuitive and physical space embedded in the philosophical views of Edmund Husserl.

§3 The Unknown Relation between Husserl and Carnap

Notwithstanding Husserl's decisive influence on Carnap's dissertation, as already pointed out above, Husserl is barely mentioned in Carnap's 'Intellectual Autobiography'. In fact, neither the 'Intellectual Autobiography' nor any of Carnap's writings can serve to arouse the suspicion that there was a personal relation between Husserl and Carnap. Let us now mention a few facts about the young Carnap.

Carnap began his studies of philosophy and physics in Jena in 1911 and also studied in Freiburg, where he attended courses by Rickert, who had been Bruno Bauch's teacher. After the war he returned to Jena and first considered writing a thesis at the physics department, but his proposal was too philosophical and was sent to the philosophy department. Thus, he ended writing a dissertation under the direction of Bruno Bauch, though there does not seem to exist any ground to make us believe that Carnap was a near student of Bauch. Interestingly enough, during the two years from 1919 to 1921, in which Carnap was working in his dissertation, he lived in Buchenbach, a town in the outskirts of Freiburg, where Husserl had replaced Rickert as full professor since 1916. It is not completely clear whether Carnap met Husserl during those two years in which he was at most a half hour by train from Freiburg, but the odds are by far in favour of having met the great philosopher. The reader can imagine himself writing a dissertation, let us say, in the 1970s mostly influenced by Quine and living for two years in the outskirts of Boston, but without having the temptation to meet the admired philosopher. That is an extremely improbable situation, as is Carnap's not having met Husserl during those two years. In any case, the fact of the matter is that after obtaining his doctor's degree in Jena, Carnap returned to Buchenbach and then took part in four of Husserl's seminars during the years 1923–1925, that is, precisely when he was writing the *Aufbau* and, according to mainstream interpretations, was either under the influence of Mach's phenomenalism and Russell's empiricism or under the influence of Kant and the neo-Kantians. Though Carnap never mentioned in his writings that he was Husserl's student, the latter's assistant during those years, the ten years younger than Carnap Ludwig Landgrebe informed Prof. Karl Schuhmann in a letter dated 6 August 1976, referred to on p. 281 of Schuhmann's *Husserl-Chronik*[15] that Carnap was in three of Husserl's seminars from 1924 to 1925. But as a matter of fact, Carnap was in four of Husserl's seminars, beginning with the winter semester of 1923–1924, as attested by the Carnap diaries[16]. Moreover, in a letter of Landgrebe to Husserl of 1932 he not only reminds Husserl of the fact that Carnap visited his seminars almost a decade earlier, but especially that he and Carnap were then in friendly terms and used to discuss philosophical matters.[17] By the way, in those days – of 1924–1925 – Landgrebe was organizing the material that much later – in fact, after Husserl's death – was published as the second volume of *Ideen*.[18] Furthermore, Carnap not only visited Husserl's seminars for two years, but he tried to present his professorship's thesis, the Aufbau, with Husserl, though the latter rejected the proposal. Moreover, as late as September 1925, and even after Moritz Schlick had accepted a similar proposal of his future partner, Carnap was asking Jonas Cohn to intercede with Husserl and try to change

---

15 *Husserl Chronik*, M. Nijhoff, Den Haag 1977.
16 Carnap's diaries are now in internet thanks to Christian Daemboeck. See the entries for 21st and 23rd November 1923.
17 Landgrebe's letter is of 11 November 1932. See *Briefwechsel IV*, p. 298.
18 *Ideen zu einer reinen Phänomenologie und phänomenologischen Philosophie II*, Hua IV, M. Nijhoff, Den Haag 1952.

his mind.[19] But before we say something about the other partner of such mysterious relation, let us mention some facts about traditional university studies in Germany that are particularly relevant to what Carnap said in his 'Intellectual Autobiography' about his relation to Frege and what he did not say about his relation to Husserl.

At German universities the academic hierarchy has traditionally been much more rigid than, for example, in the USA, and the lack of relationship between professors and students is remarkable. Full professors (ordentliche Professoren) are by far at the top of the hierarchy, whereas associate professors (außerordentliche Professoren) receive by far less respect. At the bottom of the hierarchy are the auxiliary professors (Privatdozenten) that traditionally were not even paid by the university, even though, after obtaining their doctor's degree, they had to write a professor's dissertation (Habilitationsschrift) and give a public (inaugural) lecture in order to obtain the *venia legendi*, that is, the right to teach at the university level. Courses were basically divided in lecture courses for a general public and seminars for more specialized students, including the Oberseminare for doctoral students and young doctors. In the lecture courses no questions were asked, the role of students being totally passive, and the professor sometimes did not even dare to look at the students during a whole semester and probably would not recognize them if they were to cross paths in the street. Thus, it is by no means strange that Carnap heard three of Frege's lectures, but never dared to talk to him. The opportunity to get acquainted with the professor and, especially, for the professor to acknowledge the student's existence was in the seminars, particularly in those destined for doctoral students and young doctors. It was precisely in four of those elitist courses of Husserl that Carnap took part between 1923 and 1925. Hence, even in the improbable case that Carnap had not visited other of Husserl's seminars or at least met him before obtaining his doctor's degree, he had four semesters in which he certainly had the opportunity of getting to know Husserl both as a teacher and as a person.[20] Thus, Carnap's acquaintance with Husserl was by far greater than his acquaintance with Frege – which simply consisted in having visited three of his lecture courses, without even asking him any question. Hence, there should be no doubt that in his Autobiography Carnap intentionally omitted any reference to his relation with Husserl and, of course, any reference to Husserl's influence on him. Even in the case of *Der Raum*, where Husserl was with-

---

[19] See Carnap's letter to Jonas Cohn of 26 September 1925.
[20] By the way, as stated in his Diaries, already the 23rd of November 1923 Carnap was invited to tea by Husserl, who was, by the way, an atypical "German" professor.

out doubt the greatest philosophical influence, he intentionally tried to distort the facts by referring not only to Kant's influence but also to the presumed influence of Natorp and Cassirer. Let us turn now to Husserl.

As attested by his *Briefwechsel* (10 volumes), in his relation with his students Husserl was a sort of atypical professor of German universities. There is a massive correspondence with students from his Göttingen years, with students from München – where Husserl never taught – and with students of his Freiburg years. The correspondence is not only philosophical but also personal, be it asking a former student to send him tobacco from München[21], serving as a sort of private advisor to depressed former students[22], or accepting a former Canadian student's offer to send him money, though not for himself but for Heidegger, who was having economic difficulties in post-war Germany.[23] With some of his former students Husserl developed a friendship that lasted until his death, among them probably the best known are Roman Ingarden, Hermann and Helene Weyl, and Max Born. Of all Husserl's students mentioned in the *Briefwechsel*, only in the case of a student of his Göttingen years who had tried to plagiarize Husserl, of Hugo Dingler, who took part, together with Max Born and Helene Weyl, in a seminar of Husserl's on the philosophy of mathematics, and of Carnap did Husserl show lack of sympathy. In the case of Dingler, Husserl's answers to Dingler's letters are evasive.[24] In the case of Carnap, it is interesting that Heinrich Scholz once asked Husserl how he would classify three of his former students who were candidates for a professorship, namely, Oskar Becker, Moritz Geiger and Rudolf Carnap, and – contrary to what would be an almost unanimous opinion nowadays – he put them in exactly that order, with Carnap way back last.[25] Moreover, after Husserl gave a lecture in 1935 in Prague, Husserl's wife, Malvine, wrote Husserl's former student and long time friend Roman Ingarden that she

---

[21] See Husserl's four letters to Johannes Dauben of 27 and 29 October, 11 and 18 November 1906.
[22] See his correspondence with Manke, and even some of his correspondence with Landgrebe when the latter was desperate looking for a university at which to present his professorship's thesis and be able to teach as a "Privatdozent".
[23] See Husserl's letter to Winthrop Pickard Bell of 18 September 1921, in *Briefwechsel III*, especially p. 21.
[24] See *Briefwechsel III*, pp. 59–76
[25] See letter of Husserl to Heidegger of 9 May 1928 in *Briefwechsel IV*, pp. 157–158, in which Husserl informs Heidegger of a letter of Heinrich Scholz, who was looking for a replacement in Kiel, since he had accepted a professorship in Münster. Husserl recommends Oskar Becker clearly over the other two, with Geiger in the second place and Carnap far behind, in Husserl's words: "…was aber Carnap anbelangt, so stehe er doch gar zu weit zurück" ("…with respect to Carnap, he remains by far behind").

was pleased that Husserl was able to avoid the painful situation of having to say hello to Carnap.[26] We can ask ourselves whether Carnap had fallen so low in Husserl's eyes just by abandoning phenomenology and adhering to logical empiricism, or whether there was a still stronger reason for not even wanting to see him. In the following we will show that there could have been a stronger reason for Husserl's attitude towards Carnap, namely, the latter's attempt to mask Husserl's influence on *Aufbau*. Though Husserl most surely did not read Carnap's book, it is not excluded that some assistant or former student of Husserl had read it and informed Husserl of the content.

§4 Husserl's Influence on *Aufbau*

Carnap wrote the bulk of the *Aufbau* in 1924 to 1925, that is, precisely when he was attending Husserl's seminars. Thus, it should not be surprising if the footprints of Husserl's views are present in that work. Nonetheless, very few authors seem to have detected those footprints, probably the most notable has being Verena Mayer, who in two important papers in the early 1990s[27] stressed the influence of Husserl on Carnap's *Aufbau*. In fact, as the present author has shown in his book *The Young Carnap's Unknown Master*[28] the influence is not only larger than expected but intentionally masked.

Thus, in 1926, the 35 years old Carnap went to Vienna with the whole manuscript of *Aufbau* and showed it to Moritz Schlick and Otto Neurath, who made some criticisms and forced Carnap to make some changes in the manuscript. The book that was finally published in 1928 is still very strongly influenced by Husserl but for whatever reason that influence is intentionally masked. The general strategy is to refer to two or more authors, sometimes even to seven or eight authors, one of the last of which usually is Husserl. However, when you examine the text you see that Husserl's influence is by far the strongest.

Carnap's objective in the *Aufbau* is to build a constitutional system of objects (or concepts), where constitution, contrary to Kant's notion of constitution but in perfect agreement with Husserl's usage, goes from the bottom up. In fact, the notion of constitution, in the same sense in which Carnap used it, is the basis of Husserl's phenomenology. As Carnap stresses, only an autopsychological or a

---

[26] See *Briefwechsel III*, p. 305. The letter is dated 14 January 1936.
[27] 'Die Konstruktion der Erfahrungswelt: Carnap und Husserl', in W. Spohn (ed.), *Erkenntnis Orientated* 1991, pp. 287–303, and 'Carnap und Husserl', in D. Bell and W. Vossenkuhl (eds.), *Wissenschaft und Subjektivität* 1992, pp. 181–205.
[28] *The Young Carnap's Unknown Master*, Ashgate 2008.

physicalist basis make sense, though from an epistemological standpoint an autopsychological basis is preferable.[29] Thus, on an autopsychological basis Carnap is to constitute the physicalist world, then the heteropsychological, that is, the existence of other human subjects, and finally the cultural or spiritual world. Before continuing, it should be pointed out that Carnap's constitutional system's structure is basically the same of Husserl's manuscripts on which Landgrebe was working when he was befriended with Carnap and used to have philosophical discussions with him. In *Ideen II* – published only posthumously –, whose subtitle is *Phänomenologische Untersuchungen zur Konstitution* (*Phenomenological Investigations on Constitution*)[30], Husserl proceeds from an autopsychological basis that is exactly the one chosen by Carnap, namely, the pure subject with its internal experiences of consciousness (*Erlebnisse*) flowing in the stream of the internal time of consciousness, to the physical world, from there to the heteropsychological world, and from there to the cultural or spiritual world. Furthermore, it should already be pointed out that the transit from the physical world to the heteropsychological proceeds in both authors exactly alike.

With respect to the basis, it seems pertinent to quote a passage that exemplifies Carnap's masking strategy. Thus, on p. 4 of *Aufbau* Carnap states:

> The most important motivations for the solution of the problem [of] how the scientific concepts are to be reduced to the "given" were given by Mach and Avenarius. Points of contact are also present with Husserl's indicated objective of a "mathesis of experiences of consciousness".[31]

Certainly that passage contrasts with what Carnap stated in 1961 in the Preface to the second edition of *Aufbau*, namely, that he had taken the 'Elementarerlebnisse' as the basic elements of his system in *Aufbau* but that if he were to write the book at that moment – 1961– he would follow Mach in taking sense

---

29 See *Aufbau*, p. 81.
30 By the way, *Ideen II* is divided in three main Parts, namely, (1) Die Konstitution der Materiellen Natur (The Constitution of Material Nature), (ii) Die Konstitution der Animalischen Natur (The Constitution of Animal Nature) and (iii) Dir Konstitution der Geistigen Welt (The Constitution of the Spiritual World). Moroever, the third and fourth chapters of part two are titled: (i) Die Konstitution der Seelischen Realität durch den Leib (The Constitution of the Reality of the Soul by means of the Body) and (ii) Die Konstitution der Seelischen Realität in der Einfühlung (The Constitution of the Reality of the Soul in Empathy).
31 "Die wichtigsten Anregungen für die Lösung des Problems, wie die wissenschaftlichen Begriffe auf das "Gegebene" zurückzuführen sind, haben Mach und Avenarius gegeben. Berührungspukte liegen ferner auch vor mit dem von Husserl als "mathesis der Erlebnisse" angedeuteten Ziel."

data as basis. It is clearly implicit that he did not do that in 1928. In fact, as he repeatedly states in the book, he did not follow Mach or Avenarius.

> Our use of such a form of a system [with an autopsychological basis] by no means signifies that we are presupposing a sensualistic or positivistic conception. [*Aufbau*, p. 82][32]

> After the autopsychological was chosen as basic domain, thus, the processes of consciousness or experiences of consciousness of the I, it must still be determined which formations of this region are going to serve as basic elements. One could, let us say, consider taking as basic elements the ultimate constituent parts obtained by means of psychological and phenomenological analysis of the experiences of consciousness, thus, let us say, the simplest sensory sensations (as Mach), or more generally: psychic elements of different forms, from which the experiences of consciousness are formed. On a closer examination, however, we must acknowledge that in this case not the given itself, but abstractions from it, thus, something epistemologically secondary, has been taken as basic elements.... Since we, however, wanted also to require from our constitutional system the consideration of the epistemological order of the objects, we shall, thus, start from what is epistemologically primary to everything else, from "[the] given", and those are the experiences of consciousness themselves in their totality and closed unity.... To the chosen basic elements, those experiences of consciousness of the I as unities... we refer as "elementary experiences of consciousness". [*Aufbau*, pp. 91–92][33]

> The elementary experiences of consciousness shall be the basic elements of our constitutional system. On this basis shall be constituted all other objects of our pre-scientific and scientific knowledge, including also the objects that one is accustomed to refer to as the constituent parts of the experiences of consciousness or as components of the psychic process, and which are obtained as result of the psychological analysis. [*Aufbau*, p. 93][34]

---

32 Unsere Anwendung einer solchen Systemform [mit psychischer Basis] bedeutet aber keineswegs, daß wir eine sensualistische oder positivistische Anschauung zugrunde legen."
33 "Nachdem als Basisgebiet das eigenpsychische gewählt ist, also die Bewußtseinsvorgänge oder Erlebnisse des Ich, muß noch festgelegt werden welche Gebilde dieses Gebietes als Grundelemente dienen sollen. Man könnte etwa daran denken die letzten Bestandteile, die sich bei psychologischer und phänomenologischer Analyse der Erlebnisse ergeben, als Grundelemente nehmen, also etwa einfachste Sinnenempfindungen (wie Mach), oder allgemeiner: psychische Elemente verschiedener Arten, aus denen die Erlebnisse aufgebaut werden könnten. Bei näherer Betrachtung müssen wir jedoch erkennen, daß in diesem Falle nicht das Gegebene selbst, sondern Abstraktionen daraus, also etwas erkenntnismäßig Sekundäres, als Grundelemente genommen werden.... Da wir jedoch von unserem Konstitutionssystem auch die Berücksichtigung der erkenntnismäßigen Ordnung der Gegenstände verlangen wollten, so müssen wir von dem ausgehen, was zu allem anderen erkenntnismäßig primär ist, vom "Gegebenem", und das sind die Erlebnisse selbst in ihrer Totalität und geschlossenen Einheit.... Die gewählten Grundelemente, jene Erlebnisse des Ich als Einheiten... bezeichnen wir als "Elementarerlebnisse"."
34 "Die Elementarerlebnisse sollen die Grundelemente unseres Konstitutionssystems sein. Auf dieser Basis sollen alle anderen Gegenstände der vorwissenschaftlichen und wissenschaftlichen Erkenntnis konstituiert werden, somit auch die Gegenstände, die man als Bestandteile der Erleb-

Another passage from p. 130 can be referred to in this context, and we have quoted it in the book. Nonetheless, the three passages quoted should be conclusive evidence that Carnap's constitutional system in the *Aufbau* does not have any Machian sense data basis, but a Husserlian one. Hence, the passage of p. 4 quoted above only serves to mask the fact of the matter about the influences on the *Aufbau*. By the way, in an extensive remark on pp. 163–165 of *Aufbau*, Carnap rejects on similar terms Russell's choice of an epistemological basis in *Our Knowledge of the External World*.[35] For the Carnap of *Aufbau*, as for Husserl, neither sense data nor sensations, nor any presumed minimal component of experience is really experienced, but abstracted from what is really given.[36]

It seems pertinent to quote now an extremely important passage of the *Aufbau*, important because of at least two completely different reasons. Firstly, it shows an explicit and most decisive commitment of Carnap to the core of Husserl's transcendental phenomenology, the so-called "ἐποχή". Secondly, it gives a correct rendering of the role of that phenomenological reduction, seldom understood by hard-core phenomenologists.

---

nisse oder als Komponenten der psychischen Vorgänge zu bezeichnen pflegt, und die als Ergebnis der psychologischen Analyse gefunden werden."

35 See especially p. 164 of *Aufbau*.

36 There is, nonetheless, a later passage in *Aufbau* on p. 105 that seems both to support the positivist interpretation of that book and could also make happy the Kantian and neo-Kantian interpreters. We quote this time in German and then translate into English: "Das Verdienst der Aufdeckung der nowendigen Basis des Konstitutionssystems kommt somit zwei ganz verschiedenen und häufig einander feindlichen, philosophischen Richtungen zu. Der Positivismus hat hervorgehoben, daß das einzige Material der Erkenntnis im unverarbeiteten, erlebnismäßigen Gegebenen liegt; dort sind die Grundelemente des Konstitutionssystems zu suchen. Der transzendentale Idealismus insbesondere neukantischer Richtung (Rickert, Cassirer, Bauch) hat aber mit Recht betont, daß diese Elemente nicht genügen; es müssen Ordnungssetzungen hinzukommen, unsere „Grundrelationen"." That is: The merit of having discovered the necessary basis of the constitutional system belongs to two very different and frequently adversative philosophical tendencies. Positivism has emphasized that the stuff for knowledge is the unadulterated given in experiences of consciousness; it is there that one has to look for the basic elements of the constitutional system. But transcendental idealism, particularly of the neo-Kantian variety (Rickert, Cassirer, Bauch), has correctly stressed that those elements are not enough; one has to add some order arrangement, our „basic relations"." The fact of the matter is that the stressed Carnap could have been more coherent if he had just mentioned the basis of his system, namely Husserl's "Erlebnisse" in the "Erlebnisstrom" and remembered that his basic relation of similarity between "Erlebnisse" was made possible precisely by the stream of consciousness, as emphasized *ad nauseam* by Husserl in *Ideen I*. Once more, Carnap attempts to mask Husserl's influence on him, though this time in a more grotesque fashion.

> The distinction between actually real and not actually real is not present at the beginning of the constitutional system. For the basis no differentiation will be made between the experiences of consciousness, which on the basis of later constitution will be differentiated as perceptions, hallucinations, dreams, and so forth. This distinction and with it that between actually real and not actually real objects appears for the first time in a sufficiently high constitutional level. At the beginning of the system the experiences of consciousness are to be taken as they are given; the postulations (or determinations) of reality and the postulations (or determinations) of unreality present in them will not be included, but "put in parenthesis"; thus, the phenomenological suspension ("ἐποχή") in Husserl's sense [is] exercised. [*Aufbau*, p. 86][37]

By the way, the correctness of Carnap's rendering of the phenomenological reduction not only serves to understand the fact that after the 1907 so-called "transcendental phenomenological turn" Husserl's conception of logic and mathematics, expounded in Chapter XI of his *opus magnum*, *Logische Untersuchungen*[38] did not suffer any essential change –just the clearer distinction in *Formale und transzendentale Logik*[39] between apophantic logic (syntax) and logic of truth (semantics)-, but also is confirmed by the following passage of Husserl's in *Ideen I*:

> We adhere here, but immediately stress, that the attempt at a universal doubt shall serve us only as a methodological aid, to emphasize certain points.... [*Ideen I*, p. 64][40]

With respect to consciousness and the stream of consciousness, it seems pertinent to insert here a passage of *Aufbau* followed by three passages of Husserl's *Ideen I*.

---

37 Die Unterscheidung zwischen wirklichen und nichtwirklichen steht nicht am Beginn des Konstitutionssystems. Für die Basis wird kein Unterschied gemacht zwischen den Erlebnissen, die auf Grund späterer Konstitution als Wahrnehmung, Halluzination, Traum usw. unterschieden werden. Diese Unterscheidung und damit die zwischen wirklichen und nichtwirklichen Gegenständen tritt erst auf einer ziemlich hohen Konstitutionsstufe auf. Zu Beginn des Systems sind die Erlebnisse einfach so hinzunehmen, wie es sich geben; die in ihnen vorkommenden Realsetzungen und Nichtrealsetzungen werden nicht mitgemacht, sondern "eingeklammert"; es wird also die phänomenologische "Enthaltung" (ἐποχή) im Husserlschen Sinne gemacht."
38 *Logische Untersuchungen* (2 vols.) 1900–1901, Hua XVIII and XIX, M. Nijhoff, Den Haag 1975 and 1984.
39 *Formale und transzendentale Logik* 1929, Hua. XVII, M. Nijhoff, Den Haag 1974.
40 "Wir knüpfen hier an, betonen aber sogleich, daß der universelle Zweifelsversuch uns nur als methodischer Behelf dienen soll, um gewisse Punkte hervorzuheben...."

> ... the basic domain lies only in consciousness (in the wider sense): to it belong all experiences of consciousness, no matter whether they are immediately or afterwards reflected upon. We speak therefore preferably of "stream of consciousness". [*Aufbau*, p. 86][41]

> By experiences of consciousness in the broadest sense we understand everything present in the stream of consciousness, thus, not only the intentional experiences of consciousness, the actual and the potential cogitations, [and] these taken in their complete concretion, but whatever of real moments is present in this stream and its concrete parts. [*Ideen I*, p. 80][42]

> A unity determined purely by the proper essence of the experiences of consciousness itself is exclusively the unity of the stream of consciousness... [*Ideen I*, p. 86][43]

> The stream of consciousness is an infinite unity, and the form of a stream is a form embracing necessarily all experiences of consciousness of a pure I.... [*Ideen I*, p. 200][44]

Hence, for both Husserl and Carnap the basic domain on which all other domains of objects are going to be constituted, the autopsychological basis, in Carnap's terminology, is that of consciousness, more specifically, of the stream of consciousness with its elementary experiences [Erlebnisse]. And the term "reflection" used by Carnap in the passage of p. 86 of *Aufbau* quoted above is also a technical Husserlian term, as attested by passages on pp. 180, 181 and 184 of *Ideen I* quoted on p. 54 of the present author's book *The Young Carnap's Unknown Master*.[45]

It seems appropriate to insert here some passages both of Carnap and Husserl, which show, firstly, that Carnap's and Husserl's views on constitution are very similar and, secondly, that in Carnap's constitutional system there is no such thing as an ontological reduction of the objects of higher levels to those of lower levels. The reduction amounts to an epistemological grounding of our knowledge of objects of higher level on those of lower level and ultimately on the autopsychological basis. On this point the author of *Aufbau* is once more

---

41 ".... das Grundgebiet liegt nur im Bewußtsein (im weiteren Sinne): zu ihm gehören alle Erlebnisse, ob gleichzeitig oder nachträglich auf sie reflektiert wird oder nicht. Wir sprechen deshalb lieber vom "Erlebnisstrom"."

42 "Unter Erlebnissen im weitesten Sinne verstehen wir alles und jedes im Erlebnisstrom vorfindliche, also nicht nur die intentionalen Erlebnisse, die aktuellen und potentiellen cogitationen, dieselben in ihrer vollen Konkretion genommen, sondern was irgend an reellen Momenten in diesem Strom und seinen konkreten Teilen vorfindlich ist."

43 "Eine rein durch die eigenen singulären Wesen der Erlebnisse selbst bestimmte Einheit ist ausschließlich die Einheit des Erlebnisstromes."

44 "Der Erlebnisstrom ist eine unendliche Einheit, und die Stromform ist eine alle Erlebnisse eines reinen ich umspannende Form ...."

45 See footnote 7.

in accord with Husserl, not with his later self as a logical empiricist, as attested by the following passages of both authors.

> By a "constitutional system" we understand a hierarchical order such that the objects of each level are constituted from those of the lower levels. In view of the transitivity of the reducibility, all objects of the constitutional system will in this way be constituted from the objects of the first level; the basic objects form the basis of the system. [*Aufbau*, p. 2][46]
>
> ...the constitution of an object on the basis of other determined objects not only does not mean that the object is of a similar kind as the others, but, on the contrary, if the constitution (as it frequently happens with the spiritual objects, particularly those of the higher levels) leads to the formation of new logical levels, then the constituted objects belong to a different kind of being, more precisely: to a new sphere of objects. Thus, in my kind of constitution of the spiritual objects no psychologism is present. [*Aufbau*, pp. 202–203][47]

Now let us also quote some passages of Husserl from both *Ideen I* and *Ideen II*.

> Clearly, in the case of all these forms of constitution of objects we will be brought back to objects, which do not remit to already given objects of the sort that are originated by means of some theoretical, value-giving or practical spontaneity....then we eventually arrive in a series of steps to grounding objectualities.... [*Ideen II*, p. 17][48]
>
> We know that objects, no matter how constituted (objects of completely arbitrary region, completely arbitrary genus and species), can be substrata precisely for categorial syntheses, can enter as constitutive elements in "categorial" formations of higher level. [*Ideen II*, p. 18][49]

---

46 "Unter einem "Konstitutionssystem" verstehen wir eine stufenweise Ordnung der Gegenstände derart, daß die Gegenstände einer jeden Stufe aus denen der niederen Stufen konstituiert werden. Wegen der Transitivität der Zurückführbarkeit werden dadurch indirekt alle Gegenstände des Konstitutionssystems aus den Gegenständen der ersten Stufe konstituiert; diese "Grundgegenstände" bilden die "Basis" des Systems."
47 ".... die Konstitution eines Gegenstandes auf Grund bestimmter anderen Gegenständen nicht nur nicht besagt, daß der Gegenstand mit den anderen gleichartig sei, sondern im Gegenteil wenn die Konstitution (wie es bei den geistigen Gegenständen besonders der höheren Stufen in hohem Grade der Fall ist) zur Bildung neuer logischen Stufen führt, so gehören die konstituierten Gegenstände einer anderen Seinsart, genauer: einer neuen Gegenstandssphäre an. In unserer Art der Konstitution der geistigen Gegenstände liegt also kein Psychologismus."
48 "Offenbar werden wir bei allen diesen Formen der Konstitution von Gegenständen zurückgeführt auf Gegenstände, welche nicht mehr auf vorgegebene Gegenstände der Art zurückweisen, die ursprünglich durch irgend welche theoretischen, wertenden oder praktischen Spontaneitäten entsprungen sind ..., so kommen wir ev. in einer Reihe von Schritten, auf fundierende Gegenständlichkeiten ...."
49 "Wir wissen, daß wie immer konstituierte Gegenstände (Gegenstände ganz beliebiger Region, ganz beliebigen Gattungen und Arten) Substrate für gerade kategoriale Synthesen sein

But seen free of prejudices and phenomenologically brought back to its sources, the grounded unities are both grounded and novel, the new that can be constituted with them, can ... never and nevermore be reduced to mere sums of other realities." [*Ideen I*, p. 375][50]

§5 On the Kantian- neo-Kantian Rendering of *Aufbau*

We have already shown that the positivist-sensualist Machian rendering of *Aufbau* is untenable. The only other rendering that deserves attention, not because of its presumed tenability but because it is widely spread in English speaking countries, is the Kantian or neo-Kantian rendering of Carnap's *Aufbau*. Like the parallel rendering of Frege as a Kantian or neo-Kantian, instead of what he evidently was, namely, a rationalist and Platonist, the Kantian rendering of Carnap's *Aufbau* is based on superficialities. In any case, if any of the Kantianizers of the *Aufbau* wants to prove his case, I want him to produce passages of Kant or of any neo-Kantian that run parallel to some passages of *Aufbau*, as I have done in my book already mentioned and to a lesser extent in my paper 'On the Interpretation of the Young Carnap's Philosophy' and in this paper. In fact, the last passages quoted in the preceding section should leave no doubt that when Carnap is speaking of constitution he is using the term in the same way as Husserl, and that constitution in Carnap's sense and constitution in Kant's sense are completely different notions that even go in opposite directions: from the bottom up (Husserl and Carnap), from top to bottom (Kant).

Moreover, it should be mentioned that immediately after the passage on pp. 86–87 in which Carnap declares his allegiance to methodological solipsism, he mentions eight philosophers, among them Husserl, that he considers methodological solipsists. Neither Kant nor any of the neo-Kantians, Cohen or Rickert, Natorp, Cassirer or Bauch appears in that list. On the contrary, he includes the neo-Kantians Cassirer, Natorp and Rickert, as well as Mach, in a complementary list of philosophers that explicitly rejected the methodological solipsism of his autopsychological basis. He does not mention Kant, though he could have done it, since Kant's system is clearly not autopsychological. It is also not physi-

---

können, als konstitutive Elementen in "kategoriale" Bildungen von Gegenständen höherer Stufe eintreten können."

50 "Aber vorurteilsfrei angesehen und phänomenologisch auf seine Quellen zurückgeführt, sind die fundierten Einheiten eben fundierte und neuartige; das Neue, das sich mit ihnen konstituiert, kann .. nie und niemmer auf bloße Summen von anderen Realitäten reduziert werden."

calist, but heteropsychological, since it presupposes from the very beginning that all men are similarly endowed with the same faculties of sensibility, understanding and reason, with the same two forms of pure intuition and the same twelve neo-Aristotelian categories. Hence, the problem faced by Descartes and Husserl of trying to obtain secure knowledge of the existence of other human subjects was not even a problem for Kant. Furthermore, for the Carnap of *Aufbau* only a physicalist and an autopsychological basis were possible, and, as already mentioned, he opted for the latter on epistemological grounds. Thus, for Carnap, Kant's system based on a tacit acceptance of a heteropsychological basis was no alternative at all.

But the most decisive argument against the Kantian or neo-Kantian rendering of Carnap's *Aufbau* is precisely the fact that Carnap followed in the footsteps of Descartes and most significantly of Husserl in trying to solve the problem called by Husserl of "intersubjectivity" and by Carnap of the "heteropsychological", whereas for Kant that problem was non-existent. Leaving Descartes and his attempted "solution" aside, we can concentrate on Husserl and Carnap. In fact, Husserl's and Carnap's solutions are basically the same. It would take us too long to discuss this delicate matter in some detail here. We have done it in the whole Chapter 3 of our book on Carnap and prefer to refer the reader to that chapter, in which we compare passages of the *Aufbau* with passages of Husserl's *Ideen II*, *Cartesianische Meditationen* and the three enormous volumes of *Zur Phänomenologie der Intersubjektivität*, the first of which is based on manuscripts from 1913 up to 1920, the second on manuscripts from 1921 to 1928 and the third on manuscripts from 1929 to 1935. In any case, we give here a brief survey of the Husserl-Carnap solution, or better, the Husserl solution used by Carnap without referring to Husserl.

As already mentioned, the so-called autopsychological basis consists of a consciousness – Husserl would also say transcendental *ego* – with its experiences of consciousness (*Erlebnisse*) in the flow of internal time, that is, the stream of consciousness. In the process of constituting the external world, the physicalist level, consciousness constitutes a peculiar physical object, which accompanies consciousness everywhere and moves according to the designs of consciousness. Thus is constituted the body of consciousness. Later on, consciousness will constitute other bodies, among them some that seem to be moving on their own, that is, that do not need to be pushed by the body of consciousness. Moreover, some of those bodies seem to express emotions of joy or fear, and even emit some sort of sounds, including utterances or verbal expressions. Then consciousness will assign by a sort of analogy a sort of consciousness to those bodies moving on their own and emitting utterances. In this way intersubjectivity is reached and the level of the heteropsychological is constituted.

In my book I have tried to correct Husserl's solution, adopted by Carnap, on the basis that to recognize the existence of other embodied consciousness, voluntary movements of a body accompanied by expressions of joy or fear, and sounds is not enough. Verbal expressions of the language understood by the so-called transcendental ego play the decisive role in acknowledging that the other is an embodied consciousness like myself. In such a way the social character of language is forced unto him and he acknowledges the existence of other similar embodied transcendental egos. I am not going to say anything more about this issue here, though in my book I used my modified solution of the problem of constituting the heteropsychological to try to found a sort of revised Kantian ethics that could serve as an ethical grounding for an equalitarian society as that in which I have believed since my student years.

Finally, I just want to mention that Husserl's influence on Carnap continued beyond 1928. Carnap's distinction in 'Überwindung der Metaphysik durch logische Analyse der Sprache' between two sorts of nonsensical pseudo-sentences, in one case because they contain a nonsensical word, in the other because they violate the laws for the correct grammatical construction of sentences, is Husserl's.[51] Moreover, the distinction in *Logische Syntax der Sprache* between formation rules and transformation rules is also Husserl's. Once more Carnap does not have the moral courage to acknowledge that he learned both distinctions from Husserl. On those issues, see Chapter XI of *Logische Untersuchungen I* and, especially, *Logische Untersuchungen II*, Fourth Investigation.

§6 Final Comments: Some Medicine for Empiricist Blindness

The case of the young Carnap should serve in many ways as an example of the dangers of empiricism. First of all, as shown in this paper, almost all scholars, especially those formed in the Anglo-American empiricist tradition, failed to correctly render Carnap's *Aufbau* as a book strongly influenced by Husserl, in which the still young Carnap basically tried to reshape with the help of logical-linguistic tools the Husserlian program of constitution from the autopsychological basis

---

[51] On Husserl's influence on this famous paper, see also Thomas Mormann's overview of Carnap's philosophy in his book *Rudolf Carnap*, C.H. Beck, München 2000. By the way, the distinction between two sorts of nonsense is already present in *Aufbau*, p. 254.

of the transcendental *ego* to the physical world, the heteropsychological and, finally, the cultural and spiritual world. But the positivist-empiricist dogma had an even much deeper effect on Carnap himself. Probably acquainted with the lack of sympathy that Moritz Schlick had for Husserl and also conscious of Neuraths Marxist fanaticism, Carnap masked Husserl's influence on the *Aufbau* and beyond, making him appear dishonest to the eyes of someone acquainted enough both with Husserl and Carnap. Nonetheless, when Carnap wrote his 'Intellectual Autobiography' Moritz Schlick and Otto Neurath had been dead for many years, but the author of *Aufbau* did not have the moral courage to accept Husserl's overwhelming influence in *Der Raum*, in *Aufbau* and in a lesser degree elsewhere.[52]

But if Carnap and other logical empiricists had reflected on some of Husserl's and other non-empiricist philosophers, for example, Pierre Duhem's, writings, then they would have avoided the blind alley to which their empiricism forced them. Already in the first volume of *Logische Untersuchungen* Husserl observed[53] that the most general physical laws, like the law of gravitation, are not obtained from experience by any sort of induction, but are what Husserl called *hypotheses cum fundamento in re*, that is, hypotheses with some tenuous contact with reality. Such hypotheses, or laws of higher level, serve to explain laws of lower level, and, hence, there is already in Husserl the deductive-nomological scheme of explanation, particularly, for explaining laws of lower level, and, thus, not only that of pure deductive explanation, but especially the approximate explanation scheme. In fact, Husserl stressed most forcefully, that there are other possible hypotheses that could also serve to explain the laws of lower level or, more succinctly, that there are many non-equivalent hypotheses that, nonetheless, can explain the same laws of lower level and are, therefore, empirically equivalent. Hence, such laws of higher level, such *hypotheses cum fundamento in re* are empirically underdetermined. Thus, many of the most interesting issues discussed later by logical empiricists and the Quineans, as well as their difficulties had already been briefly but pointedly discussed by Husserl, and a study of Chapter XI of *Logische Untersuchungen I* would have helped the

---

[52] Besides 'Überwindung der Metaphysik durch logische Analyse der Sprache' and *Logische Syntax der Sprache* of the early 1930s, as late as in his 1950 *Logical Foundations of Probability* Carnap tries to mask Husserl's influence using once more the strategy of mentioning other authors before Husserl – this time Langford and Kant –, whereas the decisive influence seems to come from Husserl. See p. 3, as well as Michael Beaney's paper 'Carnap's Conception of Explication: from Frege to Husserl', in Steve Awoodey and Carsten Klein (eds.), *Carnap Brought Home*, Open Court, Chicago et al. 2004, pp. 117–150.

[53] See *Logische Untersuchungen I*, Chapter IV, §23 and very especially Chapter XI, §§62–66, especially, §§63 and 64, as well as §72.

logical-empiricists avoid wasting their time and energy looking for a criterion of verification or falsification and for the so-called protocol sentences, be it in their phenomenalist or in their physicalist version.

On the other hand, if you look at Duhem's work[54], you also find enough reasons to reject the later empiricism. In a less clear way than Husserl, Duhem also saw the problem of the underdetermination of physical laws.[55] Moreover, he also stressed the fact that even in the most simple of physical experiments there are already many implicit assumptions of a physical-theoretical nature, even in the instruments used in the experiments.[56] That is the reason why he postulated the impossibility of isolating physical hypotheses, a very sound thesis that in Anglo-American empiricist circles has been muddled with something completely different and much more questionable, namely, Quine's thesis[57] that all our beliefs, from the logical truths to the most accidental empirical statements are connected in a sort of web of belief and, hence, according to Quine, there is no fundamental difference, but only one of degree between the law of commutativity of the sum in arithmetic and the proposition that says that Newton had a toothache when he discovered his law of gravitation.[58]

---

54 See his book *La Théorie Physique: son Objet, sa Structure* 1914, English *translation, The Aim and Structure of Physical Theory*, Princeton University Press, Princeton 1955, 1991, as well as his paper 'Some Reflections on the Subject of Experimental Physics' in his *Essays in the History and Philosophy of Science*, edited by Roger Ariew and Peter Baker, Hackett, Indianapolis 1996, pp. 75–111.
55 See 'Some Reflections on the Subject of Experimental Physics', pp. 90–91.
56 See ibid., pp. 75–79.
57 See, for example, 'Two Dogmas of Empiricism' 1951, reprinted in *From a Logical Point of View*, Harvard University Press, Cambridge, Ma. 1953, pp. 20–46.
58 Hereby I want to thank Prof. Verena Mayer for calling my attention both to Carnap's diaries and to Carnap's letter to Jonas Cohn referred to in footnotes 17 and 20, respectively.

Appendix I
Some Husserlian Technical Terms used in Carnap's *Aufbau*

From the Register of Elisabeth Ströker's *Husserls Werk: Zur Ausgabe der Gesammelten Schriften*, Felix Meiner, Hamburg 1992.

(The *Gesammelte Schriften* include only the nine books of Husserl published in his lifetime, which is a very small sample of Husserl's gigantic production. But since the proof is so overwhelming, it is unnecessary to refer here also to Husserl's posthumous writings.)

Konstitution, begins on the bottom of p. 174 and ends at the bottom of the first column of p. 175

Konstituiren (p. 174) – *Logische Untersuchungen I*, pp. 119, 132, 244; *Logische Untersuchungen II*, pp. 169, 223, 357 A, 361 A, 364, 389, 390 A, 397, 400, 406, 410 A, 411 A, 415, 417, 419, 423, 515, 517, 523, 526 A, 540, 674f., 684f., 688f., 703, 705, 708f., 714f., 717, 724, 729; *Ideen I*, pp. 104, 107, 109, 114ff., 131, 182, 198, 243, 263, 274, 279, 351f., 357; *Formale und transzendentale Logik*, p. 322; *Cartesianische Meditationen*, pp. 44, 80, 82, 87, 95f., 102, 107, 110, 113, 118, 122, 127, 133, 135, 153; *Krisis*, pp. 84, 114, 170, 183, 205. (There are also extensive lists for derivatives like 'konstituierend', 'konstituiert' and konstitutiv'.)

Fundierung (p. 156) – *Philosophie der Arithmetik*, p. 79; *Logische Untersuchungen II*, pp. 268, 270, 282, 286, 290, 292, 418, 432, 515, 519, 675, 708; *Ideen I*, pp. 38, 117, 237, 266, 275, 300; *Erste Philosophie*, pp. 109, 118; *Cartesianische Meditationen*, p. 85; with the adjective 'mittelbare' in *Logische Untersuchungen II*, p. 272; with the adjective 'psychologische' in *Philosophie der Arithmetik*, p. 51; with the adjective 'unmittelbare' in *Logische Untersuchungen II*, p. 272.

Fundiert (p. 156) – *Ideen I*, pp. 38, 77ff., 90, 267, 293.

Fundierungsordnung (p. 156) – *Cartesianische Meditationen*, p. 127.

Fundierungsverhältnis (p. 156) – *Logische Untersuchungen II*, pp. 268, 271, 292, 295, 300 A.

Erlebnis and its derivatives (almost the whole p. 150) – Includes, among others, references to *Logische Untersuchungen I & II, Ideen I, Cartesianische Meditationen* and *Erste Philosophie*, in all of which Husserl uses the word as a technical term.

Erlebnisstrom (p. 151) – Includes references to *Ideen I*, pp. 67, 70, 73f., 78ff., 94, 96f., 104, 119, 123, 128, 164f., 168, 181f., 184, 186f., 191f., 195, 214, 265 and 273; to *Cartesianische Meditationen*, pp. 69, 104, 106f., 130, 137; with the adjective 'absoluter' in *Ideen I*, p. 118; with the adjective 'reiner' in *Logische Untersuchungen II, U. VI*, p. 765; with the adjective 'transzendentaler' in *Ideen I*, p. 204.

Abschattung (p. 121) – *Logische Untersuchungen II, U. VI*, pp. 584, 590 ff., 613 f., 647; *Ideen I*, pp. 14, 85 f., 88, 91, 173, 226, 230 f., 92 ff., 103, 195, 117; with the adjective 'perzeptive': *Logische Untersuchungen II, U. VI*, p. 646

Wahrnehmungsabschattung (p. 123) – *Logische Untersuchungen II, U. VI*, p. 770; *Ideen I*, p. 91.

Abschattungsmannigfaltigkeit (p. 121) – *Ideen I*, pp. 85 and 230.

Abschattungsreihe (p. 121) – *Ideen I*, p. 91.

Abschattungssystem (p. 121) – *Ideen I*, p. 85.

Abschattungsweise (p. 121) – *Ideen I*, p. 94.

Appendix II
The Refutation of Carnap's Principle of Tolerance

Probably the central thesis of Carnap's *Logische Syntax der Sprache* is the well-known Principle of Tolerance, which in a style that pervades the whole of Carnap's work, tries to avoid controversies in the philosophy of logic and mathematics by postulating a sort of neutrality between intuitionism, formalism and logicism, nominalism and Platonism, first-order logic and higher-order logic. However, as happened with Carnap's criteria of empirical significance, the logic that he so eagerly propounded serves to show that the principle of tolerance is false. We will show that first-order model theory shows the falsity of nominalism and, hence, that of the Principle of Tolerance.

Let us suppose that we are working in first-order logic, since as Quine has argued and others admitted, higher-order logic commits its user explicitly to the acceptance of mathematical objects like sets. Consider a first-order language £ and an existential sentence ϕ in £ that purports to speak about mathematical entities. Let us suppose, however, that nominalism is true and that no mathematical entities exist. In such a case both ϕ and any other existential statement purporting to talk about mathematical entities is false, whereas any universal statement about mathematical entities is vacuously true.

However, in virtue of Robinson's Model-Completeness Test, a first-order theory T is model complete – that is, for any two models M and M^*, if M is a substructure of M^*, then M is an elementary substructure of M^* – if and only, if for any existential statement in the language of the theory, there exists a universal statement in the same language that is logically equivalent to it. Hence, there exists a universal statement ψ logically equivalent to ϕ and, hence, false.

Thus, not all universal statements of the language are true. Moreover, since the negation of φ is equivalent to a universal statement and the negation of ψ is equivalent to an existential one, and they are logically equivalent, there are true existential statements in the language £. Hence, there are existential true and existential false statements, as well as universal true and universal false statements in £. Therefore, nominalism has been refuted. Moreover, it follows that one cannot arbitrarily make all existential (universal) statements of £ true or all of them false. Hence, conventionalism in the philosophy of mathematics has also been refuted. *A fortiori*, the Principle of Tolerance has also been refuted. If you want to construct a first-order language including its semantics, that is, the well-rounded, extensively developed and powerful classical model theory, you cannot consistently defend either nominalism or conventionalism, and have to accept Platonism. Nominalism and conventionalism are not tolerated, and the Principle of Tolerance itself is not tolerated by first-order classical model theory.

References

Awoodey, Steve and Klein, Carsten (eds.): *Carnap Brought Home*, Open Court, Chicago et al. 2004.
Beaney, Michael: 'Carnap's Conception of Explication: from Frege to Husserl', in Steve Awoodey and Carsten Klein (eds.), *Carnap Brought Home*, Open Court, Chicago et al. 2004, pp. 117–150.
Bell, David & Vossenkuhl, Wilhelm (eds.): *Wissenschaft und Subjektivität*, Akademie Verlag, Berlin 1992.
Bonk, Thomas (ed.): *Language, Truth and Logic*, Kluwer, Dordrecht 2003.
Carnap, Rudolf: *Der Raum*, Kant-Studien (Ergänzungsheft 56) 1922, reprint, Topos Verlag, Vaduz 1991.
Carnap, Rudolf: *Der logische Aufbau der Welt* 1928, second edition, F. Meiner, Hamburg 1961.
Carnap, Rudolf : 'Überwindung der Metaphysik durch logische Analyse der Sprache' 1932, reprint in Rudolf Carnap, *Scheinprobleme in der Philosophie und andere metaphysikkritische Schriften*, F. Meiner, Hamburg 2004, pp. 81–109.
Carnap, Rudolf: *Logische Syntax der Sprache* 1934, English revised edition, Routledge, London 1937.
Carnap, Rudolf: *Logical Foundations of Probability*, University of Chicago Press 1950.
Carnap, Rudolf: 'Intellectual Autobiography', in Paul A. Schilpp (ed.), *The Philosophy of Rudolf Carnap*, pp. 3–84.
Carnap, Rudolf: 'Replies and Systematic Expositions', in Paul A. Schilpp (ed.), *The Philosophy of Rudolf Carnap*, pp. 859–1013.
Carnap, Rudolf: *Tagebücher 1908–1935*, in http://homepage.univie.ac.at/christian.damboeck/carnap_diaries_
Carnap, Rudolf: Letter to Jonas Cohn of 26 September 1925 (see Appendix II of *Husserl and Analytic Philosophy*).

Cohen, Robert: 'Dialectical Materialism and Carnap's Logical Empiricism', in Paul A. Schilpp (ed.), *The Philosophy of Rudolf Carnap*, pp. 99–158.
Dathe, Uwe: 'Eine Ergänzung zur Biographie Edmund Husserls', in Werner Stelzner (ed.), *Philosophie und Logik*, Walter de Gruyter, Berlin 1993, pp. 160–163.
Duhem, Pierre: 'Some Reflections on the Subject of Experimental Physics' 1894, reprinted in the English translation of his papers in Roger Ariew and Peter Baker (eds.), *Essays in the History and Philosophy of Science*, Hackett, Indianapolis 1996, pp. 75–111.
Duhem, Pierre: *La Théorie Physique: son Objet, sa Structure* 1914, English Translation, *The Aim and Structure of Physical Theory*, Princeton University Press, Princeton 1955, 1991.
Friedman, Michael: 'Carnap and Weyl on the Foundations of Geometry', *Erkenntnis 42*, 1995, pp. 247–260, reprint of the whole number in U. Majer and H. J. Schmidt (eds.), *Reflections on Spacetime*, Kluwer, Dordrecht et al. 1995.
Grünbaum, Adolf: 'Carnap's Views on the Foundations of Geometry', in Paul A. Schilpp (ed.), *The Philosophy of Rudolf Carnap*, pp. 599–684.
Husserl, Edmund: *Logische Untersuchungen* (two vols.) 1900–1901, Husserliana XVIII & XIX, M. Nijhoff, Den Haag 1975 & 1984.
Husserl, Edmund: *Ideen zu einer reinen Phänomenologie und phänomenologischen Philosophie I* 1913, Hua III 1950, revised edition, M. Nijhoff, Den Haag 1976.
Husserl, Edmund: *Cartesianische Meditationen* 1928 (French version), Hua I, M. Nijhoff, Den Haag 1950.
Husserl, Edmund: *Formale und transzendentale Logik* 1929, Hua XVII, M. Nijhoff, Den Haag 1974.
Husserl, Edmund: *Ideen zu einer reinen Phänomenologie und phänomenologischen Philosophie II*, Hua IV M. Nijhoff, Den Haag 1952.
Husserl, Edmund: *Zur Phänomenologie der Intersubjektivität* (three vols.), Hua XIII-XV, M. Nijhoff, Den Haag 1973.
Husserl, Edmund: *Briefwechsel* (ten vols.), Kluwer, Dordrecht 1994.
Mayer, Verena: 'Die Konstruktion der Erfahrungswelt: Carnap und Husserl', in W. Spohn (ed.), *Erkenntnis Orientated* 1991, pp. 287–303.
Mayer, Verena: 'Carnap und Husserl' in D. Bell and W. Vossenkuhl (eds.), *Wissenschaft und Subjektivität* 1992, pp. 181–205.
Mormann, Thomas: *Rudolf Carnap*, C. H. Beck, München 2000.
Rosado Haddock, Guillermo E.: *The Young Carnap's Unknown Master*, Ashgate, Aldershot 2008.
Rosado Haddock, Guillermo E.: 'On the Interpretation of the Young Carnap's Philosophy', in Guillermo E. Rosado Haddock, *Against the Current*, Ontos Verlag, Frankfurt 2012, pp. 261–284.
Russell, Bertrand: *Our Knowledge of the External World* 1914, revised edition, 1926, fifth printing, Allen and Unwin, London 1969.
Sarkar, Sahotra: 'Husserl's Role in Carnap's *Der Raum*', in Thomas Bonk (ed.), *Language, Truth and Logic*, Kluwer, Dordrecht 2003, pp. 179–190.
Schilpp, Paul A.: *The Philosophy of Rudolf Carnap*, Open Court, La Salle et al. 1963.
Spohn, Wolfgang (ed.): *Erkenntnis Orientated*, Kluwer, Dordrecht 1991.
Ströker, Elizabeth: *Husserls Werk: Zur Ausgabe der Gesammelten Schriften*, erschienen als Band X der *Gesammelten Schriften Edmund Husserls*, Felix Meiner, Hamburg 1992.

Part III: **Appendices**

Carlo Ierna and Dieter Lohmar
Husserl's Manuscript A I 35

The following pages contain a partial edition of Husserl's manuscript A I 35, pages 1a-28b.[1] The first few pages are dated on May 1927 and are included mostly for completeness' sake. The bulk of the manuscript convolute, however, is from 1912. Four pages of the convolute, 31a-34b, have been published as Beilage XII (210, 2–216, 2) in Hua XXXII.[2]

The manuscript was excluded from the text selection of Husserliana XXI[3] based on its much later date of composition. A I 35/24a is mentioned in Husserliana XXII (p. xxi, n. 4) as confirmation for Zermelo's 1902 "oral report" to Husserl of his own independent discovery of the paradox.

The text presented here for the first time has already been the target of at least three extensive commentaries, while still unpublished, by Claire Ortiz Hill and Guillermo Rosado Haddock.[4] These present a good survey in english of the central issues on the text and contain many translated quotations.

<1a *Umschlagblatt Drucksache vom August 25. 1922 1a/75a m. folgender Aufschrift m. Blaust.*>
    Menge und Begriffsumfang.
    Paradoxien, Allheit.
    Dazugehöriges über Fermat
    über Umfang und Wissenschaftsgebiet etc. in O_α II.
    Gebiet einer Wissenschaft, Allgemeines zur Lehre von den funktional-„überhaupt"-Urteilen

---

[1] Based on two partial transcriptions (one originally prepared by Martin Lang at the Husserl-Archives of Cologne University). The editors would like to thank Thomas Vongehr and Klaus Sellge for their assistance and Ullrich Melle, the director of the Husserl-Archives Leuven, for his kindly conceded permission to publish the text.
[2] Edmund Husserl *Natur und Geist. Vorlesungen Sommersemester 1927*, edited by Michael Weiler (Dordrecht/Boston/London: Springer, 2001).
[3] Edmund Husserl *Studien zur Arithmetik und Geometrie. Texte Aus Dem Nachlass (1886–1901)*, edited by Ingeborg Strohmeyer (Den Haag: Nijhoff, 1983).
[4] Claire Ortiz Hill, "Tackling three of Frege's Problems: Edmund Husserl on Sets and Manifolds", in Axiomathes 13 (2002), Guillermo Rosado Haddock, "Husserl's Philosophy of Mathematics: its Origin and Relevance", in Husserl Studies, 22 (2006), and Guillermo Rosado Haddock, "Platonism, Phenomenology, and Interderivability", in Mirja Hartimo (Hrsg.), *Phenomenology and Mathematics*, (Dordrecht: Springer, 2010). What is published here corresponds to what Haddock refers to as "part a".

auch Limes, Approximative Intentionalität
auch Überhaupt-Urteile.
<2a "1">
Mai 1927. Noten.

Die Intentionalität in der Konstitution jeder offenen Unendlichkeit mit dem Aufspringen des Und-so-Weiter.

Füge ich zu einer Kugel eine zweite hinzu, in "Gedanken", dann wieder eine, dann wieder, so kann ich mir Folgendes denken: Zu irgendeiner Kugel kann ich mir eine andere "dazu" denken, dann wieder eine andere, eine "neue", dann wieder, ich kann mir zu irgendeiner so gewonnenen Menge ein "neues" Element hinzudenken.

Ich kann mir danach eine Kette der Erzeugung denken, 1, 2, 3 usw., eine ideell praktische Intention und Verwirklichung, in der jedes Erzeugnis Durchgang ist, derart also, dass die Intention sich in ihm erfüllt, aber durch es hindurch als Intention sich auf das nächste Glied richtet als zunächst Intendiertes, sich darin in Aktualisierung Erfüllendes, das aber wieder nur Durchgang ist usw.

Auch wenn ich einen Haufen habe, eine in einem Blick erfasste sinnliche Menge, kann ich sie durchlaufen, und darin liegt: Ich erzeuge, und es konstituiert sich eine Kette praktischer Intentionalität, eine Kette von Intention und Erfüllungen derart, dass durch jedes Erfüllungsglied die Intention hindurchgeht. Indem sie aber hindurchgeht auf das Nächste, durch das, wenn es da ist, wieder durchgeht, so haben wir nicht nur unmittelbares Hindurchgehen, sondern ein Verketten der Intentionalität in einer Synthese der Durchgänge. Von Anfang an geht die Intentionalität als einheitliche so fort, dass jede Erfüllung zugleich Ende und zugleich Durchgang ist, <2b> hier so, dass jedes Mittelglied einerseits mit gilt, andererseits Mittelglied ist für die Erzeugung des nächsten usw.

Denke ich mir ein beliebiges Glied einer solchen Erzeugung, so ist es mittelbares Erzeugnis seiner Stufe, Ende einer Erzeugungsreihe und zugleich Durchgangserzeugnis für die noch folgenden Glieder. Jedes Glied a trägt in sich den intentionalen Charakter des Endes von einem Anfang an. Es ist Endglied einer Erzeugungsstrecke, als Erzeugungsreihe, die mit 1 anfängt, und ist Anfangsglied, aber nur relatives, eben Durchgangsglied für eine noch offene Reihe als zu erzeugende:

Bei der Dekadik: Eine unendliche Reihe der Erzeugung ist gedacht mit gewissen Voraussetzungen, die zu ihrer Denkmöglichkeit gehören, (dass man immer wieder "Neues" sich denken, vorgefunden denken und in die Erzeugung einbeziehen ⟨kann⟩), denn: ich fasse eine bestimmte, immer wieder zu identifizierende Reihe 1–10 zusammen. Doch nein. Ich bilde ja "Zahlen", reine Formen der Erzeugnisse in mittelbarer Intentionalität, Stellenformen in der Kettenerzeugung. Ich zähle nun selbst in Bezug auf die allgemeinen Charaktere ⟨der⟩ Reihenform; ich bilde eine Methode, eine unendliche Reihe, dekadisch durch ein immer wieder einsetzendes dekadisches Zählen als eine unendliche Erzeugungsreihe neuer Stufe zu bilden, als dekadisch gebildete Zahlenreihe usw. Das müsste natürlich ordentlich durchdacht werden.

⟨3a "2"⟩ Sind Zahlen einzeln, so sind sie zurückbezogen gedacht auf Mengen. Im Faktum sind Mengen endliche, gegebene Mengen. Ideell kann man aber Mengen auf die Form bringen (formalisieren, wie schon der Begriff der Menge selbst Form ist und als allgemeine Form das Und-so-Weiter in sich trägt, obschon die Menge, die als unbestimmte Einzelnheit daraus gedacht ist, eine "endliche" ist), das ist die "Äquivalenz"-Betrachtung. Man kann sich zu jeder Mengenform (oder einer beliebigen ⟨Menge⟩ dieser Form) ideell eine Menge denken, die "mehr" Glieder hat, die größer ist und so *in infinitum*. Und von da geht man auf die "natürlichen Zahlen" über, von den ersten Anzahlen als Mengentypen, deren erste trotz kategorialer Erzeugung der zuverlässigen Identifizierung und Unterscheidung entbehrt, zu den neuen Zahlen, die eben methodische Gebilde sind, die sich sicher identifizieren und unterscheiden lassen, freilich mit immer neuer Umständlichkeit. Alle kategorialen Gebilde werden verfügbarer Erwerb. Aber das sind sie doch nicht ohne Weiteres. Eine Rede, die ich einmal gehört und verstanden, eine Theorie mit ihren vielen Schlüssen und Beweisen, habe ich inne, und doch: Kann ich sie genau reproduzieren, sie, die ich in Erinnerung habe? Wie kann ich eine kategoriale Bildung, die selbst eine "Konstruktion" ist, rekonstruieren; wie Methoden der Konstruktion, die ich immer wieder als besondere Weisen von Konstruktion immer wieder konstruieren und wohl unterscheiden kann, ⟨das sind⟩ methodische Konstruktionsweisen, die ich immer wieder anwenden und universell entscheiden kann, ⟨3b⟩ um damit alle logischen Gebilde so aufzubauen (methodisch indiziert), dass ich aus den vagen Gebilden feste, verfügbare, identifizierbare gewinne?

Ein besonderer Fall des Ineinander der Intentionalität als Reihen-Intentionalität ist eine Bildung von Erzeugnissen, deren jedes das folgende darstellt, für dasselbe "Erscheinung" ist. Also Erscheinung von, Erscheinung von (Erscheinung von) ... Unterschied kontinuierlicher Erscheinung und Erzeugung, und diskontinuierlicher, diskreter Erzeugung. Idee der Approximation als formale Idee einer relativen Erscheinung, zugehörig zu einer Erscheinungsreihe mit den Begriffen der relativen Nähe und Ferne. Zahlbestimmung von Nähe und Ferne, Limes-Idee. Eine vorgegebene "Größe" als Pol einer "Erscheinungs"reihe, als ihr Limes. Eine Fernerscheinung als relativer Pol der Annäherung, Idee eines Limes, formal gedacht als Pol einer Erscheinungsreihe. Definitheit der irrationalen Zahl, ⟨in⟩wiefern sie zu rechtfertigen wäre.

<4a *Umschlag 4a/29a (Rückseite der Abschrift eines Briefes vom 3. Mai 1902) mit der Aufschrift:*>

Die Paradoxien. Die Insolubilia. 7.3.1912.

Insbesondere auch die Paradoxien der Mengenlehre.

Menge.

Goldstein, ⟨J.⟩, Wandlungen in der Philosophie der Gegenwart ⟨Mit besonderer Berücksichtigung des Problems von Leben und Wissenschaft⟩, ⟨W. Klinkhardt⟩ Leipzig 1911

<5a>

Identität des empirischen Gegenstandes.

Identität des idealen Gegenstandes.

Die Idee dieses Hauses, dieses empirischen Dinges, sein Wesen. Sein Wesen ist es, einmal so und das andere Mal so, in der einen Strecke der Dauer so beschaffen, in der anderen anders beschaffen zu sein.

Die Idee des Dinges in einer Zeitstrecke seines Seins ist eine andere als die Idee in einer anderen. Aber die Idee des Dinges ist Idee von etwas, das dasselbe ist in beiden Zeitstrecken. (Das Ding ist nicht in der Zeit, so wie die Zahl in der Zahlenreihe).

Das Ding hat Eigenschaften.

<u>Eigenschaft als Dingbestimmung für eine Zeit.</u>

Das Ding hat seine Zeitdauer und hat Bestimmungen für verschiedene Teile der Dauer.

Das Ding hat die Beschaffenheit a.

Das Ding hat die Eigenschaft, in einer gewissen Strecke seiner Dauer flüssig zu sein, das Ding hat wechselnde Eigenschaften sagt, es hat für verschiedene Strecken der Dauer verschiedene und solche, die sich in derselben Strecke nicht vertragen.

Logisch: Das Ding ist dasselbe. Die logische Identität ist keine andere als die dingliche Identität. Dies ⟨ist⟩ ein Spezialfall. Aber während ein idealer Gegenstand keine Zeitdauer hat und seine Beschaffenheiten keine Zeitbestimmung einschließen, tut das der empirische Gegenstand. Die Zahl 4. Sie ist gerade schlechthin.

Eine Linie ist an einer Stelle rot, an einer anderen blau, an einer Teilstrecke gerade, in einer anderen krumm. Eine Körperoberfläche ist an einer Stelle rotfleckig, dort grünfleckig, da kugelförmig, dort kantig.

<5b>Die Fläche ist ein Ganzes aus Teilen, und jeder Teil hat seine Farbenbedeckung, und das Ganze seine "Färbung". Das Ganze hat eine Form: Diese baut sich aus Teilformen ⟨auf⟩. Das Ganze mit seiner Form hat eine Färbung.

Die baut sich den Teilformen entsprechend in Teilfärbungen ⟨auf⟩.

Das Ding hat eine Oberfläche und hat Färbung, sofern es eine Oberfläche hat oder sonst Räumlichkeit.

Das Ding hat Gestalt, hat Raumkörper, hat im oder am Körper Färbung, etc. Und das Ding hat das als Dauerndes und als Dauerndes hat es das in wechselnder Besonderung in verschiedenen Phasen und Strecken der Dauer

Was ist eine Fläche für eine Sache? Eine räumliche Fläche.

Nur denkbar als Raumform eines Dauernden oder als ein "Zwischen" zwischen Dauerndem und selbst dauernd in seiner Unselbständigkeit an Dauerndem.

Das Ding ist dasselbe in allen seinen Dauern. Aber die Identität des Prädikats ist vorausgesetzt, logisch. Dasselbe Ding ist rot zur Zeit a ⟨und⟩ nicht rot (sondern blau) zur Zeit b.

Das Ding ist dauernd mit einem Bestimmtheitsgehalt. Es ist dasselbe in der Dauer, aber dasselbe ist immer wieder anders bestimmt in der Dauer.

<6a>Bestand der Relation, Existenz der Relationsglieder.

In einem Relationsurteil ist gesetzt ein relationeller Sachverhalt, und dieser besteht "zwischen" zwei oder mehreren Beziehungspunkten. Diese sind mit der Relation als seiend gesetzt, ebenso gut, wie in jeder kategorialen Prädikation, die affirmativen Inhalt hat, das Sein des Subjektes und das Sein des Prädikates gesetzt ist.

Aber alles ist dabei gesetzt in dem Sinne, den eben das Urteil und seine Bedeutungsglieder fordern.

In der Relation (dem "gegenständlichen" des Relationsurteils, dem Sachverhalt) können stehen zwei als existierend gesetzte Dinge der Natur, ein reales Dasein zu einem anderen realen Dasein. Ich sage der Kaiser und meine eben den Kaiser, das reale Objekt in der Naturwirklichkeit.

Es kann aber auch gesetzt sein ein "intentionaler Gegenstand als solcher". Ich fingiere ein Nirgendheim[5] und darin einen Kaiser in einem ganz bestimmten Sinn, und nun halte ich den Sinn fest und das Fingierte setze ich konsequent in diesem Sinn. Dann kann ich Vergleiche machen zwischen diesem Kaiser und dem Kaiser von Deutschland usw. Die Wahrheit des Relationsurteils hängt vom Sein dieser Gegenstände ab, und das Sein des Intentionalen liegt in seiner

---

[5] See Wander, Deutsches Sprichwörter-Lexikon, Vol. 3. Leipzig 1873, Sp. 1036 (http://www.zeno.org/nid/20011676612, consulted on 29.02.2016).

Möglichkeit. Ich weise sie aus in der Klärung des Sinnes, soweit er für die Ermöglichung des Relationsbestandes in Frage kommt, in der fingierenden Anschauung.

<6b>Ein rundes Viereck ist ein Gedachtes, aber ein widersinnig Gedachtes als solches. Es kann in keinen Relationen stehen, es ist nichts, ist Unmögliches. Es kann zwar gesagt werden "ein rundes Viereck" sei Vermeintheit; aber es ist nur Denkvermeintes, das sich nicht in erfüllbare Anschauung als "Mögliches" herausstellen lässt.

Denkvermeintheiten als solche (Denk-bedeutungen) lassen sich als Gegenstände in Relation setzen zu anderen, ich vergleiche dann die bloß logischen Bedeutungen, ich setze in Beziehung "Begriffe" und "Urteile" etc.

<Bl. 7a-9b "Identität und Relation" *mit Bemerkungen zum Aristotelischen Satz vom Widerspruch, unpaginiert*>

<7a> Identität und Relation.

Ich sage, ein Gegenstand habe die Beschaffenheit a, und derselbe Gegenstand habe auch die Beschaffenheit b.

Wo ich von einem Gegenstand spreche, kann ich auch von demselben sprechen, ich kann also auch sagen, derselbe Gegenstand hat die Beschaffenheit a und die Beschaffenheit b.

Wieder kann ich sagen: dieser Gegenstand etc. – derselbe Gegenstand.

Ferner: Dieser Gegenstand hat die Beschaffenheit a.

    Jener Gegenstand hat die Beschaffenheit b. Ein anderer Gegenstand, nicht derselbe.

Die Beschaffenheit b kommt dem Gegenstand G zu, und sie kommt noch anderen, nicht denselben zu. Ein Gegenstand (oder ein und derselbe oder derselbe) kann nicht die Beschaffenheit a haben und die Beschaffenheit a nicht haben. Ein Gegenstand, ein jeder überhaupt, muss entweder die Beschaffenheit a haben oder sie nicht haben.

Was setzen solche Reden für die "Einheit" oder Identität voraus? Ein individueller, ein zeitlicher Gegenstand ist seinem Wesen nach Einheit einer Dauer, er währt eine Dauer, die seine Dauer ist. Er, der dauernde Gegenstand, das Ding, hat Beschaffenheiten, wir sagen auch, hat Eigenschaften. Dasselbe Ding, dieses identische Ding, hat entweder die Beschaffenheit a oder hat sie nicht, eines von beiden. Und wenn das eine, so nicht das andere. Aber das Ding ist jetzt rot und dann nicht rot, sondern blau. Also das Ding, das dasselbe ist jetzt und dann, ist rot (nämlich jetzt, in der Zeitstrecke), <7b> und ist nicht rot (während der anderen Zeitstrecke).

Aristoteles sagt, dasselbe kann in derselben Hinsicht nicht zugleich a und nicht a sein. In Hinsicht auf die eine Dauer kann der Gegenstand nicht rot und nicht-rot sein (die ganze Dauer hindurch).

Das ist aber keine klare Rede.

Der Gegenstand während seiner ganzen Dauer: Ein Ding ist überhaupt nur möglich als dauerndes, es ist dauerndes Sein, Identisches in einer Dauer. Und das Ding hat seinen "Inhalt", seinen Gehalt an Bestimmtheiten, und mit diesen erfüllt es die Dauer. Es kann während seiner Dauer durchaus Unverändertes sein, nicht nur Identisches während der Dauer, sondern auch identisch nach dem Wesen seiner zeitlichen Bestimmtheiten, "mit sich selbst immerfort gleich"; d. h., das Ding in jeder Zeitstrecke hat dieselben Bestimmtheiten. Es kann aber auch Sich-Änderndes sein, und während es dasselbe ist, doch immer wieder andere Bestimmtheiten haben in den neuen und neuen Zeitstrecken seine Dauer. Das Ding ist nicht in der Zeit wie ein Apfel im Sack ist, der Apfel steckt bloß im Sack drin und könnte auch ohne Sack sein. Das Ding ist auch nicht "notwendig" in dem Sack Zeit, als ob es irgendwie da hineingebunden wäre, unlöslich. Ebenso wie das Haben der Beschaffenheiten bzw. Eigenschaften nicht ein Haben ist wie ein Baum den Apfel hat als etwas an ihm Hängendes und Abnehmbares.

Das Ding ist und ist als Einheit von Eigenschaften, und wieder, es ist Einheit von Eigenschaften als Einheit einer Dauer, und das wieder sagt <8a>, der Gegenstand als Einheit einer zeitlichen Ausbreitung hat in jeder Zeitphase seiner Dauer eine Gegenstandsphase und in jeder Strecke seiner Dauer eine Gegenstandsstrecke. Jede Gegenstandsphase ist eine gewisse Einheit, nämlich eine Einheit von Eigenschaften, und jede neue Gegenstandssphäre eine andere. Aber alle Gegenstandsphasen sind nicht nur einig, sofern sie kontinuierlich sich zur Dauerkontinuität vereinigen, sondern sie tragen in sich eine Einheit, ein Identisches, das seinem Wesen nach sich in solchen Phasen kontinuierlich auseinanderlegt. Und wieder, in jeder Dauerstrecke ist eine durchgehende Einheit als Einheit gerade dieser Strecke, und diese Einheit hat Eigenschaften, d. h., sie hat in jeder Phase Eigenschaften und die Eigenschaften erstrecken sich analog, aber innerhalb ihrer kategorialen Eigenschaften durch eine Dauer, oder sie wechseln, sei es plötzlich oder kontinuierlich, und je nachdem "ändert" sich die Einheit der Dauer (jeder Dauer und somit auch der Gesamtdauer) plötzlich oder kontinuierlich oder ändert sich streckenweise auch nicht, sei es überhaupt, sei es hinsichtlich irgendeiner Eigenschaft. Das alles erschauen wir als zum Wesen einer individuellen Einheit gehörig. Die Einheit ist Identisches, sie ist eben Eines.

Wenn die Logik von Einem spricht, von einem Gegenstand, der Beschaffenheiten hat, und wenn sie sagt, der Gegenstand hat die Beschaffenheit a und er habe sie nicht, das schließe sich aus, was meint sie da? Nun, sie meint: Denke ich in einem bestimmten Sinn, "der Gegenstand G habe die Eigenschaft a", so schreibt dieser Sinn, der genau festgehalten werden muss, auch dem "kontradiktorischen Gegenteil" seinen Sinn vor: Derselbe Gegenstand G hat nicht die Eigenschaft a, und beides in genau entsprechendem Sinn genommen, habe ich einen Ausschluss kontradiktorischer Prädikation, den der Satz vom Widerspruch meint. Sage ich also, der Gegenstand ist ein Ding, und dieses Ding sei rot, ⟨8b⟩ so habe ich diese Prädikation in einem bestimmten Sinn zu nehmen. Ich kann da meinen, der Gegenstand, das Ding ist seiner ganzen Oberfläche nach rot oder einem Teil nach rot, es kommt an ihm überhaupt das Rot vor, und natürlich muss ich das bei der Negation genauso fassen. Und werfe ich es durcheinander, so erhalte ich Verkehrtheit. Der Gegenstand ist rot und er ist nicht rot schließen sich nicht aus, wenn ich eben den Sinn, statt ⟨ihn⟩ genau entsprechend zu halten, vielmehr ändere.

Weiter: ich kann meinen, das Ding sei während seiner ganzen Dauer rot, oder es sei überhaupt einmal rot (wobei ich das Rotsein zugleich etwa fixiere als Ganz-und-gar-rot-Sein), sei während irgendeiner seiner Strecken rot. Natürlich muss ich mich betreffs des Sinnes entscheiden. Tue ich es, dann schließt sich natürlich jede sinnesbestimmte Prädikation mit der kontradiktorischen aus. Da das Ding in einer seiner Strecken der Dauer rot ist und in einer anderen nicht rot ist, das ist selbstverständlich nichts, was die Logik in Verlegenheit setzen kann.

Sage ich, ein Haus ist rot, oder dieses Haus ist rot etc., so ist das ein vieldeutiger Ausdruck. Meint es, muss ich fragen, dieses Haus ist überhaupt einmal rot, innerhalb der Zeit seiner Dauer? Denn das weiß ich, dass ein Haus Eigenschaften nur hat als wesentlich bezogene auf seine Dauer, und zwar, sei es auf die ganze Dauer oder auf Teile der Dauer. In jedem Teil hat es irgendwelche Eigenschaften, aber die es in einem Teil hat, braucht es in einem anderen nicht zu haben. ⟨9a⟩ Das gehört zum Ding-Gemeinten als solchem. Und nun ist es offenbar eine Unbestimmtheit des Sinnes, wenn ich sage, dieses Haus ist rot, und nicht klar sage, ob gemeint ist, es sei überhaupt einmal rot oder es sei jetzt rot, in dieser bestimmten Dauer rot etc.

Jedes kann gemeint sein (und ist sehr oft gemeint): Es ist jetzt, in der gegenwärtigen Dauer (derjenigen, in der ich die Aussage mache), beständig rot (unbestimmt, wie lange das noch weiter dauern wird); oder ob ich anderes meine. Letzteres ist für die gewöhnliche Aussage mit "ist" nicht zu befürchten. Sie bezieht sich eben auf die gegenwärtige Dauer. Anders bei den Vergangenheitsaussagen. Das Ding war rot, das Ding war nicht rot, schließt sich nicht aus, aber nur bei Sinnesänderung. Das Ding war rot besagt, das Ding in einer gewissen Strecke seiner Dauer war rot. Damit verträgt sich, das Ding in einer gewissen Strecke seiner Dauer war nicht rot. Aber das sind kontradiktorische Aussagen nur, wenn die gewisse Strecke als dieselbe Strecke gedacht ist. So ist es je auch verträglich: Ein Ding ist an einer Stelle rot, das Ding ist an einer Stelle nicht rot. Nur wenn die Stelle als dieselbe bestimmt wird, haben wir kontradiktorische Aussagen. So ist auch ⟨"⟩Irgendein Haus am Hohen Weg ist ein Ziegelbau und ist nicht ein Ziegelbau⟨"⟩ kontradiktorisch, wenn das Haus als dasselbe gesetzt und ausgesagt ist, sonst nicht. Also, das Wesentliche ist, dass in solchen Aussagen Unbestimmtheiten auftreten, und es liegt im Sinne der Logik, dass kontradiktorisch nur Aussagen sind mit Unbestimmten, wenn die Unbestimmten der einen Aussage durch Identitätsbezug verbunden sind mit denen der anderen. <9b> Wir haben also keinen Anlass, logische Identität von personaler Identität und überhaupt empirischer zu unterscheiden.

Der Mensch als Greis, sagen wir, ist ein ganz anderer Mensch als der Mensch als Kind, andererseits ist es doch dieselbe Person, derselbe Mensch.

Der Mensch ist eine Einheit "während seiner ganzen Lebensdauer", aber in der Jugenddauer hat er Jugendbestimmungen, die eben auf diese seine Dauer bezogen sind, und diese Bestimmungen sind erheblich verschieden von den Altersbestimmungen, denen der Altersdauer. Wir können auch sagen: Denken wir uns die Altersperiode für sich und den Menschen während dieser Periode; denken wir uns, es ginge keine Jugendperiode vorher, nehmen wir die Einheit Mensch rein als Einheit dieser Dauer und ebenso für die Kindheit, so hätten wir allerdings zwei Menschen und zwei verschiedene Personen mit verschiedenen Eigenschaften. Das aber ist eine Abstraktion, und die beiden gehen in eins und sind dieselben, sowie wir die Vermittlungsglieder dazu nehmen, es ist dann genau derselbe Mensch, nur verändert in seinem Habitus, in Charakterentwicklungen etc.; die Logik fordert nicht, dass ich zwei Dinge, zwei Gegenstände daraus mache, wenn ich sage, der Mensch im Alter ist ein anderer (mit anderen Eigenschaften begabter) als der in der Jugend, sie fordert nur, dass ich bestimmten Sinn erhalte und somit sage, die Eigenschaften des Menschen bezogen auf das Alter sind eben Alterseigenschaften desselben, der in seiner Jugendperiode Jugendeigenschaften hat, die selbstverständlich vielfach andere sind. Wie steht es nun mit den Relationen eines Dinges zu sich selbst?

<10a> Zur Auflösung der Paradoxien

Gegenstände stehen in Relationen hinsichtlich gewisser Eigenschaften:
Die Glocke A tönt lauter als Glocke B,
Der Mensch A läuft schneller als der Mensch B, etc.

Die Subjekte der Eigenschaften stehen in Relation; primär aber haben die den Eigenschaften entsprechenden Wesen Relation: Die Farben haben Verhältnisse der Qualität, der Helligkeit, etc.

Also unterscheiden wir Relationen, die zu Wesen (niedersten Differenzen von Spezies) gehören, und Relationen, die zu den Individuen, und zwar den konkreten Individuen (Trägern von Eigenschaften) gehören, mit Hinsicht auf irgendwelche ihrer Eigenschaften, oder begriffliche Bestimmungen überhaupt. Doch ist zu überlegen, das ist wohl zu beschränkt.

Es kommt nicht gerade auf konkrete Individuen an, sondern auf das Grundverhältnis zwischen Wesen (das seinerseits niederste Differenz ist in Bezug auf Spezies und Genera von Wesen) und singularer Einzelheit, Vereinzelung des Wesens. Es ist aber auch zu unterscheiden zwischen einem umfassenderen Kontinuum, das die unmittelbare Vereinzelung des Wesens in sich birgt (etwa ein Ding, das ein Moment Farbe hat) und der unmittelbaren Vereinzelung selbst (Moment Farbe). Alle dergleichen Verhältnisse müssen überhaupt allseitig durchdacht und klar herausgestellt werden.

Es wäre nun zu studieren, welche Grundarten von Wesensrelationen es gibt. Auch die Beziehung zwischen Wesensrelation und Wesensverbindung, bzw. Wesensganzem und Wesensgliedern wäre zu studieren.

⟨10b⟩ Eine Wesensrelation hat die Form A ρ B (die logische Pluraleinigung von mehreren Relationen der Form A ρ B_1 und B_2 ... und umgekehrt können wir ausschließen). Eine Wesensverbindung hat die Form A ist verbunden mit B, eventuell A verbunden mit B_1B_2 ... in einem und demselben Ganzen.

Eine Relation, eine Verbindung von Wesen zu einem ganzen Wesen setzt eine Mehrheit von Wesen, ursprünglich zwei Wesen voraus. Es kann nicht in einer Relation oder Verbindung ein und dasselbe Wesen als Grundglied und Gegenglied (als Teil und Ganzes) auftreten! Ein Relationsurteil, bzw. ein Relationssatz, der im Subjekt- und Prädikatglied dasselbe Wesen (denselben Begriff) enthält, ist widersinnig.

Wie steht es mit Relationen von Gegenständen in Hinsicht auf Beschaffenheiten (die als solche den Wesenskern haben), die sie haben?

Unterscheiden wir die Sache (das logische Substrat, den logischen Träger des Wesens) und das Wesen. Dieselbe Sache kann verschiedene Wesen "haben", und das Haben ist so vielfach als die Wesen sind, die gehabt werden. Es kann aber auch dasselbe Wesen von derselben Sache mehrfach gehabt werden, etwa so wie dasselbe Ding dieselbe Farbe mehrfach hat, nämlich in verschiedenen Zeiten seines dauerndes Seins, und wieder zu derselben Zeit in verschiedenen Teilen seiner Körperlichkeit. Das Haben ist dabei ein Verschiedenes: Sofern dasselbe Wesen mit verschiedenen anderen Wesen oder mit denselben in verschiedener Weise in Zusammenhang tritt, und alle diese Wesen zum "Inhalt" des Gegenstandes beitragen. Hier können wir also die Relationsformen haben: Dieselbe Sache ist hinsichtlich a größer, lauter, heller etc. als sie selbst hinsichtlich b ⟨ist⟩; dieselbe Sache ist sich selbst gleich hinsichtlich a, sie ist sich selbst gleich, was die Farbe anlangt, nämlich in allen ihren Teilen, etc. Derselbe

Mensch ist älter als er selbst: nämlich derselbe im Alter älter als derselbe in der Jugend.

<11a>Dieselbe Sache steht in Relation zu sich selbst: Das enthält notwendig eine Unbestimmtheit des Sinnes. Sachen stehen überhaupt in Beziehungen aufgrund der Wesen, deren Sachen sie sind, aufgrund der Beschaffenheiten, die sie haben, und nun müssen die Wesen ihre Relation haben und es müssen also mehrere Wesen im Spiel sein. Die Bestimmung erfordert die Angabe der Wesen, und sie ist eine volle Bestimmung, wenn die Wesen soweit gegeben (bzw. ausdrücklich angegeben) sind, dass die Hinsicht und die Art des Habens bestimmt bezeichnet ist. S ist hinsichtlich ihrer Farbe sich selbst gleich, das ist unvollständig: Es ist sich selbst gleich hinsichtlich der Farbe an diesen oder jenen Teilen ihrer Körperlichkeit oder an allen Teilen. Das S hat noch andere Wesensbestimmtheiten (es hat als Sache und ein und dieselbe Sache noch verschiedene andere Wesen, die sich mit Farbe und Körperlichkeit einigen), aber auf dies kommt es für die Bestimmtheit der Relation nicht an.

Allgemein gilt das logische Gesetz, das wie für alle Prädikate, so für Relationsprädikate gilt: Das Prädikat ist überall dasselbe Prädikat nur dann (und vertritt sich nur dann, schließt sich also in der Negation als Widerspruch nur dann aus), wenn die Unbestimmtheit, die es enthält (oder die Gruppe von Leerstellen) Identität des Sinnes hat, also als dieselbe unbestimmte Bestimmbarkeit angesetzt wird.

Allerlei Paradoxien erwachsen daraus, dass man das Unbestimmte nicht im selben Sinn nimmt, und so auch die Insolubilia.

Fragt jemand mich: was urteilst du über diese Sache, was denkst du darüber, so kann ich antworten nichts! Aber damit urteile ich doch in Betreff dieser Sache. Natürlich ist der Sinn beiderseits ein anderer.

<11b> Ich spreche die Wahrheit. Ich lüge.

Das hat den Sinn: Was ich eben gesprochen habe oder sprechen werde, ist ein wahrer Satz, ist ein falscher Satz, auch: ist ein Satz, der mit meiner wahren Überzeugung streitet, etc.

Und das hat also nur Sinn, wenn ein Satz vorliegt, der den Inhalt des "Ich spreche die Wahrheit" bestimmt. Genau so "ich nenne": Seine Ergänzung fordert etwas, das ich nenne. Ein Name kann nicht sich selbst nennen, das ist ein Widersinn. Ein Satz sich nicht selbst setzen.

Ich kann sagen: Jeder Name ist ein Wort, jede namentliche Bedeutung ist eine Bedeutung. Dann befassen diese allgemeinen Sätze mit ihrer Wahrheit auch den Namen "Namen", auch die namentliche Bedeutung "namentliche Bedeutung".

Sie befassen sie logisch, in ihrer Allgemeinheit. Aber "Name" ist eine singuläre Bedeutung, das Wort Name ist ein singuläres Wort. Es kann das Wort nicht eigennennend auf sich selbst bezogen sein und die singuläre namentliche Bedeutung nicht als Eigenbedeutung auf sich selbst bezogen sein. Das ist widersinnig. Sage ich ⟨"⟩der Name Name⟨"⟩, so habe ich einen neuen Namen, der von dem Namen "Namen" verschieden ist, ein Name zweiter Stufe, usw.

Ein Satz kann "über alles und jedes" allgemein gesprochen eine Aussage machen, und ist er ein allgemeiner Satz über Sätze überhaupt, so bezieht sich diese Allgemeinheit des Satzes überhaupt auch auf den ausgesprochenen Satz selbst. (Sowohl für logische Sätze als ⟨auch⟩ für grammatische Sätze in gewisser Weise). Wieder aber ist zu sagen, dass ein singulärer Satz, dessen Sinn es ist, über einen bestimmten, wenn auch unbestimmt bezeichneten Satz etwas auszusagen, über ein Satzindividuum, nicht über sich selbst aussagen kann. Das gehört zum Wesen des Nennens und Aussagens. Eine Aussage, die sich selbst zum Subjekt hat, ist keine Aussage, ist überhaupt nichts.

⟨12a⟩Wir haben hier Relationen:

Die namentliche Bedeutung (der logische Name) und das Genannte als solches, das sind zwei Wesen, die in Relation treten. Die Aussagebedeutung und das Ausgesagte als solches, bzw. statt des Sachverhalts, das Worüber der Aussagebedeutung, das Gegenständliche im Subjekt oder Objekt, auf das sie sich bezieht.

Es handelt sich hier um Wesensrelationen: Die namentliche Bedeutung kann sich nicht selbst nennen, sonst hätten wir, könnte man sagen, eine Wesensrelation mit identischen Termini. Wie alle Wesensrelationen, so setzen die zwischen Namen und Genanntem, Aussagen und Ausgesagtem, verschiedene Termini voraus.

Das ist richtig. Andererseits aber gehört es zum Wesen des Nennens, des Aussagens, dass aus ihm eine Beziehung "entnommen" werden kann, es liegt in seinem Wesen, das notwendig zu unterscheiden ist zwischen der Bedeutung selbst und dem, worauf sie sich bezieht, und dass sie aufhört Bedeutung zu sein, oder vielmehr, dass sie nichts mehr ist, in sich aufgehoben ist, wenn ich ein Zweites, worauf sie sich bezieht, aufheben würde. Eben weil zum Wesen des Bedeutens ein Beziehen gehört, ist hier der Satz, dass Bedeutung und Bedeutetes nicht identisch sein können, ein Spezialfall des Satzes, dass Relation zwischen Wesen verschiedene Wesen als Fundamente voraussetzt.

Also überall, wo man zeigen kann, dass im Wesen eines Phänomens eine Relation liegt, oder dass ein Wesen in sich Relation zwischen Wesen birgt, da kann ich sowohl ohne Weiteres direkt einsehen, dass die bezogenen Wesen nicht zusammenfallen können, als ⟨auch⟩ sagen: Es ist das ein Spezialfall des Gesetzes, dass eine "Relation zwischen sich selbst" für Wesen ein Unsinn ist. Bringt man sich die Wesen zur Klarheit, bzw. bei den Paradoxien den Sinn zur Deutlichkeit und Klarheit, so sieht man sofort den Widersinn. Die Lösung der Paradoxien besteht aber in der Nachweisung der Sinnesverschiebungen, die es machen, dass man den Widersinn eben nicht gleich merkt, und nicht angeben kann, wenn man ihn durchfühlt, wo er liegt.

<12b> Was aber die Mengenparadoxien anlangt, so kann man sagen: wo immer der Mathematiker von Mengen spricht, muss er, wenn der Begriff ein mathematischer sein soll, ein Wesen Menge im Auge haben. Und was immer Menge dann für ein Wesen sein mag, es drückt mit eine Relation aus, die zum Wesen gehört: die zwischen Menge selbst und "Element" einer Menge. Eine Wesensrelation schließt aus, dass die Beziehungsglieder identisch sind. Also, eine Menge, die sich selbst als Element enthält, ist widersinnig.

Aber damit ist für den Mathematiker wenig getan. Denn es handelt sich für ihn darum zu verstehen, wie er in diese Begriffsbildung hineingerät, und wie das Wesen Menge in mathematischem Sinn berechtigt zu fassen und zu bestimmen ist.

Es fragt sich, ob der Begriff Menge wesentlich bezogen ist auf den der "mathematischen" Mannigfaltigkeit oder definiten Mannigfaltigkeit.

Die Definition einer Mannigfaltigkeit dieser Art (zu welcher die so genannten "Axiome" derselben gehören) definiert nicht nur ein allgemeines Wesen überhaupt, sondern definiert zunächst einen beschränkten Inbegriff von allgemeinen Wesen, die bestimmt sind durch "Axiome", vermöge deren sie allgemein Zusammenhang haben. In diesen Allgemeinheitsgruppen, mit welchen ein allgemeiner Zusammenhang als Mannigfaltigkeit definiert ist, sind nun beschlossen in der Weise, wie ein Allgemeines überhaupt Besonderheiten einschließt, Besonderheiten, und zwar als Wesensbesonderheiten; dies aber nicht etwa so, wie der Begriff ⟨"⟩sinnliche Qualität⟨"⟩ überhaupt alle uns bekannten und noch eventuell unbekannte enthält, und so, dass, wenn die besondere sinnliche Qualität gegeben ist, sie dem Allgemeinen unterzuordnen ist. Vielmehr ist jede mögliche Besonderheit der hier definierten Allgemeinheiten durch die Bedingungen der Definition konstruierbar. Jedes bestimmte Wesen bis zur niedersten Differenz ist angebbar, d.h. ist bestimmbar durch Begriffe, die aus den Definitionen als mögliche Begriffe ableitbar sind.

<13a> Alle ableitbaren Begriffe sind nun nach den "Axiomen" zu entscheiden nach Geltung und Nichtgeltung, und so grenzt sich die Idee einer Mannigfaltigkeit von "existierenden" Gebilden ab, das ist, von Besonderungen der definierten Allgemeinheiten, die wirklich gültige Besonderungen sind. Und alle Besonderungen derselben überhaupt sind vermöge der Definitionen und Axiome einerseits konstruierbar und andererseits auswertbar als gültig und ungültig, also alle möglichen Besonderungen sind gegeben oder zu geben, und alle sind als voll gegebene entschieden nach ihren Beschaffenheiten als wahr oder falsch.

Wir haben also die gesamte Definition und die Idee einer Allheit in ihr beschlossener, konstruierbarer möglicher Besonderheiten (und alle beschlossenen sind auch konstruierbar). Vielleicht können wir so sagen:

Bei jedem gültigen Begriff wie Farbe etc. können wir von der Idee eines a überhaupt übergehen zur Idee einzelner und beliebig zu vermehrender Gruppen, Mengen von möglichen Besonderheiten, und dann die Vorstellung "Allheit" der Besonderheiten bilden als die Idee einer denkenden Umfassung, die jedes a mit jedem zusammenbegreift. Dies ist die vage Allheit. Sie kommt zur Gegebenheit nur in der Form des willkürlichen Explizierens von Gruppen und der Einsicht, dass immer wieder Neues aufweisbar, vorstellbar ist, und dass, wenn irgend etwas a ist, es "hereingenommen" sein soll. Über diese Allheit können wir nichts weiter aussagen, als was uns die Allgemeinheit selbst, die allein gegeben ist, lehrt. Sie ist ein fraglicher und in gewisser Weise symbolisierender Begriff: Sie ordnet der Allgemeinheit sozusagen bildlich eine Menge zu; eine Menge, die nicht gegeben werden kann.

<13b> Ganz anders ist die Sachlage bei der definiten Mannigfaltigkeit. Hier ist das Bild einer Menge reicher: In einer Menge haben wir alles, was zu ihr gehört, beschlossen. In der Definition der Mannigfaltigkeit haben wir beschlossen immer neue und neue Besonderheiten, und zwar notwendig beschlossen, konstruierbar, festbestimmt. Und diese Bestimmtheit ist es, die Gegebenheit jedes besonderen Wesens, die es notwendig macht, dass jede Aussage über dieses Wesen durch die Definition nach Wahr und Falsch bestimmt ist.

Die Frage ist dann, was sind die notwendigen Bedingungen der Möglichkeit einer mathematischen Mannigfaltigkeit, und ist jede solche als eine Menge zu bezeichnen, in einem spezifischen Sinne? Oder haben wir nicht zu sagen: Zu jeder mathematischen Mannigfaltigkeit gehört eine vollständige Disjunktion von sich ausschließenden Wesen, in die jedes Besondere einzuordnen ist? Aber vielleicht in vielfacher Weise, oder müssen wir nicht sagen:

Wo immer wir den Fall haben, dass ein Allgemeines so definiert ist, dass es aufgrund der Definition in eine vollständige Disjunktion sich ausschließender Besonderheiten übergeführt werden kann, die sämtlich konstruierbar sind, da hat das Allgemeine eine Menge als Umfang. Und wieder: Führt dies nicht auf rein Formales zurück, d.h. auf formale Bedingungen der Möglichkeit der Konstruktion und Disjunktion in Besonderheiten? Also alle "Mannigfaltigkeiten", alle definiten Mannigfaltigkeiten und alle wie immer gearteten zugehörigen Mengen führen auf formale Mannigfaltigkeiten und Mengen formaler Natur zurück: Es müssen die Wesensartungen, die als Materie fungieren, formalisierbar sein. Das sind die Probleme. Man wird darauf kommen, dass Bedingungen der Möglichkeit der Konstruktion und der systematischen Disjunktion konstruierter Besonderheiten in "Anzahl" und "Ordnung" und in ihren verschiedenen Gestaltungen liegen, und dass sich daran die Begriffe von Menge, unendlicher Zahl etc. zu orientieren haben.

<14a> Die Menge aller Gegenstände überhaupt P.

Sie enthält sich selbst als Element.

Sie ist die größtmögliche; und doch soll es keine größtmögliche Anzahl geben.

Die Menge aller ihrer Untermengen ist selbst wieder ein Gegenstand, also in ihr enthalten als Untermenge.

Begriff der Menge.

Es fragt sich, ob wir so vorgehen können.

Wir gehen von reinen Allgemeinheiten (überhaupt) aus, und wo immer ein universelles Urteil gültig ist, sagen wir, es existiere diese Allgemeinheit (immer in Beschränkung auf reine Allgemeinheit). In diesem Sinne "existiert" die Allgemeinheit, ein Rotes überhaupt, aber auch ein Nicht-Rotes überhaupt. Denn in letzterer Hinsicht kann ich aussagen, irgendetwas überhaupt, das nicht rot ist, ist entweder eine gerade Zahl oder es ist nicht eine gerade Zahl, ein a oder nicht ein a usw. Ich kann vielerlei rein logische Aussagen machen, aber freilich, das ist das Eigentümliche reiner Negationen, nur solche disjunktiven und allenfalls hypothetischen Aussagen. Was im Wesen des negierten p liegt (ein Etwas-überhaupt, das nicht p ist), das kann ich nicht dem p substituieren, ich kann aber sagen: Liegt es im Wesen des p, nicht q zu sein, innerhalb der Gattung g, so ist ein Nicht-p überhaupt, wenn es von der Gattung g ist, auch ein Nicht-q u.dgl. Also allerlei Aussagen, und nicht bloß rein logisch weiterführende, kann ich machen. Die Allgemeinheit des non p "existiert", wofern nur p ein einstimmiger Begriff ist.

<14b> Nun ist die Frage, wann kann ich dem Überhaupt, oder diesem Allgemeinen, eine Menge zuordnen, einen Mengen-Umfang?

Nehmen wir ein Beispiel. Ein Kegelschnitt überhaupt. Hier kann ich sagen: Er ist entweder ein Kreis überhaupt oder eine Ellipse überhaupt oder Hyperbel überhaupt oder Parabel überhaupt. In vollständiger Disjunktion in diesem Fall nennen wir das Allgemeine 〈"〉Kegelschnitt〈"〉 Gattung und sagen, sie zerfalle in die Artallgemeinheiten, und zwar in vier Arten.

Was für Gedanken legt uns solch ein Beispiel nahe? Insbesondere, wenn wir es vergleichen mit dem Beispiel der reinen und seienden Allgemeinheit 〈"〉ein Rotes überhaupt〈"〉?

Versuchen wir, folgendes anzusetzen: Zu jeder reinen Allgemeinheit gibt es einen Umfang in folgendem Sinn. Gibt es ein a in Allgemeinheit, und das gibt es für jedes einstimmige Wesen, so gibt es auch Mehrheiten von Partikularitäten, von Besonderheiten, die unter die Allgemeinheit fallen. Wir sagen, eine Besonderheit der Allgemeinheit gibt es als reine Besonderheit, wenn ein a möglich ist. Und es ist dann möglich ein a, aber auch ein a und ein anderes a, ein a und ein anderes und ein drittes a usw. Jedes Allgemeine lässt sich in Reinheit bestimmt denken, es ist in besonderer Bestimmung möglich und vielfach möglich, d. h. wir können Mehrheiten denken (Mehrheiten von a sind möglich). Und wieder gilt es, dass, wenn irgendeine Mehrheit m von a als Möglichkeit gesetzt ist, eine Mehrheit m+n als Möglichkeit zu setzen ist und so *in infinitum*. Wir können nun den Gedanken der Allheit von möglichen Besonderheiten der Allgemeinheit verstehen, erhalten aber neben diesen Denkvorstellungen von immer neuen Vielheiten keinen reinen Allheitsbegriff, der in sich einstimmig vollziehbar wäre.

<15a> Die bildliche Vorstellung einer geschlossenen Vielheit oder eines Haufens, auch eines Umkreises mit dem Gedanken, dass da alle disjunkten Vielheiten von möglichen Besonderheiten oder jede ähnliche Einzelheit hineingehören soll und keine fehlen, kann zwar gebildet werden. Aber ob sie einen logisch zulässigen und nützlichen Begriff bildet, das steht bei der Struktur dieses Begriffs in Frage (der bloße Überhaupt-Gedanke, der einmal lautet ein Besonderes überhaupt und zusammenfällt mit ein a überhaupt, das andere Mal eine Gruppe von Besonderungen der Allgemeinheit überhaupt, kann wenig helfen. Es ist eine äquivalente Allgemeinheit, aber keine "Menge"). Nun nehmen wir den Fall, dass sich eine Allgemeinheit in eine vollständige Disjunktion von Arten "einteilen" lässt, dann ordnet sich jedes Besondere unter irgendein Glied dieser Disjunktion, und so, wenn wir wieder vollständig injungieren können, immerfort.

Wir versuchen nun, den Begriff der "Menge" oder der mathematischen Allheit zu fassen als den Inbegriff der Glieder einer solchen vollständigen Disjunktion von Arten, in die sich das in Rede stehende leitende Allgemeine einteilt. Wir würden dann also den Begriff der Menge jeweils beziehen auf einen Begriff und ausschließlich auf einen solchen Begriff, der sich einteilen lässt.

Die Frage ist, ob das irgendwelchen Nutzen hat. Man sieht nicht recht, welchen. Die Redeweise ist zunächst noch unbrauchbar. Denn man wird doch nicht sagen, die Menge des Begriffs Kegelschnitt, das sei die Menge seiner Arten. Und von Mengen eines Begriffs sprechen wir doch überhaupt nicht, sondern allenfalls von Mengen aller Kegelschnitte oder von der Menge der Arten der Gattung Kegelschnitt.

Tasten wir uns weiter. Wir nehmen gar nicht den "Umfang" von Kegelschnitt <15b> im Bild etwa eines Haufens "aller einzelnen Kegelschnitte", vielmehr nehmen wir die Gattung Kegelschnitt in Hinsicht auf ihre Arten und verstehen "alle Kegelschnitte" als alle Arten. Wir schreiben also nur Gattungsbegriffen, nicht allen Allgemeinbegriffen, einen Mengen-Umfang zu, und zwar mit Beziehung auf seine Einteilung in Arten: nur dann, wenn eine solche Einteilung gegeben bzw. aufweisbar ist, in Form einer vollständigen Disjunktion.

Wenn die Disjunktion in reinem Denken ausweisbar, also das disjunktive Urteil in seiner Vollständigkeit begründbar ist, so ist uns die Menge des Umfangs gegeben. Natürlich: Wenn wir annehmen, es gebe solch ein Urteil oder solch eine disjunktive Wahrheit, so nehmen wir damit an, der Begriff habe einen Mengenumfang (wirklich einen Umfang) etc.

Welche Möglichkeiten für solche disjunktiven Wahrheiten haben wir nun?

Zwei Möglichkeiten: Entweder die Anzahl der Glieder der Disjunktion ist eine "endliche", oder sie ist eine unendliche.

Oder deutlicher: Entweder wir kommen auf eine "geschlossene" Disjunktion, mit der uns ein geschlossener Inbegriff von Disjunktionsgliedern, eine einheitliche Kollektion, und in dieser jedes Glied wirklich gegeben ist;

oder wir kommen auf eine Disjunktion, die ein notwendiges "Usw." oder mehrere solche Usw., deren jedes die Idee der Bestimmtheit der fortgehenden Konstruktion mit sich führt, enthält, diesen Index der Unendlichkeit.

Im ersten Fall entspricht der Disjunktion eine Anzahl von Disjunktionsgliedern, eine Anzahl als die Form eines geschlossenen Plurals. Im zweiten Fall entspricht ihr eine einfache oder mehrfache unendliche "Zahl", eine Anzahl im erweiterten Cantorschen Sinn, oder eine Mannigfaltigkeits-Zahl.

<16a> So ist die Anzahl der Anzahlen (d. h. die zur Gattung Anzahl gehörige Form der einteilenden Disjunktion in Arten) eine "unendliche Anzahl"; jede Anzahl (d. h. jede Art der Gattung Anzahl im gewöhnlichen Sinn der Form einer geschlossenen Mehrheit) entweder 2 oder 3 oder 4 "usw.", und das ist eine vollständige Disjunktion. Nicht nur kann ich von jedem Möglichen aussagen, ob es Zahl ist oder nicht (ob etwas einem Begriff gemäß ist oder nicht, das "kann" ich von jedem aussagen, das ist allweil objektiv, nämlich bestimmt, und nur darauf kommt es an), sondern ich kann, *a priori* dem Wesen der Zahl nachgehend, die Reihe der Zahlen erzeugen, in die sich jede Zahl notwendig einordnet.

Ich kann nicht nur zu jeder vorgegebenen Vielheit von Anzahlen noch neue Anzahlen hinzufügen, die als leere Möglichkeiten unter die Idee Anzahl fallen; sondern die Idee der Anzahl schreibt deduktiv-gesetzlich die Notwendigkeit für alle Besonderheiten vor, und diese Besonderheiten sind gegeben als im gleichen Sinne existierend wie die Idee Anzahl selbst, und sie existieren in der Einheit der Anzahlenreihe, die unendlich ist, aber trotzdem ein Feld vollständiger Disjunktion darstellt. Es handelt sich um ein bestimmtes Usw., mit dem wir die Anzahlreihe aussprechen: Aus jeder Anzahl geht nach demselben Relationsgesetz ein bestimmtes Glied als neue und nächste Anzahl fort "usw.".

Nun wäre zu erforschen, was die Bedingungen der Möglichkeit solcher vollständigen und apriorischen Einteilung sind, und damit zusammenhängend: was für Formen von "Mengen", von Mannigfaltigkeiten es prinzipiell geben kann.

Und weiter ist zu erklären, warum wir uns auf diese reine Sphäre beschränkt <16b> haben, da doch auch empirische Begriffe eventuell einen zählbaren Umfang (da ist eine Menge von Begriffsgegenständen) haben können.

Weiter sind die Cantorschen Gesetze der Mannigfaltigkeitslehre abzuleiten, die offenbar auf die Zusammensetzung vollständiger Disjunktionen zu umfassenden vollständigen Disjunktionen zurückgehen, parallel mit der Einordnung der Leitbegriffe unter einen umfassenden Begriff, der sie selbst als Glieder einer Disjunktion, und einer einteilenden, befasst.

Oder auch umgekehrt: Wenn wir schon die Mengenformen als Formen, die vollständige Disjunktion ermöglichen, haben, können wir ideell diese Formen kombinieren, zusammensetzen, multiplizieren etc., immer geleitet von der Idee von möglichen reinen Begriffen, der in diesen Formen eben Formen reiner Einteilungen hat.

Nach dem Gespräch mit Koyré[6] scheint es mir aber doch, dass auch ein weiterer brauchbarer Begriff von Menge möglich und für den Mathematiker zu Anfang nötig ist. Es scheint, dass Koyrés Begriff darauf hinauskommt, dass ein Klassenbegriff als ⟨"⟩Gesamtheit der A⟨"⟩ überall berechtigt ist, wo das Partikularurteil, ⟨"⟩es gibt ein A⟨"⟩ (wo *ein* ein positiver Begriff ist), wahr ist. ⟨"⟩Etwas, das nicht A ist⟨"⟩, das gibt keinen berechtigten Begriff, da mit der Negation "paradoxe Mengen" hineinkommen, die auf sich selbst bezogen wären. Doch muss das noch überlegt werden.

<17a>
Menge P aller Gegenstände überhaupt.
Das Russell'sche Paradoxon.

Alle Mengen zerfallen in zwei Klassen:
a) Mengen, die sich selbst als Element enthalten,
b) Mengen, die es nicht tun, die unter ihren Mengen nicht vorkommen.

---

6 Alexandre Koyré (1892–1964) had studied with Husserl in Göttingen from the Winter Semester 1908/09 to 1912 and again in the Summer Semester 1913.

Betrachten wir nun die Mengen aller Mengen b), d.h. die nicht sich selbst enthalten: $\mathcal{M}$.

Gehört $\mathcal{M}$ zu a) oder b)?

Nach dem Satz vom ausgeschlossenen Dritten: eins von beiden.

Man kann aber zeigen, dass keines von beiden oder auch beides gelten müsste.

Denn gehörte sie zu a), so hieße das, sie enthielte sich selbst, das widerspräche ihrer Definition. Ist sie also von der Art b)? Aber dann wäre $\mathcal{M}$ nicht die Menge *aller* b's.

Einwand von Schoenflies[7]: Es gibt keine Mengen, die sich selbst als Element enthalten.

Er müsste nur sagen, dass das widersinnig ist.

Und in der Tat geht aus dem Paradoxon hervor, wenn keine Begriffsverschiebung nachzuweisen ist, dass eine Menge der Art a) oder eine Menge der Art b) ein Widersinn sein muss. Dann ist auch die Einteilung widersinnig. Oder endlich, wenn beides nicht der Fall wäre, ob die $\mathcal{M}$ nicht widersinnig ist.

(Da das eine Glied ganz sicher Sinn hat, so haben wir zwei Fälle: entweder der Begriff a) ist widersinnig, oder der Begriff der $\mathcal{M}$.)

Die Einteilung soll als mathematische den Sinn haben einer Einteilung aller <u>möglichen</u> Mengen überhaupt unabhängig von Fragen realer Existenz, die auf reale Dinge des Daseins statt auf mögliche Dinge überhaupt, mögliches Gezähltes, Kollidiertes überhaupt geht.

<17b> Russell. Die Menge aller nicht-roten Dinge.

Die Menge aller nicht im Meer lebenden Dinge.

Die gehören sich selbst als Elemente an, da sie nicht selbst rote Dinge, im Meer lebende Dinge sind.

Hier stehen wir aber entweder in der real-existenzialen Sphäre, und die geht uns gar nichts an, oder in der idealen Sphäre. Dann aber ist die Frage, ob die betreffenden reinen Mengen überhaupt Ideale "Existenz", ob sie Möglichkeit haben.

---

7 Arthur Schoenflies (1853–1928), had studied mathematics in Berlin under Weierstrass, shortly before Husserl, 1870–1875 and was professor in Göttingen until 1899. The reference here is to his 1911 "Über die Stellung der Definition in der Axiomatik" in *Jahresbericht der Deutschen Mathematiker-Vereinigung* 20, 222–255, specifically his critical discussion of Zermelo's appropriation of Russell's "aεa" on p. 243 and its explicit exclusion on p. 245.

Richard's Paradoxon.

Irgendeine Zahl kann auf viele mögliche Weisen definiert werden. Im Allgemeinen brauchen wir mehr Worte, je größer die Zahl ist.

Wir ordnen nun so, dass wir anfangen mit der Definition, die die kleinste Zahl von Worten braucht, und dann weiter nach der Zahl der Worte. So bekommen wir eine bestimmte Anordnung der Zahl selbst. Unter den Zahlen, die mindestens 100 Worte zur Benennung fordern, gibt es sicher eine kleinste:

Die kleinste mit mindestens 100 Worten benennbare Zahl (nicht unter 100 Worten benennbar).

1   2   3   ⟨4⟩   5   6   7   8

Aber jede Zahl ist doch mit 8 Zahlworten nennbar. Widerspruch.

Englisch: die kleinste Zahl, die nicht nennbar ist mit 19 Silben: 11777 (auszusprechen!) Der eine Ausspruch ist aber mit 18 Silben (englisch).

⟨18a⟩Im Begriff der Menge liegt, dass die Menge eine Einheit ihrer Elemente ist.

Einheit, was besagt das? Warum ist die Menge aller Mengen, die Gesamtheit des Seienden überhaupt, der gesamte Inbegriff aller Möglichkeiten, keine Menge?

a und b und c,   (a), (b), (a und b)
Mengen, Zahlen   0 1 2 3 4 ... (ω)
Ganze (Einheiten, Vereinigungen) _____.

_____.

(alle Mengen) M'

1) Jedes Element einer Menge von jedem anderen verschieden (disjunkt),

2) jedes Element ⟨ist⟩ in der Menge enthalten. Die Menge eine Einheit aus den Elementen, die charakterisiert sind als die ihren,

3) und jedes einzelne, was zur Menge gehört, ist als solches irgend ausgezeichnet und unterschieden von jedem, das nicht zu ihr gehört.

[4] Jede Menge hat mehr als ein Element (mindestens noch eins)]

5) Hat eine Menge Teilmengen, so hat sie neben den Elementen der Teilmengen noch mindestens ein Element, hat sie mehrere Teilmengen, so ist notwendig eine Teilung der Menge in disjunkte Teilmengen (und einzelne Elemente) möglich.

⟨18b⟩[8]
⟨first group⟩

$$\frac{A}{\frac{+V}{\subseteq F}}$$

$$\frac{A}{\mathcal{A} \cdot V \subseteq F}$$

$$\frac{\mathcal{A} \subseteq \mathcal{F}1}{\mathcal{A} \subseteq (V \subseteq F)}$$

$$\frac{A \subseteq \mathcal{F}1}{A \subseteq V \subseteq (\mathcal{F} \cdot \mathcal{F}1)}$$

$$\mathcal{A} \subseteq \underbrace{V \subseteq 0}$$

⟨second group⟩
  A / $a \; \varepsilon \; \mathcal{L}$
    $a \; \varepsilon_0 \; \mathcal{L}$

$a = a_{\alpha\beta} \ldots$
$A \subseteq x_\alpha$ so $x_{\beta 0}$, x_β so $x_{\alpha 0}$
$x_{\alpha\beta} \ldots$ ist ein "widersprüchlicher Begriff"

⟨third group⟩

Ind⟨irect⟩ $A \subseteq B$ B_0!

---

[8] Page 18b of the manuscript contains various formulae which are not readily decipherable and do not have an obvious link to each other or the surrounding text. They might be annotations relating to another text. We can distinguish three groups among the formulae. The first seems to deal with the relation of a set and its subsets, perhaps related to the argument that a set cannot be its own subset. The second appears to deal with a set and its elements and how specific combinations of elements might yield a contradictory concept. The third might have to do with existential axioms in set theory. The three groups contain too little actual text to support a univocal interpretation. We reproduce here, insofar as possible, the three groups. Husserl has horizontal lines instead of the slashes and uses Schröder's notation (an equals sign drawn through a subset symbol, which looks almost like an Euro sign) instead of the modern symbol.

	A_0!	
Axiom.	Existenzbeweis:	$\mathcal{A} \subseteq$ existiert ein A+B für jedes A und B
$G_{\alpha\beta...\mu}$	$(\varepsilon \subseteq \alpha \cdot \alpha_0 \subseteq 0) \subseteq \varepsilon_0$!	

<19a>Satz vom Widerspruch.

Jedem Gegenstand kommt jedes beliebige Prädikat entweder zu oder nicht zu.

Ist G irgendein Gegenstand und p irgendein Prädikat, so gilt eins von beiden und nur eins von beiden: G ist p, oder G ist nicht p.

Irgendein Gegenstand heißt nicht irgendein Ding, sondern irgendein Seiendes, irgend etwas, das ist, irgend etwas überhaupt.

Ist G irgendetwas = Ist G, entspricht dem Begriff G ein Etwas, ein Seiendes – ist ein Rundes nicht rund, =R, also ist R.

So ist eins und nur eins von beiden, R ist rund, R ist nicht rund.

Ist aber R, so ist es rund und ist es nicht rund.

Also ist R, so ist nur eins von beiden, ist beides ⟨R ist rund, R ist nicht rund⟩, so ist R nicht;

ist R, so ist nicht nur eins von beiden (sondern beides), also ist R, so ist R nicht. Ist R nicht, so sind beide Sätze falsch.

Der gegenwärtige Kaiser von Frankreich ist blond, ist nicht blond.

Beide Sätze sind gegenstandslos; sage ich, der gegenwärtige Kaiser ist blond, so liegt darin, dass Frankreich gegenwärtig einen blonden Kaiser hat, und es hat überhaupt keinen Kaiser.

 a) gegenstandslose Sätze,
 b) falsche im eigentlichen Sinn.

Der Satz ist falsch, d. h., sich auf den Boden des Redners stellen, der da voraus angenommen und hingestellt hat ⟨"⟩der französische Kaiser⟨"⟩ der Gegenwart als den wirklich Seienden. Diese Assertion als kategorisch nehme ich nicht an. Daher komme ich gar nicht in die Logik, sie hat das ⟨, was⟩ in der Prädikation liegt, überhaupt zu erwägen. (Dazu ist kein Anlass mehr. Der Satz gilt nicht, weil er gegenstandslos ist.

<19b>[9] Ein Satz gilt nicht, weil er gegenstandslos ist (faktisch oder vermöge eines Widerspruchs im Subjektterminus). Ein Satz gilt nicht, weil er von seinem

---

9 On the top right side of the page, clearly an older text: "Berlin Samstag 7.II.1880". In 1880 Husserl was still studying mathematics and philosophy in Berlin.

Gegenstand etwas behauptet, was ihm nicht zukommen kann, der Satz ist widersinnig hinsichtlich seiner Prädikation.

Ein Satz gilt nicht, weil er von seinem Gegenstand, dessen Existenz gilt oder als gültig zugestanden wird, etwas aussagt, was Gegenständen dieser Art überhaupt nicht zukommt, oder was diesem Gegenstand allein faktisch nicht zukommt.

<20a> Kann eine Menge sich selbst als Teilmenge enthalten?

Verstehen wir unter Teilmenge jede Menge, die überhaupt nur Elemente von $\mathcal{M}$ enthält (als ihre Elemente), so hat jede Menge sich selbst als Teilmenge.

Verstehen wir unter Teilmenge nur jede Menge, die nur Elemente von $\mathcal{M}$ enthält unter ihren Elementen, aber mindestens ein Element von $\mathcal{M}$ unter ihren Elementen nicht enthält, so enthält keine Menge sich selbst als Teilmenge.

Kann eine Menge ⟨sich⟩ selbst als Element enthalten?

Gelten könnte das natürlich nur von Mengen von Mengen (unter den Elementen Mengen vorkommend). Denn Mengen sind Allheiten von Elementen irgendeines Merkmals µ.

Also müsste das betreffende Element eine Allheit sein.

Gesamtmenge aller Mengen (aller möglichen Mengen, aber auch aller realen Mengen), Gesamtheit alles Möglichen überhaupt: Dies ist ja selbst ein Mögliches, wenn diese Gesamtheit zugelassen werden soll; entweder sie ist etwas Widerspruchsvolles oder sie ist selbst Element.

Zur Intention der Rede von einem Inbegriff, einer Vielheit ... gehört, dass aus Denkobjekten ein Neues gebildet werden soll, das durch die vorgegebenen bestimmt ist, aber erst durch die Bildung erwächst. Es widerspricht diesem Gedanken, dass unter den Objekten das Resultat der Bildung vorkommen könnte. Gehen wir von Begriffen aus, so kann dergleichen wohl vorkommen, dass die unter den Begriff zu Summierenden und das Bildungsresultat unter demselben Begriff stehen <20b> oder deutlicher, dass das Bildungsresultat sich dem Begriff unterordnet, dass die Bildung selbst geleitet oder in derselben die Einheit zu bestimmen hätte. Dann ist solch ein Begriff aber zur Inbegriffsbildung unbrauchbar.

Ich würde also sagen: Zur Idee der Menge gehört es, eine Einheit zu sein, ja gleichsam ein Ganzes, das gewisse "Elemente" als Teile umfasst, aber so, dass sie den Elementen gegenüber ein Neues ist, das erst durch sie gebildet wird. Ein Ganzes kann nicht sein eigener Teil, eine Vielheit ⟨kann⟩ nicht ihr eigenes Element, ⟨Element⟩ ihrer eigenen Einheit sein.

So wie es widersprechend ist, dass ein Ganzes zugleich sein eigener Teil, so ist es widersprechend, dass ein Mengenganzes sein eigenes Element sei. Daraus, dass ich von allen Mengen, allen Möglichkeiten sprechen kann, folgt nicht, dass die Allheit der Mengen wieder als Menge, die Allheit der Möglichkeiten wieder als eine Möglichkeit angesehen werden könnte.

Alle mathematisch-logischen Operationen, die mit Mengen gemacht werden, hängen daran, dass Mengen sich als eine Art von Ganzen ansehen lassen, als neue Einheiten, Gebilde, die etwas Neues sind gegenüber ihren fundierenden Einheiten, so dass aus diesen Gebilden dann wieder als Einheiten neue Gebilde usw. gebildet werden können.

Die Einheit einer Ordnung ist etwas Neues gegenüber den geordneten Elementen. Es wäre ein Widersinn, dass die Ordnungseinheit selbst eines unter den Elementen derselben Ordnung sein könnte, auf die sich die Ordnung gründet. Aber Ordnungseinheiten können selbst wieder geordnet werden und begründen dann höhere Ordnungsformen, sie treten dann aber als Elemente in neue Ordnungsganze.

<21>

Elemente haben die logische Priorität vor dem Ganzen, vor der Einheit im weitesten Sinn. Sie sind vorgegeben. Wir müssen ein Gesetz haben, dass sie einheitlich bestimmt, oder wir müssen ein Gesetz supponieren können, das sie alle (d.h. jedes) ergibt. Derweil können wir einen Mengenbegriff bilden als Gesamtheit der durch das Gesetz vorgegebenen und in eins gesetzten Elemente. Haben wir ein Prinzip, das die Möglichkeit jedes einzelnen Falls und der Einheit der Verträglichkeit jedes beliebigen mit jedem beliebigen gewährleistet, dann gibt dieses eine hinreichende Einheit zur Mengenbildung. Jedes einzelne "ist" dasselbe und ist verträglich mit jedem anderen, und so ist die Einheit des sie umfassenden Gedankens und Inbegriffs eine Verträglichkeit.

Bloße Reden wie die: "eine Menge, welche jede ihrer Teilmengen als Elemente enthält", verbürgen nichts. Im Voraus kann ich nicht vermeiden, gelegentlich von Mengen im Allgemeinen zu reden. Dann bin ich aber gebunden an die Logik, die verlangt, dass Mengen, echte Mannigfaltigkeiten, sicher den formalen Regeln der Ganzen unterstehen müssen. Verträglichkeit in der Einheit muss bestehen oder vielmehr: Jede mögliche Einheit verbürgt Verträglichkeit, und Verträglichkeit sagt nichts als Möglichkeit in einer Einheit. Zur Möglichkeit in der Einheit gehört aber auch die Vermeidung des Widerspruchs, dass das geeinigte Ganze nicht selbst sein Element sein soll, das Ganze sein eigener Teil.

<22a>

I. $\mathcal{M}$, welche jede ihrer Teilmengen als Element enthält.
1) nehme ich ein Element (z.B. eine beliebige Teilmenge) dieser Menge weg,

1) hat eine Menge von vornherein die Eigenschaft $\mathcal{M}$, so kann sie sie auch nicht verlieren, wenn wir ein Element von ihr wegnehmen. Der Beweis wird

so hat $\mathcal{M}$-1 entweder wieder die Beschaffenheit $\mathcal{M}$ oder nicht.
α) hat sie es nicht, so hätten wir eine Menge $\mathcal{M}_0$, welche die Eigenschaft hätte, dass die Hinzufügung eines einzigen Elements ihr die Eigenschaft $\mathcal{M}$ gibt. Das ist widersinnig. Denn wenn $\mathcal{M}$ mehr als ein einzelnes Element überhaupt hat, so erwachsen durch das neue Glied sicher Teilmengen, Mengen, die in $\mathcal{M}$ noch nicht enthalten waren. Jede Verknüpfung mit einem bisherigen Element ergäbe eine Menge und eine neue. Denn wäre e_a ein letztes Element, und e das neue, und wäre $e_a e$ schon da, so müsste es auch e sein, weil jede Teilmenge von Teilmengen, dem Begriff von $\mathcal{M}$ gemäß, in $\mathcal{M}$ enthalten sind.
β) also müsste die Wegnahme eines Elements aus $\mathcal{M}$ wieder ein $\mathcal{M}$ machen. Und so könnte jedes Element, jede beliebige Gruppe (Menge) von Elementen herausgenommen werden, ohne Störung des Charakters von $\mathcal{M}$. Halte ich nur eine endliche Zahl von Elementen, etwa 2 übrig, so hätte ich also eine endliche $\mathcal{M}$. Das ist aber absurd. (M. a. W., jede Teilmenge müsste die Eigenschaft $\mathcal{M}$ haben.)

aber besser gleich so geführt, dass man statt eines Elements eine beliebige Menge µ nimmt. Der Beweis bleibt im Wesen derselbe, es gilt wohl auch der Satz: hat $\mathcal{M}$ die Eigenschaft, so verliert sie sie sofort durch Hinzusetzung eines neuen Elements.

1) hat eine Menge von vornherein die Eigenschaft $\mathcal{M}$, so kann sie sie auch nicht verlieren, wenn wir ein Element von ihr wegnehmen. Der Beweis wird aber besser gleich so geführt, dass man statt eines Elements eine beliebige Menge µ nimmt. Der Beweis bleibt im Wesen derselbe, es gilt wohl auch der Satz: hat $\mathcal{M}$ die Eigenschaft, so verliert sie sie sofort durch Hinzusetzung eines neuen Elements.

2) hat eine Menge M nicht von vornherein die Eigenschaft $\mathcal{M}$, so kann sie diese Eigenschaft nicht durch Hinzufügung eines einzigen Elements erhalten, (nach α). Aber auch nicht durch Hinzufügung einer beliebigen wie immer defi-

nierten Mannigfaltigkeit μ. Angenommen M+ μ hatte die Eigenschaft $\mathcal{M}$. Ist nun ε irgendein Element von M, so ergibt ε+μ wieder eine Menge, die Teilmenge von M+μ sein müsste (denn $\mathcal{M}$ hat ja die Eigenschaft, jede ihrer Teilmengen zu enthalten, εμ wäre aber eine Teilmenge), usw.

<22b>Folge: Es kann überhaupt keine Menge $\mathcal{M}$ geben, denn jede Menge enthält Mengen, nämlich andere Mengen, etwa Paare, die nicht die Eigenschaft $\mathcal{M}$ haben. Aus Mengen, die diese Eigenschaft nicht haben, kann ein $\mathcal{M}$ aber nicht entstehen.

Man kann auch hübsch so argumentieren:

1) Jede Teilmenge müsste schon die Eigenschaft $\mathcal{M}$ haben, z. B. μ, denn jede Menge kann ich zerlegen in μ+M, und wenn μ sie schon nicht hätte, könnte M+μ sie nicht erlangen (nach 2).

2) keine Teilmenge von $\mathcal{M}$ kann die Eigenschaft $\mathcal{M}$ haben, denn wenn sie sie hätte, so könnte keine aus ihr durch Addition entstandene sie noch besitzen (nach α).

<23a>
Gesetz = Formel

1) Aus einer Beziehung ρ (einem Gesetz dafür) folgt durch Besonderung, Substitution nur wieder eine Beziehung ρ, aber eine besondere. Also eine neue Beziehung folgt daraus nie, also kann keine der Substituierungen einer neuen Beziehung – nie – Widerspruch hereinbringen.

2) Wenn man ein zweigliedriges Beziehungsgesetz hat, so kann man daraus durch Substitution einer definierten Verknüpfung von zwei Gliedern dreigliedrige ableiten, und kann kombinatorisch alle dreigliedrigen Formeln aufstellen, die daraus folgen. Wird also ein neues dreigliedriges Gesetz als Axiom aufgestellt, so ist seine Independenz und Widerspruchslosigkeit gesichert, wenn es in diesen Konsequenzen nicht vorkommt.

3) Widersprüche können überhaupt nur entstehen, wenn neben einem Beziehungsgesetz für ρ auch ein Gesetz aufgestellt ist für nicht-ρ (= nicht=), oder wenn neue Beziehungen eingeführt werden, die, sei es überhaupt, sei es für gewisse angegebene Fälle (gattungsmäßig bestimmte) das nicht-ρ bedingen (das ρ ausschließen).

4) Wenn eine neue dreigliedrige Beziehung die Form nicht-ρ haben soll, so darf sie sich nicht in der Gruppe der dreigliedrigen ρ-Folgerungen befinden, und jede nicht darin enthaltene dreigliedrige Beziehung kann als eine Nicht-ρ⟨-Beziehung⟩ angesetzt werden.

Überhaupt also: Kombinatorisch kann ich aus den bereits angesetzten verträglichen Formeln alle möglichen für den Typus ableiten, den eine neu festzusetzende ρ oder nicht-ρ Formel haben soll. Der besondere Typus, den ich festsetze, darf dann nicht unter den schon implizite festgelegten Typen liegen: Entweder er ist überflüssig oder widersprechend.

<23b>
$a+b=b+a$
$(a+b)+c=a+(b+c)$

$ab=ba$ $\qquad$ $a(b+c)=ab+ac$

Widerspruch $a=b$, $a>b$, nicht $b>a$.
$a =$ oder $>$ oder $< b$, $a+b>a$, $b \gtreqless 0$, $a+0=a$

Gebiet der unmittelbaren und mittelbaren logischen Einsichten
gleich $\quad$ 1 $\quad$ 2 $\quad$ 3 $\quad$ 4
$\qquad\quad$ 1+1 $\quad$ 2+1 $\quad$ 3+1
a $\quad$ a+c
b $\quad$ b+c
a+b $\;$ (a+b)+c

$(a+c)+b = b+(a+c)$
$a+(b+c) = (b+c)+a$
$(a+b)+c = c+(a+b)$

Verteile alle möglichen Änderungen in den Klammern, so bekomme ich alle möglichen dreigliedrigen Gleichungen kombinatorisch. Darunter findet sich das assoziative Gesetz nicht. Ebenso folgt aus dem assoziativen das kommutative ⟨Gesetz⟩ ohne Nullsetzung nicht, mit Nullsetzung etc.

<u>Menge</u>
$A+B$

Allheit der α als Menge
1) die als Einheit, als Ganzes betrachtet werden kann,
2) jedes solche Ganze soll mit jedem zum Ganzen derselben Art verbindbar sein. $M+M'=M''$
3) Jede Allheit, die aus A durch Ausschluss von Elementen hervorgeht, soll wieder ein Ganzes derselben Art sein. $M-M'=M''$

<24a>

Zermelo argumentiert:

Eine Menge M, welche jeder ihrer Teilmengen als Elemente enthält, ist eine inkonsistente Menge.

1) wir betrachten diejenigen Teilmengen, welche sich selbst nicht als Element enthalten,
   2) diese bilden in ihrer Gesamtheit eine Menge M_0, die in M enthalten ist.
      Definition: M_0 ist die Gesamtheit (=Menge) der Teilmengen von M, die sich selbst nicht als Element enthalten.
   3) M_0 ist also Element von M,
   4) M_0 ist nicht Element von M_0.

Beweis: wäre M_0 Element von M_0, so würde es eine Teilmenge von M enthalten (nämlich M_0), die sich selbst als Element enthält.

Aber M_0 soll ex definitione nur Teilmengen von M enthalten, die sich nicht als Element enthalten.

5) also M_0, da es nicht Element von M_0 ist, ist eine Teilmenge von M, die sich selbst nicht als Element enthält. Aber alle solche Mengen sind ex definitione im Begriff von M_0 befaßt, also im Gegensatz zu 4: M_0 ist doch Element von M_0. Wir kommen zum direkten Widerspruch.

Gehört es wesentlich zum Begriff der Menge, dass (ohne Widerspruch) keine Menge sich selbst als Element enthalten kann, so ist M_0 und M identisch dieselbe Menge, und die ganze Schlussweise wird hinfällig.

<25a>
<u>Zur Lehre vom Definiten.</u>
Zu Weyl, Brouwer, "Entscheidungsdefinitheit".
Hat sicher die formale Logik der Existenzsätze und somit auch <u>meine Paradoxie</u>. [Wenn etwas a ist, ist es b = es "gibt" kein a̶b̶, ergibt: es <u>kann</u> ein a geben b̶ ≠ es <u>gibt</u> ein a̶b̶]
Beziehung: Diese Paradoxie muss also mit erwogen werden.
Protagoras' Angriff gegen die rein geometrischen Gebilde.
Aristoteles, Metaphysik B 3 (?) 997b 32.[10]

<26a>
Russell'sches Paradoxon.

---

[10] The reference is mostly correct, 997b contains critical remarks on Plato's doctrine of ideas, Protagoras is then explicitly mentioned on 998a.

Alle Mengen zerfallen in solche, die sich selbst als Element enthalten, und solche, die das nicht tun. Als was ist die Menge aller Mengen anzusehen, die sich selbst nicht als Element enthalten? Enthält sie sich selbst nicht als Element, so ist sie nicht die Menge aller Mengen, die sich nicht selbst enthalten. Enthält sie sich aber selbst, so ist unter der Menge aller Mengen, die sich <26b> nicht selbst als Element enthalten, eine, die sich selbst als Element enthält.

<27a>
Logik
Russell: Vortrag "L'importance Philosophique de la Logistique" Conférence faite à l'École des Hautes Études sociales le 22 mars 1911. Revue de Métaphysique et de Morale 19 (Mai 1911) <281–291>.

Annahme, dass alle Zahlen "der vollständigen Induktion genügen".
Def: eine "erbliche Eigenschaft" einer Zahl ist eine solche, die sich auf $n+1$ bezieht, vorausgesetzt, dass sie sich auf n bezog.
So ist die Eigenschaft, >100 zu sein, eine erbliche Eigenschaft: Wenn sie irgendeiner Zahl zukommt, so kommt sie der nächstgrößeren Zahl zu.
Wir verstehen unter einer "induktiven Eigenschaft" eine erbliche Eigenschaft, welche die Zahl Null besitzt. (D.h. wohl jede erbliche Eigenschaft, die der Zahl Null zukommt.) Eine solche Eigenschaft kommt dann natürlich allen Zahlen der gewöhnlichen Zahlenreihe zu.
Eine solche "induktive Eigenschaft" ist die folgende:
Wenn irgendeine Menge die Anzahl n hat, so hat kein Teil dieser Menge dieselbe Anzahl n.
Da jede induktive Eigenschaft Eigenschaft aller Zahlen ist, so ist es ein Widerspruch mit dem eben angegebenen Satz, dass es eine Menge geben sollte, die dieselbe Anzahl hat als irgendeiner ihrer Teile.
Dieser Widerspruch besteht nicht mehr, wenn es Zahlen geben sollte, welche nicht alle induktiven Eigenschaften haben. Und dann findet man, dass im Begriff einer unendlichen Zahl kein Widerspruch existiert (im Gegensatz zu Leibniz, der eben einen Widerspruch in ihr finden wollte, darin bestehend, dass sie mit den angegebenen Sätzen in Widerspruch käme <Russel a.a.O., p. 282>). Cantor hat eine ganze Arithmetik der unendlichen Zahlen geschaffen und vollständig die alten Probleme über die Natur des Unendlichen gelöst <a.a.O., p. 283>. Mit ihnen innig verbunden sind die Probleme des Kontinuums, und ⟨sie⟩ kommen damit zu ihrer vollen Lösung. Zeno's Argumente, die Probleme von Raum, Zeit und Bewegung, eine widerspruchslose Theorie, welche das Kontinuum komponiert aus einer unendlichen Anzahl von disjunkten Elementen; was man früher für unmöglich gehalten hätte.

<27b>
Folge: eine Revolution in der Philosophie des Raumes und der Zeit. Man hätte die "realistischen" Theorien für Widersprüche gehalten, sie sind es aber – wie sich zeigt – nicht, und die "idealistischen" Theorien haben ihre Kraft verloren.

Die Theorie der unendlichen Zahlen und der Natur des Kontinuums, die mathematische Theorie der Bewegung und anderer Kontinua verbindet zwei korrelative Begriffe: den der Funktion und den der Variablen.

Beispiel: Wenn dieselbe Ursache sich reproduziert, so muss sich derselbe Effekt wiederholen. Aber dieselbe Ursache, sagt man zugleich, kehrt nie wieder. Was in Wahrheit statthat, ist eine konstante Beziehung zwischen Ursachen einer bestimmten Art und den Wirkungen, die daraus resultieren. Dass eine solche konstante Beziehung statthat, ist die Wirkung – "Funktion" der Ursache.

Durch das Mittel einer konstanten Beziehung resümiert man unter einer einzigen Formel eine Unendlichkeit von Ursachen und Wirkungen. Diese Idee der Funktion, das ist dieser Begriff der konstanten Ursache, ⟨er⟩ ist es, welcher das Rätsel der Macht der Mathematik auflöst, simultan eine Unendlichkeit von Tatsachen zu beherrschen. Um die Rolle der Idee der Funktion in der Mathematik zu verstehen, bedarf es eines Verständnisses der mathematischen Deduktion. Die mathematischen Demonstrationen, so zeigt es sich, (auch diejenigen, welche der vollständigen Induktion folgen) sind immer deduktiv, denn die Gültigkeit der Deduktion hängt nicht am Sujet, von dem man spricht, sondern einzig und allein an der Form.

"Um einen Satz der reinen Mathematik zu erhalten, oder was dasselbe ist, der mathematischen Logik (logique mathématique)" ... von dem Moment, als ein Argument gültig bleibt, wenn man einen seiner Termini ändert, muss man den Terminus durch eine Variable ersetzen, d. i. durch ein indeterminiertes Objekt.

<28a>
Man kommt dann schließlich zu einem rein logischen Satz (*proposition de logique pure*), welcher keine anderen Konstanten enthält als logische Konstanten. Die Definition der logischen Konstanten ist nicht leicht.

Etwa so: Nimmt man irgendeine Deduktion und ersetzt man ihre Termini durch Variable, so kommt man nach einer bestimmten Zahl von Schritten dahin, dass die Konstanten, die übrig bleiben, in der Deduktion zu einer bestimmten Gruppe gehören, und wenn man dann versucht, die Generalisation dann noch weiter zu verfolgen, so bleiben immer wieder Konstanten übrig, die zu derselben Gruppe gehören. Das ist die Gruppe der logischen Konstanten. Diese sind es, welche die reine Form konstituieren. Eine formale Proposition ist eine solche, welche keine anderen Konstanten enthält als logische Konstanten.

Ist eine gültige Deduktion gegeben, welche auch immer, so hängt ihre Gültigkeit an der Form. Diese Form erhält man durch Ersatz der Termini der Deduktion durch Variable, bis keine anderen Konstanten mehr übrig bleiben als logische.

Umgekehrt: Jede gültige Deduktion kann man gewinnen durch Ausgang von einer Deduktion, welche operiert mit Variablen mittels logischer Konstanten, indem man den Variablen die bestimmten Werte gibt, durch welche die Hypothese (die Prämissen) wahr wird. Mittels dieser Operation der Generalisation separiert man das strikt deduktive Element eines Arguments von dem Element, das von der Besonderheit abhängt, von der die Rede da ist.

Die reine Mathematik beschäftigt sich ausschließlich mit dem deduktiven Element. Man erhält die rein mathematischen Propositionen durch einen Prozess der Reinigung. Angewandte Mathematik.

<28b>

Der rein hypothetische Charakter der reinen Mathematik: Sie hat es ausschließlich mit irgendwelchen indeterminierten Objekten zu tun, mit "Variablen".

Warum gibt man sich die Mühe, die Deduktionen auf solche reine Form zurückzuführen?

1) weil es gut ist, jede Wahrheit so weit zu verallgemeinern als irgend möglich.

2) Ökonomie der Arbeit.

(287) Die Mathematik setzt sich ganz aus Propositionen zusammen, welche ausschließlich Variable und logische Konstanten enthalten, d.i. aus Propositionen der reinen Form.

Die mathematische Erkenntnis bedarf der Prämissen, die nicht basiert sind auf sensiblen Prämissen. Jede allgemeine Erkenntnis entbehrt der Quellen der sinnlichen Erkenntnis, diese geben nur Individuelles, sie können nicht durch Induktion erwiesen werden.

Primitive (nicht-demonstrierte) menschliche Erkenntnis teilt sich in zwei Teile:

1) Erkenntnis partikulärer Tatsachen, nur diese Erkenntnis affirmiert Existenz,

2) Erkenntnis von logischen Wahrheiten, welche Erkenntnis nur räsonieren kann über Gegebenheiten. Prämissen der Logik (die reine Mathematik)

A Letter of Rudolf Carnap to Jonas Cohn from 26 September 1925

an ihn wenden möchte. Ich wäre Ihnen daher sehr dankbar, wenn Sie mir ganz im Vertrauen Ihre persönliche Meinung über die Möglichkeiten (selbstverständlich ohne jede auch nur moralische Verbindlichkeit) sagen und einen Rat geben würden.

Ich habe inzwischen von einer anderen Universität ohne mein Zutun eine Aufforderung zur Habilitation erhalten, die ich aber aus persönlichen Einstandnahme in die dortigen Verhältnisse nicht gefolgt bin. An einer anderen Universität hat man mir Hoffnung gemacht und mir vorgeschlagen, im Laufe dieses Winters eine Hab.-schrift einzureichen. Dort glaube ich auch, günstige Wirkungsbedingungen finden zu können. Trotzdem würde ich Freiburg vorziehen, wenn sich hier die Möglichkeit ergäbe.

Falls Sie glauben, mir über die augenblicklichen Verhältnisse hier etwas sagen zu können, so bin ich bereit, Sie aufzusuchen Montag vorm., bin ich in Freiburg und könnte zu Ihnen kommen, falls ich Sonntag früh Ihre Antwort erhalte. Doch ist mir auch jeder spätere Tag recht. (Montag kann ich zu jeder Stunde von 9 Uhr ab kommen; an anderen Tagen am besten um 12 Uhr oder nachm.)

Mit ergebensten Grüße
Ihr Rudolf Carnap

Thomas Vongehr
Jonas Cohn und Edmund Husserl.
Eine Skizze ihrer Beziehung

Jonas Cohn (1869–1947) und Edmund Husserl (1859–1938) waren 12 Jahre lang Kollegen an der Philosophischen Fakultät der Universität Freiburg, und zwar von 1916 an bis zu Husserls Emeritierung im Jahr 1928. Bevor ich die Beziehung der beiden Philosophen skizziere, soll der akademische Werdegang von Cohn zusammengefasst werden.[1]

Cohn studierte zunächst Biologie, später Philosophie und Pädagogik. Nach seiner Promotion in systematischer Botanik an der Universität in Berlin war er von 1892 bis 1894 wissenschaftlicher Mitarbeiter am berühmten experimental-psychologischen Laboratorium von Wilhelm Wundt in Leipzig. Im Jahr 1897 habilitierte er sich bei Wilhelm Windelband und Heinrich Rickert in Freiburg mit einer Arbeit aus dem Gebiet der Wertphilosophie. Cohn blieb als Privatdozent an der Freiburger Universität und erhielt dort 1901 zunächst eine außerplanmäßige außerordentliche Professur für Philosophie und Psychologie, und 1919 dann ein planmäßiges Extraordinariat für Philosophie und Pädagogik. Cohn, dem nach eigener Aussage „jedes Gefühl der Zugehörigkeit" zur jüdischen Religion fehlte,[2] wurde 1933 als „Nicht-Arier" zwangspensioniert. Er emigrierte 1939 nach England, wo er 1947 starb. Cohn stand dem Neukantianismus, speziell der „Badischen" bzw. „Südwestdeutschen Schule" von Windelband und Rickert, nahe.[3] Unter dem Einfluss Hegels bemühte er sich, wie es in einer zeitgenössischen Darstellung heißt, „Dialektik und strengen Kritizismus zu vereinen"[4].

Ein erster Kontakt fand wahrscheinlich im Jahr 1904 statt, als Cohn an Husserl seinen Aufsatz „Psychologische oder kritische Begründung der Ästhetik?"[5]

---

[1] Vgl. J. Cohn, „Jonas Cohn". In: *Die Philosophie der Gegenwart in Selbstdarstellungen*, R. Schmidt (Hg.), Leipzig 1923, S. 1–21.
[2] Vgl. M. Heitmann, „‚Jedes Gefühl der Zugehörigkeit fehlt.' Jonas Cohn (1869–1947) – Einblicke in ein deutsch-jüdisches Gelehrtenleben". In: *Kalonymos*. Heft 4, 2001, S. 1–4.
[3] Vgl. M. Scheler, „Die deutsche Philosophie der Gegenwart". In: *Deutsches Leben der Gegenwart*, P. Witkop (Hg.), Berlin 1922, S. 129–224.
[4] S. Marck, *Die Dialektik in der Philosophie der Gegenwart*, 2. Halbband, Tübingen 1931, S. 1; dort auch: „Das Postulat, nachhegelisch, gerade deswegen aber nichthegelisch zu philosophieren, kennzeichnet [Cohns] Programm."
[5] J. Cohn, „Psychologische oder kritische Begründung der Ästhetik?" In: *Archiv für systematische Philosophie* 10 (1904), S. 131–159 (in Husserls Bibliothek, Signatur SA 89, Husserl-Archiv Leuven).

schickte. Darin richtet er sich gegen den Psychologismus in der Ästhetik. Das an Husserl gesendete Exemplar trägt die dem Adressaten zugedachte handschriftliche Widmung: „Dem energischen Bekämpfer des Psychologismus in vorzüglicher Hochachtung". Dieser bedankte sich dafür freundlich mit einer Postkarte. In den folgenden drei Jahrzehnten erhielt Husserl die jeweils neuesten Publikationen. So befinden sich in seiner Privatbibliothek, aufbewahrt im Husserl-Archiv Leuven, fast alle Veröffentlichungen Cohns, viele mit dessen handschriftlicher Widmung.[6]

Es ist zu bedauern, dass sich – mit einer Ausnahme, auf die ich gleich eingehen werde – weder in Husserls veröffentlichten, noch in seinen nachgelassenen Schriften philosophisch relevante Bezugnahmen auf Cohns Werk finden. Selbst der umfangreiche Briefwechsel Husserls, in dem doch viel Privates zur Sprache kommt, gibt keinen näheren Aufschluss über die persönliche Beziehung der beiden Freiburger Professoren.

Reinhard Klockenbusch, der 1989 eine vergleichende Untersuchung über das Werk der beiden Freiburger Philosophen verfasst hat, deutet zu Recht an, dass eine Auseinandersetzung zwischen Husserl und Cohn zu Lebzeiten hätte „fruchtbar" sein können.

> Fruchtbar scheint der Vergleich Husserls mit Cohn deshalb, weil die Position des einen durch die des anderen weiter geklärt werden kann. Daß diese Klärung durch Husserl und Cohn nicht selbst erfolgte, liegt daran, daß beide Denker von der jeweilig anderen Position nur unzulänglich Kenntnis hatten und Unverständnis, wenn nicht Vorurteile eine Auseinandersetzung verhinderten.[7]

Eine Ausnahme bildet nun die Auseinandersetzung, die sich im Anschluss an Cohns Buch *Voraussetzungen und Ziele des Erkennens. Untersuchungen über die Grundfragen der Logik*[8] entwickelt hat. Cohn hat sein Buch kurz nach der Veröf-

---

[6] In Husserls Bibliothek befinden sich etwa 30 Titel Cohns. Die letzte Veröffentlichung, die er Husserl zukommen ließ, ist wohl der Sonderdruck seines 1936 erschienenen Aufsatzes „Kritische Bemerkungen zur neupositivistischen Erkenntnislehre, namentlich zu der Carnaps (Methodenmonismus und Problemabweisung)". In: *Philosophische Hefte*, M. Beck (Hg.), 5. Jg., Heft 1/2, Prag 1936, S. 51–74. – Dieser Aufsatz wurde ein Jahr zuvor von Rudolf Carnap für eine Veröffentlichung in der von ihm und Hans Reichenbach begründeten Zeitschrift *Erkenntnis* abgelehnt (vgl. den Brief von Carnap an Cohn, 14.III.1935, Jonas Cohn-Archiv, Salomon Ludwig Steinheim Institut für deutsch-jüdische Geschichte, Essen; siehe auch den darauf Bezug nehmenden Brief von Carnap an Reichenbach vom 1.II.1935, Rudolf Carnap Papers, 1905–1970, ASP.1974.01, Special Collections Department, University of Pittsburgh, Box 102d, Folder 64, 05).

[7] R. Klockenbusch, *Husserl und Cohn. Widerspruch, Reflexion und Telos in Phänomenologie und Dialektik*, Dordrecht/Boston /London 1989 (*Phaenomenologica* 117), S. 2 f.

[8] J. Cohn, *Voraussetzungen und Ziele des Erkennens. Untersuchungen über die Grundfragen der Logik*, Leipzig 1908. Das von Cohn an Husserl gesendete Exemplar trägt seine handschriftliche

fentlichung 1908 an Husserl geschickt – mit dem Wunsch, dieser möge sich darüber äußern. Er nahm wohl an, dass sich Husserl für die von ihm behandelten Themen aus der Mathematik, der Logik, der Urteilslehre und der Theorie der Zahlen etc. interessieren würde, zudem bezieht er sich mehrfach auf dessen *Logische Untersuchungen*. Tatsächlich ist dies die einzige Schrift Cohns, die von Husserl aufmerksam gelesen wurde, wie man aus den zahlreichen Annotationen und Anstreichungen in seinem Exemplar schließen kann.

Etwa zeitgleich mit der Lektüre von Cohns Buch hat Husserl ein 8-seitiges Manuskript verfasst. Es trägt den Titel: „Meine transzendentalphänomenologische Methode und Kants transzendentallogische Methode. Reflexionen mit Beziehung auf Jonas Cohn"[9]. Er setzt sich darin allerdings nicht direkt mit Cohn auseinander, sondern nimmt dessen Buch nur zum Anlass, sich über die Tragweite der transzendental-phänomenologischen gegenüber der transzendental-logischen Methode klarer zu werden. Nur an einer Stelle des Manuskripts bezieht sich Husserl namentlich und kritisch auf Cohn, und zwar bemängelt er in dessen Darstellungen „reichlich<e>" „Vagheiten".[10]

Dennoch klingt Husserls Urteil über Cohns Buch, das er ihm in einem Brief vom Oktober 1908 mitteilt, zumindest dem Grundton nach anerkennend und wohlwollend. Er schreibt:

> Ich zweifle nicht, daß Sie mit diesen Untersuchungen der lebendigen Erkenntniskritik unserer Zeit wertvolle Dienste erwiesen haben u. daß dem Werke vermöge vieler vortrefflicher Ausführungen Wirksamkeit beschieden ist.[11]

Obwohl sich allerlei Anknüpfungspunkte geboten hätten, geht Husserl im weiteren Verlauf des Briefes, wie schon im oben genannten Manuskript, kaum auf den Inhalt des Buches ein. Er berichtet eher darüber, was ihn selbst zur Zeit be-

---

Widmung „Herrn Prof. Dr. Husserl in vorzüglicher Hochachtung" (Signatur BQ 78, Husserl-Archiv Leuven).

9 Unveröffentlichtes Husserl Manuskript (Signatur B IV 1/89–96, Husserl-Archiv Leuven).

10 Die betreffende Stelle in Husserls Manuskript lautet: „Kann man deduzieren, dass es eine Ordnung geben muss, die ein Analogon der räumlichen ist? Hat nicht schon die Deduktion einer ruhenden Welt seine Bedenken? Wie kommt man über Vagheiten hinaus (derart wie sie sich bei Cohn, S. 234 ff., ja auch reichlich finden)?" (Husserl Manuskript, Signatur B IV 1/92b, Husserl-Archiv Leuven) – Korrespondierende Anmerkungen und Anstreichungen finden sich in Husserls Leseexemplar von Cohns *Voraussetzungen und Ziele des Erkennens* auf der angegebenen Seite („S. 234 ff.").

11 Cohn an Husserl, Brief vom 15.X.1908, in: Edmund Husserl, *Briefwechsel*, *Husserliana Dokumente III*, in Verbindung mit E. Schuhmann hrsg. von K. Schuhmann, Dordrecht/Boston/London 1994 (im Folgenden abgekürzt als *Husserl-Briefwechsel* unter Angabe des Bandes), Bd. V, *Die Neukantianer*, S. 14.

schäftige, nämlich dass er versuche, sich über eine phänomenologisch konzipierte Kritik der Vernunft klarzuwerden. Daher interessiere ihn besonders Cohns Bestimmung der transzendental-logischen Methode. Er bevorzuge aber, so Husserl, die transzendental-phänomenologische Methode, nämlich als „Methode einer rein immanenten Wesenslehre der Intentionalität hinsichtlich ihrer beiden Evidenzseiten, der Bewußtseinsseite u. der Gegenstandsseite (,phänologisch' – ,ontologisch')"[12]. „Von dieser Methode", so heißt es in einem wohl aus derselben Zeit stammenden Forschungsmanuskript, „haben Kant und der ganze von ihm abhängige Neukantianismus und Neuidealismus keine Ahnung gehabt."[13]

Husserls Interesse an Cohn erwächst also auf dem Hintergrund seiner Beschäftigung mit Kant und dem Neukantianismus. Die frühesten Manuskripte, in denen sich Husserls Wendung zum transzendental-phänomenologischen Idealismus abzeichnet, sind übrigens fast zur gleichen Zeit entstanden wie die Auseinandersetzung mit Cohn.[14] Im genannten Brief schreibt Husserl über Cohns Buch:

> Ich fühle mich dadurch, jedenfalls, sehr angeregt u. zu Danke verpflichtet. Es kam mir sehr gelegen, da ich eben daran war, wiederholte Erwägungen der letzten Jahre über ‚Voraussetzungen u. Ziele' bzw. Sinn und Grenzen der transcendental-logischen Methode (wie sie im alten u. neuen Kantianism u. Fichteanism gehandhabt worden ist) nachzuprüfen, bzw. abzuschließen.[15]

Am Ende holt Husserl dann noch zu einem Rundumschlag bezüglich der Kritik an kantischer Transzendentalphilosophie und am Neukantianismus aus. Dabei trifft sein Vorwurf auch Cohn, dem er mangelnde „Klarheit und Exactheit"[16] vorwirft. Husserl bedauert jedoch, dass er das in seinem Brief nicht ausführlicher erläutern könne, aber er schlägt Cohn noch vor: „Vielleicht können wir uns einmal persönlich darüber unterhalten: das wäre mir eine Freude!"[17] Die Gelegenheit dazu bot sich wohl erst einige Jahre später, als Husserl nach Freiburg berufen wurde.

Seltsamerweise hat sich Cohn fast drei Jahre Zeit gelassen, bevor er auf die Kritik Husserls reagierte. In einem Brief von Ende März 1911 begründet er das

---

12 Ebd., S. 15.
13 E. Husserl, *Erste Philosophie (1923/24). Erster Teil: Kritische Ideengeschichte*, *Husserliana* VII, R. Boehm (Hg.), Haag 1956, S. 382.
14 Vgl. E. Husserl, *Transzendentaler Idealismus. Texte aus dem Nachlass (1908–1921)*, *Husserliana* XXXVI, in Verbindung mit R. Sowa hrsg. von R. D. Rollinger, Dordrecht/Boston/London 2003.
15 Husserl an Cohn, a.a.O., S. 14.
16 Ebd., S. 14.
17 Ebd., S. 15.

damit, dass er sich erst einmal vertrauter mit dessen Phänomenologie hätte machen wollen. Unmittelbarer Anlass für seine Reaktion scheint jedoch das Erscheinen von Husserls Schrift „Philosophie als strenge Wissenschaft" (1911) in der Zeitschrift *Logos* gewesen zu sein.[18] Trotz einiger Differenzen mit Husserl betont Cohn eine „weitgehende Übereinstimmung in vielen Fragen, vor allem bei gleicher Kampfstellung gegen Naturalismus u. Historicismus"[19].

Neben dem eben Genannten, das leider nur spärlichen Aufschluss gibt über die philosophische Auseinandersetzung, sollen wenigstens noch einige konkrete berufliche Berührungspunkte zwischen beiden erwähnt werden. Husserl, der in den Jahren nach der Veröffentlichung der *Logischen Untersuchungen* (1900/01) darum bemüht war, sich von der Tradition der deskriptiven Psychologie der Brentano Schule zu lösen und die Phänomenologie von der Psychologie zu emanzipieren, übernahm mit Amtsantritt 1916 als Nachfolger von Rickert auch dessen Position als Direktor des Freiburger Psychologischen Laboratoriums.[20] Cohn, der ja schon in frühen Jahren am Psychologischen Laboratorium Wundts in Leipzig gearbeitet hatte, war seit 1903 in Freiburg der Assistent des Direktors des Psychologischen Laboratoriums und übte diese Funktion dann auch unter Husserls Leitung aus. Und im Jahr 1920 – wahrscheinlich im Zusammenhang mit einer 1919 erfolgten Beförderung – wurde Cohn offiziell neben Husserl zum Mitdirektor des Laboratoriums ernannt.

Im Jahr 1913 unterschrieben Cohn und Husserl einen in der Zeitschrift *Logos* veröffentlichten Aufruf. Sie opponierten damit (wie auch andere Philosophen) gegen die zunehmende Besetzung der traditionellen philosophischen Lehrstühle durch Psychologen bzw. Experimentalpsychologen.[21] Aus der Zeit ihrer Zusam-

---

18 E. Husserl, „Philosophie als strenge Wissenschaft". In: *Logos* 1 (1911), S. 289 – 341 (auch in *Husserliana* XXV, S. 3 – 62). – Vgl. Cohns Überlegungen in „Der Sinn der gegenwärtigen Kultur. Ein philosophischer Versuch", Leipzig 1914.
19 Ebd., S. 17. – Es handelt sich um einen auf den 31.III.1911 datierten Entwurf eines Briefes von Cohn an Husserl.
20 Vgl. J. Fahrenberg, J. R. Stegie, „Beziehungen zwischen Philosophie und Psychologie an der Freiburger Universität: Zur Geschichte des Psychologischen Laboratoriums/Instituts". In: J. Jahnke, J. Fahrenberg, R. Stegie & E. Bauer (Hg.), *Psychologiegeschichte – Beziehungen zu Philosophie und Grenzgebieten*, München 1998, S. 251 – 266.
21 Cohn und Husserl gehören zu den insgesamt 106 Unterzeichnern der 1913 veröffentlichten „Erklärung von Dozenten der Philosophie in Deutschland gegen die Besetzung philosophischer Lehrstühle mit Vertretern der experimentellen Psychologie" (veröffentlicht in: *Logos. Internationale Zeitschrift für Philosophie der Kultur.* 4. Bd. Hrsg. von R. Kroner und G. Mehlis unter Mitwirkung von R. Eucken, O. v. Gierke, E. Husserl, F. Meinecke, H. Rickert, G. Simmel, E. Troeltsch, M. Weber, Windelband, H. Wölfflin, Tübingen 1913, S. 115 – 116). – Husserl hatte sich schon Ende 1912 mit einer Art Privat-Petition für dasselbe Ziel engagiert (vgl. den Brief von Husserl an H. Knittermeyer, 31.X.1912. In: *Husserl-Briefwechsel*, Bd. V, S. 23 f.). Gegenüber August Messer be-

menarbeit ist auch ein gemeinsam entworfener und an die Philosophische Fakultät in Freiburg gerichteter Vorschlag (vom Juni 1920) erhalten, der darauf zielt, das Fach Experimentalpsychologie im Studium auch als Nebenfach zuzulassen.[22] Daneben existieren Korreferate Husserls zu von Cohn geleiteten Dissertationen.[23] Bei dem von Rudolf Carnap in einem Brief an Cohn erwähnten Schüler Husserls, der eine „Habilitation vorhabe", weshalb er selbst sich diesbezüglich „einstweilen keine Hoffnungen machen dürfe"[24], handelt es sich wahrscheinlich um Fritz Kaufmann (1891–1958), der 1924 bei Husserl promoviert hatte und 1926 seine Habilitation abschloss.[25]

Das trotz aller Kritik weitgehend positive Urteil, das Husserl Cohn in seinem Brief von 1908 anlässlich der Übersendung des Buches *Voraussetzungen und Ziele des Erkennens* mitteilte, hat sich durch den seit 1916 möglich gewordenen persönlichen Umgang mit Cohn in Freiburg wohl eher verstärkt als gemindert. Als Natorp bei Husserl im Juni 1917 wegen einer frei werdenden Professur in Marburg um Ratschläge für geeignete Kandidaten nachfragt, da schlägt Husserl Cohn vor, der

> als Philosoph doch sehr schätzenswert [sei], ein feinsinniger Vermittler der südwestdeutschen und Marburger Richtungen [des Neukantianismus], ein Mann von weitem Blick, von allseitiger, reicher wissenschaftlicher Bildung, nach einer systematisch geschlossenen Weltanschauung strebend. Seine ‚Voraussetzungen und Ziele des Erkennens' enthalten ausgezeichnete Kapitel und auch seine sonstigen philosophischen Schriften lese ich mit Belehrung. Er hat doch überall Blick für Principielles, obschon er kein führender Arbeiter an den Fundamentalproblemen ist.[26]

Die persönliche und philosophische Wertschätzung, die Cohn Husserl entgegenbrachte, hat er in seinen Tagebüchern mehrfach zum Ausdruck gebracht. Einer

---

tonte Husserl, dass bei ihm „von einer Feindschaft gegen die <e>x<perimentelle> Ps<ychologie> keine Rede" sein könne (Husserl an A. Messer, 19.II.1914. In: *Husserl-Briefwechsel*, Bd. VII, S. 176).
22 Vgl. *Husserl-Briefwechsel*, Bd. VIII, S. 170f.
23 Vgl. z. B. *Husserl-Briefwechsel*, Bd. VIII, S. 164, 190.
24 Vgl. den im vorliegenden Band abgedruckten Brief von R. Carnap an J. Cohn, 26.IX.1925. – Carnap besuchte während eines früheren Aufenthaltes in Freiburg (1911–1912) die psychologischen Vorlesungen von Cohn. Er stand mit ihm wohl noch in den 1920er Jahren in gelegentlichem persönlichen Kontakt.
25 In Frage käme evtl. auch Dietrich Mahnke (1884–1939): 1922 Promotion bei Husserl, 1926 Habilitation in Greifswald.
26 Brief von Husserl an Natorp, 3.VI.1917, in *Husserl-Briefwechsel*, Bd. V, S. 128. – Das Engagement Husserls führte nicht zum gewünschten Erfolg. Auf das Marburger Extraordinariat wurde Max Wundt berufen.

dieser Tagebucheinträge Cohns – niedergeschrieben kurz nach dem Tod Husserls – soll hier zitiert werden:

> Am 27. April [1938] starb nach langer Krankheit Edmund Husserl, ein weiser, gütiger Mensch, überzeugt, ja besessen von seiner Mission, die Philosophie durch Phänomenologie zur strengen Wissenschaft zu erheben. [...] einer der wenigen Denker von Rang in unserer Zeit, durch logische Untersuchungen und den Geist der positiven Aufnahme dessen, was sich uns gibt, von bleibender Bedeutung. Mir war er ein wohlwollender Kollege, ich liebte sein reines Wesen [...][27]

Zum Schluss bleibt nichts übrig, als das Bedauern zu wiederholen, dass der philosophische Dialog zwischen den beiden Freiburger Philosophen nicht mehr Gestalt angenommen hat.

---

[27] Zitiert nach M. Heitmann: „Jedes Gefühl der Zugehörigkeit fehlt.'", a.a.O., S. 4.

Name Index

Ajdukiewicz, Kazimierz v, 8
Angelelli, Ignacio 17, 19, 29
Anscombe, G. E. M. 84
Ariew, Roger 282
Avenarius, Richard 6, 196, 261–262, 272–273
Awoodey, Steve 281

Baker, Peter 282
Baron, Lawrence 249
Bauch, Bruno 180, 186, 250–251, 264–265, 267–268, 274, 278
Bauer, E. 327
Beaney, Michael 281
Becker, Oskar 270
Bell, David 271
Bell, Jeffrey A. 173, 271
Bennett, M. R. 62, 64–65
Benoist, Jocelyn 37, 187
Bergmann, Hugo 125–127, 134
Bergson, Henri 191–192
Bernays, Paul 163
Betti, Arianna 148
Beyer, Christian 159
Biemel, Marly 193
Boehm, Rudolf 326
Bolzano, Bernard 17, 31, 53, 98, 124–126, 131, 136, 146, 152, 154, 156–157, 160
Bonk, Thomas 260, 263
Born, Max 4, 270
Bourbaki, Nicholas 5, 10, 22, 28
Brentano, Franz 3, 8, 61, 119–120, 124–127, 129, 134, 138, 147–148, 194, 241, 243–244, 327
Bühler, Karl 191
Burg, Josef 246

Cairns, Dorion 128
Cantor, Georg 3, 91, 111, 121, 124, 135, 137, 155, 160, 317
Carnap, Rudolf vi, viii, 2, 4, 7–10, 25–27, 31, 148, 155–158, 160, 163–165, 175–224, 226–256, 261–272, 274–276, 278–284, 321–322, 324, 328

Carus, André 179, 183
Cassirer, Ernst 178, 181, 240–241, 250–251, 261, 263, 270, 274, 278
Cavallès, Jean 28
Centrone, Stefania 28, 31, 98, 120
Coffa, J. Alberto 155–156
Cohen, Hermann 278
Cohen, Joseph 185, 207–208, 250–251
Cohen, Robert 262–263
Cohn, Jonas vi, viii, 9–10, 178, 187–190, 193, 254, 268–269, 282, 321, 323–329
Couturat, Louis 125, 181
Creath, Richard 195

Da Silva Casari, Jairo J. vii, 7, 28
Dathe, Uwe 265
Dauben, Johannes 27
Davidson, Donald 148, 151
Demopoulos, William 90
Dennett, Daniel C. 7, 61, 64
Descartes René 36, 58, 68, 279
Dingler, Hugo 201, 224, 270
Dreyfus, Hubert L. 145
Driesch, Hans 196, 200, 224, 231, 238, 263, 266
Duhem, Pierre 23–24, 281–282
Dühring, Eugen 181
Dummett, Michael 37, 90–91

Ebbinghaus, Heinz-Dieter 121
Ehrenfels, Christian von 136
Englisch, Paul 176
English, Jacques 38
Erhard, Christopher 214, 242–243
Eucken, Rudolf 265, 327

Fahrenberg, J. 188, 327
Farber, Marvin 61, 68
Feferman, Anita Burdman 148, 157, 164
Feferman, Solomon 148, 157, 164
Fodor, J. A. 1
Føllesdal, Dagfinn 145
Fonfara, Dirk 178, 203

Name Index

Frege, Gottlob v, vii, 2–3, 5, 7–9, 15–21, 23, 26–27, 29–31, 37, 39–40, 46, 89–92, 95, 97–98, 103–114, 120, 131, 139, 145–146, 152, 154–156, 160, 165, 167, 181, 194, 228, 236, 240, 261, 265, 269, 278, 281, 289
Friedman, Michael 155–156, 165, 195, 239, 246, 248, 250, 252, 255, 263

Gander, Hans-Helmuth 185
Geiger, Moritz 270
Gierke, O. v. 327
Gödel, Kurt 6, 10, 28, 149, 160
Goldstein, J. 292
Gomperz, Heinrich 191, 201
Goodman, Nelson 198
Grelling, Kurt 127
Grünbaum, Adolf 262–263

Hacker, P. M. S. 62, 64–65
Harman, Gilbert 62
Hartimo, Mirja 120, 289
Häusser, Hans-Dietrich 251
Heidegger, Martin 180, 232, 241, 246, 270
Heilner, R. 89
Heitmann, Margret vi, 178, 188, 323, 329
Hempel, Carl G. 25
Hilbert, David 3–4, 6, 10, 28, 90–91, 97, 111, 120–122, 127, 155, 160, 163, 181, 240
Hintikka, Jaakko 151, 155, 166–168
Hopkins, Burt 121
Hume, David 36, 129
Husserl, Malvine 17

Ierna, Carlo vi-viii, 8–9, 119–120, 127, 129, 135–136, 289
Ingarden, Roman 233, 270

Jacoby, Günther 201
Jahnke, J. 327
Jaspers, Karl 180
Jourdain, P. 98

Kant, Immanuel 1–2, 7, 9–10, 21, 23, 31, 36–38, 155–158, 160, 165, 261–268, 270–271, 278–279, 281, 325–326
Katz, Jerrold J. 1
Kauffmann, Max 224, 231, 238
Kaufmann, Felix 248, 261, 328
Kern, Iso 206, 250, 253
Klein, Carsten 281
Klein, Felix 3, 10, 120, 181
Klein, Jacob 181
Klockenbusch, Reinhard 324
Knittermeyer, H. 327
Knoblauch, Hubert 121
Köhler, Wolfgang 261–262
Köhnke, Klaus Christian 251
Königsberger, Leo 3, 91, 119
Kotarbinski, Tadeusz 148
Koyré, Alexandre 8, 121–125, 127–128, 130–135, 137–138, 306
Kraus, Oskar 126, 193–194
Kreis, Friedrich 255
Kripke, Saul 151, 155
Kronecker, Leopold 3, 91, 119
Kroner, R. 327

Landgrebe, Ludwig 26, 187, 193–194, 201–203, 231, 248, 256, 268, 270, 272
Lang, Martin 289
Leibniz, Gottfried 8, 10, 36, 93, 167, 317
Lesniewski, Stanislaw v, 8, 163
Lessing, Theodor 249
Lipps, Hans 121, 124, 134
Lohmar, Dieter vi, viii, 9, 119, 178, 206, 212, 289
Lotze, Hermann 92–93, 160
Lukasiewicz, Jan 163
Lynch, Michael P. 144, 150

Mach, Ernst 2, 6, 181, 194, 196, 261–262, 268, 272–273, 278
Mahnke, Dietrich 328
Majer, Ulrich 28, 263
Mally, Ernst 137
Mayer, Verena vi-vii, 9, 175, 192, 222, 242, 271, 282
McIntyre, Ronald 81, 146, 151, 159, 167
Mehlis, G. 327

Meinecke, F.   327
Meinong, Alexius   74–78, 84, 119–120, 129, 136, 147–148, 244
Meixner, Uwe   vi-vii, 7, 55
Melle, Ulrich   289
Merten, Bernhard   187
Messer, August   327–328
Miller, J. P.   120
Misch, Georg   114
Mohanty, J. N.   243
Montague, Richard   148
Moran, Dermot   185, 207–208, 250
Mormann, Thomas   183, 186, 230, 248, 280

Natorp, Paul   181, 241, 250–254, 261, 263, 270, 278, 328
Nelson, Leonard   127, 181
Neurath, Otto   v, 4, 271, 281

Ortiz Hill, Claire   vii, 8, 21, 23, 28–29, 89–91, 94–95, 97, 106, 108–113, 119, 146, 289
Osborn, Andrew   91
Ostwald, Wilhelm   181

Panzer, Ursula   98
Parakenings, Brigitte   178
Parker, Rodney   121–123
Patzig, Günther   9, 179
Pavlov, Ivan P.   2
Peckhaus, Volker   121
Pickard Bell, Winthrop   270
Plato   10, 102, 316
Poincaré, Henri   23, 125–126, 181
Popper, Karl   1, 25
Putnam, Hilary   4, 7, 49–52

Quine, Willard van Orman   1–2, 4, 36–37, 40, 45, 51–53, 157, 268, 282, 284

Reichenbach, Hans   180, 188, 249, 324
Reinach, Adolf   121–124, 128, 130, 134
Reininger, Robert   191
Richardson, Alan   195, 239, 248, 252
Rickert, Heinrich   178, 183, 230, 250–251, 267–268, 274, 278, 323, 327
Riemann, Bernhard   4, 22

Rollinger, R. D.   326
Rosado Haddock, Guillermo E.   vii-viii, 1, 15, 23, 29, 39–40, 146, 178–179, 182, 194, 222–223, 231, 261, 289
Roy, Jean-Michel   197
Russell, Bertrand   v, vii, 2, 4, 8–10, 89–91, 108–110, 113–114, 119–128, 131–132, 134, 137–138, 181, 194, 197, 224, 239–240, 244–245, 255, 261–263, 268, 274, 306–307, 316–317
Ryle, Gilbert   4, 7, 57, 59–65, 68–72, 74–76, 78

Sainsbury, R. M.   168
Sarkar, Sahotra   9, 182, 263
Scheler, Max   229, 323
Schilpp, Paul A.   236, 238, 261–262
Schirn, Matthias   21
Schlick, Moritz   v, 4, 7, 10, 35, 49, 180, 183, 188–194, 202, 206–207, 218, 236, 239, 241, 245–247, 249, 268, 271, 281
Schmidt, H. J.   263
Schmidt, R.   323
Schmit, Roger   119, 135
Schoenflies, Arthur   307
Scholz, Heinrich   186, 270
Schröder, Ernst   17–19, 112, 309
Schuhmann, Elisabeth   20, 127, 325
Schuhmann, Karl   25–26, 91, 98, 121–123, 127–128, 134, 187, 193, 249, 268, 325
Schuppe, Wilhelm   261
Scott, Dana,   148
Sellge, Klaus   289
Sieg, Ulrich   251
Simmel, Georg   327
Sluga, Hans   21
Smith, Arthur. D.   67
Smith, Barry   121, 136
Smith, David Woodruff   vii, 8, 80, 143–146, 148–149, 151, 156, 158–159, 165, 167
Sowa, R.   326
Spohn, Wolfgang   271
Stadler, Friedrich   249
Stegie, J. R.   327
Stein, Edith   193, 201–203, 248
Stelzner, Werner   265
Stepun, Fedor   187

Ströker, Elisabeth   206, 283
Stumpf, Carl   3, 119

Tarski, Alfred   vii, 8, 28, 143–155, 157–166, 168–169
Theodorou, Panos   42
Tieszen, Richard   154, 158
Troeltsch, Ernst   327
Tschichmanoff, Ivan   187
Twardowski, Kazimierz   8, 119, 147–148
Tye, Michael   62

Urbach, B.   125–127, 131, 134

Vaihinger, Thomas   183
Varga, Peter Andras   119
Volkelt, Johannes   201
Vongehr, Thomas   vi, viii 10, 178, 187–188, 229, 249, 289, 323
Vossenkuhl, Wilhelm   271

Weber, Max   327
Weierstrass, Karl   3, 91, 98, 119–121, 135, 307
Weiler, Michael   289
Wertheimer, Max   261–262
Weyl, Helene   270
Weyl, Hermann   4, 6, 51, 89, 98, 114, 155, 160, 263, 270, 316
Whitehead, Alfred North   90–91, 109–110, 197
Willard, Dallas   111
Windelband, Wilhelm   323, 327
Witkop, P.   323
Wittgenstein, Ludwig   v, 4, 7, 55–60, 62, 64, 83–84, 192–193, 249, 261
Wölfflin, H.   327
Wundt, Max   328
Wundt, Wilhelm   323, 327

Zambelli, Paola   121, 123, 125, 138
Zermelo, Ernst   8, 10, 120–122, 127, 134, 137, 289, 307, 316
Ziehen, Theodor   196, 201, 238

Subject Index

Abschattung 284
Ähnlichkeitserinnerung 176, 234–235
Analytic v, vii, 1–2, 4–5, 7–9, 15, 19, 31, 35–46, 48–53, 87, 91–92, 97–98, 156–158
Analyticity 2, 5, 7, 22, 31, 35–36, 39–40, 43–44, 51, 52–53, 89–90, 113, 156
Analytic philosopher v, vii, 1–2, 4, 7–9, 15–17, 19, 21, 23, 25, 31, 37–38, 40, 45–46, 51–52
Analytic philosophy v, vii, 1, 6, 8, 13, 16–17, 21, 37, 87, 90–91, 114
Assertion 1, 28–29, 35–36, 38–39, 41–50, 146, 266, 310
Ausdrucksbeziehung 175, 222–223, 226, 237
Autopsychological 271–273, 276, 278–280

Behaviouristic 1

Categorial abstraction 6
Categorial intuition 5–6, 10, 23, 38, 51–52
Categorial objectualities 6
Class 37, 39, 43–44, 50, 66, 108–111, 126, 131, 134, 161
Concept 18–19, 24, 27, 30–31, 35, 39–43, 45, 48–52, 59–61, 64, 77, 89–90, 92–99, 101–108, 111–114, 120, 123–124, 126–127, 129–130, 132–136, 145–146, 148–149, 155–157, 161, 207, 238, 271–272, 309
Concept, logical 39, 42, 49, 52
Concept, mathematical 18, 27
Concept, physical 24
Conceptual content 30
Conceptual truth 40
Conceptual word 19
Consciousness 7, 16, 46–48, 55–58, 60–62, 64–65, 67, 72–73, 79, 81–82, 94–95, 113, 143–148, 151–153, 155–162, 164–165, 167–168, 170–171, 208, 272–276, 279–280
Constitution 46, 49, 83, 155–156, 238, 271–272, 275–278, 280

Constitutional system 255, 262, 271–277
Constructivism 2
Constructivist 2, 135
Contemplation of essences 264–267
Content 19, 30, 36, 39–43, 48–49, 52, 61, 65, 67–71, 73, 92, 97, 99–102, 104, 110–112, 127, 129, 136, 144–148, 152–154, 157–160, 165, 167, 169–170, 244, 271
Content, judgeable 30
Content, noematic 145, 152–153, 168, 170
Context principle 30
Continental philosophy 1
Countersense 4, 26–27, 130, 132, 137
Conventionalism 285

Deductive-nomological 25, 281
Ding 128, 160, 175, 183, 202, 204–205, 209–211, 214–215, 217–220, 225, 227, 229–230, 233, 243, 246, 253, 292–298, 307, 310
– Physikalisches Ding 209, 217 f.
– Physisches Ding 211, 218, 220, 229 f., 233, 253

Eigenpsychische Basis 175, 199–200, 239, 251
Einfühlung 175, 209, 222–226, 237, 272
Elementarerlebnis 184, 195, 203, 205, 213–214, 220, 226, 229, 238, 246, 251, 262, 272–273
Empfindung 175, 183–185, 196, 203, 211, 214, 216–217, 223, 231
Empiricism v, 2, 8, 10, 16, 36, 40, 51–52, 156, 164, 271, 268, 280–282
– Empiricism, logical 155–156, 165, 262, 271
Empiricist v, 1–2, 5, 9, 16, 51, 156, 164, 261, 277, 280–282
– Empiricist, logical 1, 25, 281–282
Epoché 56–57, 66, 143–144, 151, 153, 156, 158–160, 163, 169–170, 175, 199–200, 205, 227, 231, 251, 253, 255
εποχη 199

Equivalence class   20–21
Erlebnis   57–58, 69, 72, 175, 183, 187, 192–193, 195–198, 200, 205,–207, 213–214, 218–220, 223–225, 230, 234–235, 237, 242–244, 247, 251, 256, 262, 272–276, 279, 283
Erlebnisstrom   175, 197, 199–200, 218–220, 262, 274, 276, 283
Essence   22–23, 37–38, 40–43, 45, 47–50, 52, 66, 69–70, 83, 92–93, 95–98, 100, 127, 129–133, 151, 157–158, 263–267, 276
Euclidicity   267

First philosophy   15–16, 58
Formal apophantics   39, 42
Foundation   5, 15, 20, 23 f., 27, 31, 61 f., 64 f., 68, 89–91, 96, 98, 111–114, 121, 124–127, 129 f., 135, 137 f., 149, 152, 161 f., 262 f., 281
Function   vii, 8, 31, 89–90, 92, 95, 98–114, 131, 137
Fundierung   182, 229, 231, 238, 255, 283

Gegebenheit   198, 225, 233, 245, 264, 302, 319
Gegebenheitsweise   81, 83, 235
Gegenstand   17–18, 72–73, 128, 132–133, 189, 193, 195, 200, 203–215, 217–218, 221, 223, 225–226, 228–230, 232, 235, 237–238, 242–243, 245, 247–248, 252–253, 266, 273, 275, 277–278, 292–298, 303, 310–311
– Geistiger Gegenstand   228
– Quasi-Gegenstand   190, 204
Gegenständlichkeit   70, 233, 235, 277
Gegenstandsbereich   196, 201, 232
Genus   59, 133, 277
Gestalt   136–137, 228, 230, 261–262, 293, 329
Gestaltpsychologie   254
Gestalttheorie   194
Gestaltic   135–136
Grammar   52, 57–59, 103, 150, 163
– categorial grammar   39
– logical grammar   5, 22, 26

Grounding   1, 15, 27, 114, 156, 262, 276–277, 280

Heteropsychological   272, 279–281
Horizon / Horizont   98, 167, 185, 214
Hypotheses cum fundamento in re   4, 24, 281

Identität   130, 218, 222, 292–294, 297, 299
Indexical   5, 8
Indexic ality   168
Insolubilia   122–125, 128, 130, 132–134, 292, 299
Intentional act   5, 37, 43, 45–46, 65, 152
Intentionality   vii, 7–8, 55–58, 60–65, 68–77, 79–81, 143–146, 148, 151–162, 164–170, 243
Intentional object   65–67, 69–70, 72–74, 76–83, 128
Intersubjective   60, 83, 162
intersubjectivity   279–280
Intuition   22–23, 39, 41–42, 48–49, 51–52, 60, 64, 129, 152, 157, 192, 237, 245–246, 264, 279
Intuitionism   284
Intuitive space   261–263, 265–266

Judgment   35–36, 39, 44, 71, 89, 95–96, 98–104, 113–114, 122, 128, 130, 134, 158, 169

Kantian / Kantianism   2, 9, 28, 155–157, 159–160, 165, 261, 265, 274, 278–280, 326
Konstituieren   195, 200, 205, 207, 209, 212 213, 216, 218, 222, 224–225, 227, 229, 318
Konstitution   155, 175, 178, 182, 193, 196–197, 199, 201, 202–204, 206–209, 212–213, 215–216, 218, 220–230, 232, 234, 237–238, 240, 243, 252, 254, 256, 272, 275, 277, 283, 290
Konstitutionssystem   175–176, 186, 190–191, 194–196, 200, 202–204, 206–209, 213, 218, 223, 226–227, 230–232, 234–235, 237–240, 247, 251–255, 273–275, 277

Konstitutionstheorie   155, 183, 187–189, 191–193, 196, 206, 208, 234, 243, 246, 253, 255

Language   2, 5, 9–10, 15, 22, 29, 37, 46, 61, 63–64, 84, 95, 101, 103–104, 106, 113, 143–163, 165–166, 168–169, 263, 280, 284–285
– metalanguage   143–144, 149–151, 153, 157, 160, 164–165
– object language   149–150, 153–154, 160, 164–165, 168–169
– ordinary language   1, 7, 95, 103, 149
Law   4, 15–16, 22, 24–27, 38, 41–45, 48–50, 52, 90–92, 94–95, 97–98, 107–109, 112–113, 280–282
– analytic law   39, 41–44, 46, 48
– synthetic *a priori* law   41–42, 48
Logic   1–2, 4, 7–8, 15–16, 21–22, 24–31, 36–42, 46, 49, 51–52, 58, 79, 89–99, 102–103, 106, 108–109, 111–114, 119–122, 131, 134, 143–146, 148–149, 151–166, 168, 263, 275, 284
– apophantic logic   38–39, 97, 275
– pure logic   92–93, 95, 97, 112, 146–148, 154, 157–158, 162, 165
Logical empiricism / logical empiricist   1, 25, 155–156, 165, 262, 271, 277, 281–282
Logical positivism / logical positivist   1, 37, 156
Logical syntax   27, 158, 163
Logicism / logicist   2, 5, 27, 29, 91, 284
Logic of truth   154, 157, 275

Manifold   4, 22, 28–29, 67, 96–97, 99, 111–112, 114, 132–133, 149, 158, 289
Mathematical intuition   5–6, 23
Mathesis der Erlebnisse   175, 196–198, 272
Mathesis universalis   28–29, 38
Meaning   5, 17–19, 25–27, 30, 35–37, 40–41, 43–46, 48–53, 56, 58–59, 61–62, 65, 67, 71–73, 78, 90, 92–95, 97–98, 100–102, 105–107, 112, 129–132, 135, 144–149, 151, 153–154, 156–160, 162–163, 165
Mental representationalism   68–69, 73

Mereological   136
Mereology   v, 5, 22, 135
Metalevel   154
Methodological solipsism   156, 164, 278
Methodology   143–144, 152, 158–160, 162–165, 171

Naturalistische Einstellung   175, 204, 209, 211, 227
Neo-Kantian / Neukantianer / Neukantianismus / neukantianisch   v, 1–2, 9, 155, 157, 165, 176, 179–180, 187, 195–196, 230, 248, 250–254, 261, 264–265, 268, 274, 278–279, 323, 325–326, 328
Noema   61, 145, 152, 156, 159–160, 165, 243, 252
Noesis   243, 252
Nominalism   v, 2, 10, 284–285
Nominalist   8, 16, 151, 236
Nonsense   4, 9, 25–27, 112, 280

Object   5–6, 16–18, 24, 37–41, 43–45, 49–51, 57–58, 65–83, 90, 93–95, 97, 103–109, 111–114, 119, 127–133, 135, 137, 143–148, 150–157, 159, 161–167, 169–170, 243f., 265, 271, 273, 275–277, 279, 284
Objectuality   5–6, 264, 277
Ontological nexus   4, 23–24
Ontology   22, 94, 97, 114, 146, 148–149, 151, 156, 158
– formal ontology   22, 38–39, 42, 44, 267
– regional ontology   267

Paradox / Paradoxie   vi, 8, 10, 49, 76, 111, 121–127, 130–132, 134, 136–137, 168, 289, 292, 297, 299–301, 306–307, 316
– Liar Paradox   121, 152, 168–169
– Richard's Paradoxon   308
– Zermelo-Russell Paradox / Russell's Paradox   vii, 8–9, 119–120, 123–128, 131, 134, 137–138
Phenomenological reduction   66, 274–276
Phenomenology   vii, 3, 8, 10, 16, 22, 35, 42, 47, 51, 55–57, 61, 64–65, 68, 71, 74, 94–95, 119–123, 127, 134, 143–145,

Subject Index

151–165, 167, 169–171, 175, 197, 238, 261–262, 264, 271, 289
– transcendental phenomenology 3–4, 7–8, 16, 89, 94, 114, 121, 127, 145, 151, 164–165, 274
Platonism 10, 23, 160, 284–285, 289
Platonist v, 2, 5, 16, 23, 160, 278
Positivism / Positivismus 2, 199, 274
Positivist 2, 5–6, 23, 261, 274, 278, 281
Power set 137
Presentation 98, 129, 147, 154, 161, 163
Principle of Tolerance 284–285
Probabilistic-nomological 25
Psychologism 2, 4, 18, 21–22, 31, 36, 92, 135, 277
Psychologistic 145–146

Rationalism / Rationalismus 2, 10, 240
Rationalist v-vi, 8, 16, 21, 278
Reductionism 2
Reductionist 5, 40
Referent 2, 5, 7–8, 17–21, 30, 7–79.
Relation v, 1, 5–10, 20, 24–25, 28, 39, 44–46, 49, 59, 65, 69–73, 80, 89–90, 95–96, 101, 103–104, 107–108, 124–25, 128–132, 136, 143, 145–147, 149–151, 153–155, 159, 161–162, 164, 166–167, 169–170, 184, 190, 234, 237–238, 243–244, 246, 261, 263, 267, 269–270, 274, 293–294, 297–301, 309
relativism, individual 22
relativism, specific 22
Robinson's Model-Completeness Test 284

Semantics 2, 5, 8, 21–22, 27, 39, 143–149, 151–155, 157, 161–167, 275, 285
Sense perception 5–6
Set 5–6, 16, 27–28, 40, 91, 93, 97, 111, 113, 121–124, 127, 132–138, 148, 151, 154, 166, 284, 289, 309
Situation of affairs 20–21, 30
Species 59, 133, 263–264, 277
State of affairs 6, 20–21, 30, 75–76, 146–147, 151–152, 154, 159, 170
Structure 4–5, 37, 96, 98, 124, 132, 138, 143–144, 146, 148–149, 153–160, 162–166, 168, 170, 208, 263, 265–266, 272, 282
Syntax 4, 9, 25–27, 38–39, 100, 150, 154–158, 162–165, 194, 261, 275, 280–281, 284
Synthetic *a priori* 2, 5, 7, 35, 37–42, 44, 47–51, 53, 156, 266–267

Theory of truth 143–144, 147–152, 154, 161–162, 164–166, 168
Transcendental idealism 156, 164–165, 274
Truth-condition 145, 148–151, 153–154, 157, 159, 166–168
Truth(s) vii, 16, 24, 27, 30, 35–44, 47–48, 51–53, 59, 61, 65, 72, 80, 92, 94–97, 102, 106, 109, 143–145, 147–155, 157–162, 165, 168–170, 262–263
– analytic truth 35–37, 39–44, 48, 50–52, 156–158
– contingent material truth 39
– necessary material truth 39
– nexus of truth 4, 24
– synthetic *a priori* truth 7, 35, 37–40, 42, 47, 51, 53, 156
– synthetic a posteriori truth 7, 39, 47, 51,
truth-value 19–21, 105–106, 112

Underdetermination 4, 282

Wahrnehmung 196, 198, 206, 211, 214–216, 219–221, 223, 229–230, 233–235, 242, 252–253, 263, 266, 275
Welt 182–183, 195, 200, 205, 207, 209, 211, 213, 225–228, 231, 238–239, 247, 255–256, 325
– Geistige Welt 175, 190, 203, 227
– Intersubjektive Welt 175, 185, 225, 227
– Physikalische Welt 211, 218
– Wahrnehmungs-Welt 211, 217, 224
Wert 175, 195, 199, 203, 209, 227, 229–230, 253, 319
Wertphilosophie 323
Wesenserschauung 210, 234, 245, 264–266

www.ingramcontent.com/pod-product-compliance
Lightning Source LLC
Chambersburg PA
CBHW030432300426
44112CB00009B/963